# C/C++

# C/C++

## Dirk Louis

Prentice
Hall

An imprint of PEARSON EDUCATION

PEARSON EDUCATION LIMITED

Head Office:
Edinburgh Gate
Harlow CM20 2JE
Tel:  +44 (0)1279 623623
Fax:  +44 (0)1279 431059

London Office:
128 Long Acre
London WC2E 9AN
Tel:  +44 (0)20 7447 2000
Fax:  +44 (0)20 7240 5771

First published in Great Britain in 2001
© Pearson Education Limited 2001

First published in 1999 as C++: *Reference & Praxis*
by Markt & Technik Buch-und Software-Verlag GmbH
Martin-Kollar-Straße 10–12
D-81829 Munich
GERMANY

ISBN 0-130-90459-7

British Library Cataloguing in Publication Data
A CIP catalogue record for this book can be obtained from the British Library.

The programs in this book have been included for their instructional value. The publisher does not offer any warranties or representations in respect of their fitness for a particular purpose, nor does the publisher accept any liability for any loss or damage arising from their use.

Many of the designations used by manufacturers and sellers to distinguish their products are claimed as trademarks. Peason Education Limited has made every attempt to supply trademark information about manufacturers and their products mentioned in this book.

10 9 8 7 6 5 4 3 2 1

Translated and typeset by Cybertechnics, Sheffield.
Printed and bound in Great Britain by Biddles Ltd, Guildford & King's Lynn.

The publishers' policy is to use paper manufactured from sustainable forests.

# Contents

Preface ................................................................... xv

## Reference ............................................................... 1

new reference .............................................................. 1

## Basics ................................................................... 2

The C and C++ programming languages ....................................... 2
    Features ............................................................. 3
    The ANSI standard ................................................... 3
    Notational conventions in C/C++ ..................................... 5
    Structure of a C/C++ program ........................................ 5
    Typical components of C/C++ programs ................................ 8
    Larger programs and modularisation ................................. 13
    Object-oriented programming ........................................ 15
    Use of standard libraries .......................................... 16
    Input and output ................................................... 18
    Program flow ....................................................... 20
    Program creation ................................................... 21

## Language concepts and syntax ........................................... 27

Language elements ......................................................... 27
    Character set ...................................................... 27
    Trigraph sequences ................................................. 29
    Keywords and symbols ............................................... 30
    User-defined identifiers: definition and declaration ............... 32
Variables and data types .................................................. 34
    Variables and data types ........................................... 34
    Elementary data types .............................................. 36
    Memory representation of integer types ............................. 37
    Representation of floating point numbers ........................... 38

# Contents

Signs of integer data types . . . . . . . . . . . . . . . . . . . . . . . . . . . . . . . . . . . . . . . . . . . . . . . . . 39
Declaration of variables . . . . . . . . . . . . . . . . . . . . . . . . . . . . . . . . . . . . . . . . . . . . . . . . . . . 40
Scope . . . . . . . . . . . . . . . . . . . . . . . . . . . . . . . . . . . . . . . . . . . . . . . . . . . . . . . . . . . . . . . . . . . 43
Namespaces . . . . . . . . . . . . . . . . . . . . . . . . . . . . . . . . . . . . . . . . . . . . . . . . . . . . . . . . . . . . . 45
Visibility and hiding . . . . . . . . . . . . . . . . . . . . . . . . . . . . . . . . . . . . . . . . . . . . . . . . . . . . . . 48
Life span . . . . . . . . . . . . . . . . . . . . . . . . . . . . . . . . . . . . . . . . . . . . . . . . . . . . . . . . . . . . . . . . 49
Combined data types . . . . . . . . . . . . . . . . . . . . . . . . . . . . . . . . . . . . . . . . . . . . . . . . . . . . . . . 50
Combined data types . . . . . . . . . . . . . . . . . . . . . . . . . . . . . . . . . . . . . . . . . . . . . . . . . . . . . 50
Enumeration types . . . . . . . . . . . . . . . . . . . . . . . . . . . . . . . . . . . . . . . . . . . . . . . . . . . . . . . 51
Arrays . . . . . . . . . . . . . . . . . . . . . . . . . . . . . . . . . . . . . . . . . . . . . . . . . . . . . . . . . . . . . . . . . . 53
Multidimensional arrays . . . . . . . . . . . . . . . . . . . . . . . . . . . . . . . . . . . . . . . . . . . . . . . . . . . 55
Strings . . . . . . . . . . . . . . . . . . . . . . . . . . . . . . . . . . . . . . . . . . . . . . . . . . . . . . . . . . . . . . . . . 58
Structures . . . . . . . . . . . . . . . . . . . . . . . . . . . . . . . . . . . . . . . . . . . . . . . . . . . . . . . . . . . . . . 60
Bit fields . . . . . . . . . . . . . . . . . . . . . . . . . . . . . . . . . . . . . . . . . . . . . . . . . . . . . . . . . . . . . . . 62
Unions . . . . . . . . . . . . . . . . . . . . . . . . . . . . . . . . . . . . . . . . . . . . . . . . . . . . . . . . . . . . . . . . . 64
Pointers and references . . . . . . . . . . . . . . . . . . . . . . . . . . . . . . . . . . . . . . . . . . . . . . . . . . . . . 66
Pointers . . . . . . . . . . . . . . . . . . . . . . . . . . . . . . . . . . . . . . . . . . . . . . . . . . . . . . . . . . . . . . . . 66
Special pointers . . . . . . . . . . . . . . . . . . . . . . . . . . . . . . . . . . . . . . . . . . . . . . . . . . . . . . . . . . 70
References (C++ only) . . . . . . . . . . . . . . . . . . . . . . . . . . . . . . . . . . . . . . . . . . . . . . . . . . . . . 73
Type definitons and type conversions . . . . . . . . . . . . . . . . . . . . . . . . . . . . . . . . . . . . . . . . . . 75
Type definitions . . . . . . . . . . . . . . . . . . . . . . . . . . . . . . . . . . . . . . . . . . . . . . . . . . . . . . . . . . 75
Default conversions . . . . . . . . . . . . . . . . . . . . . . . . . . . . . . . . . . . . . . . . . . . . . . . . . . . . . . . 76
Type conversion . . . . . . . . . . . . . . . . . . . . . . . . . . . . . . . . . . . . . . . . . . . . . . . . . . . . . . . . . 78
Constants . . . . . . . . . . . . . . . . . . . . . . . . . . . . . . . . . . . . . . . . . . . . . . . . . . . . . . . . . . . . . . . . . 80
Constants . . . . . . . . . . . . . . . . . . . . . . . . . . . . . . . . . . . . . . . . . . . . . . . . . . . . . . . . . . . . . . . 80
Literals . . . . . . . . . . . . . . . . . . . . . . . . . . . . . . . . . . . . . . . . . . . . . . . . . . . . . . . . . . . . . . . . . 80
#define – symbolic constants . . . . . . . . . . . . . . . . . . . . . . . . . . . . . . . . . . . . . . . . . . . . . . . 82
const – constant variables . . . . . . . . . . . . . . . . . . . . . . . . . . . . . . . . . . . . . . . . . . . . . . . . . 83
Operators . . . . . . . . . . . . . . . . . . . . . . . . . . . . . . . . . . . . . . . . . . . . . . . . . . . . . . . . . . . . . . . . . 84
Operators . . . . . . . . . . . . . . . . . . . . . . . . . . . . . . . . . . . . . . . . . . . . . . . . . . . . . . . . . . . . . . . 84
Signs . . . . . . . . . . . . . . . . . . . . . . . . . . . . . . . . . . . . . . . . . . . . . . . . . . . . . . . . . . . . . . . . . . . 87
Arithmetic operators . . . . . . . . . . . . . . . . . . . . . . . . . . . . . . . . . . . . . . . . . . . . . . . . . . . . . . 87
Increment and decrement operator . . . . . . . . . . . . . . . . . . . . . . . . . . . . . . . . . . . . . . . . . . 88
Assignments . . . . . . . . . . . . . . . . . . . . . . . . . . . . . . . . . . . . . . . . . . . . . . . . . . . . . . . . . . . . 90
Comparative operators . . . . . . . . . . . . . . . . . . . . . . . . . . . . . . . . . . . . . . . . . . . . . . . . . . . . 92
Logical operators . . . . . . . . . . . . . . . . . . . . . . . . . . . . . . . . . . . . . . . . . . . . . . . . . . . . . . . . . 92
Data access . . . . . . . . . . . . . . . . . . . . . . . . . . . . . . . . . . . . . . . . . . . . . . . . . . . . . . . . . . . . . . 95
Bitwise operators . . . . . . . . . . . . . . . . . . . . . . . . . . . . . . . . . . . . . . . . . . . . . . . . . . . . . . . . . 99
Stream operators . . . . . . . . . . . . . . . . . . . . . . . . . . . . . . . . . . . . . . . . . . . . . . . . . . . . . . . . 102
The new and delete operators . . . . . . . . . . . . . . . . . . . . . . . . . . . . . . . . . . . . . . . . . . . . . . 103
Type conversion and identification . . . . . . . . . . . . . . . . . . . . . . . . . . . . . . . . . . . . . . . . . . 106
Other operators . . . . . . . . . . . . . . . . . . . . . . . . . . . . . . . . . . . . . . . . . . . . . . . . . . . . . . . . . . 111
Synonyms . . . . . . . . . . . . . . . . . . . . . . . . . . . . . . . . . . . . . . . . . . . . . . . . . . . . . . . . . . . . . . . 113
Precedence and associativity . . . . . . . . . . . . . . . . . . . . . . . . . . . . . . . . . . . . . . . . . . . . . . . 114
Overloading of operators . . . . . . . . . . . . . . . . . . . . . . . . . . . . . . . . . . . . . . . . . . . . . . . . . . 115
Program control . . . . . . . . . . . . . . . . . . . . . . . . . . . . . . . . . . . . . . . . . . . . . . . . . . . . . . . . . . . . 118

Program control . . . . . . . . . . . . . . . . . . . . . . . . . . . . . . . . . . . . . . . . . . . . . . . . . . . . . . . . . . 118
The if condition . . . . . . . . . . . . . . . . . . . . . . . . . . . . . . . . . . . . . . . . . . . . . . . . . . . . . . . . . . 119
The if-else statement . . . . . . . . . . . . . . . . . . . . . . . . . . . . . . . . . . . . . . . . . . . . . . . . . . . . . 120
if-else chains . . . . . . . . . . . . . . . . . . . . . . . . . . . . . . . . . . . . . . . . . . . . . . . . . . . . . . . . . . . . . 120
switch statements . . . . . . . . . . . . . . . . . . . . . . . . . . . . . . . . . . . . . . . . . . . . . . . . . . . . . . . . 121
loops . . . . . . . . . . . . . . . . . . . . . . . . . . . . . . . . . . . . . . . . . . . . . . . . . . . . . . . . . . . . . . . . . . . . . 123
The for loop . . . . . . . . . . . . . . . . . . . . . . . . . . . . . . . . . . . . . . . . . . . . . . . . . . . . . . . . . . . . . . 124
The while loop . . . . . . . . . . . . . . . . . . . . . . . . . . . . . . . . . . . . . . . . . . . . . . . . . . . . . . . . . . . 126
The do-while loop . . . . . . . . . . . . . . . . . . . . . . . . . . . . . . . . . . . . . . . . . . . . . . . . . . . . . . . . 127
Break statements for loops . . . . . . . . . . . . . . . . . . . . . . . . . . . . . . . . . . . . . . . . . . . . . . . 128
Functions . . . . . . . . . . . . . . . . . . . . . . . . . . . . . . . . . . . . . . . . . . . . . . . . . . . . . . . . . . . . . . . . . . . 129
Functions . . . . . . . . . . . . . . . . . . . . . . . . . . . . . . . . . . . . . . . . . . . . . . . . . . . . . . . . . . . . . . . . . 129
Function declaration and definition . . . . . . . . . . . . . . . . . . . . . . . . . . . . . . . . . . . . . . . . 131
The main() function . . . . . . . . . . . . . . . . . . . . . . . . . . . . . . . . . . . . . . . . . . . . . . . . . . . . . . 133
Data exchange between functions . . . . . . . . . . . . . . . . . . . . . . . . . . . . . . . . . . . . . . . . . 135
The return value . . . . . . . . . . . . . . . . . . . . . . . . . . . . . . . . . . . . . . . . . . . . . . . . . . . . . . . . . 136
Parameters . . . . . . . . . . . . . . . . . . . . . . . . . . . . . . . . . . . . . . . . . . . . . . . . . . . . . . . . . . . . . . . 136
Function arguments and the default . . . . . . . . . . . . . . . . . . . . . . . . . . . . . . . . . . . . . . . 139
Functions and the stack . . . . . . . . . . . . . . . . . . . . . . . . . . . . . . . . . . . . . . . . . . . . . . . . . . 139
Functions with any number of arguments . . . . . . . . . . . . . . . . . . . . . . . . . . . . . . . . . 143
Inline functions (C++ only) . . . . . . . . . . . . . . . . . . . . . . . . . . . . . . . . . . . . . . . . . . . . . . . . 144
Specifiers for functions . . . . . . . . . . . . . . . . . . . . . . . . . . . . . . . . . . . . . . . . . . . . . . . . . . . 145
Overloading . . . . . . . . . . . . . . . . . . . . . . . . . . . . . . . . . . . . . . . . . . . . . . . . . . . . . . . . . . . . . . 146
Overloading of functions . . . . . . . . . . . . . . . . . . . . . . . . . . . . . . . . . . . . . . . . . . . . . . . . . 147
Overloading of methods . . . . . . . . . . . . . . . . . . . . . . . . . . . . . . . . . . . . . . . . . . . . . . . . . . 148
Overloading, overriding, hiding . . . . . . . . . . . . . . . . . . . . . . . . . . . . . . . . . . . . . . . . . . . 149
Classes . . . . . . . . . . . . . . . . . . . . . . . . . . . . . . . . . . . . . . . . . . . . . . . . . . . . . . . . . . . . . . . . . . . . . . 150
Classes . . . . . . . . . . . . . . . . . . . . . . . . . . . . . . . . . . . . . . . . . . . . . . . . . . . . . . . . . . . . . . . . . . . . 150
Classes and OOP . . . . . . . . . . . . . . . . . . . . . . . . . . . . . . . . . . . . . . . . . . . . . . . . . . . . . . . . . . 152
Encapsulation . . . . . . . . . . . . . . . . . . . . . . . . . . . . . . . . . . . . . . . . . . . . . . . . . . . . . . . . . . . . . 153
Data elements . . . . . . . . . . . . . . . . . . . . . . . . . . . . . . . . . . . . . . . . . . . . . . . . . . . . . . . . . . . . . 154
Static data elements . . . . . . . . . . . . . . . . . . . . . . . . . . . . . . . . . . . . . . . . . . . . . . . . . . . . . . 154
Constant data elements . . . . . . . . . . . . . . . . . . . . . . . . . . . . . . . . . . . . . . . . . . . . . . . . . . . 155
Class instances as data elements . . . . . . . . . . . . . . . . . . . . . . . . . . . . . . . . . . . . . . . . . . . 156
Local and embedded classes . . . . . . . . . . . . . . . . . . . . . . . . . . . . . . . . . . . . . . . . . . . . . . . 158
Methods . . . . . . . . . . . . . . . . . . . . . . . . . . . . . . . . . . . . . . . . . . . . . . . . . . . . . . . . . . . . . . . . . . . 158
Static methods . . . . . . . . . . . . . . . . . . . . . . . . . . . . . . . . . . . . . . . . . . . . . . . . . . . . . . . . . . . . 160
Constant methods . . . . . . . . . . . . . . . . . . . . . . . . . . . . . . . . . . . . . . . . . . . . . . . . . . . . . . . . . 161
Access specifiers . . . . . . . . . . . . . . . . . . . . . . . . . . . . . . . . . . . . . . . . . . . . . . . . . . . . . . . . . . 162
Access within the class . . . . . . . . . . . . . . . . . . . . . . . . . . . . . . . . . . . . . . . . . . . . . . . . . . . . 164
Access from outside the class . . . . . . . . . . . . . . . . . . . . . . . . . . . . . . . . . . . . . . . . . . . . . . 164
Access to base class elements . . . . . . . . . . . . . . . . . . . . . . . . . . . . . . . . . . . . . . . . . . . . . . 166
The constructor . . . . . . . . . . . . . . . . . . . . . . . . . . . . . . . . . . . . . . . . . . . . . . . . . . . . . . . . . . . 168
The copy constructor . . . . . . . . . . . . . . . . . . . . . . . . . . . . . . . . . . . . . . . . . . . . . . . . . . . . . . 170
The destructor . . . . . . . . . . . . . . . . . . . . . . . . . . . . . . . . . . . . . . . . . . . . . . . . . . . . . . . . . . . . 171
Default methods . . . . . . . . . . . . . . . . . . . . . . . . . . . . . . . . . . . . . . . . . . . . . . . . . . . . . . . . . . . 172

The this pointer .......................................................................172
Instance formation ...................................................................173
Inheritance and polymorphism ...........................................................174
Inheritance ..........................................................................174
Inheritance versus embedding ........................................................176
Access restrictions in inheritance ....................................................177
Relaxing access rights for individual elements ........................................179
Inheritance and constructor ..........................................................180
Methods which cannot be inherited ...................................................182
Polymorphism .......................................................................183
Overriding and virtual methods .......................................................184
Inheritance and destructor ...........................................................186
Abstract methods and classes .........................................................186
Base class pointer ...................................................................187
RTTI – Runtime Type Identification ....................................................188
Multiple inheritance .................................................................190
Virtual base classes .................................................................191
Templates ...............................................................................192
Templates ...........................................................................192
Function templates ..................................................................194
Class templates .....................................................................195
Methods in class templates ..........................................................196
Instantiation and specialisation .....................................................197
Implicit instantiation ...............................................................198
Explicit instantiation ...............................................................199
Explicit specialisation ..............................................................200
The preprocessor ........................................................................202
Inserting and replacing source code ..................................................203
Defining macros .....................................................................204
Arguments in macros .................................................................205
Directives for conditional compilation ................................................206
String formation and base symbol combination .........................................208
Other directives and symbols .........................................................209
Exception handling ......................................................................211
Exception handling ..................................................................211
Triggering exceptions ................................................................214
Catching exceptions ..................................................................216
Determining the handler scope ........................................................217
Related functions ....................................................................218
Strings .................................................................................219
C strings ............................................................................219
The string class .....................................................................221
Wide character and multibyte characters ..............................................222
Input and output (I/O) ..................................................................223
Formatted and unformatted I/O ........................................................223
Streams in C .........................................................................224

Streams in C++ ................................................................. 226
Buffering ..................................................................... 230

**The C standard library** ...................................................... 233

The header files ............................................................... 233
  assert.h ..................................................................... 233
  ctype.h ...................................................................... 234
  errno.h ...................................................................... 234
  float.h ...................................................................... 235
  ios646.h ..................................................................... 236
  limits.h ..................................................................... 237
  locale.h ..................................................................... 237
  math.h ....................................................................... 238
  setjmp.h ..................................................................... 239
  signal.h ..................................................................... 240
  stdarg.h ..................................................................... 241
  stddef.h ..................................................................... 241
  stdio.h ...................................................................... 242
  stdlib.h ..................................................................... 244
  string.h ..................................................................... 245
  time.h ....................................................................... 247
  wchar.h ...................................................................... 248
  wctype.h ..................................................................... 250
The functions of the C standard library ....................................... 251

**The C++ standard library** .................................................... 317

Overview of the standard library .............................................. 317
Header files .................................................................. 318
  algorithms ................................................................... 318
  bitset ....................................................................... 320
  complex ...................................................................... 321
  deque ........................................................................ 322
  exception .................................................................... 323
  fstream ...................................................................... 324
  functional ................................................................... 324
  iomanip ...................................................................... 326
  ios .......................................................................... 327
  iosfwd ....................................................................... 328
  iostream ..................................................................... 329
  istream ...................................................................... 330
  iterators .................................................................... 330
  limits ....................................................................... 332
  list ......................................................................... 333
  locale ....................................................................... 333
  map .......................................................................... 335
  memory ....................................................................... 336

new . . . . . . . . . . . . . . . . . . . . . . . . . . . . . . . . . . . . . . . . . . . . . . . . . . . . . . . . . . . . . . . . . . . . . . . 336
numeric . . . . . . . . . . . . . . . . . . . . . . . . . . . . . . . . . . . . . . . . . . . . . . . . . . . . . . . . . . . . . . . . . . 337
ostream . . . . . . . . . . . . . . . . . . . . . . . . . . . . . . . . . . . . . . . . . . . . . . . . . . . . . . . . . . . . . . . . . . 338
queue . . . . . . . . . . . . . . . . . . . . . . . . . . . . . . . . . . . . . . . . . . . . . . . . . . . . . . . . . . . . . . . . . . . . . 338
set . . . . . . . . . . . . . . . . . . . . . . . . . . . . . . . . . . . . . . . . . . . . . . . . . . . . . . . . . . . . . . . . . . . . . . . . 339
sstream . . . . . . . . . . . . . . . . . . . . . . . . . . . . . . . . . . . . . . . . . . . . . . . . . . . . . . . . . . . . . . . . . . . 340
stack . . . . . . . . . . . . . . . . . . . . . . . . . . . . . . . . . . . . . . . . . . . . . . . . . . . . . . . . . . . . . . . . . . . . . 341
stdexcept . . . . . . . . . . . . . . . . . . . . . . . . . . . . . . . . . . . . . . . . . . . . . . . . . . . . . . . . . . . . . . . . . 341
streambuf . . . . . . . . . . . . . . . . . . . . . . . . . . . . . . . . . . . . . . . . . . . . . . . . . . . . . . . . . . . . . . . . . 342
string . . . . . . . . . . . . . . . . . . . . . . . . . . . . . . . . . . . . . . . . . . . . . . . . . . . . . . . . . . . . . . . . . . . . . 342
typeinfo . . . . . . . . . . . . . . . . . . . . . . . . . . . . . . . . . . . . . . . . . . . . . . . . . . . . . . . . . . . . . . . . . . 343
utility . . . . . . . . . . . . . . . . . . . . . . . . . . . . . . . . . . . . . . . . . . . . . . . . . . . . . . . . . . . . . . . . . . . . . 344
valarray . . . . . . . . . . . . . . . . . . . . . . . . . . . . . . . . . . . . . . . . . . . . . . . . . . . . . . . . . . . . . . . . . . . 344
vector . . . . . . . . . . . . . . . . . . . . . . . . . . . . . . . . . . . . . . . . . . . . . . . . . . . . . . . . . . . . . . . . . . . . . 346
The container classes . . . . . . . . . . . . . . . . . . . . . . . . . . . . . . . . . . . . . . . . . . . . . . . . . . . . . . . . 347
General characteristics . . . . . . . . . . . . . . . . . . . . . . . . . . . . . . . . . . . . . . . . . . . . . . . . . . . . . 347
bitset . . . . . . . . . . . . . . . . . . . . . . . . . . . . . . . . . . . . . . . . . . . . . . . . . . . . . . . . . . . . . . . . . . . . . 350
deque . . . . . . . . . . . . . . . . . . . . . . . . . . . . . . . . . . . . . . . . . . . . . . . . . . . . . . . . . . . . . . . . . . . . . 352
list . . . . . . . . . . . . . . . . . . . . . . . . . . . . . . . . . . . . . . . . . . . . . . . . . . . . . . . . . . . . . . . . . . . . . . . 355
map and multimap . . . . . . . . . . . . . . . . . . . . . . . . . . . . . . . . . . . . . . . . . . . . . . . . . . . . . . . . . 358
priority_queue . . . . . . . . . . . . . . . . . . . . . . . . . . . . . . . . . . . . . . . . . . . . . . . . . . . . . . . . . . . . 362
queue . . . . . . . . . . . . . . . . . . . . . . . . . . . . . . . . . . . . . . . . . . . . . . . . . . . . . . . . . . . . . . . . . . . . . 364
set and multiset . . . . . . . . . . . . . . . . . . . . . . . . . . . . . . . . . . . . . . . . . . . . . . . . . . . . . . . . . . . 365
stack . . . . . . . . . . . . . . . . . . . . . . . . . . . . . . . . . . . . . . . . . . . . . . . . . . . . . . . . . . . . . . . . . . . . . 368
vector . . . . . . . . . . . . . . . . . . . . . . . . . . . . . . . . . . . . . . . . . . . . . . . . . . . . . . . . . . . . . . . . . . . . . 369
The iterator classes . . . . . . . . . . . . . . . . . . . . . . . . . . . . . . . . . . . . . . . . . . . . . . . . . . . . . . . . . . 372
General points . . . . . . . . . . . . . . . . . . . . . . . . . . . . . . . . . . . . . . . . . . . . . . . . . . . . . . . . . . . . . 372
reverse_iterator . . . . . . . . . . . . . . . . . . . . . . . . . . . . . . . . . . . . . . . . . . . . . . . . . . . . . . . . . . . 374
insert iterators . . . . . . . . . . . . . . . . . . . . . . . . . . . . . . . . . . . . . . . . . . . . . . . . . . . . . . . . . . . . . 376
stream iterators . . . . . . . . . . . . . . . . . . . . . . . . . . . . . . . . . . . . . . . . . . . . . . . . . . . . . . . . . . . . 378
Supporting user-defined implementations . . . . . . . . . . . . . . . . . . . . . . . . . . . . . . . . . . . . . 381
The algorithms . . . . . . . . . . . . . . . . . . . . . . . . . . . . . . . . . . . . . . . . . . . . . . . . . . . . . . . . . . . . . . 382
The stream classes . . . . . . . . . . . . . . . . . . . . . . . . . . . . . . . . . . . . . . . . . . . . . . . . . . . . . . . . . . . 391
Overview . . . . . . . . . . . . . . . . . . . . . . . . . . . . . . . . . . . . . . . . . . . . . . . . . . . . . . . . . . . . . . . . . . . 391
ios_base . . . . . . . . . . . . . . . . . . . . . . . . . . . . . . . . . . . . . . . . . . . . . . . . . . . . . . . . . . . . . . . . . . . 393
basic_ios . . . . . . . . . . . . . . . . . . . . . . . . . . . . . . . . . . . . . . . . . . . . . . . . . . . . . . . . . . . . . . . . . . 395
basic_streambuf . . . . . . . . . . . . . . . . . . . . . . . . . . . . . . . . . . . . . . . . . . . . . . . . . . . . . . . . . . . . 396
basic_istream . . . . . . . . . . . . . . . . . . . . . . . . . . . . . . . . . . . . . . . . . . . . . . . . . . . . . . . . . . . . . . 398
basic_ostream . . . . . . . . . . . . . . . . . . . . . . . . . . . . . . . . . . . . . . . . . . . . . . . . . . . . . . . . . . . . . . 400
basic_iostream . . . . . . . . . . . . . . . . . . . . . . . . . . . . . . . . . . . . . . . . . . . . . . . . . . . . . . . . . . . . . 402
basic_stringbuf . . . . . . . . . . . . . . . . . . . . . . . . . . . . . . . . . . . . . . . . . . . . . . . . . . . . . . . . . . . . . 402
basic_istringstream . . . . . . . . . . . . . . . . . . . . . . . . . . . . . . . . . . . . . . . . . . . . . . . . . . . . . . . . . 404
basic_ostringstream . . . . . . . . . . . . . . . . . . . . . . . . . . . . . . . . . . . . . . . . . . . . . . . . . . . . . . . . 405
basic_stringstream . . . . . . . . . . . . . . . . . . . . . . . . . . . . . . . . . . . . . . . . . . . . . . . . . . . . . . . . . 406
basic_filebuf . . . . . . . . . . . . . . . . . . . . . . . . . . . . . . . . . . . . . . . . . . . . . . . . . . . . . . . . . . . . . . . 406
basic_ifstream . . . . . . . . . . . . . . . . . . . . . . . . . . . . . . . . . . . . . . . . . . . . . . . . . . . . . . . . . . . . . 408

basic_ofstream .................................................................. 409
basic_fstream ................................................................... 410
The string classes ................................................................ 411
Overview ...................................................................... 411
char_traits .................................................................... 411
basic_string .................................................................. 412
Classes for local settings ......................................................... 417
Overview ...................................................................... 417
locale ........................................................................ 418
Auxiliary classes for individual categories .................................... 419
The numeric classes .............................................................. 435
complex ...................................................................... 435
valarray ...................................................................... 436
Subsets of valarray objects ................................................... 439
numeric_limits ............................................................... 443
Classes and functions for exception handling ...................................... 445
exception ..................................................................... 445
Derived exception classes .................................................... 445
Functions for exception handling ............................................. 448
Runtime type identification ...................................................... 449
type_info ..................................................................... 449
Utilities ......................................................................... 450
The pair structure ............................................................ 450
Function objects .............................................................. 451
Memory allocation ............................................................... 456
allocator ..................................................................... 456
auto_ptr ...................................................................... 457
Functions and iterators ...................................................... 457

Practice ..........................................................................459

Category: variables and data types ................................................ 459
Value ranges of integer data types ............................................... 460
Value range and precision of floating point numbers ............................. 463
The std namespace of the runtime library ......................................... 464
Using elements from namespaces .................................................. 466
Introducing namespaces into local validity ranges ............................... 468
Namespaces in extensive software projects ....................................... 469
Enumeration types in switch statements .......................................... 470
Enumeration types as sets ........................................................ 471
Arrays and dynamic fields ........................................................ 473
Sorting arrays ................................................................... 475
Searching arrays ................................................................. 477
Arrays as function parameters .................................................... 478
Arrays with elements of different data types ..................................... 480

Contents

Arrays of structures ................................................................483

Recursive structures ...............................................................484

Category: pointers and dynamic memory management .......................................487

Memory allocation with malloc() .........................................................488

Memory allocation with new..............................................................490

Error handling for new ................................................................492

Pointer arithmetic....................................................................494

Dynamic memory in functions ...........................................................495

Dynamic memory in classes ............................................................497

Dynamic memory and exception handling ...............................................498

auto_ptr ...........................................................................499

Pointers versus references..............................................................501

References as parameters ..............................................................502

References as return values of operators ..................................................503

Category: operators .................................................................507

The efficient use of operators ..........................................................508

Overloading of operators ..............................................................509

Overloading the increment operator ++ ...................................................510

Overloading the arithmetic operators +, +=..................................................511

Overloading the [] operator ............................................................512

Overloading the () operator ............................................................513

Overloading the assignment operator = ...................................................514

Overloading new and delete ...........................................................516

Overloading the stream operators << >> ...................................................518

Category: program  control .........................................................519

Infinite loops .......................................................................520

Menus with switch ...................................................................521

Category: functions .................................................................523

Pointers and references as parameters ....................................................524

Local static variables .................................................................526

Recursive functions ..................................................................527

Functions with any number of arguments .................................................528

Overloading ........................................................................530

Category: classes ..................................................................533

Class definition .....................................................................534

Default constructor...................................................................535

Private data – public methods...........................................................538

Copying class objects: copy constructor and assignment operator ...........................541

Pointers as instance variables ..........................................................543

Overloading operators: +, << ..........................................................545

Conversion methods .................................................................546

Persistent classes . . . . . . . . . . . . . . . . . . . . . . . . . . . . . . . . . . . . . . . . . . . . . . . . . . . . . . . . . 548

## Category: inheritance and polymorphism . . . . . . . . . . . . . . . . . . . . . . . . . . . . . . . . 551

Inheritance as an extension of existing classes . . . . . . . . . . . . . . . . . . . . . . . . . . . . . 552
Inheritance and polymorphism . . . . . . . . . . . . . . . . . . . . . . . . . . . . . . . . . . . . . . . . . . 553
Guidelines for inheritance . . . . . . . . . . . . . . . . . . . . . . . . . . . . . . . . . . . . . . . . . . . . . . 555
Base class pointers and arrays . . . . . . . . . . . . . . . . . . . . . . . . . . . . . . . . . . . . . . . . . . 556
Base class pointers as parameters . . . . . . . . . . . . . . . . . . . . . . . . . . . . . . . . . . . . . . . 558
RTTI with virtual methods . . . . . . . . . . . . . . . . . . . . . . . . . . . . . . . . . . . . . . . . . . . . . . 559
RTTI with dynamic_cast . . . . . . . . . . . . . . . . . . . . . . . . . . . . . . . . . . . . . . . . . . . . . . . 561
Type identification at runtime: RTTI with typeid . . . . . . . . . . . . . . . . . . . . . . . . . . . . 562

## Category: templates . . . . . . . . . . . . . . . . . . . . . . . . . . . . . . . . . . . . . . . . . . . . . . . . . . 565

Type-independent functions . . . . . . . . . . . . . . . . . . . . . . . . . . . . . . . . . . . . . . . . . . . . 566
Type-independent classes . . . . . . . . . . . . . . . . . . . . . . . . . . . . . . . . . . . . . . . . . . . . . . 568

## Category: preprocessor directives . . . . . . . . . . . . . . . . . . . . . . . . . . . . . . . . . . . . . . 571

Compiler switches . . . . . . . . . . . . . . . . . . . . . . . . . . . . . . . . . . . . . . . . . . . . . . . . . . . . 572
Debugging with conditional compilation . . . . . . . . . . . . . . . . . . . . . . . . . . . . . . . . . . 573
Portability with conditional compilation . . . . . . . . . . . . . . . . . . . . . . . . . . . . . . . . . . 574

## Category: exceptions . . . . . . . . . . . . . . . . . . . . . . . . . . . . . . . . . . . . . . . . . . . . . . . . . . 577

Catching exceptions . . . . . . . . . . . . . . . . . . . . . . . . . . . . . . . . . . . . . . . . . . . . . . . . . . . 578
Triggering exceptions . . . . . . . . . . . . . . . . . . . . . . . . . . . . . . . . . . . . . . . . . . . . . . . . . 579
Passing exceptions . . . . . . . . . . . . . . . . . . . . . . . . . . . . . . . . . . . . . . . . . . . . . . . . . . . 579
Defining exception classes . . . . . . . . . . . . . . . . . . . . . . . . . . . . . . . . . . . . . . . . . . . . . 581

## Category: strings . . . . . . . . . . . . . . . . . . . . . . . . . . . . . . . . . . . . . . . . . . . . . . . . . . . . . 583

Programming with C strings . . . . . . . . . . . . . . . . . . . . . . . . . . . . . . . . . . . . . . . . . . . . 584
Programming with the string class . . . . . . . . . . . . . . . . . . . . . . . . . . . . . . . . . . . . . . 586
Analysing (parsing) strings . . . . . . . . . . . . . . . . . . . . . . . . . . . . . . . . . . . . . . . . . . . . 588

## Category: input and output . . . . . . . . . . . . . . . . . . . . . . . . . . . . . . . . . . . . . . . . . . . . 591

Formatted input and output in C . . . . . . . . . . . . . . . . . . . . . . . . . . . . . . . . . . . . . . . . 592
Formatted input and output in C++ . . . . . . . . . . . . . . . . . . . . . . . . . . . . . . . . . . . . . . 594
Using manipulators . . . . . . . . . . . . . . . . . . . . . . . . . . . . . . . . . . . . . . . . . . . . . . . . . . . 595
Error handling for streams . . . . . . . . . . . . . . . . . . . . . . . . . . . . . . . . . . . . . . . . . . . . . 596
Text files in C . . . . . . . . . . . . . . . . . . . . . . . . . . . . . . . . . . . . . . . . . . . . . . . . . . . . . . . . 598
Binary files in C . . . . . . . . . . . . . . . . . . . . . . . . . . . . . . . . . . . . . . . . . . . . . . . . . . . . . . 600
Random access in C . . . . . . . . . . . . . . . . . . . . . . . . . . . . . . . . . . . . . . . . . . . . . . . . . . 602
Text files in C++ . . . . . . . . . . . . . . . . . . . . . . . . . . . . . . . . . . . . . . . . . . . . . . . . . . . . . 604
Binary files in C++ . . . . . . . . . . . . . . . . . . . . . . . . . . . . . . . . . . . . . . . . . . . . . . . . . . . 606
Random access in C++ . . . . . . . . . . . . . . . . . . . . . . . . . . . . . . . . . . . . . . . . . . . . . . . . 608
Dividing stream buffers . . . . . . . . . . . . . . . . . . . . . . . . . . . . . . . . . . . . . . . . . . . . . . . 610
String streams . . . . . . . . . . . . . . . . . . . . . . . . . . . . . . . . . . . . . . . . . . . . . . . . . . . . . . . 612

Category: the STL (Standard Template Library) ............................................... 613
   Data management with containers ........................................................ 614
   Iterators ................................................................................. 617
   Algorithms ............................................................................... 619
   Preparing classes for containers and algorithms ...................................... 623
   Creating function objects .............................................................. 624
   Function adapters ....................................................................... 628

Category: multiple file programs ............................................................. 631
   Modularisation .......................................................................... 632
   Constructing a header and an implementation file ..................................... 633
   Preventing multiple calls of header files ............................................. 636
   Cross-module use of elements .......................................................... 637
   Restricting elements to one module .................................................... 639

Category: libraries ........................................................................ 641
   Using libraries ......................................................................... 642
   Creating user-defined libraries ....................................................... 643

Category: internationalisation and localisation .............................................. 645
   Special characters in MS-DOS ........................................................... 646
   Wide characters ......................................................................... 647
   Localising output ....................................................................... 649
   Local environment ....................................................................... 650
   Querying the settings of a locale ..................................................... 653

Category: miscellaneous ..................................................................... 655
   Random numbers .......................................................................... 656
   Assembler ............................................................................... 657
   Windows programming ..................................................................... 659
   Database programming .................................................................... 663

Appendix ................................................................................... 667
   Compatibility between C++ and C ........................................................ 668
   ASCII table ............................................................................. 669
   ANSI table .............................................................................. 670
   Glossary ................................................................................ 672

Table Index ................................................................................ 677

# Preface

It is always a difficult matter to write a reference to C/C++. How does one squeeze information that could fill 2,000 pages without effort, into a book of a few hundred pages?

- One must condense the information. Thus, language concepts and syntax are assumed to be understood. After a brief and concise introduction of the individual elements and concepts of C/C++, a clear overview is given of their syntax and other relevant information, followed by practical examples and tips for their application.

- One must do without redundant information. A complete reference of the C and C++ runtime libraries would by far exceed the scope of this book, and is unnecessary because most compilers contain an extensive on-line reference for these libraries. The Reference part of this book is intended to accomplish two tasks:

  1. Give you, the reader, an overview of the header files of the libraries and the distribution of the library elements across the header files.

  2. Show you the individual functions or classes and explain their usage.

- One must make a choice. In the Practice section, typical tasks and techniques involved in programming in C/C++ are described and explained. Here, the number of possible subjects is practically unlimited. I have therefore limited myself to subjects that are suitable as a problem-oriented complement to the Reference section (such as sorting of arrays, overloading of operators, programming with STL containers) and/or important for daily programming work or of general interest (such as dynamic memory management, recursive functions, multi-file programs and libraries).

- The book is rounded off by a section that includes an introduction to C/C++ and the structuring and creation of programs; an Appendix with ASCII/ANSI tables, a glossary and a list of the most important differences between C and C++.

Should you have suggestions or criticism to this book, email me at rdlouis@compu-
serve.com or visit my Website http://www.civilserve.com/rdlouis.

I wish you success with C/C++ and this book.

Dirk Louis

# Reference

## new reference

This section explains all the important terms and

instruments needed for successful programming

and illustrates their functioning using

examples.

# Basics

## The C and C++ programming languages

In contrast to other high-level languages such as Pascal or Basic, which were originally designed as pure teaching languages, C owes its existence to the fact that Bell Laboratories were looking for a higher-level programming language for the implementation of a newly developed operating system. Until then, the whole operating system, later to be known as UNIX, was programmed in assembler. To facilitate their work, people began to write a new programming language of their own which was to be highly efficient, portable and easy to compile.

Brian W. Kernighan and Dennis M. Ritchie finally led these efforts to success and at the same time created one of the most powerful programming languages of all times: the C programming language. C quickly became popular because of its qualities – and despite the difficulties (particularly for beginners) of learning this language – became increasingly widely used.

Over time, the demands on a professional programming language changed. The generation of fast and compact code remained a high priority, but the maintenance and reusability of existing code became more and more important, and with this came an interest in object-oriented concepts.

During the mid-1980s, Bjarne Stroustrup began to extend C with object-oriented concepts. The emphasis lies on the term 'extend', because compatibility with C was a priority design feature. One of the first steps, on the way to the new programming language, was therefore still called 'C with classes'. In 1985 a version appeared which could be considered as an object-oriented programming language and became known as C++. Today, C++ is as is successful as C.

One reason for this is certainly the (practically) complete downward compatibility with C, which greatly facilitates a C programmer the migration to object-oriented programming and guarantees the usability of existing C code.

In contrast to purely object-oriented languages such as Modula or Smalltalk, there is, however, the danger of employing C++ merely as a more relaxed version of C. Programming in C++ should not be automatically considered as being equivalent to object-oriented programming.

# Features

C was originally designed as a high-level language for system programming, in particular for the development of the UNIX operating system. In this respect, C was simply a tool, and C programs had to be easy to compile and fast. The result was a language which excelled through

- its limited number of language elements,
- the fast runtime behaviour of its programs,
- its support for modular programming and
- its good portability combined with a close proximity to the system.

Today, computing time is becoming increasingly cheaper and programming cost increasingly expensive. The aim of object-oriented programming in C++ is therefore to write source code which excels through

- safe and easy use,
- high reusability,
- simple maintenance and
- good comprehension and readability.

# The ANSI standard

The success of a programming language does not only depend on the language itself, but also on the availability of suitable compilers (or interpreters) and support libraries. The latter have been of particular importance for the diffusion of C, because for many central tasks (input/output, string handling, dynamic memory management) there are no elements anchored in the C language itself.

Its dependency on standard libraries, however, also means additional dependency on compiler manufacturers. In order to act against this influence and to prevent every compiler manufacturer from defining their own C dialect, a committee was formed in the American National Standard Institute (ANSI) in 1983, in which compiler manufacturers, software developers and hardware manufacturers came together to create a standard for the C programming language. This standard, ratified in 1989 (reference number ISO/IEC 9899:1990) defines both the syntax and semantics of the language, together with the components of the standard library.

Programmers who adhere to the rules established by the standard and do not use platform-specific functions (for example, programming with DOS interrupts) can be sure, thanks to the ANSI standard, that their programs can be generated by any ANSI-compatible compiler. This also means that a program can be ported to any platform (computer/operating system) as long as there is a suitable ANSI-compatible compiler for this platform.

In 1995 the C standard library was extended with a collection of functions for programming with so-called wide characters, that is, characters encoded with 16-bit or 32-bit character codes. Most of these functions, which are declared in the new `wchar.h` and `wctype.h` headers, are adaptations of existing C functions to the `wchar_t` character type. These extensions are summarised in the ISO/IEC 9899:1990/Amd.1:1995(E) amendment.

Today there is also an ANSI standard for C++. The most important new features, with respect to Bjarne Stroustrup's quasi standard valid until then, should be the introduction of namespaces as freely definable global scopes and the standardisation of the C++ runtime library. Explanations and descriptions in this book follow the new C++ standard. In the Practice section of this book you will find many sections that show how you can use the classes of the C++ runtime library in your daily programming work.

Although downward compatibility to C was very important in the development of C++, a few of the concepts taken over from C have been changed in their semantics (see the Appendix). Should a C program behave differently after compilation with a C++ compiler, you should check whether the program is affected by these changes.

## Sources

The C and C++ standard documents can be requested on-line at the ANSI Institute or the IHS (Information Handling Service) at:

```
www.ansi.org
www.ihs.de
```

Copies of the standards can also be obtained from the following address in Switzerland:

ISO/IEC Copyright Office
Case Postale 56
CH-1211 Genève 20
Switzerland

or from Munich:

IHS Information Handling Services
Tel. 089 / 89526999

Currently, the final C++ draft can still be downloaded from the Internet from:

```
ftp://ftp.maths.warwick.ac.uk/pub/c++/std/cd2/
```

# Notational conventions in C/C++

In the construction of names of identifiers, that is, names of variables, functions, classes, types and macros, the following characters may be used:

- all letters of the English alphabet (a to z, A to Z)
- the digits 0 to 9
- the underscore (_)

In addition, the following rules apply:

- The name of an identifier must start with a letter or with an underscore. The use of a digit as the first character of an identifier is not allowed.
- Umlauts, accents and other foreign language special characters are only allowed in comments and in character strings.
- The maximum length of an identifier is not prescribed, but according to ANSI C at least the first 31 characters may be used for distinction.

## Warning

The C language differentiates between upper case and lower case spelling. Thus, the identifiers `var1` and `Var1` can be used for two different variables.

# Structure of a C/C++ program

```
#include <stdio.h>
int main()
    {
    /* statements */
    return 0;
    }
```

## Description

C/C++ programs consist of a collection of declarations and definitions of data types, variables, functions and classes (plus some special directives for the preprocessor). Statements that specify what a program does can be found in function definitions (in C++ also in the methods (element functions) of the classes). Every C/C++ program must define a `main()` function with whose execution the program starts.

## Application

In the simplest case, a C/C++ program consists of

- one or more `include` directives, which allow access to specific functions and classes of the C/C++ standard library, together with

- the mandatory `main()` function which contains all statements needed to execute the program,
- variables which are declared to represent and store or buffer values, and
- statements in which the values of the variables are processed.

## Example

To set up a simple program that multiplies two numbers and outputs their product, you might proceed as follows:

In order to be able to manage two integer values in the program, you declare two variables of the `int` data type (data type for integer values). For the result, a third variable is defined:

```
int main()
{
  int number1, number2;
  int result;
```

With the aid of the assignment operator, you can assign values to the variables:

```
int main()
{
  ...
  number1 = 120;               /* assign values */
  number2 =   4;
```

To multiply two `int` values, you use the `*` operator. The result of the calculation is directly assigned to the third variable:

```
  result = number1 * number2;
```

To output the values, you can use a special function called `printf()`, which is a part of the C runtime library:

```
  printf("The product of the numbers is: %d\n", result);
```

Before you call a function, the function must be made known to the compiler by a declaration. The declarations for the functions of the runtime library are combined in a series of header files. Once you have found out in which header file the required function is declared, you integrate the header file by using an `#include` statement at the beginning of the program:

```
#include <stdio.h>
```

## Warning

Readers who wish to program with C/C++ for Windows should note that Windows programs use the `WinMain()` function instead of `main()`. Depending on the compiler and class library used, `WinMain()` can in turn be replaced with another function (for example `OwlMain()` for Borland C++ with OWL) or a class instance (for example, a global object of the MFC class `CWinApp` in Visual C++).

Console programs executed under Windows (that is, programs running in a MS-DOS Prompt window and without a Windows interface of their own), however, use the `main()` function, as do pure DOS or UNIX programs.

## Example

After compilation, the following program can be called and executed from the console of your operating system (under Windows, the MS-DOS Prompt).

```c
#include <stdio.h>

int main()
  {
  int number1, number2;        /* factors */
  int result;                  /* product */

  number1 = 120;                    /* assign values */
  number2 =   4;
  result = number1 * number2;   /* calculate value */

  printf("The product of the numbers is: %d\n", result);

  return 0;
  }
```

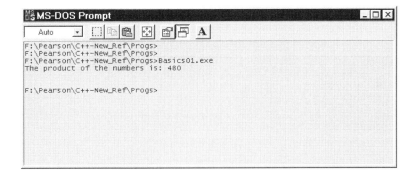

## References

See the following sections for additional introductory information on the structure of C/C++ programs:

See the section on use of the standard library for problems with the inclusion of header files;

See the Reference section on the language for detailed information on variables, data types, operators and functions;

See the Practice section, category input/output.

# Typical components of C/C++ programs

```
                /* The first C program */  ──── Comment
                #include <stdio.h> ───────────── Preprocessor directive
 Function
                int main()
             ┌─ {
 Statement   │    printf("Hello World\n");  ──┐
 block       │    return 0;                   ├─── Statements
             └─ }
```

Typical components of a C/C++ program

## Description

The functionality of a program is determined by the data it processes and the operation(s) it performs on data. In this respect, one might think that a program consisted only of variable definitions and statements. This is, however, not the case. The compiler differentiates between many more elements.

From the compiler's view, a program consists of:

− definitions

− declarations

− statements

− preprocessor directives

− comments

## Definitions and declarations

When executing a program, code and data of the program need to be loaded into the computer's working memory. Which code and which data belong to a program is specified in the source code.

The program code consists of the source code statements translated into machine code. In C/C++ statements may only be placed in function definitions. By defining a function, for example the main() function of the program, you tell the compiler that it should reserve memory for the function and take care that the code of the function is loaded into the appropriate memory area.

Variables are defined for the management of data. Behind the variables, you will find memory areas in RAM reserved by the compiler for this purpose. In the variables, you can store your program's data.

With a definition, you introduce new elements (functions, variable, data types) into a program. At the same time, during the definition, the element is associated with an identifier (variable name, function name, etc.), which is used in the program source text to access the element.

Since the definition of functions and variables entails the allocation of memory areas, these elements must be uniqe; that is, they must be defined only once in a program (otherwise there would be identifiers associated with several memory areas). On the other hand, the compiler requires that all elements to be used are made known to it beforehand. Thus, before a variable is used, the compiler must be told the data type of the variable; before a function is used, the compiler must be told which parameter the function takes and which return type it yields. This way of making elements known is called a declaration. There is, however, also a possibility of declaring elements without declaring them. For variables, you prefix the 'definition' with the keyword extern, while for functions, you simply specify the function head (return type, name, parameter list) without the statement part.

## References

See the Reference section, language category.

See Practice section, category multi-file programs for more information on declaration and definition.

### Variables and constants

Fixed values which do not change during the course of the program or which are only used once can be directly entered in the source text in the form of literals.

Variables, instead, are defined for values that are subject to change. The compiler allocates the variable a memory area in which different values can be stored during the course of the program.

A variable can, however, only take values of one data type (with the exception of unions). The reason is that different data (characters, integer values, floating point values) need different amounts of memory. Also the coding of the values in binary representation for storage in RAM is different for the individual data types. Therefore, each variable belongs to a data type which is specified by the programmer in the definition of the variable.

```
int var1;        // declaration of a variable for integer values
double var2;     // declaration of a variable for floating point values
char var3;       // declaration of a variable for characters
var1 = 3;        // assignment of an integer constant
var2 = 3.14;     // assignment of a floating point constant
var3 = 'c';      // assignment of a character constant
```

## References

See the Reference section, category variables and data types.

## Statements                                                                :

The code proper of the program. Statements are translated by the compiler into machine instructions which, during execution of the program, are processed one after the other by the computer's CPU. Statements always end with a semicolon.

- Statements may only occur inside statement blocks of functions.

- Each program statement must be terminated with a semicolon.

- Several statements can – separated by semicolons – share the same line.

- As well as the statements, declarations are also terminated with a semicolon.

```
var1 = 3 * var2;        // assignment of a value
                        // to a variable
printf("Hello");        // call of a function
return 0;               // keyword for terminating
                        // a function
```

## Statement blocks                                                          {}

In C/C++ statements are combined into statement blocks. A statement block begins with an opening brace (curly bracket) and ends with a closing brace.

Blocks of statements can be nested. The outermost block is always the definition block of a function. Inside the statement block of the function, additional blocks can be defined, for example, to implement a loop or a branching of the program flow independent of an if condition.

```
void func()                             // function
{                                       // statement block for loop

  long loop = 1;

  while (loop <= 10)                    // loop and loop condition
    {                                   // statement block for loop
    // calculate exponentiations
    printf("%d ^ %d = %f\n", loop, loop, pow(loop,loop));
    loop++;
    }
}
```

## Functions

Functions support modularisation of the source code. Instead of packing all statements into the main() function, related statements that fulfil a common task can be dislocated as functions.

A function consists of

- a statement block,
- an interface to other parts of the program and
- a name via which the function can be called.

The `compare()` function defines two parameters which can be passed values at the time of the function call. As a result, by means of the keyword `return`, the function returns an integer value which indicates whether the two values passed are equal or different.

Function definition:

```
int  compare (int parameter1, int parameter2)
{
   if (parameter1 == parameter2)
      return 1;
   else
      return 0;
}
```

Function call:

```
int result;
int var = 25;

result = compare(23, var);    // assigns result the value 0
```

## References

See the Reference section, category functions.

## Preprocessor directives                                                    #

Preprocessor directives are special instructions to the preprocessor, which are carried out prior to the translation of the program into machine code. Preprocessor directives always begin with a hash (#) and occupy one line each.

The most important preprocessor directive is `#include`. It is used to copy the contents of a text file into the source text of the current file. In C/C++ even beginners are immediately shown this concept, because this is the only way to access functions/classes of the standard library. The standard libraries of C and C++ are present in the form of compiled LIB files and contain the definitions of a series of useful functions (and classes). To be able to call one of the functions in a program, it must first be made known to the compiler. This is achieved by means of a declaration.

To save the programmer the typing effort for the declaration of the library elements, the ANSI standard provides a series of header files that contain the declarations of the library elements. Each header file is dedicated to a specific subject area. The `printf()` function for text output, for example, belongs to the input/output (I/O) area, and its declaration is included in the `stdio.h` header file. Instead of declaring `printf()` and further input/output functions in the program itself, it is sufficient to include the `stdio.h` header file:

```
#include <stdio.h>
```

## References

See the section on the use of standard libraries and problems with the inclusion of header files.

See Practice section, category libraries.

## Comments                                                   /* */ and //

Comments are pieces of text which are ignored by the compiler. They allow the programmer to integrate notes into the source text – usually to explain the adjacent or subsequent C/C++ code.

```
C
```

In C, comments begin with the character combination slash – asterisk (/*) and end with the character combination asterisk – slash (*/). The characters enclosed by these delimiters are ignored by the compiler. This also applies to end-of-line characters, so comments can extend over several lines. According to the ANSI standard, however, comments may not be nested. (Some compilers allow nesting of comments.)

```
/* This is a comment which extends over several - more
precisely, over two - lines */

/* The following program outputs a greeting */
/* on the screen of your computer.          */
#include <stdio.h>
int main()
    {
    printf("Hello!\n");  /* call of a function */
    return 0;
    }
C++
```

In C++, comments can also be initiated with a double slash (//). The subsequent comment reaches to the end of the line. In C++, both commenting concepts can be used independently from each other.

```
/* The following program outputs a greeting */
/* on the screen of your computer.          */
#include <stdio.h>
```

```
int main()
    {
    printf("Hello!\n");  // call of a function
    return 0;
    }
```

## Tip

An idea that suggests itself in C++ is to use // comments inside the statement blocks and to reserve the /* and */ parentheses for commenting out larger blocks for the purpose of debugging.

# Larger programs and modularisation

## Description

When writing larger programs, it is recommended that the code should be modularised instead of being written statement after statement in the main() function.

Modularisation and structuring of the code should be done in such a way that

— statements and code are organised in the form of functions and classes (C++ only), and

— the source text itself is distributed across several files.

## Subdivision in functions and classes

Larger programming tasks are usually solved by formulating partial tasks and solving these in the form of separate functions. A program which reads two data items, performs a calculation of the basis of this data and then outputs the result could be split into three sub-tasks:

- read data,
- perform calculation and
- output data.

For each of these sub-tasks a separate function could be defined (where in the case of input/output the corresponding functions of the runtime library can be directly used for simple tasks).

The subdivision in functions has the advantage that

- the source text becomes clearer, and
- the source text is easier to debug and maintain.

The latter applies in particular when one of the sub-tasks needs to be executed several times. Instead of typing the corresponding statements every time, the appropriate function is called. The code is written only once, in the function definition. If the function turns out to be faulty or needs extending, this can be centrally done in the function definition.

In C++, code cannot only be organised in functions, but also in classes (data types in which variables and functions are combined).

## Subdivision into several source text files

Long code can be split across several source text files. This is sensible when one wishes to store a collection of useful functions in a separate file, for example, (often the first step to an own user library), or when several people work together on a larger program project. It is then the task of the compiler and linker to combine the individual source text files into one program.

All source text files which are together, in one step, translated and compiled into one object file by the compiler are called modules or translation units. A translation unit consists of implementation files (which have the extension .c or .cpp) and all source text files whose contents are directly or indirectly integrated via #include statements.

## Example

For a program that reads two numbers from the keyboard and calculates both the product and the average of the two numbers, one could, for example, write two special functions for calculating the product and the average and call them up in the main() function. (In practice, nobody would write separate functions for such simple calculations as product and average. The point here is, however, to illustrate the principle of modularisation.)

```c
#include <stdio.h>

int calculate_product(int z1, int z2) {
  int result;

  result = z1 * z2;    /* calculate product */
  return result;       /* return result */
}

double calculate_average(int z1, int z2) {
  double result;

  result = (z1 + z2)/2.0;    /* calculate average */
  return result;             /* return result */
}
```

```
int main(int argc, char **argv)
{
  /* variable declarations */
  int number1, number2;
  int product;
  double average;

  /* read numbers */
  printf("Enter two numbers between 0 and 100: \n\n");
  scanf("%d %d", &number1, &number2);
  fflush(stdin);

  /* calculate results */
  product = calculate_product(number1, number2);
  average = calculate_average(numebr1, number2);

  /* output results */
  puts("\n");
  printf("Product = %d\n", product);
  printf("Average = %f\n", average);

  return 0;
}
```

## References

See the Reference section, on language, for more detailed information on functions and classes.

See Practice section, category multi-file programs and libraries.

# Object-oriented programming

Object-oriented programming (OOP) does not simply mean exploiting the amenities of C++ as opposed to C or using the class libraries instead of the C libraries. In this sense, the following sample program, in which the cout class instance and the overloaded << operator are used instead of the C function printf(), cannot be considered to be programmed in an object-oriented manner.

## Example

```
/* The first C++ program */
#include <iostream>
using namespace std;
```

```
int main() {
    cout << "Hello world!" << endl;
    return 0;
    }
```

Object-oriented programming as such only begins where classes are defined and the important concepts of encapsulation and polymorphism are sensibly employed, and it finds its justification in particular where class libraries are created which can be easily and safely used.

Ultimately, all essential concepts of object-oriented programming aim to accelerate the process of program development under various aspects:

- reusability of already implemented code,
- faster development of data types through inheritance and polymorphism,
- reduced susceptibility for errors through encapsulation or
- improved readability of the programs, thanks to the object-oriented view.

Where these criteria do not apply, an implementation in C may be indicated, where the abandonment of object-oriented concepts entails a reduced code size and an improved runtime behaviour.

### References

See the Reference section, category classes.

See Practice section, category input/output.

See the section on the use of standard libraries and problems with the inclusion of header files.

# Use of standard libraries

`#include`

## Description

C and C++ have an extensive collection of functions and classes which can be used to carry out the most important programming tasks, such as input and output of data, programming with character strings (text), the use of mathematical functions such as sine, cosine, exponentiation, etc.

## Application

C/C++ uses a fairly small set of keywords, a number of operators, and an extremely extensive collection of syntax rules that specify how keywords, operators and user-defined identifiers are combined into correct C/C++ programs.

The potential of these language elements and rules is enormous, but the development of even the simplest programs with these language elements alone would be a cumbersome task, because these language elements offer no support even for the most elementary programming tasks. Therefore, one would need to

- program loops for copying character strings (that is, pieces of text), in which the strings are copied character by character,
- look up a maths textbook to find out how the sine of a number can be determined by approximation through the calculation of a trigonometric progression, and
- program input and output at operating system level.

Far-sighted programmers will implement such frequently occurring programming tasks in the form of separate functions so that – for example in the calculation of the next sine – they do not need to execute the whole calculation process again, but can call the appropriate function.

Smart programmers know that this has already been done for the most important programming tasks. Before they can call and use these functions (in C++ also classes), they need to

- inform themselves which function/class might be able to solve their problem (see the runtime libraries reference),
- inform themselves how the function/class is used (see the runtime libraries reference). For functions, it is important which arguments are passed to the function at call time and which type of result the function will return, and
- make the function (class) known to the compiler that translates their program source text.

## Warning

According to ANSI C, all header files for the C runtime library have the file name extension .h.

According to ANSI C++, however, the header file names have no extension, and the old C headers are prefixed with the letter c (`cstdio` instead of `stdio.h`). Furthermore, all library elements are declared in the `std` namespace. The correct inclusion of the header files in C++, for example the `iostream` header file with the stream classes for input and output, would therefore look as follows:

```
#include <iostream>
using namespace std;
```

Some compilers currently still support older versions of `iostream` or do not have the stream classes declared in the `std` namespace. In such cases, one is forced to follow the syntax prescribed by the compiler, usually:

```
#include <iostream.h>
```

or

```
#include <iostream>
```

## References

See Practice section, category libraries.

# Input and output

```
printf() / scanf()
cout / cin
```

## Description

To be able to interact with the user, a program must be capable of accepting information and data from the user and must in turn output information and data via the screen.

## Application

In contrast to languages such as Fortran or Basic, the C language does not have language elements of its own for input or output. This does not mean that no I/O operations can be carried out with C or C++ programs; one must simply call a suitable function of the runtime library instead of a keyword of the language.

C mainly uses the functions

- `printf()` for output on the console (screen), and
- `scanf()` for reading from the keyboard.

C++ makes use of the classes

- `cout` (console output) and
- `cin` (keyboard input)

and the stream operators << and >>.

## Warning

According to ANSI, the above functions and classes are part of the standard libraries of C/C++ and therefore always available. The exchange of information between user and program via these functions and classes is, however, restricted to console programs. Programs with graphical user interfaces (GUI), which run under Windows, X Windows or OSF Motif, use other input and output methods which are supported and implemented by means of special APIs (collections of functions and classes for specific programming tasks).

# Examples

Input and output under C:

```c
#include <stdio.h>

int main()
{
  int number1, number2;

  /* read data */
  printf("Enter two numbers between 0 and 100: \n\n");
  scanf("%d %d", &number1, &number2);
  fflush(stdin);

  /* ouput data */
  puts("\n");
  printf("1st number = %d\n", number1);
  printf("2nd number = %d\n", number2);
  printf("Product = %d\n", number1 * number2);
  return 0;
}
```

Input and output under C++:

```cpp
#include <iostream>
using namespace std;

int main()
{
  int number1, number2;

  /* read data */
  cout << "Enter two numbers between 0 and 100: \n\n";
  cin >> number1 >> number2;
  /* output data */
  cout << endl;
  cout << "1st number = " << number1 << endl;
  cout << "2nd number = " << number2 << endl;
  cout << "Product = " << number1 * number2 << endl;
  return 0;
}
```

# References

See Practice section, category input and output, and category miscellaneous, Windows programming.

# Program flow

C/C++ programs consist of a collection of declarations and definitions. Statements can only be found in functions (and in C++ also in the methods (element functions) of classes). This opens the question with which statement the execution of a program begins.

- Every C/C++ program begins with the function main(), which must be defined in the source text of the program.
- The statements in the main() function are executed one after the other.
- By calling a function from inside another function, including main(), for example, the program flow can be controlled and the source code modularised by splitting it across several functions.
- Inside a function, the program flow can be controlled via branches (if, switch) and loops (for, while).

## Warning

Readers who wish to use C/C++ to program for Windows should note that Windows programs use the WinMain() function instead of the main() function. Depending on the compiler and class library used, WinMain() can in turn be replaced with another function (for example OwlMain() for Borland C++ with OWL) or a class instance (for example a global object of the MFC class CWinApp in Visual C++).

Console programs executed under Windows (that is, programs running in the MS-DOS Prompt window and without a Windows interface of their own), however, use the main() function, as do pure DOS or UNIX programs.

## References

See the Reference section, categories program control, functions, exception handling.

# Program creation

## Description

In order to make an executable program out of a program source text formulated in C/C++, the source needs to be compiled; that is, converted into machine code by the compiler. In cooperation with the linker, this machine code is used to generate an executable file (in Windows, this has the extension .exe) which can run only on specific platforms (combinations of processor and operating systems, for example, an Intel-compatible processor and the Windows 98 operating system).

## Application

The creation of a program is not finished by entering the source text in an editor. Before a program can be executed, it needs to be converted into machine code. When a program consists of several modules, these must be linked. These tasks are accomplished by the compiler and the linker.

1. **Enter the source text in an editor.** In principle, this can be done with any ASCII text editor. PC compilers usually dispose of an integrated development environment (IDE) with its own editor, which offers additional support with the program creation.

2. **Copy header files.** At the beginning of the compilation, the source text of the header files listed in the #include directive(s) is copied into the source text of the program file.

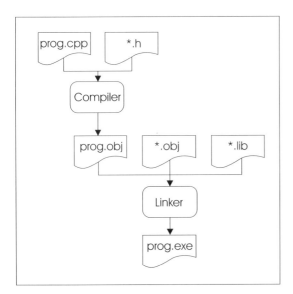

The sequence of program generation

3. **Compile source text files.** The compiler translates the source text into the computer's object code. Object code is usually adapted to a specific environment (computer configuration) and is not portable between different environments (platforms). Syntax errors in the program are signalled by the compiler and must be corrected.

4. **Link object code files (.obj) and libraries (.lib).** When a program consists of several source text files, these are individually translated by the compiler into object code. The linker then has to link together these object code files and the object code of the library functions used into one program file (.exe in Windows).

5. **Debug.** After compiling and linking, an executable program is present which may contain bugs. With executable programs, a distinction is made between runtime errors, which usually manifest themselves through program crashes or endless loops, and logical errors, when the program runs but does not fulfil its purpose. To detect these errors, a debugger is usually used which allows the programmer to execute and check the program step by step.

## The most popular compilers

### The GNU compiler

The GNU compiler is a freely available compiler, which can be downloaded from the Internet free of charge (http://sources.redhat.com). The GNU compiler is available for UNIX as well as for Windows.

A slightly awkward feature for Windows users is the fact that the GNU compiler does not dispose of an integrated development environment and must therefore be called explicitly from within the MS-DOS Prompt.

1. Write your source text with the aid of an arbitrary ASCII editor and save the file.

2. Provided you have included the /bin directory of the compiler in your path, so that the gcc or g++ compiler can be called from everywhere, change to the directory where you have stored the source text file.

3. Call the C++ compiler with the file name of the source text file:

```
g++ sourcetext.cpp
```

or

```
gcc sourcetext.c
```

for calling the pure C compiler.

The finished program will be called a.exe (a.out under UNIX) and can be executed.

If you wish, you can also specify an explicit name for the executable file.

```
g++ sourcetext.cpp -o progname
```

Programs that consist of several modules are created by listing all source files involved (without including the #include files).

```
gcc sourcetext1.cpp sourcetext2.cpp -o progname
```

If you wish to pass the compiler any options (for example -ansi for strict ANSI-compatible code or -c for compiling without linking), you write these after the file name.

```
gcc sourcetext.cpp -ansi -c
```

For the generation of Windows programs, various libraries must be explicitly linked:

```
gcc winprog.cpp -lkernel32 -luser32 -lgdi32
```

Information on which other libraries may have to be included can be found in the compiler documentation.

## The Borland C++ compiler

In the IDE (Integrated Development Environment) of the Borland C++ compiler, programs are managed in the form of projects. Although console applications which consist of only one file can be created without project management, there is no reason why one should not use the options provided.

1. Create a new project (File/New/Project in Borland C++ 5.0; in version 4.5 the command was still to be found in the Project menu). The Target Expert appears, in which you can specify which kind of application you want to create.

2. Enter the project directory and a name for the executable file. Select Application as the target type, Win32 as the environment and Console as the target model (or DOS as the environment if you still work with a Win16 operating system). The subsequent settings are automatically adjusted for you, but make sure that OWL is not linked.

3. Open a new source text file. In the project window that appears, click on the node of the .cpp file. (If additional nodes have been created (.rc, .def) you can delete them with commands in the context menu). An editor window appears for your source text file.

4. Enter your source text and save the file.

5. Call the compiler (Project/Compile Project in Borland C++ 5.0).

6. Execute the program (Debug/Execute in Borland C++ 5.0). Under Win32 the program runs in an MS-DOS window, which disappears immediately after the program is terminated. To prevent this, you can extend the sample programs by calling the getchar() function prior to the return statement of main(). This

causes the program to wait for keyboard input, and the DOS window remains visible.

The settings for compiler and linker are specified in the corresponding dialogs (Options/Project in Borland C++ 5.0).

For the generation of Windows programs, select the target type Application, the Win32 environment and the GUI target model (instead of Console) in the Target Expert. Ensure that no additional class library (OWL, OCF, MFC, etc.) is linked, since this book only describes pure API programs.

## The C++Builder

Borland's C++Builder also works with project management. While C++Builder 1.0 used to manage the projects individually, version 3.0 now provides the option of managing several related projects together in a project group (in analogy to the working areas in Visual C++).

1. Create a new console project (File/New in C++Builder 3.0). A multi-page dialog window appears in which you change to the New page.

2. Double-click on the Console Expert icon (text screen application for 1.0).

3. The source text editor of the C++Builder appears directly with an extra page for your source text. Save project and source text (File/Save All).

4. Enter your source text – either by fitting it into the predefined frame or by deleting the predefined frame and then typing your text.

5. Execute the program (Start/Start). Under Win32 the program runs in an MS-DOS window, which disappears immediately after the program is terminated. To prevent this, you can extend the sample programs by calling the getchar() function prior to the return statement of main(). This causes the program to wait for keyboard input, and the DOS window remains visible.

The settings for compiler and linker are specified in the corresponding dialogs (Options/Project in C++Builder 1.0 or Project/Options in 3.0).

For the generation of Windows programs, double-click on the Application icon in step 1 instead of Console Expert.

## Warning

When you work with C++Builder 3, you may have to include the <condefs.h> header file in your console application.

## Tip

The main advantage of the C++Builder lies in the RAD (Rapid Application Development) environment for the development of Windows programs, that is, the visual, component-based creation of programs.

### The Visual C++ compiler

Microsoft's Visual C++ compiler also works with project management. In addition, in Visual C++ projects are managed in workspaces (in this way, for example, the projects for a Windows application and support DLLs and LIBs can be managed together in one workspace).

1. Create a new console project (File/New in Visual C++ 5.0 and later versions). A multi-page dialog window appears in which you change to the Projects page.

2. Enter a project name, select the path under which the directory for the project's source files will be created, activate the option Create new workspace and double-click on the Win32 Console application icon. (In Visual C++ 6, a dialog window appears in which, besides an empty project, you can also have projects created for you with a file and a basic frame. Steps 3 and 4 can then be omitted.)

3. Open a new source text file (File/New, page Files since Visual C++ 5.0). Enter a file name and then double-click on the C++ source code file icon.

4. After the file has been created, double-click in the working area window (page Files) to load the file into an editor window.

5. Enter your source text and save the file.

6. Compile and link the project (Create/Create <TARGETFILE>).

7. Execute the program (Create/Execute <TARGETFILE>).

The settings for compiler and linker are specified in the corresponding dialogs (Project/Settings in Visual C++ 5.0 and later versions).

For the generation of Windows programs, double-click on the Win32 Application icon in step 1 instead of Win32 Console Application.

# Language concepts and syntax

## Language elements

## Character set

### Description

Two character sets must be distinguished:

- The **base character set**, which is provided by every ANSI-C/C++ compiler to write the program code.
- The **target or environment character set**, which the program uses during execution, for instance for input and output.

### The base character set

The base character set, which is recognised by every C/C++ compiler and with whose characters the program source text is written, contains the following characters:

| a | b | c | d | e | f | g | h | i | j | k | l | m | n | o | p | q | r | s | t |
|---|---|---|---|---|---|---|---|---|---|---|---|---|---|---|---|---|---|---|---|
| u | v | w | x | y | z | | | | | | | | | | | | | | |
| A | B | C | D | E | F | G | H | I | J | K | L | M | N | O | P | Q | R | S | T |
| U | V | W | X | Y | Z | | | | | | | | | | | | | | |
| 0 | 1 | 2 | 3 | 4 | 5 | 6 | 7 | 8 | 9 | | | | | | | | | | |
| _ | { | } | [ | ] | # | ( | ) | < | > | % | : | ; | . | ? | * | + | - | / | ^ |
| & | \| | ~ | ! | = | , | \ | " | ' | | | | | | | | | | | |

as well as:

| | |
|---|---|
| Space | New page (FF) |
| Horizontal tab (HT) | New line (NL) |
| Vertical tab (VT) | |

## Source and target character set

The target character set is compiler-specific. Compilers that run under Windows at present usually use the Windows ANSI character set, whose first 128 characters are equivalent to the characters of the traditional ASCII character set (see the Appendix). In future, UNICODE (which is already supported by Windows NT 4.0) will undoubtedly take over.

You can use the characters of this character set in comments and in character or string literals.

Furthermore, you can also use the following escape sequences in character and string literals:

| Character | | Escape sequence |
|---|---|---|
| New line | NL (LF) | \n |
| Horizontal tab | HT | \t |
| Vertical tab | VT | \v |
| Backspace | BS | \b |
| Carriage return | CR | \r |
| New page (form feed) | FF | \f |
| Bell | BEL | \a |
| Backslash | \ | \\ |
| Question mark | ? | \? |
| Single quote | ' | \' |
| Double quote | " | \" |
| Octal code | | \ooo |
| Hexadecimal code | | \xhhh |

## Examples

```
#include <stdio.h>
#include <string.h>

int main(int argc, char **argv)
{
  char horriblehaegar[100];            // no umlauts in identifiers
                                       // (only base character set),
  strcpy(horriblehaegar,"Hägar");      // but OK in string literals

  printf("Grandpa Hägar's nephew: %s\n", horriblehaegar);
  return 0;
}
```

## References
See Practice section, category internationalisation and localisation.

# Trigraph sequences

## Description
Trigraph sequences are series of three characters each which can be used to substitute certain characters of the base character set.

## Application
The base character set is closely tied to the English language and the English keyboard layout. Due to language-specific keyboard layouts, programmers from other countries might find entering certain characters inconvenient, or even only possible using the ALT+ASCII code. For this reason, the ANSI standard defines a range of trigraph sequences, which the compiler transforms into the corresponding characters of the base character set at the start of the compilation process.

| Synonym | Meaning | Synonym | Meaning |
|---------|---------|---------|---------|
| ??= | # | ??! | \| |
| ??/ | \ | ??< | { |
| ??' | ^ | ??> | } |
| ??( | [ | ??- | ~ |
| ??) | ] | | |

## Tip
The trigraph sequences do not always provide much help with foreign language keyboard layouts. To keep the program code legible, it is advisable to use trigraph sequences as sparingly as possible.

## Examples
```
??=include <stdio.h>

int main(int argc, char **argv)
??<
  printf("Hello??/n");
  return 0;
??>
```

# Keywords and symbols

## Description

C and C++ recognise a range of keywords and symbols, which have a fixed meaning within the language.

## Keywords

| | | |
|---|---|---|
| asm (C++ only) | false (C++ only) | sizeof |
| auto | float | static |
| bool (C++ only) | for | static_cast (C++ only) |
| break | friend (C++ only) | struct |
| case | goto | switch |
| catch (C++ only) | if | template (nur C++) |
| case | inline (C++ only) | this (C++ only) |
| class (C++ only) | int | throw (C++ only) |
| const | long | true (C++ only) |
| const_cast (C++ only) | mutable (C++ only) | try (C++ only) |
| continue | namespace (C++ only) | typedef |
| default | new (C++ only) | typeid (C++ only) |
| delete (C++ only) | operator (C++ only) | typename (C++ only) |
| do | private (C++ only) | union |
| double | protected (C++ only) | unsigned |
| dynamic_cast (C++ only) | public (C++ only) | using (C++ only) |
| else | register | virtual (C++ only) |
| enum | reinterpret_cast (C++ only) | void |
| explicit (C++ only) | return | volatile |
| export (C++ only) | short | wchar_t (C++ only) |
| extern | signed | while |

## Warning

Keywords cannot be used as identifiers for variables, functions, and so on.

## Symbols

C and C++ recognise a surprisingly large number of meaningful symbols, the majority of which are made up of the many operators of the language.

| Symbol | Brief definition | Symbol | Brief definition |
|---|---|---|---|
| ; | End of a statement or declaration | -- | Decrement |
| { } | Define statement block | -> | Element pointer selector |
| [ ] | Array definition | . | Dot operator |
| [ ] | Array indexing | * | Pointer declaration |
| ( ) | Type conversion | * | Dereference operator |
| ( ) | Parameter list of functions | == | Test for equality |
| ... | Variable parameter numberl | < | Less than comparison |
| = | Assignment | > | Greater than comparison |
| + | Addition | <= | Less than or equal comparison |
| += | Addition and assignment | => | Greater than or equal comparison |
| - | Subtraction | << | Bitwise left shift |
| -= | Subtraction and assignment | <<= | Bitwise left shift and assignment |
| * | Multiplication | >> | Bitwise right shift |
| *= | Multiplication and assignment | >>= | Bitwise right shift and assignment |
| / | Division | ?: | Conditional operator |
| /= | Division and assignment | ^ | Bitwise exclusive OR |
| % | Modulus operator | ^= | Bitwise exclusive OR and assignment |
| %= | Modulus operator and assignment | \| | Bitwise OR |
| ! | Logic negation | \|= | Bitwise OR and assignment |
| != | Test for inequality | \|\| | Logical OR |
| & | Reference declaration | ~ | Complement |
| & | Unary: address of operand | : | Class initialiser |
| & | Binary: bitwise AND | :: | Scope operator (C++ only) |
| &= | Bitwise AND and assignment | .* | Dereferencing of pointers to class elements (C++ only) |
| && | Logical AND | ->* | Dereferencing of pointers to class elements (C++ only)) |
| , | Sequential evaluation | # | String formation |
| ++ | Increment | ## | Base symbol operation |

## Alternative characters

There are alternative character sequences for a few symbols which can be used by programmers with inconvenient national keyboard layouts (similar to the trigraph sequences).

| Alternative | for | |
|---|---|---|
| <% | { | Start of statement block |
| %> | } | End of statement block |
| <: | [ | Array definition and indexing |
| :> | ] | Array definition and indexing |
| %: | # | String formation |
| %:%: | ## | Base symbol combination |
| and | && | Logical AND |
| and_eq | &= | Bitwise AND and assignment |
| bitand | & | Bitwise AND |
| bitor | \| | Bitwise OR |
| compl | ~ | Complement |
| not | ! | Negation operator |
| not_eq | != | Compares two arithmetic operands for inequality |
| or | \|\| | Logical OR |
| or_eq | \|= | Bitwise OR and assignment of result |
| xor | ^ | Bitwise exclusive OR |
| xor_eq | ^= | Bitwise exclusive OR and assignment of result |

# User-defined identifiers: definition and declaration

## Description

It is not possible to write programs using only the keywords and operators of C/C++. This is why C/C++ allow you to introduce your own elements into a program. All elements introduced by a programmer must be declared and defined.

## Application

The most important elements a programmer can introduce into a program are:

- Variables, to store data temporarily,
- Uer-defined data types, to organise and facilitate data management (including the definition of classes), and

- **Functions**, to combine related statements and modularise the source text.

## Warning

The two terms declaration and definition are often used synonymously, even though their meanings are quite different.

## Declaration

A declaration means to make the name (identifier) of a variable, function, class, template, data type or label known to the compiler. Besides the name of the new element, the declaration also contains all the necessary information that enables the compiler to control the proper use of the element in the program source text, and to translate statements, in which the element is used, into machine code.

- By declaring a variable, the name, type, memory class and visibility of the identifier are specified.
- By declaring a function, its name, return value, parameter list and visibility are specified.
- A declaration does not use up any memory.
- A variable declaration is automatically also a definition, unless the declaration is marked as `extern` and does not contain an explicit initialisation, or a static element of a class is being declared.

## Definition

Only through the definition does the compiler allocate memory for an element.

- For variables, this memory location stores the value of the variable.
- For functions, this memory location stores the code of the function.
- The allocation of names to memory areas has to be unique; that is, one name cannot refer to two different memory areas at the same time.

In C, this means, that each identifier can only be defined once within a scope.

In C++, it is possible to use function identifiers and operators in several definitions within one scope thanks to overloading. (The compiler solves this by extending the names by a coded form of the parameters and operands, so that each extended name is assigned exactly one memory area.)

## References

See scope, visibility, life span.

# Variables and data types

## Variables and data types

### Description

No matter what type of program you are writing, the main task of a program is always to process data. While the program is running, this data is stored at different places in the working memory. Variables are employed to access the data without having to bother with memory addresses.

### Variables

A variable is a name for a memory area in which a data abject can be stored (for example, an integer, a floating point number, a string, and so on). Via the variable name, the memory area can be accessed to read the existing data in it or to write new data into it. To do so the compiler creates a symbol table, in which the initial address of the corresponding memory area is noted for each variable name. During compilation it is then able to substitute each occurrence of a variable name with the appropriate address. To create this symbol table, it is essential that each variable is declared before it is used, for example:

```
int first_number;
```

Apart from the name of the variable, the most important specification in the declaration is the data type.

### Data types

Depending on the type of data that can be stored in a variable, different data types can be distinguished, for example:

- `int` for integers,
- `double` for floating point numbers,
- `char` for characters (letters, digits, special characters), and
- `bool` for Boolean variables, which can adopt a truth value (`true`, `false`).

The data types determine

- The **internal representation** of the variable values in the processor. (Remember that all the data in the memory have to be represented by a sequence of zeros and ones. The coding of a character into a bit sequence is carried out according to different rules than, for example, the coding of an integer or a floating point number.)

- The size of the **memory area**. (A floating point number requires more memory than a single character, and a structure variable usually requires more memory than a floating point number.)
- The range of **values**. (This ultimately results from the size of the memory area and the coding type.)
- The **operations** that can be carried out on the values of the data type. (For example, integers can be added, but not strings.)

C and C++ distinguish between elementary data types, which are rooted in the language (int, float, double, char, wchar_t and bool in C++), and combined data types, which are defined by the programmer (lists, arrays, structures and classes in C++).

According to their shared characteristics and operational areas in programming, the data types can be further classified:

- **Integral types**. The data type bool, the data types char and wchar_t, the data types int and long, lists (enum), bit fields. Integral data types are allowed as a data type for switch variables.
- **Arithmetic types**. All integral types plus the data types float, double and long double. They are permitted as operands for the arithmetic operators (+, --, *, /).
- **Scalar types**. Arithmetic data types and pointers. These may be used as loop variables for for.

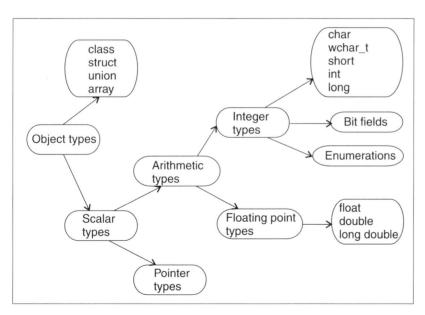

# Elementary data types

```
short, int, long
float, double, long double
char, wchar_t
bool
```

## Description

Elementary data types are firmly rooted in the language in the form of keywords.

## Application

With the help of elementary data types the programmer can declare variables for the various types of data (numbers, characters, logical values). Furthermore, it is also possible to define your own combined data types on the basis of elementary data types.

The programming languages C and C++ know the following elementary data types:

- the data types `short`, `int` and `long` for integer values,
- the data types `float`, `double` and `long double` for floating point numbers,
- the data types `char` and `wchar_t` for characters (letters, digits, punctuation marks, and so on), and
- the data type `bool` for logic values (C++ only).

The range of values of the data types – that is, the range of values which can be assigned to variables of this data type – depends on the number of bytes which the compiler provides for variables of this data type in its memory.

Apart from the `bool` data type, all these data types are signed, which means that it is possible to assign negative or positive values to these variables. By prefixing the keyword unsigned it can be determined that only positive values be permitted for the data type. The keyword signed explicitly states that a data type is signed and is usually redundant, since data types are signed by default. The only exception is the data type `char`.

## Warning

According to ANSI, for `char` it is not predetermined whether the data type is signed or not. When in doubt an explicit declaration as signed `char` or unsigned `char` is recommended when declaring the variable.

| Identifier | Bytes | Value range* |
|---|---|---|
| bool | 1 | false, true |
| signed char | 1 | -128 to 127 |

| Identifier | Bytes | Value range* |
|---|---|---|
| unsigned char | 1 | 0 to 255 |
| wchar_t | 2 | 0 to 65.535 |
| int signed int | 4 | -2.147.483.648 to 2.147.483.647 |
| unsigned int | 4 | 0 to 4.294.967.295 |
| short, short int | 2 | -32.768 bis 32.767 |
| short, short int | 2 | -32.768 to 32.767 |
| unsigned short int | 4 | 0 to 65.535 |
| long, long int signed long int | 4 | -2.147.483.648 to 2.147.483.647 |
| floatt | 4 | ca. -3.4E +38 to 3.4E+38 |
| double | 8 | ca. -1.8E +308 to 1.8E+308 |
| long double | 10 | ca. -ca. -3.4E +4932 to 3.4 E+4932 |

* The stated value ranges are typical value ranges for 32-bit systems. However, it should be noted that the value ranges depend on the coding of the values in binary representations. This binary coding is not predetermined in every detail by the ANSI standard, and is therefore implementation-specific, which means it ultimately depends on the respective compiler.

## Tip

The minimum and maximum values for the individual data types are determined in the ANSI C header files `limits.h` and `float.h` or, in C++, in the specialisations of the template class numeric_limits (from `limits`), and can be accessed from there.

## References

See Practice section, category variables and data types.

# Memory representation of integer types

`short, int, long`

## Description

Signed integer values are usually binary-coded according to the second complement. The first bit to the left codes the arithmetic sign: 0 represents positive numbers, 1 negative numbers. Multiplication by −1 is equivalent to inverting all bits with a subsequent addition of 1.

$$\partial\left(a_n, \underline{\quad}, a_0\right) := \begin{cases} \sum_{i=0}^{n-1} a_i \cdot 2^i & \text{for } a_n = 0 \\ \sum_{i=0}^{n-1} a_i \cdot 2^i - 2^n & \text{for } a_n = 1 \end{cases}$$

## Memory representation

```
int i=3;
```

| 00000000 | 00000000 | 00000000 | 00000011 |

&i

## References

See Practice section, category variables and data types.

# Representation of floating point numbers

`float, double, long double`

## Description

Floating point numbers are coded by two values, one of which is known as mantissa, and the other exponent. In this exponential script, for example, the number 54.123 appears as follows: 0.54123*10e4. The number 0.54123 is in this example the (normalised) mantissa, the number 4 the exponent to the base 10 (however, compilers usually use the base 2).

The ANSI standard does not explicitly prescribe how floating point numbers should be coded. However, the coding has to follow the floating point model prescribed by ANSI, and the characteristics of the coding have to be recorded in the constants from the header file `float.h` (`numeric_limits<float>` and `numeric_limits<double>` from the header file limits for C++).

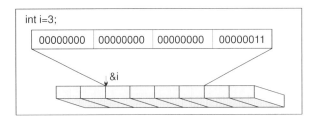

$$x = s \cdot b^e \cdot \left[\sum_{k=1}^{p} f_k \cdot b^{-k}\right], \; e_{\min} \leq e \leq e_{\max}$$

```
s = sign
b = base of the exponent
e = exponent
p = number of positions of the mantissa (determ
f_k = mantissa
```

## Memory representation

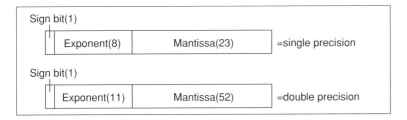

## References

See Practice section, category variables and data types.

# Signs of integer data types

## Description

By stating the keywords as being unsigned or signed, it can be determined in the variable declaration whether the arithmetic sign has to be coded or not. The value range of the data type changes accordingly.

## Application

Value range changes due to signed/unsigned keywords:

| Data type | Signed | Unsigned |
|-----------|--------|----------|
| charr | –128 to 127 | 0 to 255 |
| short | –32768 to 327677 | 0 to 655355 |
| int | –2.147.483.648 to is 2.147.483.647 | 0 to 4.294.967.2955 |
| long | –2.147.483.648 to 2.147.483.647 | 0 to 4.294.967.295 |

## Warning

- Variables of unsigned data types cannot overflow. When trying to assign values to it that are outside its scope, the modulus operator is automatically used for the value.

- Note that in C/C++ the data types are internally adapted by operands (arithmetical conversions). For example, if you compare a signed value with an unsigned value, the signed will be interpreted as an unsigned value. Thus in this way a small negative value can become a large positive value. (Note also that the return value of the `sizeof` operator is `unsigned`.)

- When there is a signed `char` variable in the range from −128 to 127, there will be a corresponding unsigned `char` variable in the range from 0 to 255. This may cause problems when porting. It can be prevented by prefixing one of the qualifiers `signed` or `unsigned`.

# Declaration of variables

`data type variable name;`

## Description

Variables are identifiers introduced by the programmer to which values can be assigned. Which values can be assigned to a variable depends on the data type of that variable. The compiler links the variable with a memory area in which the current value of the variable is stored.

## Application

To a program variables are like temporary storage, where data can be stored, accessed when required, and processed. A variable is introduced by means of a declaration and is, in principle, available from the place of its declaration onwards.

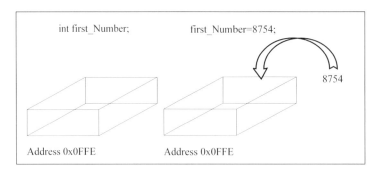

## Warning

The availability of a variable depends on several factors: the place of declaration, the specifiers used in the declaration, the scope and the life span of the variable.

## Syntax

```
data type variable name;
data type var1, var2, var2;
```

- **data type**: in the declaration the data type is stated first by employing the corresponding type identifier. Those permitted are elementary as well as previously defined, combined data types.
- **variable name**: separated by at least one space, the type identifier is followed by the name of the variable. Several variables may be declared at once. Here the identifiers are separated by commas.

## Initialisation

Variables can be assigned a value during declaration.

```
int month = 12;
```

## Specifier

```
specifier data type variable name;
```

The variable declaration can be specified further by means of a range of keywords:

| | |
|---|---|
| keyword `const` | Determines that no other value can be assigned to the variable after initialisation (value assignment during declaration). `const int month = 12;` |
| keyword `volatile` | Informs the compiler that this variable may not be sacrificed to possible optimisations during compilation. `volatile double var;` |
| memory class specifier | Explicitly assigns a memory class. Together with the place of declaration the memory class determines the visibility and life span of the variable. `auto` `extern` `register` `static` |

## Memory class                                                                    auto

The keyword `auto` explicitly assigns the automatic memory class to a variable. This memory class specification can only be used within block areas (and for parameters) and is superfluous elsewhere, as local variables are `auto` by default.

Memory for automatic variables is created on the stack when the block in which they are declared is processed, and is freed up again when the block is left.

## Memory class                                                       register

Fundamentally, the specifier `register` is equivalent to the keyword `auto`. Furthermore, it informs the compiler that the variable which has been declared in this way has to be accessed as quickly as possible.

For PCs this means that the variables must be loaded into the `register` of the processor. However, the compiler does not have to do this.

In contrast to C++, in C it is not possible to find out the address of an object that has been declared with the register, no matter whether this object is in the processor register or not. Thus, there are no pointers to register variables in C.

In principle, you should leave the division of the registers to powerful compilers and do without the specification of the keyword `register`.

## Memory class                                                         static

The keyword `static` implies local validity and a one-off statement (that is, static elements are not created on the stack).

This results in three important operational areas:

**Identifiers, which have been declared globally, usually have an external linkage** (that is, in programs which are linked together from several modules, they identify the same object in all modules). If they have been declared as `static`, they are only valid within their module.

**Local variables** of functions are reallocated when calling the function and are destroyed when leaving the function. If such a variable has been declared as `static`, memory is only reserved and initialised for the variable at the initial call of the function. Additionally, its life span only ends with the program and not with the function. The visibility remains unchanged.

Classes cannot be declared as `static`, yet class elements can (see category classes).

- A static class-data element fulfils similar tasks as a global variable. Such a data element is only initiated once (and that is outside the class!) and then shared by all the instances of the class. (Usually each instance of the class has its own copy of the class elements.)

- A static class method is one which can only access static class elements and, like a static data element, can be called by all the instances of the class, or through the class name.

Declarations of function parameters and function declarations in a single block area cannot be specified as `static`.

## Memory class                                                    extern

By means of the specifie `extern` an external linkage can be assigned to an object or a function. An external linkage means that all occurrences of an identifier with an external linkage refer to the same object. In an internal linkage only the identifiers from a single file refer to the same object. Identifiers without linkage identify definite objects.

- Objects and functions, which have been declared in a namespace or globally, automatically have an external linkage, unless they have been previously declared with a different memory class specifier. (Furthermore, in C++ global objects that have been declared as `const` also have an internal linkage.)

- Class elements and function parameters cannot be declared as `extern`.

- Object definitions without simultaneous initialisation are marked as a pure declaration by the specifier. In this way an object with an external linkage can be made known in all modules without this resulting in multiple definitions.

- C++ permits multiple definitions of functions with the same name, as far as these are distinguished by number and types of parameters. Internally this name ambiguity is solved by the compiler in such a way that it assigns new names to the individual function definitions into which the parameters are included in coded form. This is not always desirable; for example, when functions of compiled C code are used. Therefore, the name extension can be suppressed by means of the linkage specifier external `"C"`.

## Examples

```
short int week;
char     character;
int      day, month;
int      year = 1998;   // initialisation
const int months = 12;  // constant variable
```

## References

See scope, visibility, life span.

# Scope

## Description

In C/C++ a scope is assigned to each variable, depending on the position in the program in which the variable has been declared.

## Application

The scope of a variable is the range of a program in which a variable is valid. Variables can only be used within their scope and after their declaration.

## Tip

The programmer can adapt the automatic assignment of scopes by integrating certain memory class specifiers into the declaration.

## Scopes

- **Block area**: Variables which are declared within a statement block (defined by the curly brackets {..}) have local validity. They are only known within the block, and exist only as long as the block is being processed. The compiler creates these variables dynamically. After the block has been finished, the memory of the local variables is freed up again. With this their value is lost. Local variables are usually declared within functions.

- C only permits declarations at the beginning of a block; that is, before any statements. However, C++ permits declarations at any position within the block (even in loop headers).

- **File scope**: Variables which are declared outside of statement blocks, classes and namespaces have global validity and can be used from the position of their declaration onwards. They have a global life span; that is, they exist from the start of the program to its end.

- **Function area**: This area is only valid for the assignment of marks for the `goto` statement, since marks must not point out of the function in which they have been declared.

- **Class scope** (C++ only): Elements of classes are – except for static elements – only valid within their class. They are created during instance formation and are destroyed when the instance is resolved.

- **Namespace** (C++ only): In C++ it is possible to divide the global scope by declaring namespaces. The declaration of a namespace puts together a number of declarations in curly brackets. The declaration starts with the keyword `namespace`.

## Example

```
#include <stdio.h>

namespace Specials   // declarations in namespace
  {
  int var1;
```

```
class demo {            // declarations in class scope
    int wert;
  public:
    demo(): wert(3) {}
  };
}

void func(int param)    // declarations in block scope
  {
  int var;
  }

int var;                // declarations in file scope

int main()
  {
  ...
  return 0;
```

## References

See namespace.

See visibility, life span.

# Namespaces

```
namespace {   }
```

## Description

By means of the keyword `namespace` the programmer can divide the global scope (file scope) into sub-areas.

Furthermore, namespace declarations can be introduced specifically into particular scopes (such as into the block area of a function or into a different namespace).

## Application

The division of the global scope is particularly interesting for programmers, who work together with other programmers in the development of bigger software projects. If in such a case all programmers declared their global variables in a shared global scope, this could quickly result in error messages from the linker, due to several global variables with the same name created when joining the source text files into one program. This can be prevented by creating individual namespaces.

Furthermore, a programmer who wants to use elements from a namespace is free to call them up, individually if necessary, or by means of a keyword to introduce all declarations from the namespace with a statement into his own global scope or into the block area of a special function.

## Declaration of namespaces

```
namespace identifier
{
  // declarations
}
```

- Namespaces can only be declared in the global area or within another namespace.
- Namespaces that have been declared without their own identifier are assigned the identifier unique, which is replaced by a non-ambiguous identifier during compilation. This identifier is different in each translation unit (file). Therefore, the declaration of an object in an unnamed namespace is equivalent to a declaration as static in the global area.
- Elements of a namespace can be defined directly within the declaration of the namespace, or outside by using the namespace identifier and the area operator.

## Using namespaces

```
using namespace NameOfTheNamespace;
```

By means of the keyword using a namespace can be introduced into a different scope. Subsequently all elements of the newly introduced namespace are also identified in the scope, in which the namespace has been introduced.

After introducing the namespace it is possible to directly access the elements of the namespace in the surrounding scope through the identifier of the element (without prefixing the namespace).

- If there is an element in the surrounding scope which has the same name as one of the elements of the introduced namespace, the element from the surrounding scope will hide the element from the namespace. By prefixing the namespace the namespace element can be accessed.
- Unnamed namespaces are always idenified in the surrounding namespace.
- Namespaces cannot be introduced into classes, only into methods of classes.

## Extending namespaces

```
namespace identifier {
  // declarations
}
```

```
namespace identifier {
  // further declarations
}
```

Namespaces can be declared several times, in which the following declarations are treated as extensions.

In this way namespaces can be declared, switched and extended beyond file boundaries.

## Access to elements in namespaces

Elements which have been declared in namespaces cannot simply be called outside the namespace by the name under which they have been declared within the namespace. Either:

- the complete identifier (including the name of the namespace) has to be used, or

- the identifier has to be introduced through a using statement. This is equivalent to a new declaration. After the new declaration the element of the namespace can be accessed without prefixing the namespace. However, if there is already an identifier with the same name in the surrounding scope the new declaration will fail, or

- the namespace and all declarations it contains have to be introduced through a using statement. Subsequently, it is possible to access the elements of the namespace without prefixing the namespace. However, this is not a new declaration. If there are identifiers with the same name in the surrounding scope and in the namespace, the identifiers from the surrounding scope will hide the namespace elements. With a complete qualification (prefixing the namespace to the identifier), however, it is also possible to access the hidden elements.

## Synonyms

```
namespace Declarations_for_special_purpose
namespace Spec1 = Decarations_for_special_purpose
```

It is possible to introduce synonyms for the identifiers of namespaces. Thus, aliases can be defined for namespaces with very long names.

## Examples

```
namespace A {           // definition of a namespace
   int i = 1;
   }
namespace B {
   int i = 2;
   using namespace A;  // introduction of a namespace
   }
```

```
int main() {
   //cout << i;        // error because i is not declared globally
                       // and no namespace has been switched on
   cout << A::i;       // ok, access via complete qualifier
   using namespace A;
   cout << i;          // ok, yields A::i
   using namespace B;
   //cout << i;        // error, can be A::i or B::i
   return 1;
   }
```

The second example shows the options and pitfalls when extending namespaces:

```
namespace Demo {
   int i = 1;          // demo::i
   void func1(int);
   void func2(int);
   class X {
      int i = 2;       // demo::X::i
      };
   }
namespace demo {       // extension
   //int i = 3;         // error: double definition
   void func1(float);  // overloading
   void func2(int);    // ok: redeclaration
   namespace {
      int i = 4;        // demo::unique::i
      }
   }
```

## References

See Practice section, category variables and data types.

See bases section, using the standard libraries.

# Visibility and hiding

## Description

In principle every element which has been introduced by means of a declaration is visible in its scope from the point of declaration – which means it can be called and used by its name.

## Hiding

If the same identifier is used several times to declare elements in embedded scopes (for example, for a global variable and a local variable with the same name in a function), the variable of the innermost scope hides all variables of the enclosing scopes.

In C++ it is possible to access hidden variables from the global scope by means of the scope operators:

- for global variables from the file scope the identifier is simply prefixed to the operator `::var_name`
- for variables from namespaces the namespace is also to be specified: `namespace::var_name`

Furthermore, in derived classes hidden elements of the base classes can be accessed with the scope operator: `baseclass::element`.

## Warning

The multiple use of an identifier within one scope is only possible in exceptional cases:

- Classes and `enum` identifiers can be hidden by identifiers for variables, functions and `enum` elements in the same scope.
- The overloading of functions in C++ is based on the use of the same identifier for the definition of several functions in one scope. (The compiler internally resolves the names by using the parameter list.)

## Examples

```
int value = 1;          // globally declared
void func()  {
 int value = 2;          // locally declared, hides global value
 cout << "  value = " << value << endl;        // output: 2
 cout << "::value = " << ::value << endl;        // output: 1
};
```

# Life span

## Description

When you define a variable, the compiler creates an object in the memory (which you can access through the name of the variable) for this variable. Similarly, objects are created in the memory when the dynamic memory is reserved, parameters are created during a function call, and instances of classes are formed (in which class objects only exist after they are called by the constructor).

How long these objects are available and exist depends on various factors.

## Application

- **Place of declaration.** Variables (including instances of classes), which are defined in a block area, only exist until the end of the block area and are deleted when leaving the block (this is because the memory for the variables is filed on the stack). Variables that have been declared globally exist until the end of the program.

- Memory class specifier `static`. The memory for variables which have been declared as `static` within a block area, is not reserved on the stack. These variables exist until the end of the program.

- Type of memory reservation. For objects for which memory has been reserved dynamically (with `malloc()` or `new`) memory is reserved on the heap and is only freed up when the programmer explicitly demands this (`free()` or `delete`) or the program is terminated.

## References

See functions, functions and the stack.

See Practice section, category pointer and dynamic memory management, dynamic memory in local functions.

# Combined data types

## Combined data types

### Description

With elementary data types the foundation for data processing in programs has already been prepared. In fact, it would be possible to do without defining further data types. However, in many cases this would make programming very unwieldy.

For this reason C/C++ provides various options to define your own data types. However, before we have a closer look at all of these, it should be made clear that with the definition of a new data type you have to satisfy not only your requirements but also those of the compiler.

Specifically, this means that the compiler needs to know how memory should be occupied for variables of this data type, how the values of the variables should be coded and stored in the memory, which operations are permitted on the variables of this data type, and finally how type conversions can be carried out.

All these requirements might lead you to believe that the options for defining your own data types are either very limited or very labour-intensive. Neither is true. The way to go about this is to derive the new self-defined data types from the elementary data types.

You have the following options to define your own data types:

- Defining data types by listing the set of values of the data type (`enum`)
- Defining a data type by putting together several variables of a data type (array)
- Defining a data type by putting together several variables of different data types (structures)
- Defining a data type by putting together several variables of different data types, and by providing type-specific functions and operators (classes). This is the least unrestricted and furthest reaching form of type definition.

Finally, there is also an option to define pointers, with which you can directly access memory areas and manipulate objects in the memory.

# Enumeration types

```
enum {element1, element2, ...};
enum type_identifier {element1, element2, ...};
```

## Description

Enumeration types are data types whose possible values are determined by explicit enumeration of integer constants. The enumerated values can be used like constants which are defined in the surrounding scope.

## Application

In all other data types the value ranges are predetermined by the internal coding of the values in binary representation. Which values, for example, an `int` variable can adopt does not depend on you but on your compiler. At best you can influence the value range through specifiers such as `short`, `long` or `unsigned`.

In an enumeration type you can specify through explicit listing which values belong to the value range of the new enumeration type. This may make the program code more legible and easier to understand. In addition, in C++ the compiler can ensure that variables of an enumeration type are only assigned values from their respective value ranges.

Since internally all the values of an enumeration type are represented by integer constants, it is also possible to use values from enumerations in `switch` statements.

## Syntax

```
enum {element1, element2, ...};
enum type_identifier {element1, element2, ...};
```

- **elements:** The elements which have been defined in an enumeration type are treated like integer constants. To prevent the constants from adopting undefined values, the compiler automatically initialises them. Non-initialised elements are assigned the value of their predecessor +1. The value 0 is assigned to the first element. With the help of the assignment operator the programmer can assign values to the elements. However, only integer values, or values which can be interpreted as integer values, are permitted. Different elements may have the same value.

- **type identifier:** If a `type identifier` has been specified, this is equivalent to a type definition. Later you can then define variables of this type. In C the type is called `enum type identifier`, in C++ simply `type identifier` is sufficient.

## Variable declaration

```
enum {elem1 = 1, elem2 } var1, var2;
```

or

```
enum typeident {elem1 = 1, elem2 };
enum typeident  var1, var2;
```

## Value assignment

```
var1 = elem2;
var1 = typeident(3);
```

## Warning

The compiler reserves memory for `enum` variables. This has to be big enough to contain all the integer values between the smallest and the greatest value of the `enum` type. In principle it is possible to assign any value within this value range to `enum` variables, even if the value is not explicitly defined in the list (this requires an explicit conversion in C++).

## Examples

```
#include <stdio.h>
enum {ERROR_READ = 101,ERROR_WRITE  = 102};

void error_message(int error_number)   {
   switch(error_message)   {
      case ERROR_READ:    /* statements */ break;
      case ERROR_WRITE:   /* statements */ break;
      default:            break;
      }
   }
```

```
int main() {
   error_message(ERROR_NO_MEM);
   return 0;
   }
```

## References

See Practice section, category variables and data types.

# Arrays

```
type fieldname[size];
```

## Description

An array, also called a data field or field, is the compilation of several pieces of the same type of data as a variable.

## Application

Arrays permit you to define an (almost) unlimited number of variables of the same data type in a block:

```
int i[100];
```

The advantage of the array declaration lies not only in saving typing effort. The individual elements of an array are stored in sequence in the memory in a connected block. This results in a range of advantages, for example the option to access individual elements in the block through an index:

```
i[3] = i[2]+i[1];
```

## Syntax

```
type fieldname[size];
```

- **type**: The type specification determines from which elements the array is formed, and provides (together with the size) information about the memory requirements (size * sizeof(type)).

- The following data types are not permitted as elements of an array: references, functions, abstract classes.

- **fieldname**: A name for the array variable can be chosen freely. Array types are always tied to variables. This is a peculiarity of arrays.

- **size**: The size determines the number of elements which make up the array. Only constant expressions which are greater than zero are permitted as size specifications. The size specification is not obligatory. In such a case a complete declaration has to follow, otherwise the array has to be initialised with the help of an initialisation list during the declaration. (The size will then be calculated from the number of initialisation values.)

## Variable declaration

```
int field[3];              // Array for three int-Objects
struct person reader[40];  // 40 Elemente of type struct person
```

or

```
#define NUMBER 400;
double field[NUMBER];
```

## Initialisation

It is possible to carry out initialisations when defining arrays. In these cases the name of the array is followed by an equals sign, and the individual values which have to be assigned in curly brackets.

- It is not necessary to initialise all elements. Elements which have not been initialised automatically receive the value 0.

- If the size specification is missing, the size is calculated from the number of elements.

```
float values[3] = { 2.34, 5.76 }; /*corresponds to:
                                     values[0] = 2.34;
                                     values[1] = 5.76;
                                     values[2] = 0;    */
float values[] = { 2.34, 5.76 };   /* corresponds to float values[2] */
```

## Access to array elements

The individual elements of the array are accessed through an index, which is written in square brackets. The first element of an array always contains the index 0. The last element has the index size - 1.

```
field[0] = 13;
```

or

```
#define ARRAY_SIZE 20
int array[ARRAY_SIZE];
for (i=0; i < ARRAY_SIZE; i++)
    array[i] = i;
```

## Warning

The indexing of the elements in the array always begins with 0, which is why the indices for an array which has been declared a field[20] run from 0 to 19. Access through higher indices is possible (the compiler does not control the use of correct indices), but leads to runtime errors. If you define the array size as well as an initialisation list, the latter should not contain more elements than is determined by the array size.

## Examples

```
#include <stdio.h>
#include <stdlib.h>
#include <mem.h>
#define MAX  100                    // number of elements in array

int main()
  {
  int field[MAX];                   // declaration of array
  int i;

  memset(feld, 0, sizeof(field));   // initialisation of array

  // iterate through entire array and assign random values
  for (i = 0; i < MAX; i++)
     {
     field[i] = rand() % 100;
     }

  // iterate through array and output values
  for (i = 0; i < MAX; i++)
     {
     printf("Element %d \t = %d\n", i, field[i] );
     }

  return 0;
  }
```

## References

See multidimensional arrays.

See strings (Strings).

See Practice section, category variables and data types; and category inheritance and polymorphism, base class pointer.


# Multidimensional arrays

```
type fieldname[dim1][dim2];
```

## Description

Two or multidimensional arrays are arrays whose elements are in turn arrays.

Multidimensional arrays are also stored in sequence in memory. The principle works in such a way that the last index changes fastest. The elements of the array

```
int matrix[3][2];
```

would be stored in the following sequence in memory:

```
matrix[0][0]
matrix[0][1]
matrix[1][0]
matrix[1][1]
matrix[2][0]
matrix[2][1]
```

## Application

Multidimensional arrays are best used where data are managed which are in themselves already multidimensionally organised, so that there is a 1:1 correspondence between the natural order of the data and their storage in the array.

An example would be the elements of a two-dimensional matrix, which can be well managed in a two-dimensional array.

## Syntax

```
type fieldname[dim1][dim2];
```

- **type**: The type specification determines which elements constitute the array.
- **field name**: A name for the array variable which can be chosen freely.
- **dim**: The definition contains as many pairs of square brackets with size specifications as the array has dimensions. In multidimensional arrays the first square bracket may remain empty. This is because a multidimensional array is viewed as a simple array, whose elements are also arrays. The size of the array may be declared later, but the size of the elements must be fixed at the point of declaration.

## Variable declaration

```
int field[3][2];
```

## Initialisation

Multidimensional arrays can be initialised in two ways. Either a separate initialisation list, which is surrounded by curly brackets, is used for each component, or each component of the subordinated aggregate type is assigned a value individually.

```
int matrix[][2] = {   { 1, 2 },
                      { 10, 20 },
                      { 100, 200 } };
```

or

```
int matrix[3][2] = { 1, 2 , 10, 20, 100, 200 };
```

## Access to array elements

To access an element of a multidimensional array, an index has to be specified for each dimension.

```
var = matrix[2][0];
```

The above statement accesses the first element of the third sub-array (indexing begins with 0!). (This would be the element with the value 100 in the example from the initialisation paragraph.)

## Examples

```c
#include <stdio.h>
#define COLUMNS   10
#define ROWS   5

int main()  {
  int x[ROWS][COLUMNS];
  int i = 0;
  int j = 0;

  for (i = 0; i < ROWS; i++)
    {
    for (j = 0; j < COLUMNS; j++)
      {
      x[i][j] = 'a' + i;
      }
    }

  for (i = 0; i < ROWS; i++)
    {
    for (j = 0; j < COLUMNS; j++)
      {
      printf("%c ",x[i][j]);
      }
    printf("\n");
    }

  return 0;
  }
```

## Output

```
a a a a a a a a a a
b b b b b b b b b b
c c c c c c c c c c
d d d d d d d d d d
e e e e e e e e e e
```

## References

See arrays.

# Strings

```
charType str[size];
```

## Description

Arrays also offer themselves as variables for strings. In this case the elements of the arrays are the characters of the string.

## Application

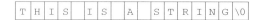

ANSI C/C++ uses the so-called ASCIIZ strings for the representation of text. These are strings which end in the character \0. Variables which can contain such a string can be declared in different ways:

- as array elements of a `char` type.
- as pointers to a `char` type, and
- as instances of a `string` class (C++ only).

The decision to use an array has the advantage that together with the array declaration the memory for the string is reserved. However, you have to be careful not to assign a string which consists of more characters than the array has reserved to the array variable.

## Warning

Note that a string in C/C++ must always end with the character \0. This termination character has to be counted when calculating memory requirements.

## Syntax

```
charType fieldname[size];
```

- **char type**: Choose in this case `char`, `signed char`, `unsigned char` or `wchar_t` as element types.
- **field name**: A name for the array variable which can be chosen freely.
- **dim**: Number of characters for which memory is reserved and which can be used in the array.

## Initialisation

```
char str[ ]  = {'o', 'n', 'e', '\0'}; // with initialisation list
```

or

```
char str2[50] = "This is a string";   // with string literal
wchar_t str3[10] = L"two";             // wide characters (UNICODE)
```

During initialisation with string literals the final zero termination character \0 is automatically attached by the compiler.

## Assignment

Assignment with the help of the assignment operator is only possible during initialisation. Subsequently it is best to use the functions of the runtime library (C header file string.h).

```
strcpy(str2, "New text");             // copy
strcat(str1, str2);                   // attach
```

## Access to individual characters

```
str1[4] = 'c';
```

## Examples

```
#include <stdio.h>
#include <string.h>

int main()  {
  char string1[] = "C and C++";
  char string2[] = "C++ and C";
  if(strcmp(string1, string2) > 0)
    printf("%s is greater than %s\n",string1,string2);
    else
    printf("%s is smaller than or equal to %s\n", string1, string2);
  return 0;
  }
```

Output

```
C and C++ is smaller than or equal to C++ and C
```

## References

See arrays.

See strings, C strings.

See Practice section, category strings, programming with C strings.

# Structures

```
struct type_identifier
   {
   type1 element1;
   type2 element2;
   };
```

## Description

Structures group together data, which may belong to different data types, into a variable. In C++ a structure is a special case of a class, in which all elements are `public` by default.

## Application

Structures are data types, in which several variables of diferent data types can be put together. The 'variables' which are grouped together in the structure are called fields or elements of the structure. The advantage of this is that logically connected data can be united in one data type.

A typical example would be the definition of variables for the storing of vectors. For a two-dimensional vector two `int` values for the x and y axes are required. To define these as individual `int` variables is inconvenient and confusing:

```
int v1_x, v1_y;      // first vector
int v2_x, v2_y;      // second vector
```

The introduction of a structure type for vectors is a better solution:

```
struct vector {
   int x;
   int y;
   };
struct vector v1, v2;
```

## Warning

- A structure must not contain a variable of its own type as an element. However, a pointer or references to variables of its own type are permitted.

- In C++ structures are classes with public access to the structure elements. Therefore, structures may also contain functions as elements in C++.

## Syntax

```
struct type_identifier {
   type1 element1;
   type2 element2;
   /* further elements */
   };
```

- **type identifier**: If a `type identifier` has been specified, this is equivalent to a type definition. Later variables of this type can be identified. In C the type is `struct type identifier`, in C++ it is simply `type idenitifer`.

- **type element**: The elements of the structure are declared within the brackets.

## Definition of structure variables

Structure variables can be defined either according to the definition of the structure with the help of the `type identifier` (provided a `type identifier` was specified) or directly during the structure definition.

```
struct person { /* definition */ };
struct person reader;
person author;            // only C++
struct person reader[40]; // 40 elements of struct person type
```

or

```
struct {
    int x;
    int y;
    float length;
    } vector1, vector2;
```

## Initialisation

Structure variables can be initialised directly during their definition. This requires the listing of the values with which the structure elements are to be initialised in curly brackets and their assignment to the variable by means of the assignment operator.

- It is not necessary to initialise all the elements of the structure.

```
struct person {
    char   name[20];
    int    postcode;
    char   town[20];
    char   street[20];
    };
struct person reader = {"Luke Skywalker",
                        S9 3QS, "Sheffield", "Attercliffe Road"
                        };
```

## Access to structure elements

There are two options for accessing the elements of a structure. The process used depends on whether the elements are accessed through a structure variable or a pointer to a structure.

```
structure_variable.structure_element
structure_pointer->structure_element
```

## Examples

```
struct person {
    char    name[20];
    int     postcode;
    char    town[20];
    };
int main() {
    struct person reader;
    struct person *preader;

    preader = &reader;
    reader.postcode = S9 3QS;

    strcpy(reader.name, "Skywalker");
    strcpy(preader->town, "Sheffield");
    printf("Reader: %s, Postcode: %d Town: %s\",
            reader.name, reader.postcode, reader.town);
    printf("reader: %s, postcode: %d town: %s\",
            preader->name, preader->postcode, preader->town);
    return 0;
    }
```

## References

See Practice section, category variables and data types, arrays of structures; category variables and data types, recursive structures.

# Bit fields

```
struct type_identifier
    {
    inttype1 element1    : number;
    inttype2 element2    : number;
    };
```

## Description

Bit fields are special elements in structure types, where you can explicitly specify how many bits are required for the element.

## Application

Bit fields are used when data are to be stored which require less than 1 byte memory. Examples of this type are 1 bit sized flags, which are sufficient to represent logic values. After the type specification and the optional name of the element there is a colon. This is followed by an integer value, which determines how many bits have to be provided for this element.

Traditionally bit fields are often used to save memory. The idea behind this is that the bits of the bit fields are stored in sequence, so for example a structure with two bit fields of 3 and 5 bit length would only use 8 bits in a row (1 byte). However, whether this is correct depends on the compiler. For this reason and because RAM is relatively cheap nowadays, using bit fields to save memory is not recommend.

## Warning

- According to ANSI C a single bit field always has to have the data type `int`, `signed int` or `unsigned int`. In contrast C++ permits any data type which can be interpreted as an integer, therefore also `char`, `short`, `long` and list types.
- Pointer and references cannot be declared for bit fields.
- Unnamed bit fields of size 0 cause the next bit field to begin in a new statement unit (mostly `int` or `word`).

## Syntax

```
struct type_identifier {
    intType1 element1 : number;
    intType2 element2 : number;
    /* further elements */
};
```

- **type identifier:** If a `type identifier` has been specified, this is equivalent to a type definition. Later variables of this type can also be defined. In C the type is `struct type identifier`, in C++ simply `type identifier` is sufficient.
- **type element:** number: The bit fields are declared within the brackets. Only `int` types may be used as the type. The element name is followed by a colon and the specification of the bits which are to be reserved for the bit field. If no name is specified this results in an unnamed bit field, with which the alignment of the bit fields in the memory can be controlled. An unnamed bit field of size 0 instructs the compiler to align the next element at the byte boundaries which are internally used for the memory division by the compiler (this reduces access time).

## Examples

```
struct s_cards {
    unsigned int value    : 3;
    unsigned int suit     : 2;
    unsigned int player   : 2;
    unsigned int played   : 1;
} cards[32];
```

```
int main()  {
  int suit, value, loop;
  for(suit=0; suit<4; suit++)
    for(value=0; value<8; value++) {
        cards[8*suit+value].suit = suit;
        cards[8*suit+value].value = value;
        cards[8*suit+value].player = 0;
        cards[8*suit+value].played = 0;
      }
  for(loop=0; loop < 32; loop++)
    printf("Suit = %d, Value = %d\n",cards[loop].suit,
                              cards[loop].value);
  return 0;
  }
```

## References

See structures.

# Unions

```
union type_identifer {
    type1 element1;
    type2 element2;
    };
```

## Description

A union is a data type, which is declared for different elements, but whose variables may only accommodate one of the elements. The size of a union variable is equivalent to the size of the largest element.

## Application

Unions save memory in comparison to structures. They can be used if only one element is required whose type type cannot be predicted by the programmer.

## Warning

A union cannot contain a variable of its own type as an element. However, pointers or references to variables of its own type are permitted.

If a union variable is initialised during its definition, it is only possible to assign the value to the first union element.

In C++ there are several features to look out for:

• In C++ unions are classes and also may contain functions as elements.

- Virtual element functions are not permitted.

- Unions cannot be elements of class hierarchies.

- Classes with their own definitions for constructor, destructor, copy-constructor or assignment operators cannot be elements of a union.

## Syntax

```
union type_identifier {
    type1 element1;
    type2 element2;
    /* further elements */
    };
```

- **type_identifier**: If a `type identifier` has been specified, this is equivalent to a type definition. Later variables of this type can be defined. In C the type is union `type identifier`, in C++ it is simply `type identifier`.

- **type element**: The elements of the union are declared within the brackets.

## Definition of union variables

```
union Login { /* definition */ };
union Login user;
```

or

```
union Login{
    char password[10];
    int  userid;
    } user1, user2;
```

## Initialisation

During initialisation it is only possible to assign a value to one element of the union.

```
union Login user = {"Secret"};
```

## Access to structure elements

```
unionvariable.structure_element
unionpointer->structure_element
```

## Examples

```
#define USERNAME

union Login{
    char password[10];
    int  userid;
    };
```

```
int main()
  {
  union Login user1;

#ifdef USERNAME
    printf("Please enter your PIN: \n");
    scanf("%d",&user1.userid);
    fflush(stdin);
#else
    printf("Please enter your password: \n");
    scanf("%s",user1.password);
    fflush(stdin);
#endif

  printf("\n");
  printf("size of union:      %d\n",sizeof(Login));
  return 0;
  }
```

## References

See structures.

# Pointers and references

## Pointers

```
type* pointer variable;
```

### Description

A pointer is a variable which contains the address of a data object or function. The use of pointers has various advantages.

### Application

Operational areas for pointers:

- **Saving in memory.** Pointer variables store addresses. Their memory requirements are therefore fixed to 16 or 32 bit, whereas the objects to which they point may be substantially larger.

- **Passing to functions.** By passing pointers to functions the function is enabled to access objects which lie outside its scope. The passing of pointers is significantly faster than the copying of large data objects. (For the same reasons references are often passed in C++.)

- **Dynamic memory management.** By means of pointers the programmer can decide for himself when memory should be reserved and freed. Pointers allow the implementation of dynamic data structures such as lists and trees.

- **Recursive data structures.** Pointers can be defined for data types which are declared but not yet defined. In this way a class may have, for example, a pointer to its own instances.

- **Arrays** of pointers to functions are permitted, unlike arrays of functions.

- **Generic implementations.** Many problems can be solved more efficiently with pointers. For example, you can use pointers to void, pointers to functions, pointers to pass functions as arguments to other functions, a base class pointer to derived objects for the management of objects of various derived classes in an array, and the use of virtual methods instead of explicit running time identification.

## Warning

A pointer can point to any data object with two exceptions:

- references and
- bit fields.

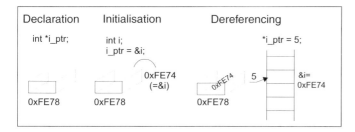

## Syntax

`type* pointer_variable;`

- **type**: data type of the objects to which the pointer points. This specification is required for the correct dereferencing of the pointer.

- **\***: marks the variable as a pointer and can stand after the type specification as well as before the pointer name.

- **pointer_variable**: name of the pointer.

## Initialisation

The initialisation of a pointer is made through the assignment of an address and a memory area which is connected to that address. The initialisation can happen in various ways.

1. Assignment of the address of an existing object.

- The address of a variable can be established through the address operator &.
- Pointers are addresses in themselves.
- The names of arrays and functions also constitute addresses.

```
int i_var = 13;
int *ptr1 = &i_var;
int *ptr2 = ptr1;
int field[10] = {11,11,11};
ptr3 = field;
```

2. Assignment of ZERO.

Pointers that do not point to an object should be initialised with the ZERO address. In this way it can be easily checked whether the pointer points to an object or not.

```
double *ptr4 = ZERO;
```

3. Statement through malloc() or new.

- The malloc() function and the new operator are used to reserve memory and to pass the address to the pointer. In this way objects are created which can only be accessed through the pointer.

```
double *ptr5 = new double;
int *ptr6 = (int*) malloc(3*sizeof(int));
```

Non-initialised pointers contain undefined bit patterns, which are interpreted as addresses during dereferencing. This inevitably leads to program errors and often to program crashes.

## Dereferencing

Pointers are addresses. Dereferencing means to access the referenced object through this address. The dereferencing operators *, ->,.* and ->* are used for this.

- *: the dereferencing operator.
- ->: a combination of dereferencing and dot operator, which dereferences a pointer to a class type and simultaneously accesses an element of the dereferenced object.
- .*: dereferences a pointer to a class element for a given class object.
- -->*: dereferences a pointer to a class element for a given pointer to a class object.

# Example

```
#include <stdio.h>

int main() {
  int i;
  int *p_i = &i;                // declaration and initialisation

  struct coord {
    int x,y;
    } pos;
  struct coord *p_pos1 = &pos;  // declaration and initialisation

  // Dereferencing
  *p_i = 2;
  (*p_pos1).x = 3;              // dereferencing a structure with *
  p_pos1->y = p_pos1->x+1;      // dereferencing a structure with ->

  printf("x = %d; y = %d\n",pos.x, pos.y);

  return 0;
  }
```

yields the following output::

```
x = 3; y = 4
```

# Warning

- The character * is also used in the declaration to specify a pointer variable. In statements it informs the compiler, that the object which is stored in the pointer variable is required.

- A pointer name is an adddress. This address refers to the memory cell in which the value of the pointer is stored. The value of a pointer is also an address. This address is used to point to other data objects.

- Never dereference pointers which contain invalid addresses (non-initialised pointers, pointers to objects, which do not exist anymore, and so on.).

# References

See Practice section, category pointer and dynamic memory management.

# Special pointers

## Pointers to strings                                              char*

A pointer of the type char* points to a single character. Many library functions that process strings (strcpy(), strlen() etc.), expect that a pointer to the first character of a string has to be processed as an argument. The string passed in this way begins with the address provided by the pointer, and ends with the first appearance of the zero character '\0'.

When using the corresponding library functions, ensure that the presented pointers always point to zero-terminated strings, and that strings are only copied or written into memory areas which are large enough to incorporate the complete string inclusive of the zero-termination character. Otherwise this results in unwanted memory access – usually accompanied by program crashes.

```
char str[20] = "Hello World!";
// reserve memory as large as the string in str plus '\0'
p_str = (char*) malloc(strlen(str)+1);
strcpy(p_str,str);
```

## Pointers to void                                                void*

A void* (pointer on void) is a universal pointer without a type. It is used when the type of the pointer is not determined or is to be kept general. It can be determined in a subsequent explicit type conversion how the memory which belongs to the pointer has to be interpreted, whether it be a float value or a string.

```
// comparative function for use with qsort()
// compares two addresses by name
int cmpr(const void* p1,const void* p2)  {
  struct address* adr1,*adr2;
  adr1=(struct address*)p1;
  adr2=(struct address*)p2;
  return strcmp(adr1->name,adr2->name);
  }
```

## Pointers to functions                                           func

Pointers to functions are required to pass functions as parameters to other functions.

```
return_type (*pointername) (Parametertypes);
```

- **return_type**: Specifies the return type of the functions to which the pointer can be directed.

- **pointername**: The name of the pointer.

- **Parametertypes**: Lists the parameter types of the functions to which the pointer can be directed.

```
void func(int i, class person reader)   {...};
void (*func_ptr) (int, class person) = func;
```

## Constant pointers                                              *const

The pointer declaration distinguishes between const pointers, which cannot be diverted to other objects, and pointers to const objects. The latter are often used in function definitions to prevent the object to which the pointer refers from being changed in the function through the pointer parameter.

```
char c = 'A';
const char *ptr_c;                  // pointer to const object
char const *ptr_c;                  // pointer to const object
char *const ptr_c = &c;             // const pointer
int func (int par1, const char *par2);
```

## Pointers to data elements                                      class::*

With the help of the area operator :: a pointer can be assigned to a class.

Here, only the name of the class is used to define and initialise the pointer. Only when accessing classes using the pointer are instances or pointers to instances required.

```
// definition:
int person::* int_ptr;         // person is a class

// initialisation:
int person::* int_ptr = &person::postcode;

// access:
class person reader, *p_reader;
reader.*int_ptr      = 66111;
p_reader->*int_ptr = 66111;
```

## Pointers to methods                                            class::*func*

By means of the area operator :: a pointer can be assigned to a class.

Here, only the name of the class is used to define and initialise the pointer. Only when accessing classes using the pointer are instances or pointers to instances required.

```
// definition:
void (person::*func_ptr) (int);    // person is a class

// initialisation:
void (person::*func_ptr) (int) = &reader::print_address;

// access:
class person reader, *p_reader;
(reader.*func_ptr) (64);
(p_reader->*func_ptr) (64);
```

## Pointers to static class elements                     class::static*

Pointers to static class elements are treated like non-element pointers, which means
that the pointer is dereferenced without a class specification:

```
int *int_ptr = &classname::static_dataelement;
int a = *int_ptr;
```

## base class pointers                                        (basis*)

In C++ every derived element can also be viewed as an object of its non-ambiguous
base classes. Correspondingly, a pointer to a derived object can be transformed
into a pointer to one of its non-ambiguous base classes without any problems. For
example, this allows the management of derived objects of different classes as basic
class objects in a shared array.

Base class pointers are usually employed in connection with virtual methods.

```
class Basis {...};                    // class hierarchy
class Der1 : public Basis {...};
class Der2 : public Basis {...};

class basis  *field[10];              // array

field[0] = new Der1;                  // include pointer in array
field[1] = new Der2;                  //
```

## this-pointers                                                 this

Every non-static method of a class is internally assigned an additional parameter by
the compiler. This is the this- pointer, which points to the initial address of the
instance for which the method is called.

```
#include <iostream>
using namespace std;

class demo
  {
  public:
   void func()     {cout << this;}
  };

int main()
  {
  class demo d1,d2;
  cout << "This-pointer of instance d1 = " << d1.func() << endl;
  cout << "This-pointer of instance d2 = " << d2.func() << endl;
  return 0;
  }
```

## References

See Practice section, category pointer and dynamic memory management; category strings, programming with C-strings; and category inheritance and polymorphism, base class pointer.

# References (C++ only)

```
type& reference_name = var;
```

## Description

References, like pointers, refer to objects. However, they can only be initialised once with an object, and subsequently cannot be diverted to other objects. Furthermore, references do not require the typical pointer syntax – they are used like normal variables, as synonyms of the variables to which they refer.

Technically speaking a reference is thus equivalent to a `const-` pointer, which is automatically dereferenced every time it is accessed.

## Application

References, also called aliases, are related to pointers and are used in similar ways for the passing of variables to functions, when the functions directly change the presented variables or when running time increases are to be avoided. Here references have the following advantages:

- they can be called like normal variables (the typical pointer dereferencing syntax is not required); and
- they are more reliable than pointers (since they always point to a single precisely defined object).

## Warning

A reference variable has to be initialised immediately during its declaration, unless

- it has been explicitly declared as `extern`,
- it is a function parameter, or
- it is a class element.

A reference variable can only be set to one variable.

It is not possible to define pointers to references.

It is not possible to form arrays from references.

There are no references to references.

References cannot be of the type void&.

## Syntax

```
typ& referencename = var;
```

- **type**: Data type of the object to which the reference refers.
- **&**: Reference operator &, which marks a variable as a reference in declarations.
- **reference_name**: The name of the declared reference variable.
- **= var**: References have to be directly initialised during definition.

## Examples

The following example illustrates the passing of arguments to reference parameters.

```
#include <iostream>
using namespace std;

class people {
    int age;
  public:
    people(int age)
    void agen()  {age++;}
    int get_age() {return age;}
  };

// function with reference parameter
void submitt_reference(people& par)
  {
  par.agen();
  }

int main()
  {
  people dennis(30);
  cout << "Dennis is " << dennis.get_age()
       << " years old\n";

  // passing of class object to the reference parameter
  submitt_reference(dennis);
  cout << "Dennis is " << dennis.get_age()
       << " years old\n";
  return 0;
  }
```

Output

```
Dennis is 30 years old
Dennis is 31 years old
```

## Warning

With parameter submission the data type of the reference parameter and the argument have to be identical. Otherwise the following points have to be noted:

- For const reference parameters the compiler carries out a type conversion and creates a temporary variable which is appropriate for the reference parameter. The reference parameter then points to this temporary variable. The return of values through the parameter to the call argument is therefore no longer possible.

- For non-const reference parameters the compiler issues an error message. (Some older compilers issue a warning and create a temporary variable.)

## References

See the Practice section, category pointer and dynamic memory management.

# Type definitions and type conversions

## Type definitions

typedef

### Description

C permits the definition of any data types on the basis of the types contained in the scope of the language. In a type definition a new type is specified and is connected with the identifier for the type. Such a type definition can be carried out with the keywords struct, union, class or typedef.

### Application

New types are not actually defined with typedef; this creates synonyms for type specifications already available. This may be necessary for two reasons:

- A type definition should be adaptable through the preprocessor switch (see first example).

- a complex type definition should be represented by a simple synonym (see second example).

## Warning

typedef types cannot be extended:

```
typedef int INT;
unsigned INT x;        // not permitted
```

## Syntax

```
typedef type_specification type_identifier;
```

- **type_specification**: Here the new type is defined. The form of the type specification is equivalent to the specification in variable declarations.

- **type_identifier**: The name of the new type.

## Examples

Type definitions subject to compiler switches:

```
#if defined (LONG)
   typedef wchar_t long;
#else
   typedef wchar_t int;
#endif
```

Type definitions as simplifications:

```
typedef unsigned int UINT;           // example from windows.h
typedef void (*func_typ) (int, int);   // defined func_typ
```

# Default conversions

## Description

In various situations the compiler carries out automatic type conversions..

## Application

The most important automatic conversions are as follows:

## Identifiers

- On the right-hand side of assignments the identifiers are understood as R-values (value, not memory address).

- On the right-hand side of statements array names are understood as pointers to their first element (inclusive of function calls).

- On the right-hand side of statements function names represent the return value of the function.

## Type adaptations

- Arithmetic data types can be converted into each other if the data type, which is the target of the conversion, can incorporate the value which is to be converted (when converting floating point numbers into integer values the digits after the point are lost).
- The compiler automatically adapts the types of both operands for binary operators, which adopt arithmetic operands. This is called the default arithmetic conversion.

## Boolean values

- Zero-pointer and zero-representations of arithmetic data types can be converted into the Boolean value false; correspondingly other values of these data types are interpreted as true.
- Conversely the Boolean value false can be converted into an arithmetic zero, and true into a one.

## Pointers and classes

- On the right-hand side of statements (including function calls) array names are understood as pointers to their first element.
- Function names can be understood as pointers to themselves.
- Pointers to special data types can be converted into pointers to void (the reverse path is only possible through explicit type conversion).
- A pointer to a derived class can be converted into a pointer to a non-ambiguous, accessible base class.
- Under the same conditions the instance of a derived class can be interpreted as the instance of a base class.
- Pointers to elements of a base class can be converted into pointers to elements of a non-ambiguous, accessible derived class.
- When you assign a value to a class instance and a corresponding constuctor is defined in the class, which is called with exactly one argument of the type, to which also the value belongs, then the constructor is used to automatically convert values of the corresponding data type into objects of the class where necessary. (This can be stopped through explicit declaration.)

## Const and volatile

- The qualifiers const and volatile can be added automatically, but cannot be taken out (thus, a nonconst argument can be passed to a const parameter, but not vice versa).

# Examples

Operand conversion

```
float f = 3/4;      // yields 0.0;
                    // integer division of 3/4 yields 0
                    // 0 is changed to 0.0 for the assignment
float f = 3/4.0;    // yields 0.75;
                    // 4.0 is floating point number, thus the integer
                    // operand 3 is changed to floating point number.
                    // A floating point division is executed
```

Constructors with one argument

```
class field  {
  public:
    int amount;
    field(int a) {amount = a;}
  };
...
field stack(3);
stack = 13;         // implied call: stack = field(13);
```

# Type conversion

```
(type) value
```

## Description

A variable of a specific data type can be treated as belonging to a different data type. This is done through the C cast-operator () or the C++ operators const_cast, dynamic_cast, static_cast and reinterpret_cast, which have been adopted into the language as keywords.

## Application

There are five main reasons for type conversions:

- You want to convert a floating point number into an integer, or vice versa.

- The latter is required, for example when you want to divide an integer by another integer, and you want the result to be stored with the division remainder in a floating point.

- You have a `void` pointer which you want to convert into a pointer to a particular data type.
- You have a base class pointer to a derived object, which you want to convert into a pointer to the derived class.
- You want to force a particular memory interpretation through the type conversion of a pointer. This option is only rarely required, and is very prone to errors.

## The C cast-operator

The cast-operator can be used in a statement to convert the type of the expression on the right-hand side into the type of the identifier on the left-hand side:

```
identifier1 = (Type_of_identifier1) expression;
identifier1 = (type_of_identifier1) identifier2;
```

A second form of the syntax directly converts the type of a variable:

```
identifier = datatype();
```

## The C++ cast-operators

The C++ operators are mainly intended to categorise the various conversions according to their potential dangers, and to facilitate the text search for the conversions.

| Operator | Operational area |
| --- | --- |
| `static_cast<Type>(var)` | To convert 'closely related' types – that is, all cases in which the compiler could also carry out an implicit conversion, plus a few simple special cases. |
| `reinterpret_cast<Type>(var)` | For almost all other permitted conversions. |
| `const_cast<Type>(var))` | Removes a `const` or `volatile` declaration from a type. |
| `dynamic_cast<Type>(var)` | To convert pointers or references to class types of a shared class hierarchy. |

## Examples

```
int i = int(3.14);
double var =  (double) 13/2);
int ptr = (int *) malloc(80 * sizeof(int));

derived *p_der = new derived;
Basis   *p_bp  = p_der;

p_der = dynamic_cast <derived*> (p_bp);
```

### References

See Practice section, category inheritance and polymorphism, RTTI with `dynamic_cast`.

# Constants

## Constants

### Description

Other than variables, constants are the second option to represent data in programs. The difference between variables and constants is obvious: whereas a variable can adopt and represent different values in the course of a program, a constant always represents a fixed value.

C/C++ recognises three different types of constants:

– Literals

– Symbolic constants

– Constant variables

### Application

Constants represent the possibility to root fixed data directly in the program code: for example to build the number value of PI into a formula or in form of a string table for error messages.

## Literals

### Description

The simplest form of the constant is a constant value. To distinguish it from constant variables, constant values are also called literals.

### Application

In translation constant values are hard-coded by the compiler, which means the values are not stored somewhere in the memory, from where they can be read if necessary, but are stored directly in the relevant machine commands.

The only exception is that memory is reserved for string-literals, and the programmer usually has no access to this memory area.

```
printf("Hello World\n");
```

However, the automatic memory statement permits the assignment of string-literals to pointers to char.

```
char *str1;
str1 = "Hello World\n";
```

| Data type | Literal |
|---|---|
| bool | true, false |
| char | 'c', 'Ü', '\n', '\\', |
|  | ''ab' (multibyte character) |
| wchar_t | L'c', L'Ü', L'\n', L'\\',, |
|  | L'ab' (multibyte character) |
| strings (char*)) | "This is a string" |
| strings (wchar_t*) | L" This is a string " |
| short | 12, -128 |
| int | 12, -128, 128u, 1277U |
|  | 012, -077 (Octal) |
|  | 0x12, 0XEE (Hexadecimal) |
| long | 12l, 1400000L, 12lu |
| float | 47.11f, 12.0F, 10e-2F |
| double | 47.11, 12.0, 10e-2 |
| long double | 47.11l, 12.0L, 10e-2L |

## Warning

In the use of literals it is important to comply with the syntax for the specification of the values, so that the compiler can read the corresponding data type from the value.

## Examples

```
int i = 513;              // assignment of a constant to a variable
double field[30];         // details of array size
if( (x < 100) && (x > 50))          // to formulate
if(!strcmp(str,"comparative text");    // conditions
```

## References

See #define.
See const-variables.

# #define – symbolic constants

## Description

Symbolic constants are identifiers which are defined as aliases for a particular value.

## Application

If a constant is used several times it makes sense to declare it beforehand and to connect it with a symbolic name, which represents the constant. This is made possible by the preprocessor directive

```
#define:
#define symbolidentifier CONSTANTS
```

Subsequently the constant can be represented by the symbolic identifier in the source text which follows. During compilation all occurrences of the symbolic identifier are replaced by the corresponding constant.

The advantage of this is:

- that you can connect a constant with a meaningful name, and
- you only have to adapt the #define statement, when you want to connect the constant with a different value (for example, it makes sense to determine the upper boundaries for arrays, termination conditions for loops or switches for the conditional compilation by means of #define at the beginning of the file, so that it can be found quickly when needed and be replaced centrally).

## Predefined constants

A number of interesting constants are already predefined in the header files of the default library, for example:

| Header files | Constant | Description |
| --- | --- | --- |
| stddef.h | ZERO | Macro, which is expanded to an implementation-specific zero-pointer constant, for example 0 or 0L. |
| stdio.h | EOF | usually -1 or (wint_t)(0xFFFF) for wchar_t |
| | FOPEN_MAX | Macro, which is expanded to an integer, which shows the minimum number of files which can be opened simultaneously. |
| limits.h | CHAR_BIT | 8 (number of bits in type char) |
| | INT_MIN | -2147483647L-1 (for 32-bit system) |
| | INT_MAX | 2147483647L (for 32-bit system) |
| | FLT_RADIX | 2 (base of the exponential representation) |
| | FLT_DIG | 6 (number of decimal places) |

## Examples

```
#define HOUR 60
#define dozen 12
#define Name "C++Compiler"
```

The symbolic identifier is only an alias name for a literal. Before the translation into machine code, the preprocessor reads through the source text and replaces all the occurrences of the symbolic identifier by the corresponding constant. When the translation begins, the source text contains no symbolic constants, only literals:

Original source text:

```
#define MAX 30
double field[MAX];
...
for (int i = 0; i < MAX; i++) {...}
...
for (int i = 0; i < MAX; i++) {...}
...
if (i < MAX) {...}
After processing by the preprocessor:
double field[30];
...
for (int i = 0; i < 30; i++) {...}
...
for (int i = 0; i < 30; i++) {...}
...
if (i < 30) {...}
```

## References

See combined data types, list types.

# constant variables

## Description

The final form of constants is the constant variable — a variable whose value cannot be changed after initialisation.

## Application

Constant variables are declared with the keyword const. From the point of view of compilers they are not real constants, but rather variables, which it protects from being overridden.

In C, as in C++, you can do the following with const:

- declare any objects (therefore also variables of your own data types such as structures and classes) as constants,
- prevent function arguments which have been passed as pointers from being changed in a function,
- extend assignment options, and
- benefit from the type check of the compiler.

### Warning

In C++ a constant variable is viewed as a real constant.

In C, which also recognises the keyword const, constant variables cannot be used at points where the compiler expects a constant or a constant expression – thus,

- not when specifying the size of an array, and
- not as case marks.

### Examples

```
const int months = 12;
int func (const int par1, const char *par2);
```

### References

See literals.

See #define.

See classes, constant data elements and methods.

# Operators

## Operators

### Description

ANSI C/C++ recognises more than 40 operators. This means that in C/C++ the number of operators is greater than the number of keywords of the language, which is unusual in programming languages. The majority of operators originate from the time of the first language definition by Kernighan & Ritchie.

The forms of operators listed here represent their original definitions and not overwritten versions. Most of the operators can be overwritten by programs (however, not elementary data types, for which they are already defined by default) but only while maintaining their usual syntax.

| Operator | Brief description |
| --- | --- |
| + | Adds two operands |
| += | Adds two operands and assigns the result |
| - | Subtracts two operands |
| -= | Subtracts two operands and assigns the result |
| * | Multiplies two arithmetic operands |
| *= | Multiplies two arithmetic operands and assigns the result |
| / | Divides two arithmetic operands |
| /= | Divides two arithmetic operands and assigns the result |
| % | Modulus-operator, determines the remainder of an integer division |
| %= | Modulus-operator with simultaneous assignment |
| ! | Non-operator, negation |
| not | Non-operator, negation |
| != | Compares two arithmetic operands for inequality |
| not_eq | Compares two arithmetic operands for inequality |
| & | For one operand this operator provides the address of the operand |
| & | For two operands a bitwise AND operation is carried out |
| bitand | Bitwise AND operation |
| &= | Bitwise AND operation and assignment |
| and_eq | Bitwise AND operation and assignment |
| && | Logical AND operation |
| and | Logical AND operation |
| () | Operator for sequential analysis, point operator |
| , | Operator für sequentielle Auswertung, Kommaoperator |
| ++ | Increments the operand |
| -- | Decrements the operand |
| -> | Element pointer selector |
| . | Dot operator |
| * | Dereferencing operator |
| = | Assignment operator |
| == | Tests for equality |
| < | Smaller than |

| Operator | Brief description |
| --- | --- |
| > | Greater than |
| <= | Smaller than or equal to |
| => | Greater than or equal to |
| << | Bitwise left shift |
| <<= | Bitwise left shift and assignment of the result |
| >> | Bitwise right shift |
| >>= | Bitwise right shift and assignment of the result |
| ?: | Conditional operator |
| [] | Array indexingg |
| ^ | Bitwise exclusive OR |
| xor | Bitwise exclusive OR |
| ^= | Bitwise exclusive OR and assignment of the result |
| xor_eq | Bitwise exclusive OR and assignment of the result |
| \| | Bitwise OR |
| bitor | Bitwise OR |
| \|= | Bitwise OR and assignment of the result |
| or_eq | Bitwise OR and assignment of the result |
| \|\| | Logical OR |
| or | Logical OR |
| ~ | Complement |
| compl | Complement |
| : | Class initialiser |
| :: | Area operatorr |
| .* | Dereferencing of pointers to class elements |
| ->* | Dereferencing of pointers to class elements |
| sizeof | Determines the size of the operand in bytess |
| new | Dynamic memory reservation |
| new[] | Dynamic memory reservation for arrayss |
| delete | Frees up memory |
| delete[] | Frees up memory for Arrays |
| # | String formation |
| ## | Base symbol combination |
| defined | Tests whether a macro is defined |
| typeid | Dynamic type information |

## Classification

All operators, depending on how many operands they work with, can be assigned to one of the following groups:

- unary operators (work with one operand),
- binary operators (work with two operands) and
- ternary operators (work with three operands).

## References

See Practice section, category operators.

# Signs

### Description

A unary operator which determines whether a number value is positive or negative.

## Application

With the unary operators '+' and '−' you can assign a sign to the arithmetic types. Values without sign are automatically positive.

| Operator | Meaning |
|---|---|
| + | Positive value |
| − | Negative value |

## Examples

```
int var1, var2;
var1 = -3;
var2 = 3 * -var1;
```

# Arithmetic operators

### Description

Binary operators for the execution of the arithmetic operations addition, subtraction, etc., as well as the calculation of the division remainder.

## Application

With the arithmetic operators you can, as the name implies, carry out simple arithmetic operations, as in other programming languages.

| Operator | Meaning |
|---|---|
| + | Addition |
| − | Subtraction |
| * | Multiplication |
| / | Division |
| % | Modulus, remainder of an integer division |

## Warning

- If several operators are used in one expression, the following apply: multiplication and division are carried out before addition and subtraction; signs, increment and decrement are carried out before multiplication and division; if the priority is the same the operators are processed from left to right.

- Generally each operator is assigned a priority value, and higher priority operators are analysed before lower priority operators.

- By inserting brackets you can determine the order of the analysis of operators yourself.

## Examples

```
var1 = 5+3;
var2 = 20 % var1;      // = 4
var2 = 3 * 4 + var1;   // = 20
var2 = 3 * (4 + var1); // = 36
```

## References

See priority and associativity.

See Practice section, category operators, overloading of arithmetic operators.

# Increment and decrement operators

## Description

Increment and decrement refers to the increasing or decreasing of a value by one unit respectively.

## Application

The programming languages C/C++ provide two operators with which the value of a variable can be incremented (increased by one) or decremented (decreased by one), where the operators can be placed before or after the variable.

```
lvalue++
++lvalue
lvalue--
--lvalue
```

The position of the operators determines when the increment or decrement of the value is calculated. This is important when the operator is used in more complex expressions.

```
int var1, var2 = 12, var3 = 12;
var1 = 3 * ++var2;       // yields var1 = 39
var1 = 3 * var3++;       // yields var1 = 36
```

The notation in which the operator is placed before the variable is called prefix spelling and results in the value of the variable being calculated before it is used. In the postfix spelling (the operator is placed after the variable) the value of the operand is used before it is changed.

| Operator | Meaning |
| --- | --- |
| ++ | Increment operator, increases its operand by 1 |
| -- | Decrement operator, decreases its operand by 1 |

## Warning

- The increment and decrement operators are not defined for list types.

- The increment and decrement operators can also be used for pointers. In this case the address is increased or decreased by the size of the objects to which the pointer refers.

- The increment of a variable of the bool type equals 1; the decrement is not defined.

## Example

```
#include <stdio.h>

int main() {
    int x,y;
    x = 5;
    y = 5;
    printf("Value of ++x is %d\n", ++x);
    printf("Value of y++ is %d\n", y++);
```

```
printf("x after incrementation: %d\n", x);
printf("y after incrementation: %d\n", y);
return 0;
}}
```

The program produces the following output:

```
Value of ++x is 6
Value of y++ is 5
x after incrementation: 6
y after incrementation: 6
```

## References

See Practice section, category operators, efficient use of the operators; category operators, overloading the increment operator.

# Assignments

## Description

With assignment operators values can be assigned and changed. Apart from the simple assignment operator there are also combined assignment operators, with which a calculation as well as an assignment can be carried out in one statement.

## Application

Generally the left operand is assigned the value of the right operand. For this to be possible the left operand must be convertable, that is it must refer to an address in the memory. These expressions are called 'L values'.

### Simple assignment                                                       =

In a simple assignment the left operand receives the value of the right operand:

```
int main() {
    int inventory, receipt;
    inventory = 10;
    receipt = 20;
    inventory = inventory + receipt;
    return 0;}
```

### Combined assignments                                                 <x>=

Apart from the simple assignment operator '=' there are combined assignment operators, with which a calculation and an assignment can be carried out simultaneously through an operator.

Combined operators have the format

`<x>=`

where `<x>` can be replaced by the operators +, -, *, /, %, <<, >>, &, ^ or | .

```
int main() {
   int inventory, receipt;
   inventory = 10;
   receipt = 20;
   inventory += receipt;
   return 0;
   }
```

## Assignment to class instances                                    operator =

Assignments to class instances are carried out by calling the overloaded operator =. If the operator is not overloaded in the class, the default operator is called.

Apart from the assignment of a class instance to an instance of the same class, the default assignment operator allows the assignment of an object of a non-ambiguous class which has been derived as `public` to an object of its base class, but not the assignment of an object in a base class to an object of its derived class.

Through copy-constructors assignments are carried out at initialisation.

```
class base {
   ...
   };
class derived :  public base {
   ...
   };

int main() {
   derived der;
   base bs;

   //der = bs;    // error
   bs = der;
```

## References

See Practice section, category operators, efficient use of operators; and category operators, overloading of the assignment operator.

# Comparative operators

## Description

With the comparative operators, which are also called relational operators, a comparison is carried out between two operands. The result of this operation is either `true` or `false`.

## Application

Expressions which contain comparative operators are often used as control statement in `do-`, `while-` or `for-` loops and `if` statements.

| Operator | Meaning |
|----------|---------|
| == | Equal to |
| != | Not equal to |
| < | Smaller than |
| > | Greater than |
| <= | Smaller than or equal to |
| >= | Greater than or equal to |

## Warning

- The result of a comparison is a logical value (`true` or `false`).
- Each value which is not 0 is interpreted as `true` by C/C++.
- Two pointers of the same type, which point to the same object, are equal.
- Pointers to different elements of a class are not equal where later declarations have higher addresses. However, this only applies if there is no access specifier between the declarations. If this is the case, the result is undefined.

## Examples

```
if (var1 <= var2)
  function();
do {
  result = function();
  } while (result != 0);
```

# Logical operators

## Description

The logical operators are used to link or negate logical statements.

# Application

The programming language C recognises three logical operators: AND, OR and NOT. In the logical AND and OR operator the logical value of the operands is linked, the logical NOT operator converts the logical value of its operand into its opposite. The operands have to be interpretable as Boolean value (true, false).

| Operatorr | Meaning |
|-----------|---------|
| && | Logical AND |
| \|\| | Logical OR |
| ! | Logical NOT |

## Logical AND                                                                 &&

With the operator '&&' a logical AND operation of its operands is carried out. The result of the operation only has the value true (does not equal zero), if both operands have the value true (do not equal zero).

The operands are processed from left to right. When the first operand has the value false (zero), the second operand is not analysed. The following table illustrates the possible combinations:

| First operand | Second operand | Result |
|---------------|----------------|--------|
| true | true | true |
| true | false | false |
| false | true | false |
| false | false | false |

## Logical OR                                                                  ||

The logical OR operator links its operands, so that the result of the operation has the value true if one or both operands have the value true.

The operands are analysed from left to right. If the first operand has the value true (does not equal zero), then the second is not analysed. The following table illustrates the possible combinations:

| First operand | Second operand | Result |
|---------------|----------------|--------|
| true | true | true |
| true | false | true |
| false | true | true |
| false | false | false |

## Example

The example program displays a formatted ASCII table on screen.

In line 7 the logical AND operator is used to state that the output will only be carried out if column has a value which is smaller than 13 (13 characters are displayed per line) and the value of character is less than 256 (to display only the ASCII characters).

In line 8 the logical OR operator is used to ensure that the characters of the extended IBM character set are also displayed, since isprint() only has the result true for the ASCII characters with the codes 32 to 126.

```c
#include <ctype.h>

int main() {
  int row, column, character;
  printf("ASCII table\n");
  for(line = 0, character = 0; rows < 20; rows++)
    {
    for(column=0; column<13 && character<256; column++)
        {
        if (isprint(character) || character>127)
            printf("%3c %3d
        else
            printf("   %3d
        character++;
        }
    printf("\n");
    }
  return 0;
  }
```

## Logical NOT                                                    !

The logical NOT operator reverses the logical value of its operand. The value 0 (false) is converted into the value 1 (true) and all values not equal to 1 are converted to 0.

## Example

The following program contains an infinite loop, in which the user is asked to enter a number. The loop checks whether the number 0 was entered by means of an if query. If yes, the loop is terminated with break.

```c
#include <stdio.h
int main() {
   int number:
   for (;;) {
      printf("Please enter a number: ");
      scanf("%d", &number);
```

```
    if (!number)
        break;
    }
  return 0;
  }
```

## References

See category program control, if condition; and program control, loops.

# Data access

## Description

Several C and C++ operators are used to access data.

## Application

These operators are required to access individual elements of an array, structure, union or class. The scope operator and the operators for the dereferencing of pointers, which permit access to the objects to which the pointer points, also belong into this category.

| Operator | Meaning |
|---|---|
| * | Dereferencing operator |
| [ ] | Array indexing |
| . | Dot operator |
| -> | Element pointer selector |
| .* | Dereferencing of pointers to class elements |
| ->* | Dereferencing of pointers to class elements |
| :: | Scope operator |

## Dereferencing operator                                                    **

The dereferencing operator '*' is used to dereference a pointer and access its object.

The type of the pointer determines the type of the result. Therefore, if the operand is a pointer to int, the result has the data type int.

```
int func(int *pointer) {
   int result;
   *pointer = result;     /* assign value */
   }
```

## Warning

- The dereferencing operator cannot be used for an incomplete type, for example a pointer to void.
- The character '*' is also used for the declaration of variables, to specify that the declared variable is a pointer. In this case it is not a dereferencing operator. The meaning, thus, always depends on the context.

## Array indexing                                                    [ ]

The operator '[ ]' can be used to specifically access individual elements of an array or of a dynamically reserved field.

```
#define FIELD_SIZE 20
int array[FIELD_SIZE];
int dyn_field = (int*) malloc(FIELD_SIZE*sizeof(int));
for (i=0; i < Field_SIZE; i++) {
    array[i]     = i;
    dyn_field[i] = i;
    };
```

## Warning

- The first element of an array (field) has the index 0.
- Internally the indexing operator is resolved through a pointer calculation by the compiler. The syntax array[i] is, therefore, identical to *(array+i).

## Dot operator                                                        .

The dot operator is used to access individual elements of a class, structure or union.

```
object.element
```

- **object**: This has to be the name of a class, structure or union.
- **element**: This has to be the name of an element.

```
struct person {
    char  name[20];
    int   postcode;
    };
int main() {
    struct person reader;
    strcpy(reader.name, "Luke");
    reader.postcode = S9 3QS;
    return 0;
    }
```

## Element pointer selector                                      ->

The operator offers a simplified syntax to access the elements of class instances (including structures and unions) through pointers.

```
pObject->element
```

- **p_object:** Pointer to a variable of the type class, structure or union.

- **element:** An element.

```
struct person  {
   char   name[20];
   int    postcode;
   };

int main() {
   struct person p_reader;
   strcpy(p_reader->name, "Luke");
   p_leser->postcode = S9 3QS;
   return 0;
   }
```

## Pointers to class elements                                      >*,.*

The two operators are used to dereference pointers to class elements.

```
classobj.*p_classelement
p_classtype->*p_classelement
```

- **p_class element:** Pointer to an element of the class T.

- **classes obj:** Instance of the class T or a class derived from T, from which the element of the base class T can be reached.

- **p_ class typ:** Pointer to an instance of the class T or a class derived from T, from which the element of the base class T can be reached.

```
#include <stdio.h>
#include <stdlib.h>

// class definition
class extreme {
  public:
    // yields parameter maximum
    int maximum(int var1, int var2)
              {return ( (var1 > var2) ? var1 : var2);}
    // yields parameter minimum
    int minimum(int var1, int var2)
              {return ( (var1 < var2) ? var1 : var2);}
   };

int main() {
   class extreme extr;          // instance formation
   int extreme;
```

```
int value1, value2;
value1 = margin()%20;
value2 = margin()%40;

// definition of pointer to methods
int (extreme::*z_max) (int, int);
int (extreme::*z_min) (int, int);

// initialisation of pointer
z_max = extreme::maximum;
z_min = extreme::minimum;

// dereferencing of pointer to function call
extreme = (extr.*z_max) (value1, value2);
printf("The maximum of %d and %d is %d\n",value1,
        value2, extreme);
extreme = (extr.*z_min) (value1, value2);
printf("The minimum of %d and %d is %d\n",value1,
        value2, extreme);
return 0;
}
```

## Area operator                                                    ::

Objects and functions with the same name and signature (parameter types) from different scopes hide each other. Using of the area operator, hidden variables and functions of other scopes can be accessed from the current scope.

```
::global_name
```

The unary operator is used to access hidden global variables (see first example).

```
space::name
```

In its binary form the operator is employed to

- access specific namespaces,
- access static class elements, and
- access base class elements.

Access is only possible if the name can be resolved non-ambiguously (see second example).

## Examples

Access to hidden global variables:

```
#include <stdio.h>
int i = 1;
int main() {
  int i = 2;
```

```
  printf("i = %d\n",i);      // local i hides global i
  printf("i = %d\n",::i);    // access to global i
  return 0;
  }
```

Access to variables from a namespace:

```
namespace space1 {
   int i = 2;
   }
class basis {
  public:
    int i;
    void func()
        {cout << space1::i;};  // access to namaspace
  };
class derived : public base {
  public:
    int i;
    void func()
        {cout << base::i;};    // access to base class
  };
```

## References

See category classes, access from outside the class.

Practice section, category operators, overloading of the [ ] operator.

# Bitwise operators

## Description

Operators for the bitwise manipulation of data. Only integer values are allowed.

## Application

By means of the bit-operator certain programming tasks can be carried out elegantly and efficiently. However, for secure use of the operators, knowledge of the binary coding of the manipulated data is essential.

## Bitwise AND                                                                        &

When the operator '&' is used with two operands, it is a bitwise AND operator. The operands can be any integer values.

The two operands are compared bitwise. The bit in the result is only used when the corresponding bits are used in both operands.

This operator can be used to delete specific bits in its first operand.

In the ASCII table the lower and upper case letters of the English alphabet (no special foreign characters) are distinguished in their binary form, in that bit 5 is always set for the lower case letters (counted from the right). To convert a lower case into an upper case letter, bit 5 of the first operand must be deleted. To achieve this all bits (except for bit 5, which must be deleted) are set in the second operand, the mask. The other bits remain unchanged.

```
   0 1 1 0   0 0 0 1   letter 'a'
 & 1 1 0 1   1 1 1 1   mask (decimal 223)
   --------------------
   0 1 0 0   0 0 0 1   letter 'A'
```

## Bitwise OR                                                                    |

The operator for the bitwise OR operation '|' compares the bit patterns of its operands and sets the corresponding bit in the event that one of the bits is set in the operands.

This operand can, be used to set individual bits without changing the other bits of the first operand.

An example for this is the conversion of upper case into lower case characters. In the ASCII table the lower and upper case letters of the English alphabet (no special foreign characters) are distinguished in their binary form, in that bit 5 is always set for the lower case letters (counted from the right).

To convert an upper case letter into the corresponding lower case letter, it is only necessary to set bit 5, as is demonstrated in the following example:

```
   0 1 0 0   0 0 0 1   letter 'A'
 | 0 0 1 0   0 0 0 0   mask decimal 32
   --------------------
   0 1 1 0   0 0 0 1   letter 'a'
```

## Bitwise exclusive OR                                                          ^

The operator for the bitwise exclusive OR operation compares the bit patterns of its operands and sets the appropriate bit in the event that one of the bits in the operands, but not both, is set.

```
   0 0 0 1   1 0 0 1
 ^ 0 0 0 0   1 1 0 0
   --------------------
   0 0 0 1   0 1 0 1
```

## Bitwise complement  ~

The bitwise complement operator '~' overturns all the bits of its operand. Through inversion all the bits which were set in the operand are deleted and all the bits which were deleted are set in the result. The number 4 has the following bit pattern:

    0 0 0 0   0 1 0 0

By means of the operation  ~4 we set the following pattern:

    1 1 1 1   1 0 1 1

## Right shift  >>

In the bitwise right shift the individual bits of an operand are moved to the right by the determined number.

The operator can be used for a quick programming of the division by the powers of the number 2.

The expression 80 >> 3 corresponds to 80 / 2^3 and produces the following result:

|              | decimal | binary    |
|--------------|---------|-----------|
| before shift | 80      | 0101 0000 |
| after shift  | 10      | 0000 1010 |

## Left shift  <<

In the bitwise left shift the individual bits of an operand are moved to the left by the determined number.

The operator can, be used for a quick programming of the multiplication by the powers of the number 2.

The expression 3 << 2 corresponds to 3 * 2^2 and produces the following result:

|              | decimal | binary    |
|--------------|---------|-----------|
| before shift | 3       | 0000 0011 |
| after shift  | 12      | 0000 1100 |

## Examples

```
##include <stdio.h>
int main() {
    printf(" a  & 223  = %c\n", 'a' &  223);
    printf(" A  | 0x20 = %c\n", 'A' |  0x20);
    printf(" 25 ^ 12   = %d\n",  25 ^  12);
    printf(" 3  << 2   = %d\n",  3  << 2);
    printf(" 80 >> 3   = %d\n",  80 >> 3 );
```

```
    printf("~4           = %d\n",  ~4);
    return 0;
    }
```

The program produces the following output:

```
a   & 223  = A
A   | 0x20 = a
25  ^ 12   = 21
3   << 2   = 12
80  >> 3   = 10
~4         = -5
```

## Reference

See stream operators.

# Stream operators

## Description

In C++ the operators >> and << are used for formatted reading-in, writing and in streams.

## Application

The use of the stream operators for inputting and outputting is easy and clear.

```
int value = 3;
cout << "Value = " << value << endl;    // cout is the standard
                                        // output stream
```

Programming with stream operators is strongly object-oriented:

- the stream operators are overloaded by default for all elementary data types (int, float, char, etc.).

- by means of overloading, the operational area of the operators can be extended to self-defined class types.

The formatting of input and output can be controlled through manipulators.

## Examples

```
int value;
cout << "Please enter a value:" << endl;
cin >> value;
```

```
cout << left;
cout << "Value = " << value << endl;
```

## References

See Reference section of the C++ running time library, header files iostream, iomanip, etc.

See Practice section, category operators, overloading of the stream operators; and category classes, operators overloaded.


# The new and delete operators

## Description

The new and delete operators are used for dynamic memory management and can replace the functions malloc() and free() in C++ programs.

Internally the operators are mainly implemented with the help of the functions malloc() and free(). However, they allow an easier and extended operation.


### New operator                                                                   **new**

The new operator is used for dynamic memory statements and the implementation of the only 6 operator functions designated in the ANSI C++ standard.

The various operator functions are intended for the distinction of simple objects and arrays as operands, for controlling of error handling, and the assignment of specific memory areas.

There are two forms of call, depending on whether the type specification is bracketed or not. This is necessary to be able to recognise whether the declaration or assignment operators are meant in type specifications, which contain operators such as &, * or []:

```
new [free_arg] Type [initialiser]
new [free_arg] (Type) [initialiser]
```

- **free_arg**: Argument lists, which can be passed to overloaded forms.
- **Type**: Data type for which memory has to be reserved.
- **initialiser**: Value which is used to initialise the reserved memory.

## Example

```
1:  long double *p, *q, **pp;
2:  p = new long double;
3:  pp = new long double*;
```

```
 4:  p = new long double(1.2);
 5:  //q = new long double * 3;
 6:  q = new long double [3];
 7:  //q = new long double [3](1,2,3);
 8:  class demo {
 9:      int i;
10:      } *p_demo;
11: p_demo = new demo[10];
12: void (**func_ptr)(int);
13: //func_ptr = new void(*[3])(int);
14: func_ptr = new (void(*[3])(int));
15: char destination[sizeof(demo)];
16: p_demo = new (destination) demo;
```

## Explanation

In line 2 a pointer to objects of the data type long double is created, and in line 3 a pointer to a pointer to objects of the data type long double.

In line 4 the pointer p is created and the memory area, to which the pointer p refers, is initialised with the value 1.2.

Line 5 attempts to create a pointer to an array of 3 long double values. The syntax used is similar to the use of the function malloc(), but leads to errors in this case, as the compiler understands the call as (new long double)*3.

In line 6 the correct statement of the array is given.

Line 7: is syntactically correct; however, arrays cannot be initialised.

In line 11 an array of class objects is created.

In line 12 a pointer func_ptr to function pointers is declared. Then memory for an array of function pointers, whose first element is given to it as an address, is to be reserved for the pointer func_ptr. The assignment in line 13 leads, as in line 5, to an error of interpretation. Therefore, in line 14 the second syntax form is chosen, where the type specification is in brackets.

In line 15 memory of the size of a demo object is reserved. In line 16 the demo object is created in the memory area to which destination points.

## Warning

- Objects which have been created with new have an unlimited life span. Memory therefore has to be freed up by the delete operator.

- When reserving memory for an array, the new operator returns a pointer to the first array element.

- When reserving arrays all dimensions have to be specified by constant, positive expressions; the first dimension can be specified by a general expression.

- Arrays cannot be initialised.

- Class objects can only be created with new, if the class has a default constructor, or if the arguments for the constructor are passed with the operator.

- References cannot be created with new, since they do not have space in the memory.

- The operator calculates the memory requirements for any data type which has to be created, which is why the first parameter of a new operator function is always of the type size_t (note for overloading).

- If the new operator is overloaded, an appropriate form of the delete- operator should also be implemented.

## Delete operator                                                    delete

The delete operator is used for the dynamic freeing up of memory which has been allocated by new.

```
delete p_object
delete [] p_object
```

## Warning

- Pointers to constants cannot be deleted.

- The destructor is called for classes during deletion.

- The second version is for the release of arrays. The dimension is not specified in this.

- Calls with zero pointers have no effect.

## Example

```
class demo *p;
p = new demo[10];
delete[] p;
int **p;
p = new int*;
delete p;
```

## References

See Practice section, category pointer and dynamic memory management, memory statement with new; and category operators, overloading of new and delete.

# Type conversion and identification

## Description

With the help of the operator for type conversion it is possible – within certain limits – to convert values and objects of one data type into another data type.

The `typeid` operator allows the type of a class object to be determined at runtime.

## Application

Occasionally it may be preferred that a variable of a specific data type be treated as belonging to a different data type. This can be brought about through the C cast-operator () or the C++-operators `const_cast`, `dynamic_cast`, `static_cast` and `reinterpret_cast`, which have been adopted into the language as keywords.

The C++ operators are mainly intended to categorise the various conversions (which could also be carried out with the cast operator ()) according to their potential danger and the operational area. In the event of an error the programmer may be able to deduce the type conversion concerned from the type of error and with the help of the search function of his editor jump to all occurrences of the operator.

| Operator | Description |
|---|---|
| static_cast<type>(var)) | To convert 'closely related' types – that is all cases, in which the compiler could also carry out an implicit conversion, plus a few simple special cases. |
| reinterpret_cast<type>(var)) | For almost all other permitted conversions. |
| const_cast<type>(var)) | Removes a const or volatile declaration from a type. |
| dynamic_cast<type>(var) | To convert pointers or references to class types of a shared class hierarchy. |

## The cast operator ()

The cast-operator can be used in a statement to convert the type of the expression on the right-hand side into the type of the identifier on the left-hand side:

```
identifier1 = (type_of_identifier1) expression;
identifier1 = (type_of_identifier1) identifier2;
```

A second form of the syntax directly converts the type of a variable:

```
identifier = datatype();
```

## Examples

```
intptr = (int *) malloc(80 * sizeof(int));
printf("%f\n", (double) 13/2);
```

```
int i = int(3.14);
int i = int();            // assigns undefined value
```

## Type conversion                                      const_cast (C++ only)

The operator `const_cast` is used to remove or swap the qualifiers `const` and `volatile` from a type specification. The operator `const_cast` can be used to render convertable a variable which has been protected from involuntary overriding through a `const` declaration for a subsequent assignment.

```
const_cast < target_type > (variable)
```

- **target type:** Specification of the type in which the `variable` is to be converted. The target type has to be identical with the type of the `variable` except for the qualifiers `const` or `volatile`.

- **variable:** The object which is to be converted.

## Example

```
const int* p;
int* q;
p = q;                     // correct: assignment of an int*
                           //          object to const int*
q = p;                     // error: const int* to int*
q = const_cast <int*> (p); // ok
```

## Type conversion                                  dynamic_cast (C++ only)

It is possible to use the `dynamic_cast` operator to convert pointers (or references) to objects of a base class into pointers (or references) to objects of a derived class, and vice versa.

**UpCast.** In an object of a derived class the elements of the base class are contained as partial objects. If T is a unique `public` base class, a pointer to the whole object can be converted into a pointer to the partial object of the base class (the same applies to references). This process is part of the C++ standard conversion and thus does not require the use of the `dynamic_cast` operator.

**DownCast.** Conversely, a pointer to a base class object which is part of a derived object can be reconverted into a pointer to the derived object, if it is not a polymorphous base class (a class that contains virtual methods). (For non-polymorphous base classes it is possible to use the `static_cast` operator.)

```
class_pointer1 = dynamic_cast < destinationtype > (class_pointer2)
```

- **class_pointer1:** Pointer or reference to a class object to which the converted pointer (reference) `class_pointer2` is assigned.

- **target_type:** Specification of the type into which `class_pointer2` is to be converted (type of `class_pointer1` or `void*`).

- **class_pointer2:** Pointer (reference) which is to be converted.

# Example

```
#include <iostream>
using namespace std;
class Basis{
  public:
    virtual void func() {cout << "base class" << endl;}
  };
derived class :  public Basis {
  public:
    void func_abg() {cout << "derived class" << endl;}
  };

int main() {
  derived    *p_drv = new derived;
  Basis      *p_bp  = new Basis;

  // change pointer to derived class to base class
  // p_bp = p_drv;  also possible
  p_bp = dynamic_cast <Basis*> (p_drv);
  if(p_bp != ZERO)
      p_bp->func_drv();                    // error

  // change pointer to base class to derived class
  // p_abg = p_bp;  not possible
  p_drv = dynamic_cast <Derived*> (p_bp);
  if(p_drv != ZERO)
      p_drv->func_drv();                   // o.k.
  return 0;
  }
```

Moreover, with dynamic_cast it is also possible under certain circumstances to cause a crosscast from a base class into another base. If of an error occurs a bad_cast exception is triggered (for references) and a zero pointer is returned (for pointers).

## Type conversion                                          static_cast (only C++)

With the static_cast operator all common conversions can be carried out explicitly. It also permits a conversion of a pointer to a non-polymorphous base class into one of its derived classes, and thus supplements the operator dynamic_cast.

```
identifier1 =  static_cast < target_type > (identifier2)
```

- **identifier1**: The object to which the converted object identifier2 is assigned.
- **target_type**: Specification of the type into which the idenitifer2 is to be converted.
- **identifier2**: The object which is to be converted.

# Example

```
#include <iostream>
using namespace std;
class Basis{
  public:
    void func() {cout << "base class" << endl;}
  };
derived class :  public Basis{
  public:
    void func_drv() {cout << "derived class" << endl;}
  };

int main() {
  Derived    *p_drv = new Derived;
  Basis      *p_bp  = new Basis;

  // change pointer to derived class to base class
  p_bp = dynamic_cast <Basis*> (p_drv);
  if(p_bp == NULL)
      cout << "cast failed" << endl;
      else
      p_bp->func_drv();        // error
  // change pointer to base class to derived class
  p_drv = static_cast <Derived*> (p_bp);
  if(p_drv == ZERO)
      cout << "cast failed" << endl;
      else
      p_drv->func_drv();      // o.k.
  return 0;
  }
```

## Type conversion                    reinterpret_cast (only C++) )

The `reinterpret_cast` operator is intended for crucial conversions, for example the conversion of integer types to pointers and vice versa, as well as for the conversion of pointers to functions.

```
identifier1 = reinterpret_cast < destinationtype > (identifier2)
```

- **identifier1**: The object to which the converted object `identifier2` is assigned.
- **target_type**: Specification of the type into which `identifier2` is to be converted.
- **identifier2**: The object which is to be converted.

# Warning

- If integer types are converted into pointers or vice versa, the value of the converted object may not be interpreted correctly.

- However, in a subsequent re-conversion the original value reappears (provided, of course, that no assignment to the variable has occurred between conversions).
- The same applies when pointers to functions are converted into pointers to functions of another type or into pointers to objects.
- If pointers or references are converted, undefined class identifiers in the type specification are allowed.

## Type identification                                                    typeid

The `typeid` operator creates for the object passed to it a corresponding instance of the `type_info` class (defined in `typeinfo`). In this instance, which is returned as a reference by the operator, information is stored about the data type of the passed object. The `type_info` objects can be compared directly with the aid of the `==` and `!=` operators. Furthermore, the `name()` method can be called, which returns a string that identifies the type of the `typeid` operand.

## Warning

According to the ANSI standard, types which only differ by the CV qualifiers (`const`, `volatile`) are identical. However, some compilers differentiate between them.

## Example

```
#include <iostream>
#include <typeinfo>
using namespace std;

class demo {int value;};

int main() {
  demo d1();
  const demo d2();

  if(typeid(d1) == typeid(d2))
    cout << "equal" << endl;
  if(typeid(d1).name() == typeid(d2).name())
    cout << typeid(d1).name() << endl;

  return 0;
  }
```

## References

See Practice section, category inheritance and polymorphism, RTTI with dynamic_cast; and category inheritance and polymorphism, type identification for the running time.

# Other operators

## Sizeof operator                                              sizeof

The `sizeof` operator returns as a result the size of its operand in bytes. The return value is of a non-signed integer type `size_t`. A data type as well as a variable can be passed as the operand.

Typical operational areas for the `sizeof` operator are memory requirement calculations for the dynamic memory statement and the calculation of the number of elements in an array.

## Warning

- For references, the `sizeof` operator returns the size of the referenced object.
- Not permitted are: functions, bit fields, undefined classes, arrays with missing dimension specification as well as the `void` type.
- If one of the types `char`, `unsigned char` or `signed char` is used as an argument, the result is always 1 per definition.
- The size of a character literal (`sizeof('Z')`) is equivalent to the size of `int` in C, and the size of `char` in C++.
- If `sizeof` is used for an array, the result is the total size of the array in bytes. But beware! If `sizeof` is used within a function to determine the size of an array passed to a parameter of the function, `sizeof` will return the size of the pointer to the array, since array names are passed as pointers.
- If the argument is a class, structure or union, the actual size is returned, in which padding bytes for the alignment at memory boundaries may also be contained. The result of the `sizeof` operation may then differ from the sum of the memory requirements of the individual elements.

## Example

```
int main() {
  int field[123];

  // yields number = 123;
  int number  = sizeof(field)/sizeof(int);
  // reserved field for 123 double values
  double *ptr = (double*) malloc(anz*sizeof(double));

  return 0;
}
```

## Address operator &

When the '&' operator is used with an operand, it returns the address of its operand. Any identifier that represents an L value can be used as an operand.

## Warning

- The operator cannot be used for the element of a bit field or for an object which has been defined with the `register` memory class.
- Function and array names can be directly interpreted as addresses, which is why the use of the address operator is not required for them.

## Example

```
// input integer value of keyboard
int number;
scanf("%d", &number);

// direct pointer to a variable
int number_value;
int *number_pointer;
number_pointer = &number_value;

// passing of function demo() to func()
void demo() {...}
void func(int* i, void (*f)() ) {...}
func(&number_value, demo);
```

## Arithmetic if operator (conditional evaluation) ?:

ANSI C/C++ has a single ternary operator, also known as the arithmetic `if` operator. The arithmetic `if` operator (?:) is a short form of the `if-else` statement. The general format of this operator is as follows:

```
If-operator ? expr1 : expr2
```

## Evaluation

- If the evaluation of the condition does not yield 0 (`true`), expr1 is executed.
- If the evaluation of the condition yields 0 (`false`), expr2 is evaluated.

## Example

```
int max, one, two;
one = 1;
two = 2;
max = (one > two) ? one : two;
```

The same assignment can also be formulated as an `if-else` statement:

```
if (one > two)
   max = one;
else
   max = two;
```

## Sequential analysis (Comma operator)

If the character ',' does not separate a list of elements (function parameters, initialisation values, and so on), it is used for sequential analysis. It is usually used to analyse two or more expressions in places where only one expression is permitted.

## Warning

- The result of the expressions which are separated by the comma operator has the same value and type as the right-hand operand.
- The operands can have any type; type conversions are not carried out.
- In lists the corresponding expressions have to be enclosed in brackets.

## Examples

```
func(int par1, float par2) {..};
```

The next example uses the comma operator in the reinitialisation section of a for loop to increment both loop variables i and j in each loop.

```
for (i=j=0; i<MAXVALUE; i++, j++) { ...
```

In the third example the left-hand operand (i++) is analysed first. Subsequently the result of number2/4 of the variables number1 is assigned.

```
number1 = (i++, number2 / 4);
```

If the operator is used in lists, the statements have to be bracketed.

```
func(i, (f=3.14, f+0.0015));
```

# Synonyms

In C++ synonymous identifiers were introduced for some operators.

| Synonym | Operator |
|---------|----------|
| bitand | & |
| and | && |
| bitor | \| |
| orr | \|\| |
| xor | ^ |
| compl | ~ |

| Synonym | Operator |
|---------|----------|
| and_eq | &= |
| or_eq | \|= |
| xor_eq | ^= |
| not | ! |
| not_eq | != |

# Precedence and associativity

## Description

To be able to predict how an expression is analysed you have to know how the compiler analyses expressions.

Precedence    Every operator belongs to a specific precedence class. In an expression, the operators are processed in their order of precedence, with operators of a higher precedence being processed first.

Associativity    If there are several operators with the same precedence in the same expression, these are processed in the operators' characteristic direction.

Operands    It is not specified in which order the operands of a binary operator are evaluated (usually the left-hand operand is evaluated first, followed by the right-hand one).

For the logical operators the left-hand operand is evaluated first. If the left-hand operand of an && operator equals 0 (false), the right-hand operator is no longer evaluated. The same applies for the || operator, if the left-hand operand equals 1 (true).

Parentheses    The order in which the operators are evaluated can be influenced by adding parentheses.

Precedence and associativity of the individual operators can be looked up in the following table.

| Precedence | Operator | Associativity |
|------------|----------|---------------|
| 18 | :: (expr) | |
| 17 | [] -> . | L-R |
| | Postfix: ++ -- | |
| | typeid, cast operators | |
| 16 | unary: + − * ! ~ & () | R-L |
| | Prefix: ++ -- | |
| | new, delete, sizeof | |

| Precedence | Operator | Associativity |
|---|---|---|
| 15 | .* ->* | L-R |
| 14 | * / % | L-R |
| 13 | binary: + | L-R |
| 12 | << >> | L-R |
| 11 | < <= > >= | L-R |
| 10 | == != | L-R |
| 9 | & (bitand) | L-R |
| 8 | ^ (xor) | L-R |
| 7 | \| (bitor) | L-R |
| 6 | && | L-R |
| 5 | \|\| | L-R |
| 4 | = *= /* %= += – = <<= >>= | R-L |
| | &= \|= ^= | |
| 3 | ?: | R-L |
| 2 | throw | L-R |
| 1 | , | L-R |

# Overloading of operators

## Description

The overloading of operators is used to adapt the behaviour of an operator to the operands which have been passed to it. The advantage for the programmer is that it is possible to redefine the operators that are available for his own data types, to be precise classes. This does not result in a runtime advantage, since the overloaded operators are actually functions.

## Application

Operators can be overloaded within the declaration of their class or outside in the file scope.

If the class scope is overloaded then the first operator is automatically an object of the class and is not listed as a parameter in the definition of the operator function. Operators which have been overloaded in the class scope have access to the `private` and `protected` elements of the class (see the following examples).

If the file scope is overloaded all operands have to be listed as parameters in the definition of the operator function. Operators which have been overloaded in the file scope do not have access to the `private` and `protected` elements of the class.

However, this can be avoided by declaring the operator function in the class as `friend` (see Overloading of stream operators).

Operators, which can be put into sequence (for example `var1 = var2 = var3;`) have to return a reference to their left-hand operand as a return value for this.

## Warning

- It is not possible to define new operators.
- The following operators cannot be overloaded: `::`, `?:`, `.`, `.*`, `#`, `##`, `defined`, `typeid`, the C++ cast operators.
- The following operators can only be overloaded in a class scope: `=`, `()`, `[]`, `->`.
- At least one operand of an overloaded operator must be a class or a reference to a class. (The functionality of the operator for the elementary data types can therefore not be changed.)
- The general lay-out of the operator (number of operands, precedence, default arguments) cannot be changed.

### Overloading of unary operators

Unary operators, which are overloaded outside the class scope, expect the submission of an operand of the class type. Unary operators, which are overloaded inside a class, must only be overloaded through non-static element functions without parameters. The class instance which calls them up is automatically adopted as an operand.

Syntax: declaration in class

```
return_type  operator @()  {}              // @ equal !, ++, --, ...
```

Syntax: declaration in file scope

```
return_type  operator @(class_type) {}  // @ equal !, ++, --, ...
```

## Example

```
class person {
    int age;
  public:
    ...
    operator ++ ()     {          //prefix increment
        ++age;
        return *this;
        }
    };
```

The declaration of an `int` parameter for the postfix increment operator does not specify a real second operand, but is only used to distinguish it from the prefix increment operator.

## Overloading of binary operators

Binary operators, which are overloaded outside the class scope, expect the passing of both operands. One of the operands must be a class type. Binary operators, which are overloaded inside a class, must only be overloaded through non-static element functions with one parameter. The class instance which calls them up is automatically adopted as an operand.

## Example

```
class person { .. };
class address_book {
   /* contains many personal entries as data elements, which are
      administered not as a static array, but as dynamic lists or
      a tree */
   ...
  public:
   person& operator[] (int);
   };
person& address_book::operator[] (int i) {
   class person *found;
   /* searching dynamic structure */
   ...
   return *found;
   };

int main() {
   class address_book personal;
   class personal entry;
   ...
   entry = personal[3];
   return 0;
   }
```

## Reference

See Practice section, category operators.

# Program control

## Program control

### Description

The more complex programs become, the more often it may be required, depending on the current state of the program, to branch to different statements. To control the program course there are various concepts:

− branchings

− loops

− exceptions

− conditional compilation

### Application

- **Branchings**. Branchings enable the programmer to determine that one or several statement blocks are only carried out subject to specific conditions.

- **Loops.** Loops permit the programmer to have a statement block carried out several times in a row.

- **Exceptions**. Exceptions and the concept of exceptions handling permit the programmer to separate error handling to a large degree from the program code. This also means that the point of error genesis does not have to be the same as the point of error handling.

- **Conditional compilation**. With the help of the preprocessor directives the programmer can control which code blocks are compiled subject to preprocessor switches and are included into the final program, and which are not.

### References

See Practice section, categories program control, preprocessor directives and exceptions.

# The if condition

## Description
The `if` condition controls whether a following statement or statement block is carried out or not.

## Application
The keyword `if` is followed by a condition in brackets. During the execution of the program this condition is evaluated. If this evaluation has the result `true` (that is a value which does not equal zero), the `if` statement is carried out. If the evaluation returns the result `false`, the execution of the program is continued with the first statement after the branching.

## Syntax
```
if (condition)                  if (condition)
   statement;                      {
                                      statement block;
                                   }
```

- **Condition**: The condition which is evaluated has to return a Boolean value. Here, for example, an integer may stand as an arithmetic operation, a comparison, or the call of a function with an appropriate return type.
- **Statement/statement block**: The `if` condition can be followed by a single statement or by a statement block. A single statement always has to end in a semicolon (the statement delimiter). If a statement block has to be carried out, it has to be enclosed in curly brackets.

## Warning
Never put a semicolon behind the condition. The compiler would interpret this as an empty statement. In this case the `if` condition would only refer to this empty statement.

## Example
```
if (ccharacter == 'a')
   printf("The character is a.");
if ( isdigit(ccharacter) )
   printf("The character is a number");
```

# The if-else statement

## Description

The if-else statement determines which of two statement blocks is carried out subject to a condition.

## Application

The simple if condition can only determine whether a single statement block is carried out or not. However, there are also cases in which – depending on whether the condition returns true or false – either one or the other statement block has to be carried out.

This language construction is started by the keyword else.

```
if (Condition)                    if (condition)
  statement;                        { statement block }
  else                              else
  statement;                        { statement block }}
```

## Examples

```
if (ccharacter == 'a')
  printf("The character is a.");
  else
  printf("The character is not a.");
```

# if-else chains

## Description

Language constructs in which the else part of an if-else statement is also an if-else statement.

## Application

With the keywords if and else it is possible to construct else-if chains, in which several expressions can be checked.

```
if (condition)
    statement;
  else if (condition)
    statement;
  else if (condition)
    statement;
  else
    statement;
```

## Evaluation of the else-if chains

The conditions are evaluated in the order in which they appear in the program code. If one of the conditions has true as its result, the corresponding statement section is carried out and with it the processing of the chain is finished.

The statements of the final else are carried out if none of the previously checked conditions returns the result true.

## Example

```
printf("Please enter: Number Operator Number <Return>\n");
scanf("%f %c %f", &number1, &Operator, &number2);
if (Operator == '+')
    printf("= %f", number1 + number2);
  else if (Operator == '-')
    printf("= %f", number1 - number2);
  else if (Operator == '*')
    printf("= %f", number1 * number2);
  ...
```

## Reference

See Switch statements.

# switch statements

## Description

Complex jump statement, which branches subject to an expression to different labels in a statement block.

## Application

A simpler and usually clearer programming technique than the if-else chains described in the previous paragraph is offered by the Switch statements. With this a program can also choose between several alternatives – however, in contrast to the if-else chain, these are only subject to the value of an expression.

```
switch(expression)
{
   case constant1:statement;
     break;
   case constant2:statement;
     break;
   case constant3:statement;
     break;
   case constant4:statement;
     break;
   default:statement;}}
```

- **Expression**: An expression is an integer value (as well as a list type), which is compared to all the case marks within the Switch statements. Here the call of a function, which returns an integer as a result, can also stand. Simultaneously, as in the if statement, an assignment of the function result can follow.
- **Case constant**: Constants are compared to the expression.
- **Statement**: The statement is only carried out if the corresponding constant and the switch expression are identical. If a correspondence has been established once, all statements (including those corresponding to other constants) are carried out, until either the keyword break stops the Switch statements or the switch block is finished.
- **Default**: If the controlling of the Switch statements with the case mark does not produce a correspondence, a branching to the statement block default follows.

## Execution: evaluation of the Switch statements

- The constants in the case marks are compared with the switch expression in the order in which they appear in the program code.
- If the expression and the constant are identical in one position, a branching to the corresponding statement follows.
- If all comparisons return the result false, a branching to the statements behind default follows, if the default mark exists.
- As the constants are only used as labels, the execution is carried on after a correspondence has been found until the Switch statements is finished. That is why (unless this failure is explicitly wanted) each statement belonging to a case is terminated with the keyword break. As soon as the compiler meets the break, the Switch statements is abandoned immediately.
- No two constants within a Switch statements may have the same value. If this is the case, the compiler produces an error message.
- In switch statements character constants are automatically converted into their integer value.
- Within the switch block variables cannot be defined and initialised.

## Example

```
#include <stdio.h>
int main(){
    float number1, number2;
    char Operator;

    printf("A small pocket calculator:\n");
```

```
printf("Please enter: Number Operator Number <Return>\n");
scanf("%f %c %f", &number1, &Operator, &number2);

switch (Operator)
   {
   case '+':
      printf("= %f", number1 + number2);
      break;
   case '-':
      printf("= %f", number1 - number2);
      break;
   case 'X':
   case 'x':
   case '*':
      printf("= %f", number1 * number2);
      break;
   case ':':
   case '/':
      printf("= %f", number1 / number2);
      break;
   default:
      printf("Unknown operator");
   } // end of switch

printf("\n\n");
return 0;
}
```

## References

See if statement

See Practice section, categories program control, menus with switch.

# loops

`for, while`

## Description

Loops are used when a statement block is to be carried out several times in a row.

Loops consist of:

- a breaking-off condition, which determines when the execution of the loop is to be stopped, and

- a statement block which is enclosed in curly brackets.

## Application

In C/C++ there are `while`, `for` and `do-while` loops. Every loop can be formulated as a `while` loop. Irrespective of the loop used it can be broken in several ways:

- break condition of the loop is met,
- break through `break`, `return` or `exit()`, or
- jump out of the loop through `goto` or `longjmp()`.

## Warning

It is the responsibility of the programmer to make sure that a loop is abandoned once its purpose has been carried out, as the program may otherwise remain in an infinite loop.

## References

See practice section, category program control, infinite loops.

# The for loop

## Description

With the keyword `for` a loop is started, which is controlled by a three-part loop header. This loop header stands in round brackets and contains the three elements initialisation, condition and alteration, separated by semicolons.

## Application

The `for` loop is always used when the desired repetitions of the statement block are countable (in contrast to the `while` loop, which can also be used when the number of repetitions cannot be calculated). In practice this means that you define your own variable (the so-called loop variable), which is initialised at the start of the loop and then increased or decreased by a specific amount in each period, until it is higher or lower than a specific amount, and therefore no longer meets the loop condition. The syntax of the `for` loop is specially adjusted to this formulation of a loop.

## Syntax

```
for (initialisation; condition; reinitialisation)
    statement;
```

- **Initialisation:** The statements contained in the initialisation section are executed before the loop is started. This is where the loop or counter variables are usually initialised. It is also possible to initialise several variables in this statement. Here the assignments are separated by commas.

- **Condition**: The condition section contains an expression, which has to be true for the statement of the `for` loop to be carried out.
- **Reinitialisation**: The statements contained here are processed after each period of the statement block which pertains to `for`. Here the counter variable is increased or decreased. However, every other statement can be adopted here. If there are several statements here, they are separated by commas.
- **Statement**: The statement section can consist of a single statement or a statement block. A single statement always has to end in a semicolon (the statement delimiter). If a statement block is to be carried out, it has to be put into curly brackets.

## Warning

A special form of the `for` loop is the infinite loop.

```
for(;;)
```

This is the result when all three elements of the definition of the `for` loop are dropped, and when only the semicolons which separate the elements remain. Infinite loops of this kind can only be broken with `break`, `return` or `goto`, since there is no break condition.

## Example

```
#include <stdio.h>
int main() {
    int counter;
    for(counter = 0; counter < 10; counter++)
        printf("The value of the counter is: %d\n", counter);
    return 0;
}
```

## References

See break statements.

See while loop.

See Practice section, category program control, infinite loops.

# The while loop

## Description

The while loop is the most general form of the loop, with which a statement block can be executed several times subject to a loop condition.

## Application

The while loop has a similar syntax to the if condition. However, the condition does not check whether the statement block is carried out, but how often it is carried out.

While loops also often contain – like for loops – loop variables, which are part of the loop condition and are changed within the statement block of the loop. However, initialisation and alteration of the loop variable cannot be integrated in the loop header, as is done in the for loop.

However, the while loop is often also used when the loop break does not depend on a loop variable but on other events (for example, user input). In this case the loop is usually broken by means of a break statement.

## Syntax

```
while (condition)
    statement;
```

- **Condition**: The condition which is evaluated has to return a Boolean value. For example, here may stand an integer, an arithmetic operation, a comparison, or the call of a function with an appropriate return type.

- **Statement**: The statement section can consist of a single statement or a statement block. A single statement always has to end in a semicolon (the statement delimiter). If a statement block is to be carried out, it has to be put into curly brackets.

## Examples

The while loop is the most general type of loop. Therefore, for example the following for loop

```
for (i=1; i <= 5; i++)
    printf("%d ", i);
```

can also be formulated as a while loop:

```
i = 1;
while (i <= 5) {
    printf("%d ", i);
    i++;
    }
```

## Execution: evaluation of the while loop

- The condition of the while loop is tested before the statement pertaining to the loop is executed.
- The loop ends when the condition no longer returns the value true.
- If the evaluation of the condition of the while loop returns the value false from the start, the statements of the loop are never executed.

## References

See break statements.

See for loop.

See Practice section, category program control, infinite loops.

# The do-while loop

## Description

Apart from the while loop there is also the construct of the do-while loop, which is started with the keyword do and in which the loop condition stands at the end of the statement block.

## Application

The most important difference from the while loop is that the statement section of the do loop is executed at least once, since the expression which contains the condition is always evaluated after the statement section has been processed.

## Syntax

```
do
   statement;
   while (condition);
```

## Example

```
#include <stdio.h>
int main() {
   int number = 99;
   do {
      printf("Please enter a number. ");
      printf("99 to end the program.\n");
      scanf("%d", &number);
      printf("The number entered ");
      printf("was: %d\n", number);
      } while (number != 99);
   return 0;
   }
```

## References

See for loop.

See while loop.

# Break statements for loops

## Description

If necessary, loops can be broken off prematurely with a range of statements.

## Application

In principle the loop condition controls how often the statement block of a loop is to be executed. Furthermore, individual loop periods can also be skipped or loops broken prematurely.

| | |
|---|---|
| continue | The continue statement jumps to the end of the loop block. The execution of the statements which follow continue is dropped and the next loop period begins. |
| break | The keyword break has already been introduced in connection with the Switch statements. Apart from the termination of the Switch statements, you can also stop the execution of a loop by using break. In contrast to continue, not only the current loop period is terminated, but the loop is abandoned completely. |

Apart from continue and break, there are further keywords and functions which can be used to leave a loop or a statement block.

| | |
|---|---|
| return | With the keyword return the execution of a function can be interrupted and then continued at the position at which the function has been called. |
| exit() | With the exit() function a program can be terminated at any point. This is usually used when a serious error has occurred, which renders the further program course impossible or useless. |
| throw | Triggers an exception and jumps to the next suitable exception handler (only for the error handling). |
| goto | With goto it is possible to branch to any other point within the current function which has been marked by a label. The label receives a name and ends, like the marks of the Switch statements, in a colon. |
| longjmp() | Resets the program into a state which precviously has been saved by calling setjmp(). |

## Examples

Skip individual iterations with continue:

```
#include <stdio.h>
int main() {
   int number;
   do {
      printf("Please enter a number. ");
      printf("99 to end the program.\n");
      scanf("%d", &number);
      if (number < 0)
         continue;
      printf("The number entered ");
      printf("was: %d\n", number);
      } while (number != 99);
   return 0;
   }
```

Premature termination of a loop with break:

```
int main() {
   int number;
   for (number = 3; number < 15; number++) {
      if (number == 8)
         break;
      printf("number has the following value: %d\n", number);
      }
   return 0;
   }
```

### References

See for loop.

See while loop.

See Practice section, category program control, infinite loops.

# Functions

## Functions

### Description

C programs consist of any number of functions, whose names can be selected freely within C
(see bases section).

## Application

The object of a function definition is to connect a statement block, which executes a particular task (for example the outputting on console, a calculation, etc.) with a name. If the function is called by its name anywhere in the program, the program execution is continued with the first statement of the statement section of the function. After the function has been processed the program execution jumps back into the line of the function call. The division of the source text into functions makes it possible to avoid redundant code, to put together frequently needed functions into libraries, and to design the programs in a modular fashion to make them easier to maintain.

To exchange data with the function which is calling it up, a function can define any number of parameters and a return value.

Functions can be defined at any point in the source text (however, not within other functions). Before a function can be called, it has to be known to the compiler. This is achieved by positioning the function definition at the start of the source text file or by defining the function at any other point, and only positioning a forward declaration of the function at the program start. The latter system is also the basis of the use of header files for libraries.

## Example

```
#include <stdio.h>      /* declarations for printf, scanf, fflush */
double fact(int num);   /* forward declaration to factorial() */

int main() {
   int num;
   double fact;

   printf("Please enter the number: ");
   scanf("%d",&num);
   fflush(stdin);

   fact = fact(num);
   printf("\nThe factorial of %d is %lf\n", num, fact);
   return 0;
   }

double fact(int num) {
   int loop;
   double fact = 1;

   for(loop=num; loop>=1; loop--)
     {
     fact *= loop;
     }

   return fact;
   }
```

## References
See Practice section, category libraries.

# Function declaration and definition

## Description
The return type, name and parameters are determined with the function declaration. A function definition also contains the function body, which comprises the statements in curly brackets.

## Application
In the function definition a statement block is connected to a function name, so that when the function name is called in the program code the statement block of the function is executed. Furthermore, by specifying the parameters and the return type of the function, it is determined how the function receives and returns data when called.

## Syntax
```
Type func_name (PARAMETER_LIST)
    {
    FUNCTION_BODY
    }
```

- **type:** The `type` specification determines the return value of the function. Arrays and function types are not permitted as return types. However, pointers to these objects are allowed.

- **func_name:** The name of the function. This name has to be non-ambiguous in C, but not in C++ (see overloading).

- **PARAMETER_LIST:** The individual parameters are given here with their types separated by commas. In a declaration the specification of the parameter types are given, which the compiler requires for the type check and to resolve overloaded names (in C++). In C++ default arguments can be given to the parameters.

- **FUNCTION_BODY:** The function body is a statement block which is enclosed in curly brackets and executed when the function is called.

## Warning
- Functions have the memory class `extern` by default. Functions can also be declared as static.

- The default `extern` declaration of functions means that the functions have external linkage (unless there is a previous `static` declaration of the function in the source text). All `extern` declarations of a particular function, therefore, refer across file boundaries to the same definition of the function. In this way it is possible to create a connection to a function, which is defined in another source text file or library, through a forward declaration in a source text file.

- If a function has been declared `static`, the function has internal linkage, meaning that the name of the function is only known within its own source text file. In this way it is possible to define functions with the same name in the various source text files (however, of course, only one per file), without this resulting in linker errors due to multiple definitions.

- Functions which are not supposed to return a value receive the type specification `void`.

- Functions for which no return type has been specified are automatically assigned the return type `int` in C (in C++ this gives an error).

- In a function declaration which is not part of a definition, no parameters are specified. This is interpreted as a function with any number of parameters in C, yet as a function without parameters in C++. By specifying the keyword `void` instead of a parameter list it is possible to declare clearly in C a function without parameters.

- Apart from the superfluous keyword `auto`, `register` is the only memory class specification which can be assigned for parameters. With this the declared argument is loaded into a processor register at the call of the function, if possible.

- The specification ... at the end of the parameter list means that a number of arguments can still be assigned.

- The function name and the parameter list together form the signature of the function.

- Within the function body it is possible to define your own variables, which if not specified otherwise, have the memory class `auto` and local scope. These local variables are created on the stack at the call of the function and are removed automatically when leaving the function.

- If the value of a local variable is to be kept after leaving the function, the memory class `static` can be used. Usually this is used to pass on the values of local variables from one function call to another.

- In C++ it is possible to declare functions as `inline`, to instruct the compiler when possible to substitute the function calls directly by statements, which are identical to the execution of the function and not by a jump into the statement section of the function. However, this is only a recommendation to the compiler.

- In C++ it is possible to specify a list of exceptions which can be triggered in the function declaration by the keyword `throw`. If there are function exceptions of other types, an `unexpected` exception is triggered.

## Examples

```
int  main();
int  func1(char* s, int n);
void func2();
```

Default arguments in C++:

```
int  func3(double par, char* s = "", int n = 2);
```

Overloaded functions in C++:

```
void func(int n);
int  func(int n, int m);
int  func(float f);
```

## Warning

The old form of the function definition that goes back to Kernighan/Ritchie, where the parameters used to be defined under the function name, is obsolete in C and no longer possible in C++.

```
// func_name(a,b)
// int a, double b;
//    { ...
```

## References

See classes, methods.

See Practice section, category libraries.

# The main() function

## Description

The ANSI standard prescribes that one of the functions in a C/C++ program has to have the name `main()`. This function is the start function of a program, to which control is automatically given after the start of the program. Additionally, it provides the option to adopt command line arguments.

## Application

The ANSI standard designates the following definitions:

```
int main() {  }
int main(int argc, char *argv[]) {   }
```

However, most compilers also permit `void` as a return value:

```
void main() {   }
void main(int argc, char *argv[]) {   }
```

## main() without arguments                                          main()

Programs which do not adopt arguments from the program call define `main()` without parameters.

```
int main () {   }
void main ( ) {   }
```

## main() and its parameters                                   main(int, char**)

The ANSI standard also designates that the function `main()` can optionally submit two arguments. The names for these arguments can be chosen freely, but the names `argc` and `argv` have become standard.

```
void main(int argc, char *argv[]) {   }
```

- **argc**: (abbreviation for 'argument count') This is the standard name for the first argument of the `main()` function. The data type of `argc` is `int`. The value of `argc` is equivalent to the number of strings in the array, to which `argv` points. By definition `argc` can never have a negative value.
- **argv**: (abbreviation for 'argument vector') This is the standard name for the second argument of the `main()` function. `argv` points to an array with pointers of the type `char`. The strings are passed by the loading module of the system to the program.

The number of parameters is determined by the argument `argc`. By definition `argv[0]` (the first pointer) always points to the name of the program, whereas `argv[argc]` is a ZERO pointer.

The individual parameters are `argv[1]` to `argv[argc-1]`.

## Examples

```
#include <stdio.h>
#include <stdlib.h>

int main( int argc, char *argv[]) {
   int i;
   printf( "\nCommand line arguments:\n" );
   for( i = 0; i < argc; i++ )
      printf( "  argv[%d]  %s\n", i, argv[i] );
   return( EXIT_SUCCESS );
   }
```

In the following you can see the output of the program, where the name of the program is MAIN.EXE, and it has been called with the following command line:

```
C:\CC>main one two three
Command lines arguments:
  argv[0]  C:\CC\MAIN.EXE
  argv[1]  one
  argv[2]  two
  argv[3]  three
```

## References

See bases section, structure of a C/C++ program.

See Practice section, category other, Windows programming.

# Data exchange between functions

## Description

In principle a C source text consists of declarations and definitions. Statements can only be found in function definitions. In order for the functions to work together, they have to exchange information, or data. In C there are various concepts for this.

## Application

| | |
|---|---|
| Parameters | Parameters are special variables of a function, which are assigned values when the function is called. If parameters are defined as pointers, the function can also return values in this way. |
| Return value | An individual value returned to the caller by the function. |
| Global variables | A further option to exchange data between functions works through the global variables. This is very easy, yet has the disadvantage that the independence of the function is impaired by it. |
| Static variables | To keep a local variable after the function has been left, so that its value is still available at the next call of the function, declare the variable as static. |

## References

See following paragraphs.

# The return value

## Description

Functions can return the result of their calculation through the return value. To achieve this the type of the return value is specified in the function header. By means of the statement

```
return (result);
```

the value is returned to the function which is calling.

## Application

There are two options for using the concept of the return value efficiently:

- The result of the function is assigned to a variable of the function which is calling.
- The function reports back whether it has solved the task successfully or whether an error has occurred in the function.

## Warning

Functions which do not return a value have the return value void. Such a function can only call return without a value: return; .

## References

See parameters.

See category program control, break statements for loops.

# Parameters

## Description

Parameters are used to pass values from the function which is calling, to the function which has been called. Parameters are always local variables, whose scope is the most peripheral block of the function. To pass data to parameters by default C uses a procedure which is called 'call by value'.

## Copying a value                                                    call by value

This means that in a function call the value of the passed argument is copied into the local variable.

This concept ensures that variables which have been passed as arguments cannot be changed by the called-up functions.

# Examples

```
#include <stdio.h>
void change(int param) {
   printf("\tParam after function call: %d\n",param);
   param = param*param;
   printf("\tParam after calculation: %d\n",param);
   }

  int main() {
   int var = 10;
   printf("var before function call: %d\n",var);

   change(var);
   printf("var after function call: %d\n",var);
   return 0;
   }
```

The above provides the following output:

```
var before function call: 10
                    Param before function call: 10
                    Param after function call: 100
var after function call: 10
```

## Copying an address                                        call by reference

This is called 'call by reference'. Here the address, not the value, of an argument-variable is passed. Since the function in this case contains a reference to the call argument instead of a copy, it can alter it. Reference parameters are  thus, apart from the return value, another device to return values from the called function to the function which is calling.

For 'call by reference' passing there are the following options:

| Parameter | | Argument | |
| --- | --- | --- | --- |
| pointer: | | | |
| | Typ * | ptr | (pointer from of typ*) |
| | typ * | &var | (address of a variable of type typ) |
| Reference, C++ only: | | | |
| | typ & | var | (Variable of the type typ) |

# Examples

```
#include <stdio.h>

void change1(int param) {
   param = param*param;
   }
```

```
void change2(int *param) {
   *param = *param * *param;
   }

void change3(int &param) {
   param = param*param;
   }

int main() {
   int var = 10;
   change1(var);    printf("var : %d\n",var);
   change2(&var);   printf("var : %d\n",var);
   change3(var);    printf("var : %d\n",var);

   return 0;
   }
```

yields the following output:

```
var : 10
var : 100
var : 10000
```

## Warning

Occasionally pointers are passed, although an alteration of the passed value is not desired. For example, this could be the case in the passing of arrays, which are always passed as pointers, or when pointers to larger data structures are passed, to save copying. In such cases the corresponding variable can be saved from being overridden by the specifier const in the parameter declaration.

## Tip

Instead of pointers, references are often used to pass arguments efficiently in C++.

## References

See return value.

See Practice section, category functions, pointer and references as parameters; and pointer and dynamic memory management, references as parameters.

# Function arguments and the default

## Description

In C++ default arguments can be passed in the `function` declaration. Parameters for which default arguments have been declared do not have to be assigned further parameters at the function call.

## Application

In this way the call of arguments which are often passed can be submitted.

## Warning

- Parameters with a default argument cannot be followed by parameters without default arguments.
- In a re-declaration further default arguments may be specified, yet previously declared default arguments must not be re-declared.
- Expressions or variables can also be declared as default arguments. However, local variables must not be used.
- The order in which the function arguments are processed is not determined and can therefore vary from one compiler to another.

## Example

```
int   func1(int n, int m = 3);
void  func2(char *s = "");
char* func3(int x, int y=4);
char* func3(int x = 2, int y);      // valid redeclaration
int   func4(int a = 0, int b);      // error
```

## References

See Practice section, category functions, functions with any number of arguments.


# Functions and the stack

## Description

The stack is a dynamically expanding and contracting memory area managed by the compiler. Here the compiler stores all information which it requires for the logging and management of the function calls.

Every time a function is called, a new data block is added to the stack. In this data block the parameters of the function, the local variables of the function and some internal information (of which the return address to the code of the calling function is the most important) are stored. This data block is also called the stack frame of the function.

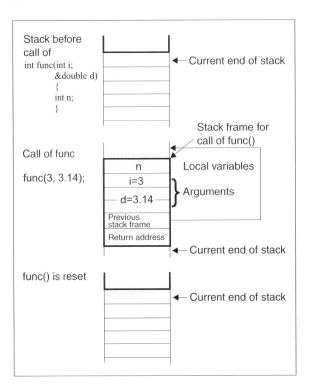

## Stack actions

- As long as a function is being processed, its stack frame remains on the stack.
- If further functions are called from within a function, their stack frames are packed onto the stack frame of the previously called-up function.
- If a function is finished, its stack frame is removed from the stack.
- The stack therefore always shows the functions which are currently being processed. The stack order of the functions shows which function has been called from which other function.

## Stack structure

For a stack which grows from top to bottom the following applies:

- The bottom function is the current function, whose statements are currently being processed.

- The function directly above has called the bottom function and is now waiting for the called-up function to be finished.
- The top function is the start function `main()`.
- The individual stack frames read from top to bottom show through which function the current function has been called.

The exact structure of the stack frames depends on the processor for which the program has been compiled. However, you can find out a little bit more about the stack management of your processor by using the debug tools of your compilers (stack display) or by examining the addresses of the parameters and local variables.

## Examples

```
#include <stdio.h>
#include <stdlib.h>

func(int par1, int par2, int par3)
  {
  int local1, local2, local3;
  printf("%d. call of func\n",par1);
  printf("\t address of par3   = %p\n",&par3);
  printf("\t address of par2   = %p\n",&par2);
  printf("\t address of par1   = %p\n",&par1);
  printf("\t address of local1 = %p\n",&local1);
  printf("\t address of local2 = %p\n",&local2);
  printf("\t address of local3 = %p\n",&local3);
  if(par1<2)
      func(++par1,0,0);
  }

int main()
  {
  func(1,0,0);
  return 0;
  }
```

output

1. Call of `func`

```
        address of par3   = 0065FE00
        address of par2   = 0065FDFC
        address of par1   = 0065FDF8
        address of local1 = 0065FDEC
        address of local2 = 0065FDE8
        address of local3 = 0065FDE4
```

2. Call of `func`

```
address of par3   = 0065FDE0
address of par2   = 0065FDDC
address of par1   = 0065FDD8
address of local1 = 0065FDCC
address of local2 = 0065FDC8
address of local3 = 0065FDC4
```

## Explanation

The above output shows a function which calls itself up.

The addresses of the parameters are delivered in inverse order, because the compiler puts the last parameter first onto the stack.

As you can see from the output, the stack in the memory is built from top to bottom, which means that the stack frame of the function, which has been called last, and which is therefore the top stack frame, lies at the lowest memory address in the memory.

The stack frame for the first call of `func()` starts at the address 0065FE00, the stack frame for the second call at the address 0065FDE0. The three `int` parameters are put first into the stack frame. Each `int` parameter use 4 bytes (as is usual for 32-bit systems). Then a space follows, in which data are deposited, to which we do not have direct access (presumably the return address and a pointer at the start of the previous stack frames). After that the local variables follow, which also use 4 bytes, according to their data type.

## Warning

- When in C/C++ a function is called, memory is reserved for the function. The creation and management of the memory of the function also costs runtime. This loss of time is called **function overhead**.

- In the memory area, which has been provided for the function, are the memory cells of the function parameters, the local variables and the return address, which ensures that after the function has been processed the compiler jumps back to the correct position in the program. When finishing the function, C/C++ frees up this memory area again. There is therefore no loss of memory. If the recursion depth is very high or the local variables of the recursive function are memory-intensive, it may be that during the recursion the memory is used completely, as for each function call memory has to be reserved. The program then crashes with a corresponding error message. This is bound to happen if your recursion does not reach a break condition.

## References

See category variables and data types, scopes.

See Practice section, category pointer and dynamic memory management, dynamic memory in functions.

# Functions with any number of arguments

```
func(typ param, ...)
```

## Description

C/C++ also permits the definition of functions with an unknown number of parameters. This is not entirely surprising as some common library functions permit a variable number of arguments: `printf()` and `scanf()`.

## Application

The implementation of functions with any number of arguments is based on two elements:

```
double centre(int amount, ...)
```

- **The ellipse.** The ellipse (...) in the list of parameters indicates that any number of arguments may follow when calling. The ellipse has to stand at the end of the parameter definition, and a regular parameter has to precede it, which indicates within the function how many parameters follow.

- The **va_makros** from `<stdarg.h>`. These are required to adopt and evaluate arguments.

## Example

```
double centre(int amount, ...)  {
  double sum = 0;
  va_list ap;
  int loop;

  va_start(ap, amount);
  for(loop=1;loop<= amount;loop++)
    sum += va_arg(ap,int);
  va_end(ap);
  return sum/amount;
  }
```

## References

See Practice section, category functions, functions with any number of arguments.

# Inline functions (C++ only)

## Description

Inline functions are functions called in the source text. The compiler, if possible, does not resolve these through real function calls and the connected creation of a stack frame, but instead integrates the statement block of the function into the source text in such a way that its execution has the same effect as if the function had been called.

## Application

Calls of functions result in time delay, the so-called function overhead. This can be avoided by using macros instead of functions. A macro call is replaced with the macro definition by the compiler during translation. However, macros entail a few problems:

- they do not carry out type checks, and
- their formulation is more prone to errors than the definition of functions.

Therefore, C++ offers the option of declaring functions as inline, simply by putting the the keyword inline at the beginning of the function header. This keyword instructs the compiler, similar to a macro, to replace the function calls by function bodies. The disadvantage in comparison with the use of macros is that the inline directive is only viewed as a recommendation by the compiler which it does not have to follow, not as a command.

## Warning

- It should be noted that although macros and inline functions speed up the runtime of a program, they also inflate the code. Therefore, they are mainly suitable for smaller functions which are not called very frequently.
- Methods of classes which have been defined within the class are automatically treated as inline functions by the compiler.
- The inline declaration is only a recommendation. For more extensive or more complex functions the compiler usually ignores the inline declaration.
- Inline functions have to be defined identically in each translation unit of the program (see Practice section, using elements comprehensively by module).

## References

See functions and the stack.

# Specifiers for functions

## Description

The operational area and functioning of a function can be manipulated by a range of special keywords, which are fixed to the function declaration.

## Specifiers for functions

Functions can be equipped with one of the memory class specifications `extern` or `static`:

| | |
|---|---|
| static | The use of `static` as a keyword before the type specification of a function narrows its visibility to the file in which it is defined. |
| extern | The use of `extern` as a keyword before the type specification of a function makes it visible in all files which belong to the program (functions are by default `extern`). |
| – | If the specification is missing, a function has by default the memory class `extern`. |

In C++, but not in C, functions can be declared as `inline`.

| | |
|---|---|
| inline | The `inline` declaration is a recommendation to the compiler to replace function calls with direct equivalent code. |

## Special specifiers for methods

| | |
|---|---|
| static | `static` methods are class-specific, but not instance-specific. |
| const | `const` methods can only change `mutable` instance variables of the class. Furthermore, only `const` methods of the class can be called for `const` instances. (However, some compilers only issue a warning in case of non-compliance.) The keyword `const` is put after the parameter list. |
| volatile | `volatile` methods. For `volatile` instances only `volatile` methods of the class can be called. The keyword `volatile` is put after the parameter list. |
| virtual | `virtual` methods are used in inheritance and switch on a late linkage for a method. |

Methods cannot be declared as `extern`. `extern` is a reference to a global declaration, which usually results in an external linkage. This is neither permitted nor useful for methods.

## Example

```
extern int func1();
static int func2();
inline int func3();
```

```
class demo {
  static int func4();
  int func5() const;
  int func6() volatile;
  virtual int func7();
  };
```

### References

See function declaration and definition.

See inline functions.

See category classes, methods.

# Overloading

## Description

C++ permits the definition of several functions (or operators) with the same name, so long as the functions are distinguished by number or type of the parameters. The definition of several functions with the same name is called overloading.

## Realisation and resolving

In C++ and C objects can be addressed with a non-ambiguous name. C++ automatically extends function identifiers with coded information about the parameters with respect to operands. In this way the programmer can assign identical identifiers, while the compiler works with non-ambiguous names. This also explains why, for example, variables or functions without parameters cannot be overloaded.

Inversely, the compiler has to be able to determine at the call of an overloaded function the function which is to be called by means of the passed arguments. This is known as the resolution of an overloading.

First the compiler looks for an overloaded function, which is identical to the arguments of the function call with regard to the data types of its parameters.

- A type T cannot be distinguished from its reference T&.
- A type T cannot be distinguished from const T or volatile T, but T* can be distinguished from const T*.

If the compiler cannot find an exact correspondence, it looks for the closest correspondence.

- First the compiler applies the arithmetic promotions on the arguments.

- Then he tries default conversions (double to int, int to double, derived* to base*, and so on),
- Finally, it takes into account user-defined conversions for classes.

## Warning

Overloaded functions have to lie in the same scope, otherwise hiding, not overloading, occurs.

The return type plays no part in overloading – overloaded functions, therefore, cannot be distinguished by their return type.

If the compiler finds two or more overloaded versions for a set of arguments, which all fit the arguments equally well, it issues an error message to inform the user that it cannot clearly resolve the overloading.

```
void func(char)  {};
void func(short) {};

void call(char c, int i, short s)
  {
  func(c);    // calls func(char)
  func(s);    // calls func(short)
  func(i);    // error: ambiguity
  }
```

The problem here is that there is no overloaded function for the data type int, however char as well as short can be converted into int through integral promotion.

## References

See category variables and data types, scopes.

See overloading, overriding, hiding.

See Practice section, category operators.

# Overloading of functions

## Description

C++ permits the definition of several functions (or operators) with the same name, so long as the functions are distinguished by number or type of the parameters. The definition of several functions with the same name is called overloading.

## Application

The overloading of functions is used to adapt the behaviour of a routine to the parameter types passed to it. The advantage for the programmer is that he does not have to assign several function names to a routine, and the compiler takes on the task for him to check the parameters and to call the correct version of the routine.

## Warning

Overloaded functions have to lie in the same scope, otherwise hiding, not overloading occurs.

## Example

```
int max(int a, int b) {
   return ( a > b ? a : b);
   }
const char* max(const char* s1, const char* s2) {
   return (strcmp(s1,s2) ? s1 : s2);
   }
int max(int a, char* s) {
   return ( a > strlen(s) ? a : strlen(s));
   }
```

## References

See Practice section, category operators.

# Overloading of methods

### Description

Methods can become equally overloaded as those functions described above. However, unusual features come to light in the overloading of inherited methods, since the base and derived classes represent different class areas.

### Warning

- Inherited functions cannot be overloaded in derived classes.
- Functions which have been declared in the derived class hide functions with the same name in the base class, which can still be called through the area operator.
- To simulate overloading, the versions of the base class have to be overridden first.

## Example

```
base class {
   public:
   void func(char * s);
   void func(char c);
   };
derived class : public base {
   public:
   void func(int value);
   }
int main() {
   derived class drv;
   drv.func("Test");              // error
   drv.func('c');                 // error
   drv.func(3.2);                 // is interpreted as 3
   drv.base::func("Test");
   return 0;
   }
```

## Reference

See Practice section, category operators.


# Overloading, overriding, hiding

## Overloaded functions

- are in the same scope,
- can be distinguished by their parameters, and
- are used to adapt a function to different parameter types.

## Overridden methods

- lie in different scopes, where the overridden method is defined in a base class and the overriding method in a class derived from the base class,
- have identical names and parameter types,
- are usually declared as virtual,
- are used for the implementation of polymorphous behaviour in class hierarchies, and
- are still available through the scope operator.

### Hidden methods

- lie in different scopes, where the overridden method is defined in a base class and the overriding method in a class derived from the base class,
- have different names and parameter types, and
- are still available through the scope operator.

# Classes

## Classes

### Description

C++ is based on the language C. Upward compatibility guarantees that C++ includes the syntax of C. Object-oriented programming is thus not to be equated with programming in C++, but begins with the use of the object-oriented concepts, with which C++ extends C. The most important of these concepts (encapsulation, inheritance, polymorphism, templates) go back to the new data type class.

### Application

Classes are used to encapsulate data elements and element functions (methods) into one data type. They allow you to assign different access rights for the individual elements, and can build up class hierarchies by means of inheritance.

### Syntax

```
class_type class_name  [: BASE_CLASSES]
    {
    ELEMENT_LIST
    } instances;
```

- **class_type:** Can be used as class type besides the keywords class, struct and union. The use of the keywords struct and union is based on the fact that in C++ structures and unions represent special classes. This facilitates the use of C modules in C++ programs, yet should not encourage the programmer to mix the concepts. It is recommended that classes always be declared as class, and only to use unions and structures according to the C convention.
- **class_name:** The name of the class to be declared.

- **:BASE_CLASSES**: A list of classes separated by commas, whose elements are adopted (inherited). The access of the derived class to the inherited elements can be modified through the specifiers public, protected and private. An entry in this list has the following syntax:

[virtual] [public, protected, private] base_class_name

- **ELEMENT_LIST**: In the element list data elements and methods of the class are declared and, if need be, also defined. Access to the elements can be controlled through the specifiers public, protected and private. All elements have their class as scope.

- **Instances**: Behind the final bracket it is possible to create instances, or variables, of the class type, separated by commas.

## Warning

- A base class has to be declared before it can be used for inheritance.

- An access specifier applies for all the following class elements up to the occurrence of a new access specifier.

- Access specifiers cannot be combined.

- Access specifiers may occur several times in the class declaration.

- Class elements at the start of the declaration, for which no access specifier has been specified, are private by default.

## Example

```
class example {
    int value;                  // private
    public:
        example() {value = 1;};    // constructor
    protected:
        int issue_value() {return value;};
    private:
        int delete_value();
    };
```

## References

See variables and data types, structures.

See variables and data types, unions.

See inheritance and polymorphism.

# Classes and OOP

## Description

The concept behind the classes and object-oriented programming is based on the fact that we judge objects of the real world by two criteria; on the one hand by characteristics such as form and colour, and on the other hand by a particular 'behaviour' an object displays, and which, for example, determines, how it has to be treated. In object-oriented terminology characteristics are equivalent to the data elements and the behaviours are equivalent to the methods (element functions).

## Example

Objects which display the same characteristics and behaviour can be put together in a class. Thus a class videorecorder could look as follows:

```
class videorecorder {
    /* features */
    char *manufacturer;
    int number_of_videorecorders;
    boolean slow_motion, long_play, two_channel_sound;
public:
    /* behaviour */
    void switch_on();
    void play();
    void record();
    void play_in_slow_motion();
    void switch_off();
};
```

When forming a variable of the class – in the following this is refered to as instance formation – values are assigned to the characteristics. In this way an instance, which only represents a particular video recorder, is created through specialisation. (A further example would be the class man and its instances, namely every single one of us – individuals. Consequently a birth would be an instance formation.)

## References

See encapsulation.

See instance formation.

# Encapsulation

## Description

The putting together of data elements and methods is called encapsulation. Two more design criteria are connected with the term:

– information hiding and

– closedness

## Information hiding

Classes should mainly be addressed through their methods. These functions form the interface between class and program. (The exact determination of the interface is carried out through the assignment of access specifiers.) After the implementation of the class it is important to the programmer that he only need use the class through its interface, without having to worry about its implementation. The interface itself is responsible for the error-free processing of the function calls and the correct behaviour of the class. If, for example, the class videorecorder has been implemented to control video recorders through the computer, the programmer only need create an instance of the class and he can then use the instance like a real video recorder:

```
my_recorder.switch_on();
my_recorder.play_in_slow_motion();
my_recorder.switch_off();
```

The class itself controls the video recorder through the parallel interface, which means it hides such details from the programmer.

## Closedness

The criterion of closedness results from the demand for information hiding. The interface of a class should be as complete as possible, in the sense that the class can be employed usefully. A class videorecorder, which does not have a function play_in_slow_motion(), would not be suitable for the control of video recorders with a slow motion function.

Conversely there should only be data and functions in a class, to characterise the objects of the class. A method calculation_break() would not make sense in the class videorecorder.

## References

See Practice section, category classes.

See access specifiers.

# Data elements

## Description

Variables, defined within a class are the data elements of that class.

## Application

If an instance is formed of the class, the instance memory is made available for the data elements. Each instance thus has its own copy of the data elements, which are therefore also called instance variables. At the same time the instance formation is used to initialise the data elements. This task is taken on by the constructor. Classes represent a separate scope, meaning the instance variables become invalid with their instance (the destructor's responsibility), and names from other scopes are hidden. Apart from the declaration of data elements of known types it is also possible to carry out a local type definition within a class.

## Warning

Data elements:

* can be declared as public, protected or private,
* are created in the instance formation and resolved together with the instance, and
* can be declared as static, const, volatile or mutable.

## Example

```
class demo {
    int amount;                 // private data
    int *field;
 public:
    char *str;                  // public data
    ...
```

## References

See constructor and destructor.

See access specifiers.

# Static data elements

## Description

Static data elements are not copied during instance formation. Instead all instances access the same variable.

## Application

Static elements have to be defined outside of the class, in the surrounding namespace (or file scope), and cannot be addressed through instances, but through the class name.

## Warning

Static elements cannot be declared as auto, register or extern.

## Example

```
class demo {
  public:
    static int instance_counter;

    demo() {instance_counter++;}
    ~demo() {instance_counter--;}
  };
int demo::instance_counter = 0;

int main()  {
  demo loc;
  cout << Demo::instance_counter << endl;
  cout << loc.instance_counter << endl;
  return 0;
  }
```

## Reference

See static methods.

# Constant data elements

## Description

Data elements declared as const cannot be changed after instance formation.

## Warning

const data elements have to be initialised in the constructor list.

## Example

```
class demo {
  public:
    const int j;         // constant instance variable
```

```
   demo() : j(2)     // initialisation
     {
      ...
  };
```

## References

See constant methods.

See category constants.

# Class instances as data elements

## Description

Instance variables can also have the data type of a class. These are called embedded objects.

## Application

Embedded objects are created in the course of the instance formation of the higher object and are resolved with it.

To create the embedded object a constructor of the embedded object has to be called. This can be a default constructor, where the programmer does not have to deal with the creation. It can also be a constructor with elements; in this case the programmer has to extend the constructor of the higher object by a constructor list, in which the constructor of the embedded object is called. (Note that the constructor is called through the object name and not as in base classes through the class name.)

To resolve the embedded object its destructor is called.

## Warning

- A class cannot contain instances of classes as elements if these classes have not been defined beforehand.

- Since the definition of a class ends in a semicolon, it follows that a class cannot contain an instance of its own type as an element. However, it is possible to define pointers or references to undefined classes, so far as the class name is known.

- The surrounding class has no exceptional access rights to the elements of the embedded object.

## Examples

Pointers to objects of undefined classes:

```
class demo;
class example {
    int a;
    class example incorrect;    // cannot be solved
                                // by the compiler
    class example* correct;
    class demo& also_correct;
    };
```

Instantiation of embedded objects through the default constructor:

```
class A {
  public:
    int i;
    A() {i = 1;}  // standard constructor
    };
class B {
  public:
    int n;
    A obj;
    B() {n = 2;}
    };
```

Instantiation of embedded objects through the constructor list:

```
class A {
  public:
    int i;
    A(int i_par) {i = i_par;}
    };
class B {
  public:
    int n;
    A obj;
    B(int p1, int p2) : obj(p1) {n = p2;}
    };
```

## References

See local and embedded classes.

See constructor.

See inheritance and polymorphism, inheritance versus embedding.

# Local and embedded classes

## Description

Classes which have been defined in the statement section of a function, are called local classes.

Classes which have been defined in the definition section of a class, are called embedded or included classes.

## Warning

- An included class can directly use types and static elements of the including class.

- Included classes must not contain static elements.

- The included class has no exceptional access rights to the elements of the including class; that is, it can only access elements of the included class through instances of that class. (In the same way, the including class has no exceptional access rights to the included class.)

## Example

```
int i;
class global {
    static int n;
  public:
    int i;
    static float f;
    class intern {
      void func(global &glob) {
          i = 3;       // error
          f = 3;       // correct
          ::i = 3;     // i from file area
          glob.i = 3; // i from class global
          n = 3;       // error
          }
...
```

## Reference

See class instances as data elements.

# Methods

## Description

Functions which are defined as elements of a class are called methods.

## Application

Methods can be defined either inside or outside a class declaration.

- Methods defined within the class definition, are automatically interpreted as `inline`. Even if the keyword `inline` is only intended as a recommendation to the compiler, it follows that within a class definition only short functions should be defined, to save memory and to keep the class definition clear.

- When defining outside of the class definition the class name has to be prefixed to the area operator.

## Definition within the class definition:

```
class demo {
     int value;
   public:
     demo()                {value = 1;}
     int submitt_value() {return value;}
   };
```

## Definition outside the class definition:

```
class demo {
     int value;
   public:
     demo();
     int func();
   };
inline demo::demo()          {value = 1;}
int demo::func() {
   ...
   }
```

## Warning

Methods:

- can be declared as `public`, `protected` or `private`,

- have access to all elements of the class,

- are the only option for accessing private elements of their class,

- can be declared as `virtual`,

- can be declared as `inline`,

- can be declared as `const`. Methods which have been declared as `const` are the only methods which can be called by instances declared as `const`. (The keyword `const` is postfixed to the parameter list.)

- can be declared as volatile. Methods which have been declared as volatile are the only methods which can be called by instances declared as volatile. (The keyword volatile is postfixed to the parameter list.), and
- can only be overloaded by methods of the same class.

## References

See overloading.

See category inheritance and polymorphism, overriding and virtual methods.

See Practice section, category classes, private data – public methods.

See Practice section, category inheritance and polymorphism, RTTI with virtual methods.

# Static methods

## Description

Static methods are methods which are declared with the keyword static. Static methods are, like static data elements, class-specific and not instance-specific.

Static methods do not have a this- pointer and, therefore, can only call other static elements (data as well as methods).

## Application

Static methods can only be called through instances or the class name.

## Warning

Static methods cannot be declared as virtual.

## Example

```
class demo {
  private:
    static int standardvalue;
  public:
    static void std_set(int i) {
       if( i > 0 && i < 100 )
          standardvalue = i;
       }
  };
int demo::standardvalue = 1;
```

```
int main()
  {
  demo obj1, obj2;
  demo::std_set(33);
  return 0;
  }
```

## Reference

See static data elements.

# Constant methods

## Description

Constant methods are methods which are declared with the keyword const. Methods declared as const cannot alter element data (unless these have been explicitly declared as mutable) and only return pointers or references to element data as const.

## Application

Const methods are the only methods which can be called by const- declared instances. (Some compilers, however, only issue a warning in the event of non-compliance.)

The keyword const is postfixed to the parameter list.

## Examples

```
class demo {
  public:
    int i;
    const int j;
    mutable int n;
    demo() : j(2) {}        // initialisation
    void incr() const {
            i++;        // error
            j++;        // error
            n++;        // ok
            }
    void func() {...}
  };
```

Constant class instances:

```
const demo obj2;
obj2.func();        // error
obj2.incr();        // o.k.
```

## Reference

See constant data elements.

# Access specifiers

## Description

The access specifiers `public`, `private` and `protected` determine how the elements of a class may be accessed from within and from outside that class.

## Application

Access specifiers are an important tool of encapsulation. Only through these specifiers can a class be protected from unauthorised access. The access specifiers are used in the class definition as well as in inheritance.

### Access specifiers in the class definition

Within the class definition the access specifiers can be used to assign the class elements which are defined afterwards to an access level.

```
class demo {
   ...
 public:
   ...
 protected:
   ...
 private:
   ...
 };
```

| Specifier | Meaning |
| --- | --- |
| public | The element can be used from every method of the own class and derived classes. Access from outside is carried out through the name of the instance and one of the access operators: |
| | `instance_name.element_name` |
| | `reference_of_instance.element_name` |
| | `pointer_to_instance->element_name` |
| private | The element can only be used by methods and friends of the class in which it has been declared. |
| protected | The same applies as for `private`. However, use through methods of classes which have been derived from the declared class is also possible. If there are no derived classes, `private` and `protected` are identical. |

## Access specifiers in inheritance

In the course of inheritance it is possible to use the access specifiers to tighten access to the inherited elements through the instances of the derived class.

```
class derived : public base_class
  {
  ...
```

| Specifier | Meaning |
|-----------|---------|
| public | The inherited elements apply the same access rights which have been determined in the base class. |
| private | All inherited elements are to be viewed as private from outside. |
| protected | Public elements are viewed as protected elements. |

Warning

- Access specifiers apply to all subsequent class elements up to the occurrence of a new access specifier.

- Access specifiers cannot be combined.

- Access specifiers may occur several times in a class declaration.

- Class elements at the start of the declaration, for which no access specifier has been specified, are automatically viewed as private.

- The keyword friend counts as an access specifier in the broader sense (see access from outside the class).

## Access to class elements

Classes are laid out in such a way that they hide their data elements through the declaration as private and only permit manipulations through a selection of particular methods which have been declared as public.

In practice there is a variety of situations with different access rights through the use of the access specifiers and the access specifier friend in the class declaration as well as in inheritance. These situations are summed up in the following pararaphs.

## References

See following paragraphs.

See inheritance and polymorphism, access restriction in inheritance.

# Access within the class

el_name

## Description

Access within a class means that other elements (data or functions) of the class are accessed by methods within the function body. This is the innermost area, and is subject to practically no restrictions. Access to the elements is made directly through their names.

## Warning

- Methods which have been declared as const can access all data elements, but can only alter mutable data elements.
- Static methods can directly address only static element data (because static methods do not have a this pointer). Non-static elements have to be addressed via an existing instance (which, for example, can be passed as an argument).
- The access rights which have been determined in the base class apply to inherited elements from base classes.

## Example

```
class demo {
  private:
   int value1, value2;
   int func1() {return value1*value2;}
  public:
   ...
   void func2(int i) {
                     value1=i+1;
                     value2 = func1();
                     }
   };
```

## References

See following paragraphs.

See this pointer.

# Access from outside the class

object.el_name

## Description

Outside access to elements of the class T is only possible through an instance of the class T in connection with one of the operators, -> ,* ->* or through friends of the class.

## Access through instances

Access is subject to the settings through the modifiers `public`, `protected` and `private`; that is, elements in the class which have been declared as `protected` or `private` (this also applies to inherited elements) cannot be addressed in this way.

```
class demo {
   int value1;        // standard private
   int func1();
  public;
   int value2;
   int func2();
   };
int main() {
   class demo d, *ptr_d;
   int dummy;
   dummy = d.value1;          // error
   dummy = ptr_d->func1();    // error
   dummy = d.value2;
   dummy = ptr_d->func2();
   }
```

## Access through pointers to class elements

Here too, only `public` elements can be accessed. The syntax for the definition, initialisation and dereferencing of pointers to class elements can be looked up in the section operators, data access.

## Access through friends                                 friend

Sometimes it makes sense to circumvent the strict rules of the access rights through `public`, `protected` and `private` and grant an arbitrary function (thus not just class functions) access to `protected` or `private` elements. The keyword `friend` permits this.

To create a `friend` function, two things are required:

- Firstly, the function has to be declared as `friend` in the class to which it is supposed to get access, and

- Secondly, a reference or instance of the class has to be passed to the function.

```
#include <iostream>
using namespaces std;

class demo {
   int wert;
   friend int func(demo&);  // friend declaration
   };
// friend function
int func(demo& object) {
   return object.value;
   }
```

```
int main() {
   class demo d;
   cout << func(d);
   return 0;
   }
```

## Warning

- Note that the `friend` declaration has to be carried out in the class. The class thus specifies which functions are `friend` and which are not, and can still protect its data from unauthorised use.
- Private elements which do not possess `public` methods can be reached through `friend` functions.
- Apart from the declaration of individual functions as `friend`, you can also declare all the functions of a class simultaneously as `friend` by declaring the whole class as `friend`.

## Reference

See category operators, data access.

# Access to base class elements

## Description

Derived classes must distinguish between their own and inherited elements, as well as between access from the methods of the derived class and access from outside.

### Access from the derived class

Methods which have been declared in the derived class can directly access their own as well as the inherited elements through the element name.

However, whereas access to a class's own elements is not subject to any restrictions, access to the inherited elements is controlled through the access specifiers from the base class declaration. A method of the derived class has access to `public` and `protected` elements, but not to `private` elements.

Inherited `private` elements can only be addressed in the methods of the derived class in a roundabout way through inherited `public` or `protected` methods.

```
class basis {
    int basis_priv;
   protected:
     int basis_prot;
```

```
    public:
      int basis_pub;
    };
class derived : private basis {
    int der_priv;
    public:
      void der_func(int n)
        {
        basis_pub   = n;
        basis_prot  = n;
        //basis_priv  = n;    // Error, no access
        }
    };
```

## Access from outside

Outwardly there is no difference between own and inherited elements of a class. It is only important which access rights for the inherited elements the derived class passes to the outside.

Basically access rights, which have been specified in the base class where elements origins are derived, are valid. However, it is possible to tighten the access rights through the access specifiers of the inheritance (see the sections on inheritance and polymorphy, and access restrictions in inheritance).

For individual elements it is possible to relax limited access rights through re-declaration or by the keyword using.

## Access to hidden/overridden methods

If an inherited method is overridden in the derived class through the declaration of a method with the same name and signature or hidden through the declaration of a method with the same name and a different signature, it is still possible to access the version of the base class with the help of the scope operator.

This works equally well from inside and outside of the class.

```
class basis {
  public:
    void func(int)    {cout << "Base version" << endl;};
  };
class derived : public basis {
  public:
    void func(char*)  {
      // access to hidden base class version
      basis::func(3);
      cout << "der. version" << endl;
      };
  };
```

```
int main() {
  class derived der;
  // access to hidden base class version
  der.basis::func(3);          // ok
  return 0;
  }
```

## References

See category inheritance and polymorphism, access restrictions and access rights.

# The constructor

```
class_name()   {}}
```

## Description

Every instance formation of a class object entails the call of a constructor.

## Application

In the statement section of the constructor the programmer can take care of the initialisation of the data elements and any initial tasks (for example, the reservation of dynamic memory).

By defining one or several own constructors (overloading) it is possible to control instance formation and to adapt it to the passing of different argument types.

### The default constructor

To ensure that every class possesses a constructor, the compiler assigns a default constructor (one which can be called without an argument) to classes without an explicitly declared constructor.

If a constructor is explicitly defined, the default constructor of the compiler is not available any longer. However, the programmer can define his own default constructor.

The default constructor facilitates the creation of embedded and inherited objects as well as arrays of class objects, which is otherwise only possible through the specification of constructor lists or initialisation lists.

### Warning

- A constructor always has the same name as its class.
- A constructor has no return value (not even void).

- Constructors cannot be declared as `virtual`, `static`, `const`, `mutable` or `volatile`.

- Constructors can be overloaded. The overloading is usually used to pass arguments for the initialisation of the data elements of the class to the constructor.

- Constructors cannot be inherited.

- It is not possible to define pointers to constructors.

- Constructors cannot be called after instance formation.

- Constructors which can be called with exactly one argument can carry out implicit conversions from the argument type into the type of their class. The compiler incorporates this conversion into the repertoire of its default conversions. To prevent unwanted default conversions, such a constructor can be declared as `explicit`.

## Example

```
class demo {
   int private;
  public:
   demo(int i) {private = i;}
   explicit demo(float f) {private = (int) f;};
   };

int main() {
   class demo instance(100);
   class demo instance2 = 100; //implicit conversion
   class demo instance3(3.2);
   class demo instance4 = 3.2; //error: explicit
   class demo instance5;       //error, standard constructor
                               //no longer available

   return 0;
   }
```

## References

See copy constructor.

See destructor.

See class instances as data elements.

See category inheritance and polymorphism, inheritance and constructor.

See  Practice section, category classes, default constructor.

# The copy constructor

```
class_identifier(class_identifier&)
```

## Description

The copy constructor creates instances of its class on the basis of other instances of the class. The instance which is to be used as the basis of the instance to be created is passed to the constructor as a parameter.

## Application

The copy constructor is called when you initialise a class instance with another class instance (of the same class). If no copy constructor has been declared in the class, the default copy constructor is called which copies the class elements 1:1.

The copy constructor is one of two options to copy class instances. The second option is the assignment operator =, which is also predefined as a 1:1 copier and has to be overloaded when required.

Copy constructors are also called implicitly when passing class objects to functions/ methods and when returning class objects as return values of functions/methods (unless pointers or references are used).

## Warning

1:1 copying as executed by the default copy constructor may result in errors if the class contains pointers. This is due to the fact that the addresses contained in the pointer are copied for a pointer, so that after the copy initialisation both pointers of the original and the copy refer to the same object.

## Example

```cpp
#include <iostream>
using namespace std;

class demo {
    int  i;
    int* p;
  public:
   demo(int value)   {
       i = value;
       p= &i;
       }
   demo(const demo& inst) {          // copy constructor
       i = inst.i; p = &i;
       }
  };
```

```
int main() {
  demo a(3);
  demo b(a);      // use of the copy constructor

  return 0;
  }
```

## References

See constructor.

See Practice section, category classes, copying class objects: copy constructor and assignment operator.

# The destructor

```
~class_name()    {}
```

## Description

Destructors are automatically called when class instances loose their validity (for example when leaving the scope or when deleting pointers to class instances). They resolve the instance and free up the reserved memory.

## Warning

For destructors apply similar rules as for constructors:

- Destructors always carry the name of their class, prefixed with a tilde (~).
- A destructor has no return value (not even void).
- Destructors cannot be declared as static, const, mutable or volatile.
- A class without an explicitly declared destructor is assigned a default destructor.
- Destructors are not inherited.
- It is not possible to define pointers to destructors.

Destructors differ from constructors in the following ways:

- Arguments cannot be passed to destructors, consequently:
- destructors can be overridden but not overloaded,
- destructors can be declared as virtual,
- when in doubt, base classes should define a virtual destructor,
- destructors of classes derived from base classes with virtual destructors, are automatically virtual, and
- destructors can be called explicitly (which, however, is rarely necessary).

### References

See constructor.

See Practice section, category pointer and dynamic memory management, dynamic memory in classes.

# Default methods

There are five methods for which the compiler automatically creates default versions if the class does not designate implementations of its own:

- default constructor,
- destructor,
- copy constructor,
- assignment operator, and
- address operator (returns the value of the this pointer).

# The this pointer

`this`

### Description

The `this` pointer is defined by the compiler. It is available in all non- static methods of a class and refers to the current object of the class, through which the method has been called.

### Application

If several instances of a class are formed, each instance receives its own copy of the data elements of the class. The methods of the class, however, only exist in the RAM and are used jointly by all instances of a class. As the methods usually operate on the element data of the class and thus should be instance-specific, it has to be ensured that the method only accesses those data which belong to the instance which is calling.

Because of this the compiler only assigns a pointer to itself to each instance – the `this` pointer. At each call of a method this pointer is automatically passed to the method. Thus, the `this` pointer is available in every method (with the exception of static methods).

## Example

```
#include <iostream>
using namespace std;

class demo {
   public:
     void func()        { cout << this; }
   };

int main() {
    class demo d1;
    cout << "This-pointer of the instance d1 = ";
    d1.func();
    return 0;
    }
```

## References

See classes, methods.

# Instance formation

```
class_type obj;
```

## Description

Instance formation is the creation of class objects (variables of a class type). During instance formation a concrete object is formed in a class by assigning values to data elements. The constructor, which is automatically called during the instance formation, is responsible for the creation of memory and the initialisation of the data elements.

## Formation of constant instances

If an instance is declared as `const` on setup, this means that all data elements not explicitly declared as `mutable` are `const`, i.e. their value cannot be altered. Declared methods can also only be called as `const`.

## Instance formation and arrays

Every array element must be set up as via a constructor on initialisation of class arrays. This can occur via a standard constructor (constructor without parameter) or through an intialisation list and explicit call for every array element.

## Example

```
class demo {
    int private;
  public:
    demo() {};        // standard constructor
    demo(int i)       {private = i;}
  };

int main() {
  class demo d[2] = {demo(10), demo(100)}; // set-up with
                                            // initialisation list
  const class demo e[200];    // set-up with standard constructor
  return 0;
  }
```

## Reference

See constructor.

# Inheritance and polymorphism

## Inheritance

### Description

Inheritance is an essential concept of object-oriented programming, and one which makes it possible to define new classes on the basis of already existing classes.

## Application

The simplest form of inheritance consists of a base class and a derived class. Through inheritance it is determined that the derived class possesses – in addition to the characteristics listed in its definition (data elements and methods) – all the elements of the base class. In this way practically every class can be derived from every other class; however, this does not always make sense.

In addition to the advantages that are associated with the class concept and encapsulation, inheritance has further benefits:

- Shared characteristics of classes only need to be implemented once through shifting into a base class, which also facilitates the maintenance of the source code.

- Conversely the derivation of base classes guarantees a unified appearance of related classes.

Different concepts allow class hierarchies to be designed flexibly:

- polymorphism (virtual functions), and
- friends.

Other concepts are used to protect the classes from unauthorised use and to organise the class hierarchies more strictly:

- access modifiers, and
- abstract classes.

## Syntax

```
class class_name : BASE_CLASS_LIST
    {
    List of class elements
    };
```

- **BASE_CLASS_LIST**: Here the base classes are listed, separated by commas, whose characteristics are to be inherited. An entry in this list has the following syntax:

```
[virtual] [public, protected, private] base_class_name
```

- In inheritance the access specifiers `public`, `protected` and `private` do not control access from the methods of the derived classes to the inherited elements (this is already carried out by the access specifiers in the declaration of the base class), but which access rights the derived class passes to the outside for the inherited elements (for example, when these elements are accessed through an instance of the derived class, or when the derived class itself is used as base class). If no access specifier is specified the class `private` is inherited.
- The keyword `virtual` is only important for multiple inheritance.

## Warning

A base class has to be declared before it can be used for inheritance.

Reasonable class hierarchies are based on the fact that:

- the shared characteristics of the derived classes are put together in base classes, and
- derived classes are natural extensions and/or specialisations of their base classes.

## Example

```
class basis {
  public:
    void func1() {cout << "Base class" << endl;}
  };
class derived :  public base {
  public:
    void func2() {cout << "Derived class" << endl;}
  };

int main() {
  derived obj;
  obj.func1();
  obj.func2();

  return 0;
  }
```

## References

See access restriction in inheritance.

See Practice section, category inheritance and polymorphism.

# Inheritance versus embedding

## Description

To be able to use the characteristics of a class in another class, there are – apart from the
friend declaration – two options: inheritance and embedding.

| Inheritance | Embedding |
|---|---|
| class X | class X |
| { | { |
| ... | ... |
| }; | }; |
| class Y: public class X | class Y |
| { | { |
| ... | class X  var; |
| }; | ... |
| | }; |

| Inheritance | Embedding |
|---|---|
| Inheritance brings with it the advantages of polymorphism, of making access restrictions and the option to treat instances of the derived class like objects of the base class. | The use of element objects, however, is easier and clearer. |

## Tip

If you are ever unsure whether to make available the functionality of a class through inheritance or through declaration of an element object, try clarify in your mind the relationship the objects which represent the classes have to each other. Simply ask yourself the question:

Is it possible to view an object of the class Y as an object of the class X, or does it look more likely that an object of the class X also belongs to an object of the class Y'?

To sum it up, this means

'is a Y an X' (inheritance)

or

'contains Y and X' (embedding)

For the three classes `Auto`, `Motor` and `Sportscar` this would mean, for example, that you would derive the class `Sportscar` from the class `Auto` (since each `Sportscar` is also a `Auto`). In contrast each `Auto` contains a `Motor`; therefore, you would embed an object of the class `Motor` in the class `Auto` (and thus also inherit to the class `Sportscar`).

## References

See Practice section, category inheritance and polymorphism.

# Access restrictions in inheritance

`public, protected, private`

## Description

The access specifiers `public`, `protected` and `private` can be used to change the access rights of the inherited elements in inheritance.

## Application

The following table shows how the access rights for the inherited elements change when using the access modifiers public, protected and private. The access specifiers of inheritance do not control access from the methods of the derived classes to the inherited elements (this is already done through the access specifiers in the declaration of the base class). The access specifiers of inheritance only concern the access rights which pass the derived class for the inherited elements to the outside (for example, when through an instance of the derived class these elements are accessed, or when the derived class itself is used as the base class). These can be tightened through the access specifiers of inheritance.

| Access specifiers of inheritance | Base class | Derived class |
|---|---|---|
| public | public | public |
| | protected | protected |
| | private | private |
| protected | public | protected |
| | protected | protected |
| | private | private |
| private | public | private |
| | protected | private |
| | private | private |

## Warning

If no access specifier is specified, the class private is inherited.

## Example

```cpp
#include <iostream>
using namespace std;

class basis {
      int w_priv;    // private
    public:
      int w_pub;
    };

class derived: private basis {
    public:
        void func() {
            w_priv = 2;      // acess denied, private element
            w_pub = 2;       // ok
            }
    };
```

```
int main()  {
  class derived obj;

  cout << obj.w_pub << endl;    // access denied, private inheritance

  return 0;
  }
```

## References

See category classes, access specifiers.

See relaxing access rights for individual elements.

# Relaxing access rights for individual elements

## Description

Access restrictions through inheritance can explicitly be relaxed again in the derived class. However, it is not possible to assign greater accessibility to an inherited characteristic than it had in the base class.

## Example

```
class basis {
      int w_priv;     // private
    public:
      int w_pub1;
      int w_pub2;
      int w_pub3;
    };
class derived: private basis {
    // redeclaration of the access rights
    public:
        basis::w_pub1;          // is public again
        using basis::w_pub2;    // is public again
    };

int main()  {
  class derived obj;
  cout << obj.w_pub1 << endl;   // access to inherited element
  cout << obj.w_pub2 << endl;
  cout << obj.w_pub3 << endl;   // no access
  cout << obj.w_priv << endl;   // no access
  ...
```

## Tip

The new ANSI standard recommends re-declaration through the using statement.

Reference

See category classes, access specifiers.

# Inheritance and constructor

## Description

Constructors and destructors cannot be inherited. It follows that, during the instance formation of a derived class, the inherited data elements have to be created by the constructor of the respective base class. In fact, the elements inherited from a base class form a kind of sub-object with their own constructors, destructors, access rights, and so on. This concept is the basis for the reduction of an object into an object of its base classes, which is common in object-oriented programming.

## Application

### Establishing base class objects                              default constructor

If there is a default constructor in the base class, the derived class does not have to deal with the establishment and initialisation of the inherited elements, but can leave this to the compiler, which in the course of instance formation automatically calls the default constructor of the base class for objects of the derived class.

```
class basis {
  public:
    int b_value;
    basis()                 { b_value = 333;}
  };
class derived : public basis {
  public:
    int der_value;
    derived(int i)      { der_value = i;}
  };

int main()
  {
  class derived obj(11);
```

### Establishing base class objects                              special constructor

To call a constructor with arguments for the establishment of the base class objects, a constructor list has to be created.

```
derived(int b1, double b2) : basis1(b1), basis(b2)  { }
```

The constructor list  is postfixed with a colon to the name of the derived constructors.

To pass arguments from the instance formation to a base class constructor, a parameter for the respective argument has to be defined in the constructor of the derived class.

```
class basis {
  public:
    int b_value;
    basis(int par)        { b_value = par;}
  };
class derived : public basis {
  public:
    int der_value;
    derived(int i)                          {der_value = i;}
    derived(int i, int n) : basis(n)        {der_value = i;}
  };

int main()
  {
  class derived obj(1,2);
```

## Establishing base class objects                                    Reinitialisation

Finally, it is possible to assign new values to the inherited elements in the constructor of the derived class. In this way the initialisation, which is carried out through the base class constructors, can be adapted to the requirements of the derived class or design the code more clearly. However, note that:

- this does not change the fact that the inherited elements have been established beforehand by a constructor of their own class, and

- the constructor of the derived class, in contrast to the constructor of the base class, cannot access elements which have been declared as private in the base class.

```
class basis {
  public:
    int b_value;
    basis)                    { b_value = 333;}
  };
class derived : public basis {
  public:
    int der_value;
    derived(int i)            { der_value = i;
                                b_value   = 0;}

  };

int main()
  {
  class derived obj(11);
```

## Multiple inheritance and constructors

### Classes with several direct base classes

If a class is derived from several direct base classes, for example:

```
class B1 {...};
class B2 {...};
class A: public B1, public B2 {...};
```

the constructors are processed in the order of their occurrence in the inheritance. Lastly the statement section of the constructor of the derived class is carried out.

### Classes with direct and indirect base classes

If a class is derived from a base class which in turn has been derived from another class, for example:

```
class B1 {...};
class B2: public B1 {...};
class A:  public B2 {...};
```

the constructor of B2 is called to establish the base class object B2. Since the B2 object in turn contains a base class object of the class B1, its constructor is called and carried out next. Then the statement section of the B1 constructor and lastly the statement section of the constructors of the class A is carried out.

## References

See category classes, the constructor.

See multiple inheritance.

# Methods which cannot be inherited

The following cannot be inherited:

- constructor,
- destructor,
- assignment operator, and
- friend declarations.

# Polymorphism

## Description
The notion of polymorphism is closely linked to the concept of inheritance. It refers to the phenomenon, that a method can be implemented differently in different derived classes of a hierarchy.

## Application

In this way similar classes can possess a range of identical and similarly used functions, which permit the programmer to treat the instances of these classes in the same way, without having to pay attention to class-specific details, which are hidden in the implementation of the methods (information hiding).

It is the obvious thing to inherit methods which are required by several classes through a common base class. In the derived classes the methods are overridden to implement class-specific handling. Methods which are to be overridden are usually declared with the keyword `virtual` in the base class.

Occasionally the overloading of functions and operators is also referred to as polymorphism.

## Example

```
class reference object {
   protected:
       struct Point reference point;
       virtual int draw(struct Point p) {
           // draw reference point to coordinate p
           ...
           }
   };

class rectangle : public reference object {
   protected:
       struct point edges[4];
       virtual int draw(struct Point p) {
           // draw rectangle with left bottom edge in
           // coordinate p
           ...
           };
   };

class Circle : public reference object {
   protected:
       float radius;
       virtual int draw(struct point p) {
           // draw circle with center in coordinate p
           ...
           }
   };
```

## References

See overriding and virtual methods.

See base class pointer.

See Practice section, category inheritance and polymorphism.

# Overriding and virtual methods

## Description

In contrast to overloading, overriding means that there is only one implementation of the method within a class. (However, the overridden base class version can be called through the name of the base class and the scope operator. This is frequently used to call the base class version within the implementation of the overriding method.)

## Application

The compiler recognises the overriding of a method by the fact that, as well as the method name, the number and types of the parameters are also identical. Overridden methods are usually declared as `virtual` in the base class as well as in the derived class. The keyword `virtual` modifies the way in which the compiler creates a linkage between an instance and its elements.

### Late linkage                                                    virtual

The keyword `virtual` is required to resolve correctly the names of overridden methods in class hierarchies.

The problem of name resolving only arises because an object of a derived class is also an object of the base class(es). This makes it possible to assign the address of an instance of the base class to a pointer or reference of the type of the derived class. If this pointer (or reference) is now used to call a method which is declared in the base class and the derived class (where the derived class overrides the declaration in the base class), the question arises, which version should be called: the method of the derived class, which corresponds to the type of the pointer (reference)? (This type of name resolving is termed early linkage, since it is carried out at compilation time.) or the version of the base class, which corresponds to the object to which the pointer (reference) points? (This type of name resolving is termed late linkage, since it is only carried out at runtime. Late linkage is agreed through the adoption of the keyword `virtual` into the function declaration (at least of the base class version).)

## Example

```
#include <iostream>
using namespace std;

class basis {
   public:
      virtual void identify()
            {cout << "This is a base class\n";};
   };

class derivedbasis : public basis {
   public:
      virtual void identify()
            {cout << "This is the derived class\n";};
   };

int main() {
  derived derived_class;
  basis *pointer = new basis;          // pointer of 'pointer to base' type

  pointer = &derived_class;
  pointer->identify();
  }
Output:    'This is the derived class'
```

## Warning

- For polymorphous classes which contain virtual methods classes the compiler creates a virtual table in which all virtual methods are listed. Moreover, the class receives a pointer to its virtual table. If a virtual method is called for an object of the class, it accesses the virtual method through this pointer and takes from it the correct address for the call of the virtual method. This ensures that the implementation which suits the object is always called, even for pointers to class objects. The late linkage, thus, produces additional object code and consequently longer runtimes.

- Constructors cannot be declared as `virtual`.

- Static methods cannot be declared as `virtual`.

## References

See inheritance and destructor.

# Inheritance and destructor

## Description

In the resolving of class objects the destructor is automatically called. This is also the case when the `delete` operator has been called for a pointer to a class object.

Here it should be ensured that the destructor of the class to which the object (and not the pointer to the object) belongs is called.

## Application

Because of the above explanations concerning late linkage, classes which are part of the inheritance hierarchy should possess a virtual destructor.

Since the destructor which is assigned by default by the compiler is not declared as `virtual`, a separate virtual destructor should be defined in the base classes of class hierarchies, even if no code is written into the statement section.

## Example

```
class basis {
    ...
  public:
    virtual ~basis() {}
    };
```

## References

See Practice section, category inheritance and polymorphism, guidelines for inheritance.

# Abstract methods and classes

## Description

Abstract methods are methods without a statement section. They must be overridden in derived classes and to be given a statement section.

## Abstract methods

Abstract methods are declared as `virtual` and set to 0. They are used as the default of an interface for derived classes and do not possess a definition body. Thus, they have to be defined in the derived classes.

```
virtual type name (PARAMETER LIST) = 0;
```

## Abstract classes

Classes which contain abstract methods automatically become abstract classes, with the result that they cannot create instances. They are always at the top of class hierarchies to predetermine suitable interfaces and, thus, confer a homogeneous character to the hierarchy.

## Warning

It has to be noted that classes which have been derived from an abstract class, and have not be overridden become abstract classes themselves.

## Example

```
class basis {
  public:
    virtual void func() = 0;
    ...
  };
class derived: public basis {
  public:
    virtual void func() { ... }
  };
```

## References

See Practice section, category inheritance and polymorphism, guidelines for inheritance.

# Base class pointer

### Description

As the elements' base classes are contained as sub-objects in a derived class, it is possible to treat a derived object like one of its base class objects; that is, reduce it to its base class sub-object.

This is a very useful concept particularly in connection with base class pointers and virtual methods, which in many cases permits extremely effective and elegant generic solutions.

### Application

A base class pointer is like a generic pointer, in that it can be assigned the addresses of derived objects (on the condition that the base class sub-object is non-ambiguously identifiable and accessible in the derived object). With the help of these generic pointers it is possible to:

- manage objects of different derived classes with a common base class in an array (or dynamic field),

```
class Reference object {  ...   };
class Rectangle : public Reference object {  ...  };
class Circle : public Reference object {  ...  };

int main()  {
  class Reference object  *geomFig[10];
  geomFig[0] = new Circle;
  geomFig[1] = new Rectangle;
```

- implement generic functions/methods, which can be assigned objects of different derived classes with a common base class as arguments.

```
void select(const Reference objet & object)  {  ...  }
```

## References

See Practice section, category inheritance and polymorphism, base class pointers and arrays, base class pointers as parameters.

# RTTI – Runtime Type Identification

## Description

To be able to work efficiently with base class pointers to derived objects, there has to be the option to re-access the functionality of the derived objects. The problem of re-conversion is the type identification: to which derived class type does the object, to which the base class pointer points, belong?

## Application

There are various options in C++ for the type identification

| Virtual methods | For a derived object a method which has been overridden in the derived class is called through a base class pointer. |
|---|---|
| | `base_ptr = &drv_obj;base_ptr->overriddenmethod();`<br>The type identification is carried out automatically by the compiler. You should use this type of type identification as far as possible. |

| | |
|---|---|
| dynamic_cast | For a derived object a method which has been redefined in the derived class, or a redefined data element is to be called through a base class pointer. |

```
base_ptr = &drv_obj;

if(drv_ptr = dynamic_cast<derived *>(base_ptr))
{

  drv_ptr->newmethod();

  drv_ptr->dataelement();

  }
```

The programmer uses the dynamic_cast operator to convert the base class pointer into a pointer to objects of a derived class and leaves the task to ensure that this conversion is correct to the operator. It is used where virtual methods cannot be used.

| | |
|---|---|
| typeid | This compares two data types, for example the type of an object to which the base class pointer refers, and the type of a derived class. |

```
base_ptr = &abg_obj;

if(typeid(*base_ptr) == typeid(derived))  {

  cout << "object is of derived type";

  }
```

The operator is used to identify types, mostly where the re-conversion of the base class pointer is not necessary (otherwise the dynamic_cast operator would be used). It should only be used sparingly. The virtual methods and the dynamic_cast operator should – whenever possible – take precedence.

## References

See Practice section, category inheritance and polymorphism, RTTI with virtual methods, RTTI with dynamic_cast, RTTI with typeid.

# Multiple inheritance

## Description

Multiple inheritance means that a class possesses more than one direct base class.

```
class derived: public basis1, public basis2
```

## Application

Multiple inheritance is interesting when it is possible to view an object of a derived class as an object of several base classes or when an object unites in itself the characteristics of several direct base classes. A typical example would be an amphibian vehicle, which is a car as well as a boat.

## Warning: Name conflicts in multiple inheritance

In multiple inheritance name conflicts can easily occur, if there are identical elements hidden in the base classes. Such name conflicts can be resolved using the area operator.

## Example

```
class basis1 {
   public:
      void func();
   };

class basis2 {
   public:
      void func();
   };

class derived: public basis1, public basis2 {
   ...
   };

int main() {
   derived abg;
   drv.func();              // error
   drv.basis1::func();      // correct
   ...
```

## Reference

See virtual base classes.

# Virtual base classes

## Description

Virtual base classes are base classes which are inherited with the keyword `virtual`. Here the compiler ensures that the elements of the base classes never occur more than once in all derived classes.

## Application

Multiple inclusion in the inheritance hierarchy causes elements to be inherited several times.

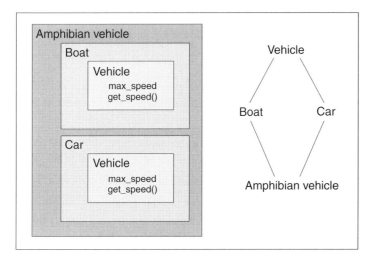

The above diagram shows how the class `amphibian_vehicle` inherits two occurrences each of the elements `max_speed` and `get_speed()` of the base class `vehicle`: once through the class `Boat` and once through `Car`. This can be useful in certain class hierarchies (for example for the amphibian vehicle, which has different maximum speeds as `Boat` and `Car`). However, this is often undesirable. It can be prevented by inheriting the base class as `virtual`.

## Examples

```
class basis   {
    ...
    };
class derived_1a : virtual public basis   {
    ...
    };
class derived_1b : virtual private basis   {
    ...
    };
```

```
class derived_2 : public derived_1a, derived_1b    {
   ...
   };
```

## Warning

Virtually inherited elements cannot be established through the direct base classes constructors. Instead a suitable constructor such as a base class constructor has to be directly incorporated into the constructor list for virtual base classes. The programmer thus has the two options:

- he can leave the initialisation to the default constructor of the virtual base class – if one is available, or

- he can incorporate a constructor of the virtual base class into the constructor list.

```
class Veicle
 class Boot : virtual public Veicle
 class Auto : virtual public Veicle
 class Amphibious veicle : public Boot, public Auto
   {
   public:
     Amphibious veicle(int price) : Veicle (price) { }
   };
```

A base class can be inherited to a derived class simultaneously virtually and non-virtually.

- Each path through which the base class is inherited non-virtually produces a separate base class object in the derived class.

- All paths through which the base class is inherited virtually, produce a common base class object in the derived class.

# Templates

## Templates

### Description

Templates are prefabricated, type-independent patterns for classes or functions. At any place within a class or function declaration where a data type is required, a wildcard can be used in the template declaration. These wildcards are listed in the header of the template declaration and are replaced with the desired types during instance formation, when the compiler creates a corresponding instance (specialisation) of the template class; that is, a class or function definition.

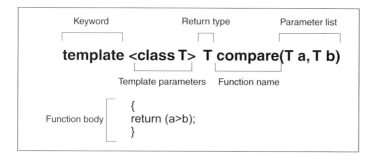

## Application

Templates are similar to macros. However, they are superior to them with respect to versatility and security. Compiler, which support templates, have therefore mostly implemented the common C macros as templates.

Templates are often implemented with the help of overloaded operators and methods to guarantee an appropriate use of these functions/operators within the template element functions.

## Warning

- If wildcards are introduced through a keyword other than class or typename, the compiler expects a corresponding constant for this wildcard. Floating point types are not permitted.

- To use a template (which is defined in a different source text file of the program) in a source text file you would, in principle, have to incorporate the template definition into the source text file through a header file. Alternatively, you can also define the template with the keyword export. To use the template in a different source text file, you then only need to specify the template declaration.

## Example

```
// Sourcetextfile.cpp
export template<class T> int func(T a, T b) // template definition
    {
    if (a == b)
      return 1;
    else
      return 0;
    }
```

```
// Sourcetextfile1.cpp
template<class T> int func(T a, T b);        // template declaration
int var1, var2;
...
func(var1, var2);
```

## References

See following paragraphs.

See Practice section, category templates.

# Function templates

## Description

Function templates are type-independent patterns for functions from which the compiler can create real functions for predetermined data types.

## Application

Function templates have, compared with overloading of functions, the advantage that the statement section only has to be written once (on condition, of course, that the statements are the same for all data types, for which the template has to be instanced). Otherwise it is naturally also possible to overload function templates.

## Syntax

```
template <TYPE_LIST>
    return_type function_name(PARAMETER_LIST) {  };
```

- **TYPE_LIST**: The type list enumerates the wildcards, which are to be replaced later on, separated by commas. Each wildcard is prefixed by the keyword class (or typename).
- The further declaration follows the syntax of function declaration, where it is possible to use wildcards instead of defined types.

## Examples

```
template<class T>  T max(T a, T b)   {
    return a > b ?: a, b;
    }
```

Instantiation:

```
cout << max(3, -14) << endl;
```

## Warning

Multiple instantiation and overloading may result in ambiguities, that is, the compiler may not be able to decide which implementation of the function has to be called for a function call.

## References

See instance formation and specialisation.

See Practice section, category templates, type-independent functions.

# Class templates

## Description

Class templates are type-independent patterns for classes, from which the compiler can create real classes for predetermined data types.

## Application

The best example for the use of class templates are the containers of the runtime library, which are all defined as templates. This defines the data type of the elements which are to be stored there, as a template parameter. The container can then be implemented independent of the type and, when required, be instanced for the desired data types.

## Syntax

```
template <TYPE_LIST> class classname {  };
```

- **TYPE_LIST**: The type list enumerates the wildcards, which are to be replaced later on, separated by commas. Each wildcard is prefixed by the keyword class (or typename).

## Warning

- Methods within class templates are automatically function templates, that is, you can use the wildcards of the class template without needing an explicit template declaration for these wildcards.

- Friend functions, which are declared in class templates, are not automatically function templates; that is, by default such functions are friends to all classes which are formed from the template. Only if a friend function contains a wildcard of the class template in its declaration is there a separate friend function for each typified class. It is also possible to declare friend functions as specialised templates to show that the friend declaration only applies for the specialisations of the template.

- Friend templates must not be defined in the template.

- If static elements are defined in a template, then each specialisation of the template receives its own set of static elements.

- Templates can be derived from templates as well as from normal classes and can in turn be used as base classes for other templates or classes.

- User-defined names in template declarations are by default understood as identifiers for variables. So that a name is recognised as a type identifier, it has to be defined within the template or in the surrounding scope or be marked by the keyword typename.

- Template class elements cannot be declared as virtual.

- Local classes must not contain template class elements.

## Examples

```
template <class T> class demo {
    T var;
 public:
   demo()    { var = 1.5;}
   T func() { T tmp;
             tmp=var++;
             return tmp;
           };
   };
```

Instantiation:

```
demo<double> obj;
```

## References

See instance formation and specialisation.

See Practice section, category templates, type-independent functions.

# Methods in class templates

## Description

Methods of class templates are automatically function templates; that is you can use the wildcards of the class template, without needing an explicit template declaration for these wildcards. Within the template their syntax is very similar to methods of ordinary classes. Outside the class template, for example for the dislocated definition, they have to be marked as elements of their class template.

## Syntax

```
template <TYPE_LIST>  return type
    class name<TYPE_LIST>::func_name(PARAMETER_LIST)
        {  };
```

## Warning

According to the new ANSI C++ standard it is also possible to declare function templates with their own wildcards within class templates. However, this concept is difficult to implement and is not supported by all compilers.

Methods of class template have to be defined in the same file as the class template. To separate both sections, keywords have to be used (see introduction to templates).

## Example

```
template<class T, class S> class demo {
    T var1;
    S var2;
  public:
    T func();
  };

template<class T, class S> T demo<T,S>::func() {
    return var1;
    }}
```

## Reference

See class templates.

# Instantiation and specialisation

## Description

A template is simply a pattern, a model for functions or classes which are to be created later on. The next step after the definition of a template is to create one or several functions (or classes) on the basis of the template, with which it is possible to work. The principal procedure is to instruct the compiler which data types it is to use for the template wildcards and then leave it to generate a real function or class from the type-independent template and the specified data types.

The functions or classes which are created on the basis of templates are called specialisations.

## Application

There are three options for indicating to the compiler that it is to produce a specialisation for a particular set of data types from a template:

- implicit instantiation,
- explicit instantiation, and
- explicit specialisation.

## Reference

See following paragraphs.

# Implicit instantiation

## Description

During implicit instance formation the programmer leaves almost all the work to the compiler. The programmer merely has to take care that the compiler has all the information it needs to be able to assign concrete data types to the wildcards.

## Application

With function templates, it is usually sufficient to call the function with appropriate arguments. The compiler gathers the type information from the arguments.

Types for classes or return values of functions cannot be derived in this way. In such a case the types for the wildcards have to be specified explicitly in pointed brackets.

## Implicit instantiation for function templates

```
template <class T1, class T2> void demo_func(T1 a, T2 b)   {
    ...
    }

int main()  {
  demo_func(13,14);
  demo_func<int>(13.2,14.3);
  return 0;
  }
```

## Explanation

```
demo_func(13,14);
```

The compiler recognises that a specialisation of the template demo_func is required. On the basis of the types of the call arguments it can determine the desired types for the wildcards `T1` and `T2`. The compiler thus produces a specialisation `demo_func<int, int>` and calls it up with the arguments `(13,14)`.

```
demo_func<int>(13.2,14.3);
```

The compiler recognises that a further specialisation of the template `demo_func` is required. It extracts the type for the first wildcard `T1` from the template arguments, which have been passed in pointed brackets. It extracts the type for the second wildcard `T2` from the type of the corresponding call argument. The compiler thus generates a specialisation `demo_func<int, double>` and calls it with the arguments `(13.2,14.3)`.

## Warning

In the instantiation of functions from function templates the compiler does not take into account default conversions. If a function template defines two parameters of the same wildcard type, the template cannot be instanced by passing two arguments of different types – even if these are convertible into each other by means of default conversions.

Once a specialisation of a function template has been produced it can be called like any other function with convertible arguments.

### Implicit instantiation for class templates

In the instantiation of class templates the data types for the wildcards must always be completely specified:

```
template<class T> class demo_class {
    T var;
  public:
    T func() { return var; }
  };

int main() {
  demo_class<int> obj;         // implicit instantiation
  return 0;
  }
```

## Reference

See explicit instantiation and specialisation.

# Explicit instantiation

Explicit instantiation is a request to the compiler to create the desired specialisation at once, even if that specialisation is not yet required.

Explicit instantiation is begun through the keyword `template`. However, arguments for the template parameters are not postfixed to the keyword `template`, but to the name of the function or class (this serves to distinguish it from explicit specialisation).

### Explicit instantiation for function templates

```
template <class T1, class T2> void demo_func(T1 a, T2 b) {
   cout << a << " " << b <<endl;
   }

// explicit instantiation
template void demo_func(int, int);
template void demo_func<int, double>(int, double);

int main()  {
  demo_func(13,14);
  demo_func<int>(13.2,14.3);
  ...
```

### Explicit instantiation for class templates

In the instantiation of class templates the data types for the wildcards always have to be completely specified:

```
template<class T> class demo_class {
    T var;
   public:
    T func() { var = 1; return var; }
   };

template class demo_class<int>;

int main()  {
  demo_class<int> obj;
  ...
```

## Reference

See implicit instantiation and specialisation.

# Explicit specialisation

## Description

Whereas we simply understand specialisation as a concrete function or class that has been generated on the basis of a template, we speak of explicit specialisation when:

- individual or all wildcards of a template are replaced with concrete data types, and when
- a separate definition is provided for this more type-dependent template.

## Syntax

The syntax of the specialisation requires two template parameter lists in pointed brackets:

```
template <first_list>   Name <second_list>>
```

- The first list, which follows the keyword `template`, contains the template parameters which are still going to be used in the specialisation.
- The second list, which follows the name of the specialisation, contains arguments for the template parameters of the primary template.

This syntax also permits partial specialisation:

```
template <class T1, class T2>  class demo          {...};
template <class T>             class demo<T, char>  {...};
template <class T>             class demo<T*, T>    {...};
template <>                    class demo<int, int>  {...};
```

The first line contains the definition of the primary template.

Below follow two partial specialisations, which only use one wildcard. The template argument list determines which data types or wildcards correspond with the wildcards of the primary template.

The final line defines a complete explicit specialisation.

## Warning

- Explicit specialisations always take precedence over implicit or explicit instantiation.
- An explicit instance formation or specialisation has to be carried out in the same namespace) as the template that is to be specialised.
- It is also possible to specialise individual methods explicitly for class templates.

The above syntax with the prefixed keyword `template` and the postfixed template parameter list is still quite new. Most compilers permit specialisations only in the form of a simplified syntax without the keyword `template`:

```
// old form of specialisation
int comparison<char*>(char *a, char *b)  {
    return(strcmp(a,b));
    }
```

## Example

```
// function template
template <class T> int comparison(T a, T b)  {
   cout << "First template:\t";
   return(a > b);
   }

// specialisation for data type char *
template <> int comaprison<char*>(char *a, char *b)  {
   return(strcmp(a,b));
   }
```

## Reference

See implicit and explicit instantiation.

# The preprocessor

## Description

Apart from the pure language definition the ANSI C standard also describes, among other things, the phrases which have to occur so that the source code of a program can be translated into a code which can be executed by the machine. One of the programs which is involved in the translation process is the preprocessor, which carries out preparation work at the source code. (In newer compilers preprocessing is not a separate process any more, but is carried out together with the compiling.) Only after the preprocessor has processed the code is it passed on to the compiler for code generation.

## Application

Apart from simple source text replacements that run automatically, the preprocessor carries out further tasks:

- Commentaries are removed (and replaced by spaces).

- String literals which are in sequence are summed up (concatenated).

- White-space characters between tokens are deleted. (A token is an identifier which has syntactic significance in the program.)

- Trigraph sequences are replaced.

These replacements are explicitly defined in the source code by preprocessor directives. With their help the programmer can:

- have header and source files be copied into the source text (`include`),
- introduce symbolic constants (`#define`), and
- control through 'switches' which code sections are to be translated (conditional compilation with `#ifdef`, and so on).

The statements to the preprocessor always begin with the character '#' and always stand in a separate line.

The following table presents an overview of preprocessor directives and operators prescribed by the ANSI standard.

| Directive | Meaning |
| --- | --- |
| defined | Operator, which tests whether a macro has been defined |
| # | Operator for the formation of strings |
| ## | Operator for the linking of base symbols |
| #define | Defines a symbol or macro |
| #elif | Else-if operator |
| #else | Else operator |
| #endif | End of the #if directive |
| #error | Produces an error message |
| #if | If operator |
| #ifdef | Equivalent to #if defined |
| #ifndef | Equivalent to #if !defined |
| #include | Integrates a file |
| #line | Changes the current time |
| #pragma | Instruction for the compiler |
| #undef | Removes the definition of a symbol |

## References

See Practice section, category preprocessor directives.

# Inserting and replacing source code

`#include`

## Description

The directive to the preprocessor that is most important to the programmer is surely `#include`. It instructs the preprocessor to copy the file specified as the argument into the current file.

## Application

Usually it is used to adopt a header file, which can contain declarations, symbolic constants, macros and/or type definitions. The integration of the file can occur at any point of the source file. However, there is general agreement that the integration takes place at the start of the file.

The use of header files is recommended particularly for programs which consist of several source text files. In this way the jointly usable type definitions, constants and function declarations can be made known to all involved files through a one-line statement.

## Syntax

Two different forms of the #include directive are possible:

```
#include <file>
```

The compiler looks for the specified file in certain directories which are specified in the development environment of the compiler.

```
#include "file"
```

The compiler looks for the specified file in a compiler-specific order. The current directory is usually searched first.

## Example

```
##include <stdio.h>
#include "subdirectory\types.h"
```

## References

See bases section, using the default libraries.

See Practice section, category libraries.

# Defining macros

```
#define macro_name
```

## Description

The preprocessor directive #define starts the definition of a macro.

## Application

A macro definition has the following form:

```
#define macro_name new_text
```

After having noted the macro definition, the preprocessor replaces each occurrence of macro_name with new_text.

The name of a macro is formed according to the same rules as a variable name. However, it has become standard to write macro names in capital letters. This nomenclature – if it is strictly adhered to – makes clear whether something is a variable/function name or a macro.

## Warning

The determination of the replacement text stops at the end of the line. To be able to write macros which are very long and complex, insert the backslash character '\' before the line break and continue the definition of the macro in the following line or lines.

If no replacement text is specified, the macro name is introduced, which can be used as a kind of compiler switch in the conditional compilation (and again be removed at any time with #undef macroname).

## Example

```
#define SIZE 20
int field[SIZE];
...
for (int i = 0; i < SIZE; i++) {  ...
```

## References

See arguments in macros.

See directives for the conditional compilation.

See category constants, #define.

See Practice section, category preprocessor directives.


# Arguments in macros

```
define name()
```

## Description

It is possible to use arguments in a macro, work with arguments within a macro and use the same macro for different arguments.

## Application

In this way functions can be replaced with macro calls, with which the function overhead can be prevented and type-independent implementations become possible.

## Warning

However, the passing of arguments may have undesirable side-effects, so that in C++ the declaration of `inline` functions for the prevention of function overhead or the programming of overloaded operators as well as of templates to achieve type-independent implementations should be preferred.

## Example

```
#define surface(a,b) (a*b)    // incorrect
result = surface(4,6);        // yields 24
result = surface(3+1,5+1);    // yields 9!
```

## Explanation

The wrong result is caused by wrongly defining the macro. The preprocessor replaces the second assignment with

```
result = 3+1*5+1
```

and this leads to the wrong result, since multiplication has precedence.

All arguments which occur in a macro definition thus should be bracketed to prevent these side-effects which are sometimes hard to find.

The correct code would be:

```
#define surface(a,b) ((a)*(b))   /* this is correct */
```

## References

See category templates, function templates.


# Directives for conditional compilation

## Description

With the directives of conditional compilation it is possible to either compile different areas of a file or to exclude them from compilation.

## Application

With the help of conditional compilation it is possible to construct different versions of a program. These versions can be:

- a version that contains debugging code,

- programs which run under different hardware or

- versions which are designated to work with different compilers.

The directives for conditional compilation evaluate a macro name, to establish which areas of the source file are to be passed to the compiler or excluded from the source code by the preprocessor.

The statement block for conditional compilation consists of several lines:

- The line containing the condition that is to be tested. It begins with #if, #ifdef or #ifndef.

- Lines which contain the code if the tested condition has the value true (optional).

- An optional else line, which begins with #else or #elif.

- Lines which contain the code if the tested condition has the value false (optional).

- A line with which the block for conditional compilation is finished; the #endif statement.

## #if

The preprocessor directive #if starts conditional compilation. It is followed by a constant expression which is evaluated. If the evaluation produces the result true, the following section is passed to the compiler (either to the next #elif, #else or to #endif).

## #elif

The directive #elif is an abbreviation for else if. This expression is only evaluated if the evaluation of the preceding directive produces the result false. #elif can occur several times in a block for conditional compilation. If the evaluation produces the result true, the following section is passed to the compiler (either to the next #elif, #else or to #endif).

## #else

#else can only occcur once in a statement block. The statements which follow after #else up to the final #endif are passed to the compiler if none of the preceding evaluations produces the result true.

## Endif and ending blocks                                                    endif

The preprocessor directive #endif has to be used for each #if, #ifdef and #ifndef to indicate the end of the block for conditional compilation.

## Conditional compilation and macro definition #ifdef, #ifndef

The directives #ifdef and #ifndef are old forms of the directives for conditional compilation. They can test whether the identifier which has been specified as an argument has been defined or not.

Furthermore, with #if defined it is possible to link the returned value, which cannot be done with #ifdef and #ifndef.

```
#ifdef identifier
#ifndef identifier
```

## The operator defined

The defined preprocessor operator returns the value true (equivalent to 1), if the identifier that has been specified as an argument has been defined with #define beforehand. If the identifier has not been defined, the operator returns the value false (equivalent to 0).

The two following statements are identical:

```
#if defined MAXROWS
#ifdef MAXROWS
```

## Example

```
#if defined(TARGETSYSTEM) && (MAXCOLUMNS==80)
    #define ARRAY_SIZE 160
#elif !defined(TARGETSYSTEM)
    #define ERROR1
    #error the file can't be compiled.
#endif
```

## Reference

See Practice section, category preprocessor directives.


# String formation and base symbol combination

## String formation #

The operator for string formation is used for macros that are similar to functions. It causes an argument which has been passed to the macro to be converted into a string.

```
#define makestring(s)    printf(#s "\n")
int main() {
    makestring(This will become a string);
    makestring("This will become another string");
    . . .
```

is transformed by the preprocessor into:

```
int main() {
   printf("This will become a string" "\n");
   printf("\"This will become another string\"" "\n");
   ...
```

The output of the program is:

```
This will become a string
"This will become another string""
```

## base symbol combination                                        ##

With the operator for base symbol combination (token-pasting operator)
individual tokens can be combined into a base symbol. The operator '##' and all
space characters which stand between the tokens are removed by the preprocessor.

```
#define pointervar(number)  printf("%d\n", var ##number)
int main() {
   int var3=3;
   pointervar(3);
```

is transformed by the preprocessor into::

```
int main() {
   int var3=3;
   printf("%d\n", var3);
   return 0;
   }
```

# Other directives and symbols

## Diagnostic messages                                           #error

The use of the preprocessor directive #error makes the compiler output the
(optional) text on the stderr device and subsequently interrupts the compilation.
The text need not be in inverted commas.

```
#error <text>
```

## Examples

```
#if !defined CAR && !defined BICYCLE
   #error Please define the desired means of transport
#endif
```

The above example could be from a program in which, through conditional
compilation, depending on the desired means of transport, a different code is
produced. As the program can only be compiled to be free of problems if either

CAR or BICYCLE is defined, the `defined` operator is used to test if the definition exists. If this is not the case the text after `#error` is outputted.

## Line-control directive                                         #line

With the line-control directive `#line` it is possible to set the line number within a file and to change the name of the file. The compiler uses this data to point to possible errors.

This directive is usually used by program generators to link errors in the generated C code with the line and file name of the file of origin.

```
#line <Line> ["filename"]
```

- **Line**: An integer constant to which the internal counter of the compiler is set.
- **File name**: This argument is optional and can contain a file name in inverted commas.

## Example

```
#line 200
#line 200 "origin.c"
```

## Pragma directives                                              #pragma

The `#pragma` directive is a compiler-specific directive; that is, the processing of the directive does not depend on the ANSI standard, but on the compiler used.

Pragma directives which do not belong to implementation are ignored. As this happens tacitly, it is necessary to proceed particularly carefully when porting code to another implementation with different pragmas.

## Pre-defined symbols and constants

According to ANSI C/C++ six different constants are predefined.

| Macro | Meaning |
| --- | --- |
| __DATE__ | Date of the compilation of the file |
| __FILE__ | Name of the source file |
| __LINE__ | Current line in the source file |
| __STDC__ | Compiler complies with ANSI C standard |
| __TIME__ | Time of the compilation of the file |
| __cplusplus | C++ code |

# Exception handling

## Exception handling

### Description

Exception handling is a form of error handling which was introduced into the language with C++. Exception handling does not rely on classes or other concepts of object-oriented programming. However, it works particularly effectively with them.

### Advantages of exception handling

Exception handling permits a separation of the cause of the error and error handling. A library function, therefore, does not have to process its errors itself. Instead it triggers an exception and leaves the handling of the error to the program which calls.

The second advantage is that the passing of the exception does not occur through the return type, the parameters or any global variables. The interface is required for the correct employment of the function is therefore not put under pressure. This is particularly important for elements such as constructors, which cannot return a value.

As exceptions are objects of a particular data type, they can transmit information from the place of the error to the place of the error handling.

Finally, the source code becomes clearer, since the actual algorithm and the error handling run separately.

### Disadvantages of exception handling

Exceptions should only be used for serious errors which cannot be repaired otherwise. Untreated exceptions lead to a program crash, unless no other exception handling has been provided by the programmer. Developers of libraries, especially should, therefore, avoid triggering an exception for every little discrepancy, which then has to be caught by the library users.

Exceptions which are not caught in the same function in which they have been triggered, lead to the resolving of the stack; that is, the functions which are on the stack are removed from it without being completely executed. This in turn can lead to problems, if resources which have been requested by the functions are not freed up at the end of the function (for example the freeing-up of dynamically reserved memory)

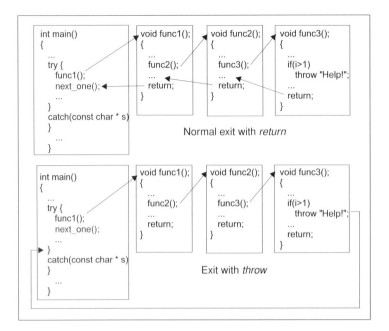

Normal exit with *return*

Exit with *throw*

There are two options for counteracting this problem:

• One option is to catch all exceptions in the function, then free up the resources and finally throw back the exceptions:

```
void func() {
FILE *fp = fopen("file.txt","rt");
try {
  func_that_may_throw(fp);
  }
catch(...) {              // ... catches all exceptions
  fclose(fp);
  throw;                  // forwarding exceptions
  }
fclose(fp);
}
```

• The other option is to encapsulate the resource in a local class instance. The destructor of the class is called for the resolving of the class instance and the programmer can ensure that the resource is freed up in the implementation of the destructor.

## Diagram of an exception handling

• Exception handling begins with the occurrence of an error, for example a division by zero.

• In reply to the error the function in which the error occurred triggers an exception. An exception is an instance of a data type. The instance usually receives information about the error. A simple exception would be a string, for example the error message 'Division by zero'. The exception is triggered with the keyword throw.

- Afterwards the surrounding block areas are searched for an exception handler. Handlers are defined for special exceptions, that is data types, and are marked by the keyword catch. The search is continued from the innermost block in which the exception has occurred to the surrounding blocks (functions on the stack), until a handler has been found or the main() function has been reached (stack resolving).

- The area for which the handler is responsible is started with the keyword try, which is enclosed in curly brackets.

## Examples

```
1:  #include <iostream>
2:  #include <string.h>
3:  using namespace std;
4:  class exception {
5:      int fact1, fact2;
6:    public:
7:      exception(int i, int j){fact1=i; fact2=j;}
8:      void output() {
9:                  cout << "fact1 = " << fact1 << endl;
10:                 cout << "fact2 = " << fact2 << endl;
11:                 }
12:  };
13: float division(int counter, int fact1, int fact2) {
14:    try {
15:      if(fact1*fact2 == 0) {
16:        throw exception(fact1,fact2);
17:        }
18:      }
19:    catch(exception& error instance) {
20:      errrorinstance.output();
21:      throw "Error occurred\n";
22:      }
23:    return counter/(fact1*fact2);
24:    }
25: int main() {
26:    try {
27:      float bruch;
28:      bruch = division(12,3,0);
29:      cout << bruch << endl;
30:      }
31:    catch (...) {
32:      cout << "Exception occurred!" << endl;
33:      }
34:    return 0;
35:    }
```

Output of the program:

```
fact1 = 3;
fact2 = 0;
Exception occurred!
```

## Explanation

The class exception is defined to be able to trigger an exception which is adapted to the error. Through its data elements the information relevant to the error is transferred. Its element function guarantees clean error handling.

In line 16 the exception of the type of the class exception is triggered and a corresponding instance is formed. The normal program course is then interrupted. Block by block is abandoned and searched for a handler, which is found in line 19.

The first error message is issued, and a second exception, this time of the char* type, is triggered. Again the program course is interrupted; the return statement is not carried out.

In line 31 all exceptions are caught. The second error message is issued.

## References

See category functions, functions and the stack.

See Practice section, category exceptions; pointer and dynamic memory management, dynamic memory and exception handling.

# Triggering exceptions

throw

## Description

Employed as a statement the keyword throw is used to trigger exceptions.

In function declarations the keyword can be used to specify which type of exception the declared function can trigger.

# Application

## Triggering exceptions                                    throw exception

To trigger an exception the keyword throw is called and passed the exception object. This triggers the exception and determines that the argument of the exception handling routine has to be of the same type as the specified throw object or at least of a convertible type. In this way it is possible to assign different throw objects to different errors (for example pointer errors, file errors and so on) and, thus, different handling routines.

After the exception has been triggered the closest handler is looked for (that is, the handler with a suitable argument) whose try block has been entered last.

Throw objects only live as long as the exception handling lasts (that is until the catch block is left).

The keyword throw without object can be used to re-trigger exceptions within a catch block or in a function which has been called in a catch block, and thus pass it to the next handler.

## Function declaration                                        func() throw;

The keyword throw can also be used at the end of function declarations to determine the list of the exceptions which are to be triggered:

```
void func() throw(exception, char*);
```

# Warning

- If an exception is triggered in a function, whose type is not contained in the throw list (presumably through a function called in the function), the function unexpected() is called.

- A function which has been declared without throw can trigger any exception.

- A function which has been declared with throw() cannot trigger an exception.

- A function which can trigger an exception of the A class can also trigger exceptions of a class derived from A.

# Examples

```
class my_exception          // definition of an exception class
{
    int fact1, fact2;
  public:
    my_exception(int i, int j){fact1=i; fact2=j;}
```

```
      void output() {
                cout << "fact1 = " << fact1 << endl;
                cout << "fact2 = " << fact2 << endl;
                }
};

float division(int counter, int fact1, int fact2)
{
   if(fact1*fact2 == 0) {                    // Division by zero!
       throw my_exception(fact1,fact2);  // Triggers exception of the
       }                                   // my_exception type
   return counter/(fact1*fact2);
}
```

# Catching exceptions

catch

## Description

The keyword catch indicates the start of a handling routine for exceptions of a certain type. The exception type which is caught is in brackets after catch.

## Application

With the keyword catch, exceptions which have been triggered in a preceding try block can be caught. The type of the triggered exception has to correspond to the type of the catch handler (certain default conversions are taken into account).

The exception type which is caught is in brackets after catch. The type of the triggered exception has to correspond to the type of the handler. The statement catch (...) catches all exceptions.

If an exception is triggered in the try block, which fits with respect to its data type to a catch handler, the statement block of the catch handler is executed.

## Warning

- Several handler definitions which each begin with catch can follow a try block. The handlers are checked one after the other until a correspondence is found.
- The statement catch (...) catches all exceptions. Therefore, the handler catch (...) should only stand at the end of a handler list.

## Example

```
try {
    ...  // Code in which in exceptions can appear
    }
catch (...) {                    //Intercepting all exceptions
    cout << "Exception occurred!" << endl;
    }
```

# Determining the handler scope

```
try
```

## Description

Scopes of handlers do not coincide with the usual blocks, but begin with the keyword `try` and are enclosed by curly brackets. The `try` block is directly followed by the keyword `catch` with the list of handlers.

## Application

Many C++ libraries are implemented in such a way that the functions and methods of the library trigger exceptions when a serious error occurs. If you want to catch these (or self-defined and -triggered) exceptions, you have to put the statements which can trigger the exceptions in a `try` block and attach one or several `catch` handler to the `try` block.

## Example

```
try {
    ...  // Code in which in exceptions can appear
    }
catch (char* s) {                // Intercepting exceptions of char* type
    cout << s << endl;
    }
catch (...) {                // intercepting all exceptions
    cout << "Exception occurred!" << endl;
    }
```

## References

See triggering exceptions.

See catching exceptions.

# Related functions

## Description

The functions unexpected() and terminate() as well as set_unexpected() and set_terminate() are connected to exception handling.

## Application

- The functions unexpected() and terminate() are required to terminate the program in case of an exception handling failure. This is the case, for example, when an exception is triggered within a function, which is not to treat the function (throw declaration). In this case the function unexpected() is called, which in turn calls terminate() by default.

- The function terminate() is directly called when there are stack problems or a handler has not been found for a triggered exception. By default the function terminate() calls the function abort() to terminate the program.

- The functions set_unexpected() and set_terminate() are used to redirect the function calls from unexpected() and terminate() to separate functions.

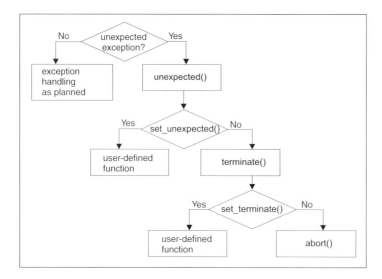

## Example

```
#include <iostream>
#include <string>
using namespace std;

// handler function for unexpected exceptions
void unexpected_exception() {
```

```
    cout << "This could not be expected!" << endl;
    terminate();
    }

// Function, which triggers an exception
void exception()  {
    throw string("Error occurred!!");
    }

// Function which should not trigger any exception
// otherwise calls unexpected().
void func() throw()   {
    exception();
    }

int main() {
    set_unexpected(unexpected_exception);   // register
                                            // unexpected handler
    func();                                 // provoke
                                            // unexpected exception

    return 0;
    }
```

## Reference
See triggering exceptions.

# Strings

## C strings

### Description
C does not recognise a separate data type for strings. Instead strings are simply interpreted as sequences of characters. Such a string begins with a particular address in the memory and ends with the zero termination character '\0'.

219

## Application

Strings are defined as pointers or arrays for one of the data types char (for 7 or 8 bit character sets such as ASCII or ANSI) or wchar_t (for 16 bit character sets such as UNICODE).

```
char *ptr;
char str1[25];
```

The declaration as array has the advantage that, together with the declaration of the string variables, memory is reserved. In the definition of a pointer to a string it has to be reserved afterwards (with malloc() or new) with the advantage that the size of the memory is determined at runtime and that, if necessary, new memory can be reserved.

In the C runtime library a range of functions, which all start with str... and are declared in the header file string.h, are defined to manipulate the strings.

## Warning

When you define a C string in the form of an array, please take care that the string does not end with the array, but with the zero termination character '\0'. Thus, if you want to copy a string into an array, make sure that the array is big enough to accommodate all characters of the string including the zero termination character '\0'. If you want to determine the length of a string which has been deposited in an array with strlen(), the number of characters in the string (without the zero termination character '\0'), not the size of the array, is returned. If you output a string, which has been deposited in an array with printf(), all the characters of the address of the array up to the next zero termination character '\0' are outputted.

The string functions of the C runtime library have the shortcoming that the memory management is left completely to the programmer. If, for example, you want to copy string B into a string A with strcpy(), you have to ensure beforehand that the memory which has been reserved for string A is big enough to accommodate string B, too. There are several options to reserve memory for strings.

## Example

```
#include <stdio.h>
#include <string.h>

int main()
  {
  char string1[] = "C and C++";
  char string2[] = "C++ and C";
```

```
if(strcmp(string1, string2) > 0)
    printf("%s is larger than %s\n",string1,string2);
    else
    printf("%s ist smaller than or equal to %s\n", string1,string2);

return 0;
}
```

## References

See the string class.

See Practice section, category strings.

# The string class

`string`

## Description

In C++ it is possible to fall back on the class `string` (`wstring` for Wide Character Strings) for programming with text.

## Application

The class string goes back to the template `base_string`, which has been defined in the header file `<string>`:

```
template<class charT, ... > class base_string;
```

Thus, what we call the `string` class, for reasons of simplicity, is actually simply an alias for the instantiation of the template for the character type `char`.

```
typedef base_string<char> string;
```

There is a corresponding `wstring` for the character type `wchar_t`..

To manipulate the strings you can use the methods and operators defined in `base_string`. The use of these methods and operators not only facilitates the work with string (in comparison to the C strings), it is also significantly more secure, as the implementation of the `string` class takes care of correct memory management.

To support existing C code the `string` has a method `c_str()`, which returns the text, encapsulated in a `string` object, as a C string.

## Example

```
#include <iostream>
#include <string>
using namespace std;

int main()
  {
  string str1("C and C++");
  string str2 = "C++ and C";

  if(str1 > str2)
     cout << str1 << " is larger than " << str2 << endl;
     else
     cout << str1 << " is smaller or equal " << str2 << endl;

  return 0;
  }
```

## References

See the string class.

See Practice section, category strings.

# Wide character and multibyte characters

wchar_t

## Description

The data type wchar_t (still defined in C by means of typedef) for 'wide characters' has been established to be able to work with character sets which, contrary to the ASCII character set, cannot be coded by 8 bit (for example UNICODE).

Wide characters must be distinguished from multibyte characters. While wide characters belong to the integer type, multibyte characters are treated as a sequence of bytes. The number of bytes in a multibyte character can vary. This can save a lot of memory, for example when mixing English text (whose characters only require 1 byte) with Chinese characters (whose coding requires at least 2 bytes) in one file. Therefore, all common multibyte coding procedures use escape sequences which serve to switch between different character sets and indicate whether the following characters are coded through 1, 2 or several bytes. Within programs, however, multibyte characters are rarely used because of their variable length and inconvenient handling. Therefore, one usually converts multibyte characters into wide characters when reading a file, works with them in that format and then writes the result back to the file as multibyte characters.

## Application

The C library contains several methods for programming with multibyte characters and wide characters. The multibyte functions can be recognised by the character sequence 'mb', as in `mblen()`, `mbrlen()`, `mbtowc()`, `wctomb()` or `mbstowcs()`, `wcstombs()`, `mbsinit()`. The wide character functions can be recognised by the 'w' in the function name, as in `wprintf()`, `wmemcpy()` or `wcscpy()`.

## References

See Practice section, category internationalisation and localisation, wide characters.

# Input and output (I/O)

## Formatted and unformatted I/O

### Description

Ultimately, data (integer values, strings, structure variables and so on) are always exchanged in form of bit streams. However, this does not mean that it is necessary to deal with bit streams when programming. C and C++ support data exchange in the form of unformatted byte streams and formatted data units.

### Application

In formatted input and output the data can be input and output in their original data format:

```
int integer = 3;
char character = 'A';
printf("%d",integer);        // output formatted in C
printf("%c",character);
cout << integer;             // output formatted in C++
cout << character;
```

In unformatted input and output, however, the data are treated as a sequence of bytes:

```
fwrite(&character, sizeof(char), 1, stdout);        // C
fwrite(&integer, sizeof(int), 1, stdout);
cout.put(character);                                // C++
cout.write((char *) &integer, sizeof(int));;
```

In the formatted input and output the data can be reformatted in the course of output through explicit type conversion. Furthermore, output can be further formatted with the help of special characters (\n for line breaks, \t for tabulator) and special formatting statements.

## Warning

Input and output are operating system-specific processes. For this reason they are not firmly rooted in the language (in the form of keywords), but are implemented through functions/classes of the runtime library. However, these support only the input and output for console programs. These functions cannot be used for Windows programs (under UNIX, XWindows or OSF Motif), but the programmer has to resort to special functions which are included in the APIs of the Windows systems.

## Examples

Reformatting in formatted output:

```
char character = 'A';
printf("%d",character);      // output: 65
cout << (int) character;     // output: 65
```

The use of special characters and special formatting statements:

```
// Setting field area of the output on 5 characters
printf("%5d",integer);
printf("%5c\n",character);     // output:     3     A

// Setting field area of the output on 5 characters
cout.width(5);
cout << integer;
cout.width(5);
cout << character << endl;     // output:     3     A     A
```

## References

See Practice section, category input and output.

See reference of the runtime libraries, examples for header files.

# Streams in C

## Description

Streams are data streams through which data are moved from a source to a target.

The stream objects with which we work always mark the end of a data stream (source or target), possess internal information about the handling of the data exchange, and are by default connected to a buffer.

## Application

In C the following default stream objects are available:

| | |
|---|---|
| stdin | Default input, typically the keyboard |
| stdout | Default output, typically the screen (to be precise, the console). |
| stderr | Default error output, typically the console, however this stream is not buffered. |

To define your own streams, especially for the input and output of files, the `<stdio.h>` defined data type `FILE` is available.

```
// possible definition for FILE:
typedef struct {
  int            level;      // filling the buffers
  unsigned       flags;      // file status
  char           fd;         // file descriptor
  unsigned char  hold;       // ungetc char, if no buffer
  int            bsize;      // buffer size
  unsigned char *buffer;     // buffer
  unsigned char *curp;       // active pointer
  unsigned       istemp;     // temporary file
  short          token;      // vlidity
  } FILE;
```

To manipulate the streams and the input and output through the streams the corresponding functions of the C runtime library are used:

| C function | Description |
|---|---|
| fclose | Closes data stream. |
| feof | Tests data stream for end of file. |
| ferror | Tests data stream for errors. |
| fflush | Empties buffer of a data stream. |
| fgetc | Reads characters from data stream. |
| fgetpos | Reads line of data stream. |
| fgets | Opens data stream. |
| fopen | Formats output to data stream. |
| fprintf | Writes character to data stream. |
| fputc | Writes a string to data stream. |
| fputs | Reopens data stream. |
| freopen | Reads formatted from data stream. |
| fscanf | Repositions file pointer. |
| fseek | Repositions file pointer. |
| fsetpos | Reads the position of file pointer. |

| C function | Description |
|---|---|
| ftell | Reads characters from data stream. |
| getc | Reads characters from data stream stdin. |
| getchar | Reads string from stdin. |
| gets | Formatted output to stdout. |
| printf | Writes characters into data stream. |
| putc | Writes characters to data stream stdout. |
| putchar | Writes string to data stream stdout. |
| puts | Formatted input from string. |
| rewind | Positions file pointer to start of data stream. |
| scanf | Formatted input from stdin. |
| setbuf | Establishes a separate data stream buffer. |
| setvbuf | Data stream buffering and change buffer size. |
| sprintf | Formatted output into string. |
| sscanf | Formatted input from string. |
| ungetc | Returns character to data stream. |

## References

See Practice section, category input and output.

# Streams in C++

## Description

Streams are data streams through which data are moved from a source to a target.

The stream objects with which we work always mark the an end of a data stream (source or target), possess internal information about the handling of the data exchange, and are by default connected to a buffer.

## Application

In C++ the following default stream objects are available:

| char | wchar_t | External device |
|---|---|---|
| cin | wcin | Default input, typically the keyboard. |
| cout | wcout | Default output, typically the screen (to be precise, the console). |
| cerr | wcerr | Default error output, typically the console, however, this stream is not buffered. |
| clog | wclog | Default log output, typically the console. |

You can establish your own streams as instances of predefined stream classes. Furthermore, there is the option to derive your own stream classes (for example for self-defined character types) from the stream templates, which are defined in the runtime library, through specialisation.

To manipulate the streams and the input and output through the streams, the methods and overloaded operators of the stream classes are used.

## Formatting

It is possible to format output by means of the following stream methods.

| Method | Description |
|---|---|
| width() | With the `width()` method it is possible to determine a minimal width for the output of the next value. |
| | If the output encompasses fewer digits than have been passed as argument to `width()`, padding characters are inserted. The final format depends on the chosen padding characters (see `fill()`) and the alignment (`left`, `right`, `internal`). |
| fill() | With the `fill()` method you can determine a padding character. Padding characters are used when you choose a field width for an output (see above), which is greater than the actual output. |
| precision() | With the `precision()` method it is possible to determine the number of digits in the output of floating point numbers. The default value is six digits. |
| | However, it has to be distinguished whether the floating point numbers are output in the default mode, or whether one of the format flags fixed or scientific has been set beforehand. |
| | In the default mode `precision()` determines the total number of digits. |
| | In the `fixed` or `scientific` mode `precision()` determines the number of digits after the decimal point. |

- by means of formatting flags, which are set and deleted through the methods `setf()` and `unsetf()`. The formatting flags are defined as elements of the class `ios_base`:

| Flag | Effect | Corresponds to in C | Default |
|---|---|---|---|
| boolalpha | Boolean values as numbers or as words | | 0 |
| left | Left-aligned output | -0 | right |
| right | Right-aligned output | | |
| internal | Gap after sign or basis | | |
| dec | Decimal representation | %d, %u | dec |
| oct | Octal representation | %o | |
| hex | Hexadecimal representation | %x | |

| Flag | Effect | Corresponds to in C | Default |
|------|--------|---------------------|---------|
| fixed | Fixed number of digits | %g, %f | fixed |
| scientific | Exponential representation | %e, %E | |
| showbase | Show basis | | 0 |
| showpoint | Show decimal point | # | 0 |
| showpos | Show plus character | + | 0 |
| skipws | Skip white-space character in input | | 1 |
| unitbuf | Empty output stream after formatting | | 0 |
| uppercase | Output certain lower case letters (for example, hex character) in upper case | %X %E %G | 0 |

- by means of manipulators. These are functions which can be passed as operands to stream operators.

| Manipulator | I/O | Effect |
|-------------|-----|--------|
| boolalpha | i/o | as setf(ios_base::boolalpha)) |
| noboolalpha | i/o | as unsetf(ios_base::boolalpha) |
| left | o | as setf(ios_base::left, ios_base::adjustfield) |
| right | o | as setf(ios_base::right, ios_base::adjustfield) |
| internal | o | as setf(ios_base::internal, ios_base::adjustfield) |
| dec | i/o | as setf(ios_base::dec, ios_base::basefield)) |
| oct | i/o | as setf(ios_base::oct, ios_base::basefield) |
| hex | i/o | as setf(ios_base::hex, ios_base::basefield) |
| fixed | o | as setf(ios_base::fixed, ios_base::floatfield) |
| scientific | | as setf(ios_base::scientific, ios_base::floatfield)) |
| showbase | o | as setf(ios_base::showbase) |
| noshowbase | o | as unsetf (ios_base::showbase) |
| showpoint | o | as setf(ios_base::showpoint)) |
| noshowpoint | o | as unsetf (ios_base::showpoint) |
| showpos | o | as setf(ios_base::showpos) |
| noshowpos | a | as unsetf (ios_base::showpos) |
| skipws | e | as setf(ios_base::skipws) |
| noskipws | e | as unsetf(ios_base::skipws) |

| Manipulator | I/O | Effect |
|---|---|---|
| unitbuf | a | as setf(ios_base::unitbuf) |
| nounitbuf | a | as unsetf(ios_base::unitbuf) |
| uppercase | a | as setf(ios_base::uppercase) |
| nouppercase | | as unsetf (ios_base::uppercase)) |
| resetiosflags (ios_base::fmtflags mask) | e/a | Delete flags |
| endl | a | New line and empty stream |
| ends | a | Output zero termination character ('\t') |
| flush | a | Empty stream |
| setbase(int base) | e/a | Basis for integer values |
| setfill(charT c)) | e/a | as fill(c) |
| setiosflags (ios_base::fmtflags mask)) | e/a | Set flags |
| setprecision(int n)) | e/a | as precision(n) |
| setw(int n) | e/a | as width(n) |
| ws | e | Skip white-space characters |

## Error handling

For error handling each stream contains the following status bits, which are set to 1 in case of an error by the streams.

| Status bit | Error |
|---|---|
| ios_base::goodbit | No error has occurred, everything is in order. |
| ios_base::eofbitt | During reading the EOF character has been reached (can be simulated if needs be by typing Ctrl+D or Ctrl+Z). |
| ios_base::failbit | When inputting the expected character could not be read (for example because of a wrong format). When outputting the desired character could not be output. |
| ios_base::badbit | The stream cannot work properly any more (usually this is the case when there are problems with the buffer it is based on (base_streambuf objects)). |

For the status bits there are the following methods, with which the status of the streams can be queried.

| Method | Description |
|---|---|
| bool good() | `true`, if no status bit has been set |
| bool eof() | `true`, if `eofbit` has been set |
| bool fail() | `true`, if `failbit` or `badbit` has been set |
| bool bad() | `true`, if `badbit` has been set |
| bool operator!() | `true`, if `failbit` or `badbit` has been set |
| iostate rdstate() | Returns the total stream status |

## References

See Practice section, category input and output.


# Buffering

## Description

Streams are buffered; that is, the input or output do not occur directly to the target of the stream, but are buffered in the memory.

The reason for the buffering is to design the input and output more efficiently. Usually external appliances (keyboard, screen, hard drive) are accessed during in- or outputting. This type of access is always a good deal slower than access to memory areas. However, it is possible to speed up data exchange by temporarily storing the data character by character in a buffer in the RAM and then transferring it in larger coherent blocks.

## Application

Each buffer has a fixed size. When the buffer is full, it empties itself. You can also empty a buffer manually.

- By calling the method `flush()`.
- The keyboard buffer (streams `stdin,cin`) can be emptied by pressing Enter.
- The console buffer (streams `stdout`, `cout`, `clog`) is emptied when the new line character is output (cout << "\n"; or cout << endl;). In addition the output buffer `cout` (`stdout`) is linked to the input buffer `cin` (`stdin`), so that before every expected input the output buffer is emptied.
- The error output `cerr` (`stderr`) is not buffered.

Behind the buffers there are classes which all go back to the class template `base_streambuf`, in C++. The connection between a stream and its buffer is created by the constructor during instance formation of the stream. After the initialisation the stream can access its buffer through the method rdbuf(),

- either to have returned a reference to its own buffer and then to manipulate it through its public interface (for example to adapt the buffer size with setbuf()),

- or to link the stream with another buffer (for example with the buffer of another stream).

## References

See Practice section, category input and output, sharing stream buffers.

# The C standard library

## The header files

To be able to call up the C functions in your programs, you first have to make the function declarations known to the compiler. This is achieved by the header files, in which the functions are ordered thematically, and which you can incorporate into your programs using the #include directive.

In the following section, the functions, ordered by header files, are introduced, and in doing so the names of the C convention have been used. According to the new C++ standard the file names of the C header files are each prefixed with a 'c' and the extension is left out (stdlib.h therefore becomes cstdlib). The difference to the C headers in this case is that the elements in the C++ headers are declared in the std namespace.

## assert.h

### Description
Only contains the assert macro, which can be used for debugging.

### Included elements
```
assert          // checks a condition and terminates the program
                // when the condition is not satisfied
```

### Example
```
#include <stdio.h>
#include <assert.h>
int main(int argc, char **argv)
  {
  int i = 3, j = 2;
  double res;
  // ... further instructions
  assert(j != 0);        // Avoid division by zero
  res = (double) i/j;
  printf("Division yields : %f\n",res);
  return 0;}
```

# ctype.h

## Description

Contains the functions for classification (is...) and conversion (to...) of simple characters.

The functions of this header file are to edit or control user input via the keyboard. Thus, you can test whether a user – as required by the program – has entered a number as a digit sequence, or has illegally written it out as a word. Or you can change user input with the functions tolower()/toupper() into lower or upper case letters.

## Included elements

```
isalnum      // tests whether a character is a number or letter
isalpha      // tests whether a character is a letter
iscntrl      // tests whether a character is a control character
isdigit      // tests whether a character is a digit
isgraph      // tests whether a character is representable
islower      // tests whether a character is a lower case letter
isprint      // tests whether a character is printable
ispunct      // tests whether a character is a punctuation mark
isspace      // tests whether a character is a space
isupper      // tests whether a character is an upper case letter
isxdigit     // tests whether a character is a hexadecimal number
tolower      // changes upper case into lower case letters
toupper      // changes lower case into upper case letters
```

## Example

```
char character, *str;
...
for(i = 0; i < strlen(str); i++)
  str[i] = tolower(str[i]);

if(isprint(character))
  putchar(character);
```

# errno.h

## Description

Contains miscellaneous macros which are used by various library functions to issue error messages.

## Included elements

```
EDOM         // copied into errno by the mathematical functions
             // in case of an invalid function argument
```

```
EILSEQ          // copied into errno by the functions mbrtowc() or
                // wcrtomb() in case of a coding error from multibyte
                // into wide character or vice versa
ERANGE          // copied into errno by the mathematical functions
                // in case of an invalid output value
errno           // set by the mathematical functions in case of
                // an error
```

## Example

```c
#include <stdio.h>
#include <math.h>
#include <errno.h>
int main(int argc, char **argv)
   {
   int    i = -3;
   double root;
   errno = 0;
   root = sqrt(i);
   if(errno == EDOM)
       puts("Domain Error on call of sqrt()\n");
    else
       printf("Root of %d is %f\n",i,root);
   return 0;
   }
```

# float.h

## Description

Contains various macros, which expand to different implementation-specific constants. Only the constants for the data type float are listed. The constants for double and long double begin with the suffixes DBL or LDBL. (FLT_ROUNDS applies to all three floating-point types).

## Included elements

```
FLT_DIG         // number of significant digits in the mantissa,
                // when represented in base 10
FLT_EPSILON     // difference between 1 and the next largest
                // representable number
FLT_MANT_DIG    // number of digits in the mantissa, when
                // represented in base FLT_RADIX
FLT_MAX         // largest positive number
FLT_MAX_10_EXP  // largest positive number for exponent of base 10
FLT_MAX_EXP     // largest positive number for exponent of
                // base FLT_RADIX
FLT_MIN         // smallest positive number (closest to 0)
FLT_MIN_10_EXP  // smallest negative number for exponent of base 10
```

```
FLT_MIN_EXP      // smallest negative number for the exponent of
                 // base FLT_RADIX
FLT_RADIX        // base of exponents
FLT_ROUNDS       // mode used for rounding the figures:
                 //   -1  indefinite
                 //    0  to null
                 //    1  to the next value
                 //    2  to +infinity
                 //    3  to -infinity
```

## Reference

See Practice section, category variables and data types, value range and precision of floating-point numbers.

# ios646.h

## Description

Synonyms for certain operators.

## Included elements

| Synonym | for | |
|---------|-----|---|
| and | && | Logical AND operation |
| and_eq | &= | Bitwise AND operation and assignment |
| bitand | & | Bitwise AND operation |
| bitor | \| | Bitwise OR |
| compl | ~ | Complement |
| not | ! | NOT operator, negation |
| not_eq | != | Compares two arithmetic operands for inequality |
| or | \|\| | Logical OR |
| or_eq | \|= | Bitwise OR and assignment of the result |
| xor | ^ | Bitwise exclusive OR |
| xor_eq | ^= | Bitwise exclusive OR and assignment of the result |

# limits.h

## Description

Contains constants which determine size and value ranges of the elementary data types (the values are implementation-specific and are determined by the compiler).

## Included elements

```
CHAR_BIT       // number of bits in smallest data type
CHAR_MIN       // smallest value for objects of type char
CHAR_MAX       // largest value for objects of type char
INT_MIN        // smallest value for objects of type int
INT_MAX        // largest value for objects of type int
LONG_MIN       // smallest value for objects of type long int
LONG_MAX       // largest value for objects of type long int
MB_LEN_MAX     // maximum number of bytes in multibyte characters
SCHAR_MIN      // smallest value for objects of type signed char
SCHAR_MAX      // Largest value for objects of type signed char
SHRT_MIN       // smallest value for objects of type short int
SHRT_MAX       // largest value for objects of type short int
UCHAR_MAX      // largest value for objects of type unsigned char
UINT_MAX       // largest value for objects of type unsigned int
ULONG_MAX      // largest value for objects of type unsigned long int
USHRT_MAX      // largest value for objects of type unsigned short int
```

## References

See Practice section, category variables and data types, value ranges of integer data types.


# locale.h

## Description

Contains the functions localeconv() and setlocale() to set and query country-specific particularities. The return type of localeconv() is the lconv structure. The LC macros can be passed as arguments to setlocale(), in order to select special facets of a locale.

## Included elements

```
LC_ALL         // all categories of country-specific settings.
LC_COLLATE     // for string comparisons
LC_CTYPE       // for character classification and conversion.
LC_MONETARY    // for currency formats
LC_NUMERIC     // for numerical formats, for example decimal
               // points in floating point numbers
LC_TIME        // for date and time input
```

```
struct lconv      // the lconv structure
localeconv        // initialise the lconv structure
setlocale         // query and modify country-specific values
```

## Examples

Querying current locale settings:

```
struct lconv ll;
struct lconv *conv = &ll;
conv = localeconv();
printf("Decimal point : %s\n", conv->decimal_point);
```

Changing locales:

```
setlocale(LC_ALL, "de_DE");
```

## References

See Practice section, category internationalisation and localisation.


# math.h

## Description

Declares mathematical functions. While under C only the `double` versions of the functions are available, under C++ the `float` and `long double` data types are also overloaded.

## Included elements

```
HUGE_VAL      // macro, expanded to a double value, returned by the
              // mathematical functions in case of an overload
acos          // calculate arc cosine
asin          // calculate arc sine
atan          // calculate arc tangent of x
atan2         // calculate arc tangent of x/y
ceil          // round to nearest integer
cos           // calculate cosine
cosh          // calculate hyperbolic cosine
exp           // calculate exponential function
fabs          // Determine absolute value
floor         // Determine largest integer smaller than or equal to
              // the argument
fmod          // calculate remainder of floating point division
frexp         // calculate exponential value
ldexp         // multiply floating point number
log           // calculate natural logarithm
log10         // calculate logarithm in base 10
modf          // parse argument in integral and divided parts
```

```
pow          // exponentiate number
sin          // calculate sine
sinh         // calculate hyperbolic sine
sqrt         // calculate square root
tan          // calculate tangent
tanh         // calculate hyperbolic tangent
```

## Example

```
double number;
printf("Enter a number: \n\n");
scanf("%lf", &number); fflush(stdin);
printf("  Square root of %lf = %lf\n",number,number*number);
printf("  %lf^3             = %lf\n",number,pow(number,3));
printf("  Log.e of %lf      = %lf\n",number,log(number));
printf("  Log.10 of %lf     = %lf\n",number,log10(number));
printf("  Sine of %lf (RAD) = %lf\n",number,sin(number));
printf("  Sine of %lf (GRAD) = %lf\n",number,sin(2*3.1415*number/360));
```

# setjmp.h

## Description

Defines the data type jmp_buf, which is used by the setjmp() macro and the longjmp()
function.

## Included elements

```
jmp_buf      // takes the number of the current environment,
             // typically the content of the processor register
             // as well as the stack and frame pointer, to enable
             // a non-local jump
longjmp      // re-establish call environment in accordance with
             // jmp_buf-argument after a non-local jump
setjmp       // safeguard call environment in jmp_buf-argument
             // environment can be re-established via longjmp()
```

## Example

```
#include <stdio.h>
#include <setjmp.h>
#include <stdlib.h>

void func(jmp_buf jump)
  {
  puts("Execute jump from funtion\n");
  longjmp(jump,1);
  }
```

```
int main(int argc, char** argv)
  {
  int value;
  jmp_buf jump;
  if(wert = setjmp(jump))
    {
    printf("returned from jump with value %d\n", value);
    exit(value);
    }
  func(jump);
  return 0;
  }
```

# signal.h

## Description

Defines constants and functions which are required for signal processing (interrupts, segmentation faults and so on). The SIG_ constants are compatible with the second parameter of signal(), which otherwise is passed a signal processing function. The SIG constants categorise the signals and serve as arguments for the first parameter of the signal() function.

## Included elements

```
SIG_DFL      // default processing
SIG_ERR      // return value of signal() in case of error
SIG_IGN      // ignore signal
SIGABRT      // abnormal program end
SIGFPE       // floating point error
SIGILL       // illegal instruction
SIGINT       // Ctrl+C interrupt
SIGSEGV      // illegal memory access (Segmentation Fault)
SIGTERM      // end query sent to program
raise        // sends a signal
signal       // installs signal handling function for the
             // processing of a SIG signal
```

## Example

```
#include <stdio.h>
#include <stdlib.h>
#include <signal.h>
void signal editing(int par) {
  /* re-install signal handling */
  signal(SIGFPE, signal editing);
  printf("Signal intercepted!\n");
  printf("Program data saved for analysis\n");
  exit(1);
  }
```

```
int main(int argc, char** argv) {
  /* re-install signal handling*/
  signal(SIGFPE, signal editing);
  int n, i = 3265;
  printf("Please enter a whole number: \n");
  scanf("%d",&n);
  fflush(stdin);
  i = i/n;
  printf("%d\n", i);
  return 0;
  }
```

# stdarg.h

## Description

Defines macros with which functions with a variable number of arguments can be processed.

## Included elements

```
va_list       // array type for va_arg, va_end and va_start
va_arg        // establishes pointer on next argument in the list
va_end        // resets pointer after editing the argument
va_start      // macro which allows the function a correct return
              // jump
```

## References

See Practice section, category functions, functions with any number of arguments.

# stddef.h

## Description

Defines a few important types and macros, which are mainly used in internal libraries.

## Included elements

```
NULL          // value of the null-pointer
offsetof      // establishes the offset of an element in a
              // structure
ptrdiff_t     // signed integer type, which can represent the result
              // of the subtraction of two
              // pointers
size_t        // unsigned integer type, which can be used as a
              // result type by sizeof
wchar_t       // character type for wide character sets (16 to
              // 32 bits)
```

# stdio.h

## Description

Contains the functions for input and output (console, keyboard, files), as well as numerous related constants and data types.

## Included macros and type definitions

```
_IOFBF       // for setbuf(); indicates that a stream is buffered (0)
_IOLBF       // for setbuf(); stream buffered in lines (1)
_IONBF       // for setbuf(); stream not buffered (2)
BUFSIZ       // the macro BUFSIZ is used by fopen(),freopen() and
             // setbuf() to determine the size of a buffer stream
             // automatically at the set-up of a buffer. (>= 255)
EOF          // negative integer constant, indicates the end of a file
FILE         // a data type which can take all information required
             // for the execution of file operations; the
             // construction of the data type is implementation-
             // specific
FILENAME_MAX // the maximum number of characetrs which may appear in
             // a filename.
FOPEN_MAX    // FOPEN_MAX contains the maximum number of data streams
             // which can be opened from one file simultaneously.
             // This value is at least 8, whereby each program
             // automatically receives the data streams stdin,
             // stdout and stderr. Programs which require more than
             // five additional data streams can be checked with a
             // macro, if they can be made available by the system.
fpos_t       // The fpos_t type is used by fgetpos() and fsetpos()
             // to specify the current position in a file
L_tmpnam     // Size of an array of data type char, which has to be
             // large enough to take filenames generated
             // with tmpnam()

// The following three macros used as an argument
// for the fseek() function determine the position
// from which the file pointer should be moved:

SEEK_CUR     // from current position (1)
SEEK_END     // from end of file (2)
SEEK_SET     // from start of file (0)
size_t       // unsigned integer type, used as a
             // result type by sizeof
stderr       // standard error stream
stdin        // standard input stream
stdout       // standard output stream
TMP_MAX      // TMP_MAX corresponds to the maximum number of
             // unique temporary file names, which can be produced
             // with the tmpnam() function. The value of
             // TMP_MAX may not be smaller than 25.
```

# Included functions

```
clearerr    // remove error condition from stream
fclose      // close stream
feof        // tests stream at end of file
ferror      // tests stream on errors
fflush      // empties buffer of a streams
fgetc       // reads characters from a stream
fgetpos     // determines the position pointer of a stream
fgets       // reads a line of a stream
fopen       // opens a stream
fprintf     // formatted output to a stream
fputc       // writes a character in a stream
fputs       // writes a string in a stream
fread       // reads data from a stream
freopen     // re-opens a stream
fscanf      // reads formatted from stream
fseek       // re-positions file pointer
fsetpos     // re-positions file pointer
ftell       // reads position of file pointer
fwrite      // writes unformatted data to a stream
getc        // reads characters from a stream
getchar     // reads characters from the stdin stream
gets        // reads string from stdin
perror      // writes error message to stdout
printf      // formatted ausgabe an stdout
putc        // writes characters to a stream
putchar     // writes characters to the stdout stream
puts        // writes character strings to the stdout stream
remove      // deletes a file
rename      // renames a file
rewind      // positions file pointer at the start of the stream
scanf       // formatted input of stdin
setbuf      // modify stream buffering
setvbuf     // modify stream buffering and buffer size
sprintf     // formatted output to a string
sscanf      // formatted input from a string
tmpfile     // create temporary file
tmpnam      // create temporary file names
ungetc      // send character back to stream
vfprintf    // formatted output to stream
vprintf     // formatted output to stdout
vsprintf    // formatted output in string
```

# Reference

See Practice section, category input and output.

# stdlib.h

## Description

Conglomeration of frequently used library functions, to which amongst others belong the dynamic memory management and the process control routines.

## Included macros and type definitions

```
div_t          // div_t is a structure returned by the div()
               // function. The structure element quot contains
               // the quotients, and rem the remainder of the
               // division
EXIT_FAILURE   // status code which can be used with the library
               // function exit() to indicate that the program
               // ended with an error
EXIT_SUCCESS   // status code which can be used with the library
               // function exit() to indicated that the program
               // ended successfully
ldiv_t         // as div_t for the function ldiv()
MB_CUR_MAX     // this macro contains the maximum number of bytes
               // per character in the current characeter set
NULL           // value of the NULL pointer
RAND_MAX       // contains the largest pseudo random number
               // which can be returned by the rand() function
size_t         // unsigned integer type used by sizeof as a
               // result type
wchar_t        // character type for wide character sets
               // (16 to 32 bits)
```

## Included functions

```
abort     // ends program immediately
abs       // determines absolute value of an integer (overload
          // for long int, float and long double in c++)
atexit    // registers function which should be executed at
          // the end of a program
atof      // converts string into a floating point number
atoi      // converts string into an integer
atol      // converts string into long int
bsearch   // execute binary search
calloc    // allocate and intialise memory
div       // execute integer division (overload for long in c++)
exit      // end program
free      // release dynamically requested memory
getenv    // read entry in program environment
labs      // determine absolute value of a number of the long int
          // type
ldiv      // integer division with numbers of the long int type
          // (overload for long in c++)
```

```
malloc      // request memory
mblen       // determine length of multi-byte character
mbstowcs    // convert character string with characters consisting
            // of several bytes into wide character string
mbtowc      // convert characters consisting of several bytes into
            // wide characters
qsort       // execute quicksort
rand        // generate pseudo random number
realloc     // re-assign memory block
srand       // generate pseudo random number
strtod      // convert string to floating point number (double type)
strtol      // convert string to long int
strtoul     // convert string to unsigned long
system      // stop program and execute other program
wcstombs    // convert character string with wide characters to
            // multi-byte string
wctomb      // convert wide characters to multi-byte characters
```

## References

See Practice section, category pointers and dynamic memory management; others, random numbers.

# string.h

## Description

Contains the functions for the manipulation of strings.

## Important elements

```
NULL        // value of NULL pointer
size_t      // unsigned integer type used by sizeof as
            // result type
memchr      // searches a memory area for the first occurrence
            // of a character
memcmp      // compares two memory areas
memcpy      // copies number of characters from one memory area to
            // another
memmove     // copies number of characters from one memory area to
            // another, which may overlap with the original area
memset      // initialises a memory area with a character
strcat      // adds one character string to another
strchr      // determines pointer on first occurrence of a
            // character in a string
strcmp      // compares two character strings
strcoll     // compares two character strings
```

```
strcpy       // copies one string into another
strcspn      // searches character strings for characters not
             // contained in other character strings
strerror     // translates an error number in a character string
strlen       // determines the length of a character string
strncat      // adds n characters of a character string to another
strncmp      // compares one string with part of another string
strncpy      // copies n characters of a string into another
strpbrk      // searches for the first occurrence of any character
             // in a specified character string
strrchr      // determines pointer on the last occurrence of
             // a character in a character string
strspn       // determines the index of the first character in a
             // character string which does not belong to the
             // character set of a second character string
strstr       // determines the first occurrence of a character
             // string inside another string
strtok       // searches for next basic symbol in a character string
strxfrm      // converts a string in view of country-specific
             // conditions
```

## Example

```c
#include <stdio.h>
#include <stdlib.h>
#include <string.h>
int main(int argc, char** argv)
  {
  char str[3][21] = {"String1", "String2", "String3"};
  char *p_str;
  int bytes;

  // Linking strings
  // determining memory area
  bytes = (strlen(str[0]) + strlen(str[1]) +
          strlen(str[2]) + 1)*sizeof(char);
  // Allocating memory
  p_str = (char*) malloc(bytes);
  strcpy(p_str,str[0]);
  strcat(p_str,str[1]);
  strcat(p_str,str[2]);
  printf("String = %s contains %d bytes\n",p_str,bytes);
  free(p_str);
  return 0;
  }
```

## Reference

See Practice section, category strings.

# time.h

## Description

Contains the data types `time_t` and `clock_t` as well as the data structure `tm` and general time functions.

## Application

For timekeeping it is usual to have the function `time()`return the start and stop time of as values of the data types `time_t`. The difference can be calculated by the function `difftime()`.

To query the time and/or date, for example, the function `asc-time()`can be used. To convert the date into a string which can be output the function `strftime()`is used.

## Included macros and type definitions

```
clock_t          // clock_t is the data type returned for the
                 // clock()function
CLOCKS_PER_SEC   // CLOCKS_PER_SEC contains the number of ticks per
                 // second. A tick is the measure with which the
                 // time of the clock() function is measured.
NULL             // value of the NULL pointer
size_t           // unsigned integer used as result type of sizeof
time_t           // the time_t type is an arithmetical type to
                 // receive time instructions
tm               // the tm structure contains all elements to store
                 // time and date information. The pattern is used
                 // by the localtime() and gmtime() functions
```

## Included functions

```
asctime    // converts s time saved as structure into a
           // character string
clock      // determines how many ticks are required from the
           // start of the called process
ctime      // converts a number of time_t type into a character
           // string
difftime   // determines the difference between the two times
gmtime     // calculates Greenwich Mean Time (GMT)
           // from local time and the time difference defined
localtime  // converts a time value of time_t type into local time
mktime     // converts time from structure into calendar time
strftime   // formats the time according to country-specific
           // conditions
time       // returns the current time to a variable of time_t type
```

## Example

```
#include <stdio.h>
#include <stdlib.h>
#include <time.h>
int main(int argc, char** argv)
  {
  time_t start, finish;
  char input[100];
  int result;
  start = time(NULL);
  puts("How many are 7 * 23: \n");
  fgets(input,100,stdin);
  sscanf(input,"%d\n",&result);
  ende = time(NULL);
  printf("You have required %d sec. \n",(int) difftime(finish,start));
  if(result == 161)
    puts("The solution is correct \n");
    else
    printf("The correct answer is 161 (not %d)\n", result);
  return 0;
  }
```

## References

See Practice section, category internationalisation and localisation, local environment.


# wchar.h

## Description

Contains the functions for the processing of wide characters and multi-byte strings (including input and output).

## Included macros and type definitions

```
mbstate_t    // type definition where information about the
             // conversion of multibyte characters into wide
             // characters and vice versa is stored
NULL         // value of the NULL pointer
size_t       // unsigned integer type; result type of sizeof
tm           // structure to store time and date information,
             // see functions localtime() and gmtime()
wchar_t      // character type for unsigned character set
             // (16 / 32 bits)
WCHAR_MAX    // WCHAR_MAX contains the largest value of the wchar_t
             // type
```

```
WCHAR_MIN    // WCHAR_MIN contains the smallest value of the wchar_t
             // type
WEOF         // constant which indicates the end of a file
wint_t       // integer type for the coding of characters from
             // extended characters sets
```

## Included functions

```
btowc        // converts a 1 multibyte character into a
             // wide character
fgetwc       // reads characters from a stream
fgetws       // reads a line from a stream
fputwc       // writes a character in a stream
fputws       // writes a string in a stream
fwide        // can set up a stream for an additional byte or
             // wide character
fwprintf     // formatted output on stdout
fwscanf      // reads formatted from the stream
getwc        // reads character from the stream
getwchar     // reads character from stdin stream
mbrlen       // determines the length of a multibyte character
mbrtowc      // converts multibyte characters into wide characters
mbsinit      // determines if its argument indicates an initial
             // conversion mode
mbsrtowcs    // converts multibyte character string into wide
             // character strings
putwc        // writes wide characters in stream
putwchar     // writes wide characters in stdout stream
swprintf     // formatted output in a string
swscanf      // formatted input from a string
ungetwc      // sends character back to a stream
vfwprintf    // formatted output to a stream
vswprintf    // formatted output in a string
vwprintf     // formatted output to stdout
wcrtomb      // converts wide characters into multibyte characters
wcscat       // adds a character string to another one
wcschr       // determines the pointer to the first occurrence of
             // a character in a string
wcscmp       // compares two character strings
wcscoll      // compares two character strings
wcscpy       // copies a string into another
wcscspn      // searches for characters in a character string which
             // are not contained in another character string
wcsftime     // formatted time according to country-specific
             // conditions
wcslen       // determines the length of a character string
wcsncat      // adds n characters of a character string to another
wcsncmp      // compares a string with a part of another string
wcsncpy      // copies n characters of a string in another
wcspbrk      // searches for the first occurence of any character
             // from a character string in another string
```

```
wcsrchr       // determines a pointer to the last occurence of a
              // character string in another string
wcsrtombs     // converts a wide character string into a multibyte
              // string
wcsspn        // yields the index of the first character in a
              // character string which does not belong to the
              // character set of another character string
wcsstr        // determines the first occurrence of a character
              // string in a second character string
wcstod        // converts a string into a floating-point number
              // (double type)
wcstok        // searches for the next basic symbol in a character
              // string
wcstol        // converts a string to long int
wcstoul       // converts a string to unsigned long int
wcsxfrm       // converts a string in view of country specific
              // conditions
wctob         // converts a character into a 1 multibyte character
wmemchr       // searches for the first occurrence of a character
              // in a memory area
wmemcmp       // compares two memory areas
wmemcpy       // copies the number character of a memory area into
              // another
wmemmove      // copies from one memory area into another, which
              // should overlap with the original area
wmemset       // initialies a memory area with a character
wprintf       // formatted input to stream stdout
wscanf        // formatted input from stream stdin
```

## References
See Practice section, category internationalisation and localisation, wide characters.

# wctype.h

## Description
Contains the functions for the classification and conversion of wide characters, as well as a few auxiliary types.

## Included elements
```
wctrans_t     // auxiliary type for character mapping
wctype_t      // auxiliary type for character classification
WEOF          // constant which indicates the end of a file
wint_t        // integer type for the coding of characters from
              // wide character sets
```

```
iswalnum       // tests if a character is a number or a letter
iswalpha       // tests if a character is a letter
iswcntrl       // tests if a character is a control character
iswctype       // tests if a character belongs to a specific class.
               // The class is specified via a call of wctype()
iswdigit       // tests if a character is a number
iswgraph       // tests if a character is printable (spaces excepted)
iswlower       // tests if a character is a lower case letter
iswprint       // tests if a character is printable
iswpunct       // tests if a character is a punctuation mark
iswspace       // tests if a character is a space character
iswupper       // tests if a character is an upper case letter
iswxdigit      // tests if a character is a hexadecimal digit
towctrans      // converts a wide character
towlower       // converts upper case to lower case letters
towupper       // converts lower case to upper case letters
wctrans        // determines a mapping of a wide character set
               // to another set (according to LC_TYPE)
wctype         // used together with iswctype(); allows a class
               // to be identified on the basis of a string
```

# The functions of the C standard library

## abort                                                    <stdlib.h>

Terminates a process

### Description

The function abort() causes a non-normal program stop, which means that in contrast to the function exit() it is not ensured that file buffers are emptied, open streams are closed, and temporary files produced with tmpfile() are removed. Moreover, the program termination routines which have been established with atexit() are not called. Instead, the function raise() is called with the constant SIGABRT as an argument, for which a signal processing routine may be established.

### Parameters

void abort(void);

### Related functions

assert(), atexit(), exit(), raise()

## abs <stdlib.h>

Calculates the absolute value

### Description

The function `abs()` returns the amount of its integer argument as a function value. The amount of a number is its distance to zero.

### Parameters

`int abs(int n);`

- **Return value.** Amount of the argument n.

### Related functions

`fabs()`, `labs()`

## acos <math.h>

Calculates the arc cosine

### Description

The function `acos()` calculates the arc cosine (inverse function of the cosine) for the passed argument.

### Parameters

`double acos(double number);`

- **number.** Argument, for which the arc cosine is calculated (has to lie between $-1.0$ and $1.0$)
- **Return value.** Arc cosine of the argument in the range [0, p].

### Related functions

`asin()`, `atan()`, `cos()`, `sin()`, `tan()`

## asctime <time.h>

Time in form of a string

### Description

The function `asctime()` converts the time information contained in the time structure `tm` into a string. The generated string has the following format (for locale "C"):

`Mon Jul 31 23:10:07 1989\n\0`

## Parameters
```
char *asctime (const struct tm *time);
```
- **Return value.** Pointer to the produced string.

## Related functions
```
ctime(), gmtime(), localtime(), setlocale()
```

## asin                                                        <math.h>
Calculates the arc sine

## Description
The function `asin()` calculates the arc sine (inverse function of the sine) for the passed argument.

## Parameters
```
double asin(double number);
```
- **number.** Argument for which the arc sine is calculated (has to lie between −1.0 and 1.0)
- **Return value.** Arc sine of the argument in the range [−p/2, + p/2].

## Related functions
```
acos(), atan(), cos(), sin(), tan()
```

## assert                                                      <assert.h>
Outputs a diagnostic message

## Description
The `assert` macro checks the value of a passed expression. If this evaluation returns the result false (0), `assert()` issues a diagnostic message on the standard error stream `stderr` and subsequently calls the `abort()` function to terminate the program. The message of `assert` contains the file name and the line number in which the macro has been called. The information is extracted from the constants `__FILE__` and `__LINE__`. By setting the NDEBUG switch (`#define NDEBUG`) further calls to `assert` can be suppressed.

## Parameters
```
void assert(int expr);
```
- **expr.** The expression to be checked.

## Related functions

abort(), exit(), raise(), signal()

## atan, atan2                                                   <math.h>

Calculates the arc tangent

## Description

The function atan() calculates the arc tangent of a number. atan2() calculates the arc tangent of number1/number2.

## Parameters

double atan(double number);
double atan2(double number1, double number2);

- **Return value.** atan() returns the arc tangent of number in the area [–p/2, + p/2], atan2() returns the arc tangent of number1/number2 in the area [–p, + p].

## Related functions

acos(), asin(), cos(), sin(), tan()

## atexit                                                        <stdlib.h>

Calls a function at exit

## Description

With atexit() you can register a function which you want to be called up at the end of the program. With it the processing of required clearing operations can be established at the end of a program.

The functions which have been registered with atexit() are called when the program is terminated with exit() or when the return statement is executed from main(). If several functions have been registered through sequential calls of atexit(), they are called in the reverse order of their registration.

## Parameters

int atexit(void (*func)(void));

- **Return value.** The function atexit() returns a zero, if the passed function is registered.

## Related functions

abort(), exit()

## atof                                    <stdlib.h>
Conversion: string to `double`

### Description
The function `atof()` (ascii to float) converts a string, pointed to by `string`, into a floating-point number of double precision and returns this number as the function value. Leading spaces and tabulators are skipped, and the conversion is terminated at the first character which is not recognised as a digit.

### Parameters
`double atof(const char *string);`
- **Return value.** Corresponding `double` value.

### Related functions
`atoi()`, `atol()`, `strtod()`

## atoi                                    <stdlib.h>
Conversion: string to `int`

### Description
The function `atoi()` (ascii to int) converts the passed string into a number of the data type `int`. Leading space characters are skipped. At the first character which cannot be identified as a digit the conversion is terminated and the number which has been determined so far is returned.

### Parameters
`int atoi(const char *string);`
- **Return value.** Corresponding `int` value or zero.

### Related functions
`atof()`, `atol()`, `strtod()`, `strtol()`

## atol                                    <stdlib.h>
Conversion: string to `long`

### Description
The function `atol()` (ascii to long) converts the passed string into a number of the data type `long`. Leading space characters are skipped. At the first character which cannot be identified as a digit the conversion is terminated and the determined number is returned.

## Parameters

```
long atol(const char *string);
```

- **Return value.** Corresponding `long` value or zero.

## Related functions

```
atof(), atoi(), strtod(), strtol()
```

## bsearch                                                    <stdlib.h>

Binary search

## Description

The function `bsearch()` carries out a binary search in a sorted data field. The comparison, which is required in the search, is carried out by a function whose address is passed to `bsearch()`. This function has to compare two elements with each other and return the following values to `bsearch()`:

| | |
|---|---|
| < 0 | The first element is smaller than the second. |
| 0 | Both elements are identical. |
| > 0 | The first element is greater than the second. |

## Parameters

```
void *bsearch (const void *searchobj, const void *basis,
    size_t number, size_t width,
    int (*cmp) (const void *elem1, const void *elem2));
```

- **searchobj.** Object for which a correspondence is searched (This is passed as the first element to `vgl()`).
- **basis.** Pointer to the start of a field which is to be searched.
- **number.** Number of the elements in a field.
- **width.** Size of each element in bytes.
- **cmp.** Pointer to a function which compares two elements of the type `const void*`.
- **Return value.** If the search is successful, the function returns a pointer to the first element in the field which meets the search criterion. If no suitable element could be found, a ZERO pointer is returned.

## Warning

If the field has not been sorted yet, the function qsort() can be called up beforehand.

## Related function

qsort()

See Practice section, category Data and data types, Arrays of structures.

## btowc                                                                <wchar.h>

Converts a 1-byte character

## Description

Converts a 1 multi-byte character into a wide character.

## Parameters

wint_t btowc(int c);

- **Return value.** Wide-character representation of the passed character. WEOF, if the chracter has not been a valid 1 multi-byte character in the initial conversion status or EOF.

## Related function

wctob()

## calloc                                                                <stdlib.h>

Allocates memory

## Description

With calloc() memory can be established for a field of number elements of the size sighz and initialised with zeros.

## Parameters

void *calloc(size_t number, size_t sighz);

- **Return value.** If the memory request could be met, the function returns a pointer to the allocated memory area, otherwise it returns a ZERO pointer.

## Related functions

malloc(), realloc()

## ceil <math.h>

Rounding function

### Description

The function `ceil()` calculates the smallest integer value which is greater or equal to its `double` argument, and returns it.

### Parameters

`double ceil(double number);`

- **Return value.** Rounded value.

### Related functions

`floor(), fmod()`

## clearerr <stdio.h>

Reset error display

### Description

The function resets the error and file-end flag for a stream.

### Parameters

`void clearerr(FILE *stream);`

### Related functions

`feof(), ferror()`

## clock <time.h>

Duration of the calling process

### Description

The function returns the used processor time of the calling process as a value of the type `clock_t`. The constant `CLOCKS_PER_SEC` corresponds to the number of ticks per second. When the value returned by `clock()` is divided by the constant `CLOCKS_PER_SEC`, the result states the processor time in seconds.

### Parameters

`clock_t clock(void);`

- **Return value.** Returns the processor time that has passed since an implementation-specific point in time. If the number of ticks cannot be determined, the value –1 is returned.

## Related functions
difftime(), time()

### cos, cosh                                                          <math.h>
Calculates the cosine

## Description
The functions cos() and cosh() calculate the cosine of the passed argument (angle in radian measure) and are defined for all real numbers.

## Parameters
double cos(double number);
double cosh(double number);

- **Return value.** cos() returns the cosine of the argument in the range [–1, 1]. cosh() returns the hyperbolic cosine of the argument in the range [1, 8].

## Warning
The hyperbolic cosine rises very quickly.

## Related functions
asin(), atan(), atan2(), sin(), sinh()

See example for header file math.h

### ctime                                                              <time.h>
Time as a character string

## Description
The function ctime() converts the calendar time, which has been passed into a string as a variable of the type time_t. The generated string possesses the locally used format, for example:

Fri Jun 30 23:10:07 1988\n\0     // for the C-Locale

Corresponds to the call-up asctime(localtime(ptr_time));.

## Parameters
char * ctime(const time_t *ptr_time);

- **Return value.** Pointer to the generated string.

## Related functions
asctime(), gmtime(), localtime()

## difftime <time.h>

Difference between two points in time

### Description

The function difftime() dtermines the difference between two points in time of the type time_t and returns the result in seconds.

### Parameters

double difftime(time_t neuetime, time_t altetime);

- **Return value.** Difference between the two points in time.

### Related functions

asctime(), ctime(), localtime(), time()

See example for header file time.h

## div <stdlib.h>

Quotient and remainder of two integer numbers

### Description

The function div() divides an integer (number1) by a second integer (number2) and returns the result as a variable of the structure type div_t.

### Parameters

div_t div(int number1, int number2);

- **Return value.** The function returns a variable of the type div_t, in which the quotient (.quot) and the division remainder (.rem) are recorded.

### Related function

ldiv()

## exit <stdlib.h>

Terminates a process

### Description

The function exit() terminates a program after the functions which have been registered with atexit() have been processed in the inverse order of their registration, the stream buffer has been emptied, open files have been closed, and temporary files, which have been generated with tmpfile(), have been removed.

The argument `status` specifies a status code (for example the ANSI C constants `EXIT_FAILURE` or `EXIT_SUCCESS`), which is passed to the program which is calling. Under MS-DOS this value can be queried in batch files with IF ERRORLEVEL

## Parameters

```
void exit(int status);
```

## Related functions

```
abort(), atexit(), system()
```

## exp <math.h>

Calculates the exponential function

## Description

The function `exp()` calculates the exponential function of its argument. It is the counterpart of the function `log()`.

## Parameters

```
double exp(double number);
```

- **Return value.** When successful, the function returns the exponential value ($e$^number), `HUGE_VAL` in case of a result value which is too high.

## Related functions

```
log(), log10(), pow()
```

See example for header file math.h

## fabs <math.h>

Calculates the absolute value of a floating point number

## Description

The function `fabs()` calculates the amount of a floating-point number and returns it.

## Parameters

```
double fabs(double number);
```

- **Return value.** Amount of the argument.

## Related functions

```
abs(), ceil(), floor(), fmod(), labs()
```

## fclose

Cloases a stream

### Description

The function closes a stream whose pointer has been passed to it as an argument. The buffer linked to the stream is emptied, the data that is in the buffer is written to a file, and read data that is in the buffer is deleted.

### Parameters

```
int fclose(FILE *stream);
```

- **Return value.** When successful the function returns a zero, and otherwise EOF.

### Related functions

```
fflush(), setbuf(), setvbuf()
```

See Practice section, category input and output, text files in C.

## feof <stdio.h>

Checks a stream for end of file

### Description

The function feof() checks whether the file-end flag of the stream, whose pointer has been passed, is set.

### Parameters

```
int feof(FILE *stream);
```

- **Return value.** If the current position is the end of the file, a value which does not equal zero is returned, and otherwise it returns zero.

### Related functions

```
ferror(), perror()
```

See Practice section, category input and output, text files in C.

## ferror <stdio.h>

Checks a stream for errors

### Description

The function ferror() checks whether a read or write error has occurred for the data stream stream. Corresponding error flags are not reset (this can be dome by calling up rewind() or closing the stream).

## Parameters

```
int ferror(FILE *stream);
```

- **Return value.** In case of an error, a value not equal to zero, otherwise it returns zero.

## Related functions

```
feof(), fopen(), perror(), rewind()
```

## fflush                                                        <stdio.h>

Empties a stream

### Description

This function empties the buffer which is linked to the passed stream. If it is an output stream, the buffered data are written into the corresponding file. According to ANSI C the behaviour is undefined, if it is an input buffer. Most compilers only empty the buffer.

## Parameters

```
int fflush(FILE *stream);
```

- **Return value.** When successful, a zero is returned, and otherwise EOF.

## Related functions

```
fclose(), setbuf(), setvbuf()
```

See Practice section, category input and output, formatted input and output in C.

## fgetc, fgetwc                                        <stdio.h><wchar.h>

Reads a character from a stream

### Description

The function reads a character from the data stream, to which stream points, and moves the file pointer forward.

## Parameters

```
int fgetc(FILE *stream);
wint_t fgetwc(FILE *stream);
```

- **Return value.** The function returns the read character as int value withour sign; EOF (WEOF) can signify an error or the end of the file.

## Related functions

```
gets(), fputc(), ungetc()
```

See Practice section, category input and output, text files in C.

## fgetpos <stdio.h>

Fetches a stream position specification

### Description

The `fgetpos()` function copies the value of the stream position pointer into the variable pointed to by `pos`. The data type of `pos` is `fpos_t`, which is defined in the header file `<stdio.h>`.

### Parameters

```
int fgetpos(FILE *stream, fpos_t *pos);
```
• **Return value.** In case of an error, a value not equal to zero, otherwise zero.

### Related functions

`fsetpos()`, `ftell()`

## fgets, fgetws <stdio.h><wchar.h>

Reads a string from a stream

### Description

The function keeps reading characters from `stream` until either `num-1` characters have been read, the line feed character (\n) has been read, or the end of file has been reached. The function automatically terminates the read string by postfixing the zero termination character (\0).

### Parameters

```
char *fgets(char *chstring, int num, FILE *stream);
wchar_t *fgetws(wchar_t *chstring, int num, FILE *stream);
```
• **Return value.** When successful the function returns a pointer to `chstring`, in case of an error or a premature file end a zero pointer.

### Related functions

`fputs()`, `gets()`, `puts()`

See Practice section, category input and output, formatted input and output in C.

## floor <math.h>

Rounding down

## Description

The function floor() calculates the highest possible integer value, which is smaller/equal to the argument, and returns it.

## Parameters

double floor(double number);

- **Return value**. Rounded down value for number.

## Related functions

ceil()

## fmod                                                          <math.h>

Calculates remainder of a floating point division

## Description

The function fmod() divides x by y and returns the remainder of the division.

## Parameters

double fmod(double x, double y);

- **Return value**. Floating-point remainder of the division.

## Related functions

ceil(), fabs(), floor(), modf()

## fopen                                                         <stdio.h>

Opening a file

## Description

The function fopen() opens a file and initialises the stream which is linked to the file. The argument modus determines in which mode the file is to be opened.

| Modus | Description |
| --- | --- |
| r | Open for reading. |
| w | Open for writing (file is overwritten or, if required, created). |
| a | Open for writing at the file end (file is created, if required). |
| r+ | Open for reading and writing, file must exist. |
| w+ | Open empty file for reading and writing (file is overwritten or, if required, created). |
| a+ | Open for reading and attaching (file is created, if required). |

## Parameters

```
FILE *fopen(const char *file, const char *modus);
```

- **Return value.** The function returns a pointer to a structure of the type FILE. This pointer is then passed as an argument to the other functions that are to operate on the stream. If the file cannot be opened, a zero pointer is returned.

## Warning

The mode specification can be opened explicitly in the text or binary mode by attaching t or b (concerns the coding of the line break).

Data streams which have been opened for reading and writing have to carry out fflush() or a function for the positioning of the file pointer (fseek(), rewind()), before it is possible to switch between reading and writing.

## Related functions

```
fclose(), ferror(), freopen()
```

## fprintf, fwprintf                                    <stdio.h><wchar.h>

Formatted output to a stream

### Description

The function generates a string of its arguments that is written into the data stream to which stream points. The formatting of the string occurs as described for printf().

### Parameters

```
int fprintf(FILE *stream, const char *format...);
int fwprintf(FILE *stream, const wchar_t *format...);
```

- **stream.** Pointer to FILE structure of the output stream.
- **format.** Format string (see printf()).
- ... . variable number of arguments.
- **Return value.** The function returns the number of the outputted characters. In case of an error a negative value is returned (mostly EOF (WEOF)).

## Related functions

```
fscanf(), fputs(), fwrite(), printf()
```

See Practice section, category input and output, text files in C.

## fputc, fputwc                                         <stdio.h><wchar.h>

Outputs a character to a stream

## Description
The function outputs a single character to a stream.

## Parameters
```
int fputc(int charac, FILE *stream);
wint_t fputwc(wchar_t charac, FILE *stream);
```
- **Return value.** The function returns the written character. If the return value is EOF (WEOF), an error has occurred.

## Related functions
```
fgetc(), fgets(), putc(), ungetc()
```

### fputs, fputws                                      <stdio.h><wchar.h>
Writes a character string to a stream

## Description
The function writes a string to a stream. The zero termination character that terminates the string is not output.

## Parameters
```
int fputs(const char *chstring, FILE *stream);
int fputws(const wchar_t *chstring, FILE *stream);
```
- **Return value.** When successful the function returns a non-negative value. If the return value is EOF (WEOF), an error has occurred.

## Related functions
```
fputc(), fprintf(), putc(), putchar(), getc(), gets()
```

### fread                                                      <stdio.h>
Reads data from a stream

## Description
For binary files. The function `fread()` reads number of elements of the sighz (in bytes) from a stream after buffer. With it it is possible to read, for example, structures which are contained in the file into a corresponding field of structures.

## Parameters
```
size_t fread (void *buffer, size_t sighz,
                        size_t number, FILE *stream);
```

- **Return value.** Number of the data elements which have been read without error.

## Related functions

fopen(), fwrite(), printf(), scanf()

See Practice section, category input and output, Binary files in C.

## free <stdlib.h>

Frees memory

## Description

The function frees up the memory which has been requested previously with one of the functions malloc(), calloc() or realloc().

## Parameters

void free(void *addr);

## Tip

The function can also be passed a pointer to zero, in which case, no code is executed.

## Related functions

malloc(), calloc(), realloc()

See Practice section, category pointer and dynamic memory management, memory allocation with malloc().

## freopen <stdio.h>

Reassigns a file pointer

## Description

The function closes the file which is linked to the passed data stream stream. Subsequently the file which has been specified through the argument pfad is assigned with the specified access rights to the stream (see fopen()). This function is usually used to carry out a redirection of the standard streams (stdin, stdout, stderr) in files.

## Parameters

FILE *freopen(const char *pfad, const char *modus, FILE *stream);

- **Return value.** When successful the function returns a pointer to the newly opened file, and when unsuccessful a zero pointer.

## Related functions

fopen(), fclose()

## frexp                                                                <math.h>

Normalises a floating point number

## Description

The function frexp() reduces a floating-point number into a normalised number and its exponent to the base 2. The number is greater /equal to 0.5 and smaller than 1.

## Parameters

double frexp(double number, int *exp);

- **Return value.** The function returns the matissa. The exponent is written into the variable to which *exp points.

## Related functions

exp(), ldexp()

## fscanf, fwscanf                                         <stdio.h><wchar.h>

Formatted reading from a stream

## Description

This function reads data formatted from the data stream stream. It uses the argument format (see scanf()) to convert the read characters into the correct data types. The read data are then written to memory positions, which are passed with the other function arguments. For each further function argument a type identifier has to be specified in the format string.

## Parameters

int fscanf(FILE *stream, const char *format,...);
int fwscanf(FILE *stream, const wchar_t *format,...);

- **stream.** Pointer to FILE structure of the input stream.
- **format.** Format string (see printf()).
- **....** variable number of arguments.
- **Return value.** The function returns the number of the successfully converted and assigned fields. If the return value is EOF, it has attempted to read the file end.

## Related functions

fprintf(), scanf(), sscanf()

## fseek             \<stdio.h\>

Positions the file pointer

### Description

The position moves the file pointer of a stream to a specific point.

## Parameters

int fseek(FILE *stream, long offset, int urprung);

- **offset.** Defines the distance in bytes, which the file pointer is to be moved from the point that is coded in the argument ursprung. For binary files this is the number of characters which the file pointer is to move (can also be negative), for text files the value zero or ftell() should have been returned, where the origin must equal SEEK_SET.

- **ursprung.** One of three constants which serve as a reference for the offset:

| | |
|---|---|
| SEEK_CUR | From the current position. |
| SEEK_END | From the end of the file. |
| SEEK_SET | From the start of the file. |

- **Return value.** The function returns a zero, if the file pointer could be moved, and otherwise a value other than zero.

## Related functions

ftell(), rewind()

See Practice section, category input and output, random access in C.

## fsetpos             \<stdio.h\>

Determines the position display

### Description

With the function fsetpos() you can reset the position display of the stream to a value, which has , for example, been determined through a call-up of the function fgetpos().

## Parameters

int fsetpos(FILE *stream, const fpos_t *pos);

- **pos.** Position to which the position pointer is to be set (saved return value of the function `fgetpos()`).
- **Return value.** When successful the function returns a zero, and in case of an error a value other than zero.

## Related functions
`fseek()`, `fgetpos()`

## ftell <stdio.h>
Determines the stream pointer position

## Description
The function `ftell()` returns the current value of the position pointer, which is linked to the argument stream.

## Parameters
`long ftell(FILE *stream);`
- **Return value.** The function returns the current position. The return value depends on whether it is a binary or a text file. For a binary file the function returns the number of bytes from the beginning of the file to the current position. For a text file the value is only suitable to be passed to `fseek()`. In case of an error the return value is −1L.

## Related functions
`fgetpos()`, `fseek()`, `rewind()`

## fwide <wchar.h>
Stream orientation

## Description
Determines and possibly changes the orientation of a a stream. If `modus` =0 the orientation is not changed, if `modus` >0 it attempts to create a wide character orientation, if modus <0 it attempts to produce a byte orientation.

## Parameters
`int fwide (FILE *stream, int modus);`
- **Return value.** A value >0 indicates that the stream is wide character-oriented, a value <0 indicates that the stream is byte-oriented.

## Related functions

```
fgetwc(), fgetws(), fwscanf(), getwc(), fputwc(), wscanf(), fwprintf(),
fputwc(), fputws(), putwc(), wprintf()
```

## fwrite                                                      <stdio.h>

Writes to a stream

## Description

For binary files. The function fwrite() writes the number of data elements of the size sighz (in bytes) from the memory area to which buffer refers into the data stream stream. After the writing process the stream position pointer is updated.

## Parameters

```
size_t fwrite (const void *buffer, size_t sighz,
                        size_t number, FILE *stream);
```

- **Return value.** Number of the data elements written.

## Related functions

```
fread(), write()
```

See Practice section, category input and output, binary files in C.

## getc, getwc, getchar, getwchar                          <stdio.h><wchar.h>

Reads one character

## Description

The functions getc() and getwc() read a from a stream, and getchar() and getwchar() read a character from the stream stdin. The macro getchar() corresponds to the call-up getc(stdin), and the macro getwchar() to the call-up getwc(stdin).

## Parameters

```
int getc(FILE *stream);
wint_t getwc(FILE *stream);
int getchar(void);
wint_t getwchar(void);
```

- **Return value.** The functions return the read character; EOF (WEOF) is returned when the file end is reached or when an error occurs.

## Related functions

```
fgetc(), putc(), putchar(), ungetc()
```

## getenv <stdlib.h>

Gets an environment value

## Description

The function getenv() examines the operation system-specific environment of a program. It searches for an entry, which is identical to the argument varname, and returns, when successful, a pointer to the corresponding environment variable.

## Parameters

char *getenv(const char *varname);

- **varname.** Searched for environment variable.

- **Return value.** Returns a pointer to the definition of the environment variable, or a zero pointer if the variable has not been defined.

## Related functions

setlocale(), localeconv()

## gets <stdio.h>

Reads a line from stdin

## Description

The function gets() reads a string from the standard input stream and stores it at the address which has been passed with str. The reading is terminated if the function detects the line feed character or EOF. The line feed character is removed and replaced with the zero termination character (\0), with which the end of the string is marked.

## Parameters

char *gets(char *str);

- **Return value.** Pointer to the read string; in case of an error this is a zero pointer.

## Warning

Note that the memory area to which str points has to be large enough to accommodate the string, as it otherwise overwrites the memory.

## Related functions

fgets(), fputs(), puts()

## gmtime                                                    <time.h>

Converts a time value into a structure

### Description

The function gmtime() expects the address of a variable of the type time_t as the argument. The calendar time which has been saved in this variable (usually received through calling up the function time()), is converted into Greenwich Mean Time by the function and stored in the structure tm.

### Parameters

```
struct tm *gmtime(const time_t *time);
```

- **Return value.** The function returns a pointer to a structure of the type tm, in which the date and the time are stored. In case of an error the function returns a zero pointer.

### Related functions

```
asctime(), ctime(), localtime(), time()
```

## is..., isw..                                    <ctype.h><wctype.h>

Character classification

### Description

The functions from the is...() group check the membership of a character to particular character groups. The corresponding isw..() functions provide the same functionality for wide characters.

```
Name        Tests for
isalnum     // letters and digits (isalpha || isdigit)
isalpha     // letters (A-Z, a-z) (isupper || islower)
iscntrl     // control characters (0x00-0x1f or 0x7F).
isdigit     // digits (0-9).
isgraph     // printable character (0x21-0x7E) (isprint
            // without isspace)
islower     // lower case letter (a-z).
isprint     // printable character (0x20-0x7E).
ispunct     // punctuation mark (isprint without isspace
            // and isalnum)
isspace     // white space (' ', '\f', '\n', '\r', '\t', '\v').
isupper     // upper case letter (A-Z).
isxdigit    // hexadecimal number (A-F, a-f, 0-9).
```

### Parameters

```
int is...(int charac);
int isw...(wint_t widecharac);
```

- **Return value.** The functions return a value equal to zero (true), if the passed character belongs to the class of characters that has been checked by the function.

## Related functions
localeconv(), setlocale()

## iswctype                                                   <wctype.h>
Determines the wide character class

## Description
Tests whether a character belongs to a particular class. The class is specified by calling wctype:

iswctype(wc, wctype("digit")) // = iswcdigit(wc)

## Parameters
int iswctype(wint_t wc, wctype_t description);
- **Return value.** Returns a value unequal to zero, if the wide-character character wc has the described characteristic.

## Related functions
wctype()

## labs                                                       <stdlib.h>
Determines the absolute value of a long number

## Description
The function determines the amount of a long integer and returns it. The amount of the number is its distance from zero.

## Parameters
long int labs(long int number);
- **Return value.** Amount of the argument.

## Related functions
abs(), fabs()

## ldexp                                          <math.h>
Calculates the exponential function

### Description
`ldexp` calculates the value of `number*2^exp`.

### Parameters
`double ldexp(double number, int exp);`
- **Return value.** Returns the value of `number*2^exp`; `HUGE_VAL` at overflow.

### Related functions
`log(), log10(), pow()`

## ldiv                                          <stdlib.h>
Quotient and remainder of two long numbers

### Description
The function `ldiv()` divides a long integer by another and returns the value in the form of a structure of the type `ldiv_t`:

### Parameters
`ldiv_t ldiv(long int number1, long int number2);`
- **Return value.** The function returns a structure of the type `ldiv_t`, which contains the quotient (`.quot`) and the division remainder (`.rem`).

### Related function
`div()`

## localeconv                                    <locale.h>
Locale setting of numeric formats

### Description
Through the function `localeconv()` local settings for the formatting of numeric values, in particular the representation of currency specifications, can be queried. The settings are stored in a `lconv` structure.

### Parameters
`struct lconv *localeconv(void);`
- **Return value.** Pointer to the filled structure `lconv`.

## Related functions

setlocale()

See example for header file locale.h

## localtime                                                                    \<time.h\>

Sets the clock to local time

## Description

The function converts the calendar time time into a structure of the type tm. Here, in contrast to the function gmtime(), the local time is taken into account.

## Parameters

struct tm *localtime(const time_t *time);

- **Return value.** Pointer to a structure of the type tm or a zero pointer if the time could not be interpreted.

## Related functions

asctime(), gmtime(), time()

## log, log10                                                                   \<math.h\>

Calculates the logarithm

## Description

The function log() calculates the natural logarithm of its arguments to the base e, while log10() calculates the logarithm of its arguments to the base 10.

## Parameters

double log(double x);
double log10(double x);

- **Return value.** The functions return the respective logarithm of $x$. As the logarithm is only defined greater than zero for positive values, EDOM is written into errno for values of $x < 0$; with 0 as argument HUGE_VAL is returned.

## Related functions

exp(), pow()

See example for header file math.h

## longjmp <setjmp.h>

Restores the program state

### Description

With the function `longjmp()` the environment is restored, which has been stored in the env array when `set-jmp()` was called-up. Afterwards the execution is not continued at the point at which `longjmp()` was called up, but where `setjmp()` has been called up.

### Parameters

```
void longjmp(jmp_buf env, int value);
```

### Warning

The function in which the preceding call-up of `setjmp()` occurred has to be active (on the stack) at the time of the jump through `longjmp()`.

### Related function

```
setjmp()
```

See example for header file setjmp.h

## malloc <stdlib.h>

Requests a block of memory

### Description

The function `malloc()` requests a memory block of the passed size. The pointer which is returned by the function has the type `*void` and has to be converted into the desired type.

### Parameters

```
void *malloc(size_t sighz);
```

- **Return value.** Void pointer to the allocated memory area or zero pointer if the memory could not be allocated.

### Related functions

```
calloc(), free(), realloc()
```

See Practice section, category pointer and dynamic location with `malloc()`.

## mblen, mbrlen <stdlib.h><wchar.h>

Length of a multibyte character

## Description

The function `mblen()` determines the length of a multi-byte character. The function `mbrlen()` determines after how many bytes the multi-byte character is complete. A maximum of n bytes are checked.

## Parameters

```
int mblen(const char *mb, size_t n);
size_t mbrlen(const char *mb, size_t n, mbstate_t *ps);
```

- **Return value.** The function `mblen()` returns the number of bytes of the multi-byte character mb. If it is not a valid multi-byte character, a negative value is returned. The function `mbrlen()` returns the number of bytes up to the end of the multibyte character mb. If it is not a valid multi-byte character or if an error occurs, a negative value is returned.

## Related functions

`mbstowcs()`, `mbtowc()`, `mbrtowc()`

## mbsinit                                                    <wchar.h>

Queries the conversion status

## Description

Determines whether the `mbstate_t` object to which the parameter refers describes an initial conversion status.

## Parameters

```
int mbsinit(const mbstate_t *ps);
```

- **Return value.** A value unequal to zero indicates that a zero pointer or a pointer to an initial conversion status has been passed; otherwise zero is returned.

## Related function

`mbstowcs()`

## mbstowcs,mbsrtowcs                                   <stdlib.h><wchar.h>

Converts a multibyte string

## Description

The function `mbstowcs()` converts the passed multi-byte string mb_string which begins in the initial shift status (the status in which the characters from the C character set are coded 1:1), into a field of elements of the `wchar_t` type. The function `mbsrtowcs()` converts a multibyte string which is in the conversion mode given by ps. A maximum of *n* wide-character characters are read.

## Parameters

```
size_t mbstowcs(wchar_t *wc, const char *mb_str, size_t n);
size_t mbsrtowcs(wchar_t *wc,const char *mb_str,size_t n,mbstate_t *ps);
```

- **Return value.** Returns the number of the converted elements (without a possible zero termination character (\0)). If invalid multibyte sequences occur, a negative value is returned.

## Related functions

```
mbstowcs(), mbtowc(), mbrtowc()
```

### mbtowc, mbrtowc                                          <stdlib.h><wchar.h>

Converts multibyte characters to wchar_t

## Description

Both functions convert the passed multibyte character mb_char into a wide character representation and store the result in wc. The function mbtowc() determines the number of bytes in the multibyte character, and the function mbrtowc() determines after how many bytes the multibyte character is complete. A maximum of *n* bytes are converted.

## Parameters

```
int mbtowc(wchar_t *wc, const char *mb_char, size_t n);
size_t mbrtowc(wchar_t *wc,const char *mb, size_t n, mbstate_t *ps);
```

- **Return value.** The function mbtowc() returns the number of bytes of the multibyte character mb. If it is not a valid multibyte character, a negative value is returned. The function mbrtowc() returns the number of bytes up to the end of the multibyte character mb. If it is not a valid multibyte character or if an error occurs, a negative value is returned.

## Related functions

```
mbstowcs(), mblen(), mbrtowc()
```

### memchr, wmemchr                                          <string.h><wchar.h>

Searches for characters

## Description

This function searches a memory area for the passed character. The search continues until either the character is found or the number of characters has been examined.

## Parameters

```
C:
void *memchr(const void *buffer, int charac, size_t number);
wchar_t *wmemchr(const wchar_t *buffer, wchar_t charac, size_t number);
C++:
const void *memchr(const void *buffer, int charac, size_t number);
const wchar_t *wmemchr(const wchar_t *buffer, wchar_t charac,
                       size_t number);
void *memchr(void *buffer, int charac, size_t number);
wchar_t *wmemchr(wchar_t *buffer, wchar_t charac, size_t number);
```

- **buffer.** Start address of the memory area which is to be searched.

- **charac.** The searched for character.

- **number.** Maximum number of characters to be checked.

- **Return value.** Pointer to the found character or zero pointer.

## Related functions

`memcmp()`, `memset()`, `memcpy()`

### memcmp, wmemcmp                                      <string.h><wchar.h>

Compares characters in memory

### Description

The function compares the content of `puf1` with that of `puf2`. The comparison is carried out until either a difference has been found or the number of characters passed with `number` has been checked.

### Parameters

```
int memcmp(const void *buf1, const void *buf2, size_t number);
int wmemcmp(const wchar_t *buf1, const wchar_t *buf2, size_t number);
```

- **Return value.** The function has three possible return values:

| negative | buf1 < buf2 |
|----------|-------------|
| 0 | buf1 == buf2 |
| positive | buf1 > buf2 |

## Related functions

`strcmp()`, `strncmp()`

### memcpy, wmemcpy                                      <string.h><wchar.h>

Copies characters to intermediate buffer

## Description

The function copies characters from one memory area into another. number of characters are copied. (The two memory areas must not overlap.)

## Parameters

```
void *memcpy(void *target, const void *source, size_t number);
wchar_t *wmemcpy(wchar_t *target, const wchar_t *source, size_t number);
```

- **Return value.** Pointer to target.

## Related functions

```
memchr(), memmove(), memset()
```

### memmove, wmemmove                                    `<string.h><wchar.h>`

Move buffer

## Description

This function copies the content of a memory area into another. (The two memory areas must not overlap). The number of bytes passed as an argument is copied.

## Parameters

```
void *memmove(void *target, const void *source, size_t number);
wchar_t *wmemmove(wchar_t *target, const wchar_t *, size_t number);
```

- **Return value.** Pointer to target.

## Related functions

```
memchr(), memchr(), memset()
```

### memset, wmemset                                      `<string.h><wchar.h>`

Set buffer

## Description

The function initialises a memory area with a particular character. The number of the memory units which are to be initialised is determined through the argument number.

```
void *memset(void *buffer, int charac, size_t number);
wchar_t *wmemset(wchar_t *buffer, int charac, size_t number);
```

- **Return value.** Pointer to buffer.

## Related functions

```
memchr(), memcmp(), memmove()
```

## mktime <time.h>

Converts time from tm to time_t

### Description

The function mktime() converts a time specification from type tm into type time_t.

### Parameters

time_t mktime(struct tm *time);

- **Return value.** The function returns the converted time specification of the type time_t. If the time specification could not be converted, −1 is returned.

### Related functions

time(), gmtime(), localtime()

## modf <math.h>

Splits a floating point number

### Description

The function modf() divides a floating-point number into a pre-point part integer and a post-point part.

### Parameters

double modf(double wert, double *p_int);

- **Return value.** The post-point part is returned. The integer is stored at the place to which p_int points.

### Related functions

fmod(), frexp(), ldexp()

## perror <stdio.h>

Issues an error message

### Description

The function perror() produces an error message in which it puts together the passed string and the error message, which corresponds to the current value of the variable errno and then outputs to the data stream stderr.

## Parameters

```
void perror(const char *chstring);
```

## Related functions

```
ferror(), clearerror(), strerror()
```

## pow                                                    <math.h>

Exponentiation

## Description

The function calculates x ^ y.

## Parameters

```
double pow(double x, double y);
double pow(double x, int y);
```

- **Return value.** When successfully executed the function returns the result of $x$ to the power of $y$. If $x < 0$ and $y$ is not an integer, EDOM is written into errno; with a too-high result value HUGE_VAL is returned.

## Related function

```
sqrt()
```

## printf, wprintf                              <stdio.h><wchar.h>

Formatted output to stdout

## Description

The function outputs formatted data to the data stream stdout. For outputting a format string is examined. Normal text and escape sequences in this string are output.

If printf() (wprintf()) finds the character % with a valid format type and optional additional specifications in the format string, the corresponding optional argument is converted into the specified type by printf() (wprintf()) and inserted into the string.

The general format for the type specification is as follows:

```
% [flag] [width] [precision] [type_prefix] format_type
```

The individual elements of the type specification and their effect:

```
Format type Data type
c           // single character
s           // null-terminated character string;
            // for wprintf() in case of type prefix l (see
```

```
                  // below) the wide character string is
                  // converted to multi-byte characters
d, i              // decimal integer number
u                 // unsigned decimal integer number
o                 // unsigned octal integer number
x                 // unsigned hexadecimal integer number without prefix
                  // (0x), output in lower case letters
X                 // unsigned hexadecimal integer number without prefix
                  // (0X), output in upper case letters
f                 // floating point number, decimal notation
e,E               // floating point number, exponential notation:
                  // [-]d.ddddexx or [-]d.ddddExx
g,G               // floating point number, shortest notation is chosen
                  // (f or e)
p                 // output as a pointer
n                 // outputs the number of characters output so far
%                 // no conversion, the % character is output
```

The following characters can also be used as a flag to extend the format element:

```
Flags      Effect
-                 // Output is left-aligned. If this character is not
                  // specified, output is automatically right-aligned,
                  // that is, leading spaces are inserted.
+                 // For numeric variables, the output is signed,
                  // that is, positive numbers are prefixed with a
                  // plus sign. The output of the minus sign for
                  // negative values is not affected by this flag
Space             // By specifying this character, positive numbers
                  // are prefixed with a blank space
0                 // Pads the field width with zeros
#                 // The effect of the formatting character # depends
                  // on the format type specified for the argument
```

- If 0 (octal integer) has been specified as the format type, zero is prefixed to the specified variable, if the value of the variable is not 0.

- The format types for hexadecimal integers (x and X) are prefixed with 0x or 0X in the output.

- For the format types e, E and f (floating-point numbers) the output of a decimal point is compelled through #.

- The effect for the format types g and G is identical for e and E.

## Width

In this field the minimum number of characters are to be output can be determined. If the number of the output characters is smaller than the value specified in [width], spaces are output (depending on whether the – flag has been set) to the left or the right, until the value specified in [width] has been reached. If the number is prefixed with a zero, zeros are added instead of spaces.

## Precision

The specification of the precision with which the number of the decimals to be output are determined has to be prefixed with a dot. In this way the parameter's width and precision can be set. The effect of the value for precision depends on the data type which is to be output.

```
Character      Effect
d,i,u,o,x,X    // The precision value specifies the minimum number
               // of digits to be output
e,E,f          // Specifies the number of digits to be output
               // after the decimal point. The last digit is
               // rounded
g,G            // The number of significant digits specified by
               // precision is output
c              // No effect: the character is output
s              // This value specifies the maximum number of
               // characters to be output
```

Various type prefixes, which give specifications with regard to the size of the parameter, can stand before the format type.

```
Type prefix    Meaning
h              // When d, i, o, x or X are specified as format type,
               // the parameter is of short int type. With format type
               // u and type prefix h, a variable of short unsigned
               // int type is expected
l              // With format types d, i, o, x or X, a parameter
               // of long int type, with u of long unsigned int type
               // is expected
               // With format types e, E, f, g and G, a variable
               // of double type is expected instead of float
               // For wprintf() for a c parameter a wint_t argument
               // is expected instead of an int argument and for
               // an s parameter a wchar_t-pointer is expected
               // instead of a char pointer. In addition,
               // automatic conversion of wide characters to
               // multi-byte is activated
L              // With format types e, E, f, g and G, a variable
               // of long double type is expected
               // For wprintf(), for an s parameter, a wchar_t
               // pointer is expected as an argument instead
               // of a char pointer
```

The following escape sequences are converted by the printf() (wprintf()) function as follows:

```
Sequence    Effect
\a          // bell
\v          // vertical tabulation
\b          // backspace
```

```
\'          // apostrophe
\f          // form feed
\"          // quote
\n          // new line
\\          // backslash
\r          // carriage return
\ddd        // ASCII character in octal notation
\t          // horizontal tabulation
\xdd        // ASCII character in hexadecimal notation
```

## Parameters

```
int printf(const char *format,...);
int wprintf(const wchar_t *format,...);
```

- **Return value.** Number of the output characters.

## Related functions

```
sprintf(), vsprintf()
```

See Practice section, category input and output, formatted input and output in C.

### putc, putwc                                        <stdio.h><wchar.h>

Writes a character to a stream

## Description

The function writes a single character into a stream.

## Parameters

```
int putc(int charac, FILE *stream);
wint_t putwc(wchar_t charac, FILE *stream);
```

- **Return value.** The function returns the written character. The return value EOF (WEOF) indicates an error or the end of the file.

## Related functions

```
putchar(), printf(), puts()
```

### putchar, putwchar                                  <stdio.h><wchar.h>

Character output to stdout

## Description

The function writes a single character to the data stream stdout. Thus, it corresponds to calling putc(charac,stdout), or putwc(charac,stdout).

## Parameters

```
int putchar(int charac);
wint_t putwchar(wchar_t charac);
```

- **Return value.** The function returns the output character. In case of an error the return value is EOF (WEOF).

## Related functions

`putc()`, `printf()`, `puts()`

See Practice section, category input and output, text files in C.

## puts <stdio.h>

Writes a character string to stdout.

## Description

The function puts() writes a string to the data stream stdout. The zero termination character (\0) of the string is replaced with the line feed character (\n).

## Parameters

```
int puts(const char *chstring);
```

- **Return value.** In an error-free execution a non-negative value is returned, otherwise it will be EOF.

## Related functions

`fputs()`, `gets()`

## qsort <stdlib.h>

Perform QuickSort

## Description

The function qsort() sorts a data field. The function uses the QuickSort algorithm. The comparison which is required for sorting is carried out by a function whose address is passed to qsort(). This function has to compare two elements and return the following values to qsort():

| | |
|---|---|
| negative | The first element is smaller than the second. |
| null | Both elements are identical. |
| positive | The first element is greater than the second. |

## Parameters

```
void qsort (void *basis, size_t number, size_t length,
            int (*vgl)(const void *elem1, const void *elem2));
```

- **basis.** Pointer to the start of the array.
- **number.** Number of array elements.
- **length.** Size of each elements in bytes.
- **cf.** Pointer to function, which compares two elements of the const void* type.

## Related functions

```
bsearch()
```

See Practice section, category input and output, binary files in C.

## raise                                                    <signal.h>

Signal to execute a program

## Description

The function `raise()` transmits a signal to the program that is calling. Through `signal()` it is possible to establish routines which are called up after the signal is resolved. The symbolic constants `SIG...` (see header `signal.h`) can be used for the signal which is to be produced (and thus for the argument `sig`).

## Parameters

```
int raise(int sig);
```

- **Return value.** Zero in a successful execution.

## Related functions

```
abort(), signal()
```

## rand                                                     <stdlib.h>

Generates a pseudo-random number

## Description

The function `rand()` produces a pseudo-random number. The produced number lies in the area from 0 to `RAND_MAX`. The function always generates the same sequence of random numbers, unless you change the initial value with the `srand()` function. Calling `rand()` without beforehand calling `srand()` has the same effect as if `srand()` had been called beforehand with the argument 1.

## Parameters

```
int rand(void);
```

- **Return value.** Generated pseudo-random number.

## Related function

```
srand()
```

See Practice section, category miscellaneous, random data.

## realloc                                            <stdlib.h>

Reallocates a block of memory

## Description

The size of a memory block, which has been requested with malloc() or calloc() before-hand, can be adapted with the function realloc(). The content of the old memory block is maintained, but its address may change.

## Parameters

```
void *realloc(void *buffer, size_t sighz);
```

- **buffer.** Pointer to the memory block which is to be extended or reduced.
- **sighz.** New size of the memory block.
- **Return value.** The function returns a pointer to the newly assigned memory block, or a zero pointer if the memory could not be created.

## Related functions

```
calloc(), free(), malloc()
```

## remove                                             <stdio.h>

Deletes a file

## Description

The remove() function deletes the file (if there is no write protection) whose name has been passed to it. The file should be closed.

## Parameters

```
int remove(const char *filename);
```

- **Return value.** The function returns zero if the file has been deleted, otherwise it returns a value not equal to zero.

## Related functions

rename(), tmpfile(), tmpnam()

## rename                                                    **<stdio.h>**

Renames a file

## Description

The function rename() changes a file name from oldname into newname. Both arguments have to contain a valid path name.

## Parameters

int rename(const char *oldname, const char *newname);

- **Return value.** The function returns zero if the file could be renamed, otherwise it returns a value not equal to zero.

## Related functions

remove(), tmpfile(), tmpnam()

## rewind                                                    **<stdio.h>**

Stream position pointer to beginning

## Description

The function rewind() sets the file position display to the beginning of the file and deletes any set error flags. The function, thus, corresponds to the call-ups:

fseek(stream, 0L, SEEK_SET);
clearerr(stream);

## Parameters

void rewind(FILE *stream);

## Related functions

fseek(), ftell()

## scanf, wscanf                                  **<stdio.h><wchar.h>**

Reads formatted data from stdin

## Description

The function reads formatted data from the data stream stdin. It uses the argument format to convert the read characters into the correct data types. The read data are then written to the memory positions, which are passed with the other function arguments. For each further function argument a type identifier has to be specified in the format string.

Type identifiers possess the following general format, where the specifications in brackets are optional:

```
%[*][width][size]type
```

- **%**: Marks the beginning of a type identifier. The % character and the type are the elements which each type identifier has to consist of.
- **\***: If the % character is followed by a star (*), the assignment of the next entry field is suppressed.
- **width**: The width is a positive decimal integer, with which the maximum number of characters to be read is specified.
- **size**: This field in the type identifier can be used to specify the size of the variables.
- **type**:

```
Format type    Data type
c              // single character
s              // character string
               // if type prefix l is set (see above), the read
               // multi-byte character sequence is converted
               // to wide characters
d              // decimal integer
i              // decimal, octal (0) or hexadecimal (0x, 0X) integer
u              // unsigned decimal integer
o              // unsigned octal integer
x              // unsigned hexadecimal integer without prefix
               // (0x), output in lower case letters
f              // floating point number, decimal notation
e,E            // floating point number, exponential notation:
               // [-]m.ddddexx or [-]m.ddddExx
g,G            // floating point number, shortest notation is chosen
               // (f or e)
p              // pointer
n              // outputs the number of characters read so far
[...]          // corresponds to the longest string that consists
               // only of the characters specified in the brackets
               // if type prefix l is set (see above), the read
               // multi-byte character sequence is converted
               // to wide characters
[^...]         // corresponds to the longest string that contains
               // none of the characters specified in the brackets
               // if type prefix l is set (see above), the read
               // multi-byte character sequence is converted
               // to wide characters
%              // no conversion: the character % is read
```

The type specifications can be prefixed with the following type prefixes to achieve a more detailed specification:

```
Typ prefix    Meaning
h             // if d, i, n, o, u, x is specified as format type,
              // the argument is of short int type
l             // if d, i, n, o, u, x is specified as format type,
              // the argument is of long int type
              // with format types e, E, f, g, and G an argument
              // of double type is expected instead of float
              // for wscanf(): with format types c, s  and [ ], an
              // argument of wchar_t type is expected and automatic
              // conversion of multi-byte to wide character
              // is activated
L             // with format types e, E, f, g and G, an argument
              // of long double type is expected
```

## Parameters

```
int scanf(const char *format, ...);
int wscanf(const wchar_t *format, ...);
```

- **Return value.** The function returns the number of the converted and read fields (can also be 0) or EOF (WEOF), if it has attempted to read the end of the string, or an error has occurred.

## Related functions

```
fscanf(), printf(), sscanf(), vsprintf()
```

## setbuf                                                    <stdio.h>

Stream buffer

## Description

With the function setbuf() a separate buffer, which replaces the automatically assigned buffer, can be established for the temporary storage of a stream. For this the function argument buffer has to point to a memory area, which is at least BUFSIZ bytes big. If the argument is a zero pointer, no temporary storage is carried out.

## Parameters

```
void setbuf(FILE *stream, char *buffer);
```

## Related function

```
setvbuf()
```

## setjmp                                                    <setjmp.h>

Stores the program status

## Description

The function `setjmp()` prepares for a non-local jump (out of a function). All the important information for a later jump back to the current position is stored in the buffer umg.

## Parameters

`int setjmp(jmp_buf env);`

- **Return value.** After the environment has been saved the return value is 0. After a later `longjmp()` call-up the function returns a value not equal to 0, to prevent an infinite loop.

## Related functions

`longjmp()`

See example for Header file `setjmp.h`

## setlocale                                   <locale.h>

Changing a local setting

## Description

With this function the local setting for the used character set, the currency specifications, and so on can be queried or changed. The LC... constants (see header file `locale.h`) can be passed to the first parameter, to select which categories are to be affected by the changes. The second parameter points to the name of the local setting, which is to be established for the specified categories (for example `"C"` for the minimum environment or `" "` for the system environment).

If a zero pointer is passed to the parameter `locale`, a string for the category of the current local setting is returned.

## Parameters

`char *setlocale(int categorye, char *locale);`

- **category.** One of the LC constants from `locale.h` for selecting of part of the local settings.
- **locale.** Name of the locale.
- **Return value.** When successful, the function returns a pointer to the string with the categories and settings. In case of an error a zero pointer is returned, and the `Locale` setting remains unchanged.

## Related function

`localeconv()`

See Practice section, category internationalisation and localisation, local environment.

## setvbuf  <stdio.h>
Stream buffering

## Description

With the function `setvbuf()` the temporary storage of a stream can be determined. Here you have more setting options than with the function `setbuf()`.

## Parameters

```
int setvbuf(FILE *stream, char *buffer,
                    int buf_typ, size_t buf_sighz);
```

- **stream**. Stream for which the buffer is to be set.
- **buffer**. Zero pointer (the buffer is established by `setvbuf`) or pointer to a self-allocated buffer.
- **buf_typ**. Can adopt the value of one of three symbolic constants, which have been defined in the file <stdio.h>. If the argument `buf_typ` has the value `_IONBF`, the options `buffer` and `buf_sighz` are ignored and the flags of the streams are set to this mode. In the two other values the value of the arguments `buffer` is checked first. If there is a zero pointer, the function allocates a buffer with the size, which is specified in `buf_sighz`. Otherwise buffer should point to a memory area which you have allocated in `buf_sighz` bytes.

| | |
|---|---|
| _IOFBF | Indicates that a stream is to be buffered fully. This means that data is stored in the buffer until it is full. |
| _IOLBF | Stream is buffered linewise. |
| _IONBF | Stream is not buffered. |

- **buf_sighz**. Size of the buffer.
- **Return value**. When successful, the function returns zero. If there is an error or invalid parameters the return value is unequal to zero.

## Warning

The function has to be called up after the stream has been linked to an open file and before any operations are carried out on the stream.

## Related function

`setbuf()`

## signal <signal.h>

Interrupt signal handling

### Description

With the function `signal()` processing routines can be determined, which are always called up when a certain signal occurs.

### Parameters

`void (*signal(int sig, void(*funct)(int)))(int);`

- **sig.** The function gets as first argument a `SIG..` constant (see header file `signal.h`), which describes the signal whose handling is to be changed.
- **funct.** The second argument is a pointer to a function which does not return a value. However, it contains the number of the signal. If this processing function calls up any function of the C runtime library other than `signal()`, the behaviour is implementation-specific. Instead of a function pointer, it is also possible to use the following constants:

| | |
|---|---|
| SIG_DFL | Identifies default processing. |
| SIG_IGN | Ignore signal. The intteruption signal is ignored. This constant should not be used together with `SIGFPE`, since it renders the floating-point arithmetic packet useless. |
| SIG_ERR | Used to indicate an error condition during execution. |

- **Return value.** When successful, the function returns the address of the previous handling routine for the signals of the specified type. In case of an error the value of the constant `SIG_ERR` is returned and the global variable `errno` set to a positive value.

### Related function

`raise()`

See example for header file signal.h

## sin, sinh <math.h>

Calculates the sine

### Description

The function `sin()` calculates the sine, and `sinh()` the hyperbolic sine of its argument.

### Parameters

`double sin(double x);`
`double sinh(double x);`

- **Return value.** sin() returns the sine of the argument in the range [–1, 1]. sinh() returns the hyperbolic sine of the argument in the range [-8, 8].

## Warning
The hyperbolic sine rises and falls very quickly.

## Related functions
asin(), cos(), cosh()

See example for header file math.h

## sprintf, swprintf                                    <stdio.h><wchar.h>
Write formatted data to a string

## Description
The function carries out a formatted output into a string. The format string has the structure described for printf().

## Parameters
```
int sprintf(char *chstring, const char *format, ...);
int swprintf(wchar_t *chstring, size_t n, const wchar_t *format, ...);
```
- **chstring.** Pointer to the string into which the output is to be made.
- **n.** Maximum number of characters that are written for (only for swprintf()).
- **format.** Format string (see printf()).
- **....** variable number of arguments.
- **Return value.** The function returns the number of output characters, without the final zero. In case of an error EOF (WEOF) is returned.

## Related functions
printf(), sscanf(), vprintf(), vsprintf()

## sqrt                                                  <math.h>
Calculates the square root

## Description
The function sqrt() calculates the square root of its argument and returns the value.

## Parameters
```
double sqrt(double number);
```

- **Return value.** Square root of the argument. As the root is only defined greater than zero for positive values, EDOM is written into errno for values of $x < 0$.

## Related function

pow()

## srand                                                                 <stdlib.h>

Initialises the random number generator

## Description

The function srand() uses its argument to determine the starting point of a set of random numbers, which are then returned by rand(). If the function is called up twice with the same value, it produces the same sequence of random numbers.

## Parameters

void srand(unsigned int number);

## Related function

rand()

## sscanf, swscanf                                                  <stdio.h><wchar.h>

Reads formatted data from a string

## Description

The function reads formatted data from a string. It uses the format string to convert the read data into the correct types. The other optional arguments have to be addresses to which the read data are to be written.

The format string can contain the same pattern as described under scanf().

## Parameters

int sscanf(const char *str, const char *format, ...);
int swscanf(const wchar_t *str,  const wchar_t *format, ...);

- **buffer.** Pointer to the string from which the data are read.
- **format.** Formatting string (see scanf()).
- **Return value.** The function returns the number of the converted and read fields or returns EOF (WEOF), if it has attempted to read the end of the string.

## Related functions

fscanf(), scanf(), sprintf()

See Practice section, category input and output, formatted input and output in C.

## strcat, wcscat <string.h><wchar.h>

Appends a character string

## Description

The function copies all the characters of the string, to which source points (including the \0 character that terminates the string), to the end of the string, to which target points. The termination character of the first string is overwritten.

## Parameters

```
char *strcat(char * target, const char * source);
wchar_t *wcscat(wchar_t * target, const wchar_t * source);
```

- **Return value.** Pointer to the linked string.

## Related functions

```
strncat(), strcpy(), strspn()
```

See Practice section, category strings, programming with C strings.

## strchr, wcschr <string.h><wchar.h>

Finds a character in a string

## Description

The function searches for the first occurrence of a character in a string. The zero termination character at the end of the string is included in the search.

## Parameters

```
C:
char *strchr(const char *chstring, int charac);
wchar_t *wcschr(const wchar_t *chstring, wchar_t charac);
C++:
const char *strchr(const char *chstring, int charac);
const wchar_T *wcschr(const wchar_t *chstring, wchar_t charac);
char *strchr(char *chstring, int charac);
wchar_t *wcschr(wchar_t *chstring, wchar_t charac);
```

- **Return value.** The function returns a pointer to charac; otherwise a zero pointer.

## Related functions

```
strrchr(), strcspn(), strpbrk(), strspn()
```

## strcmp, wcscmp                                    <string.h><wchar.h>

Compares character strings

### Description

The function compares each character of chstring1 with the character at the corresponding position of chstring2. The comparison is continued until either two different characters have been found or the end of the string has been reached.

### Parameters

```
int strcmp(const char *chstring1, const char *chstring2);
int wcscmp(const wchar_t *chstring1, const wchar_t *chstring2);
```

- **Return value.** The function has three possible return values, in which the result of the comparison is coded:

| | |
|---|---|
| < 0 | chstring1 <  chstring2 |
| 0 | chstring1 == chstring2 |
| > 0 | chstring1 >  chstring2 |

### Related functions

strncmp(), strcoll()

## strcoll, wcscoll                                   <string.h><wchar.h>

Copies a character string

### Description

The function compares the string chstring1 with the string chstring2 according to the local settings of the category LC_COLLATE.

### Parameters

```
int strcoll(const char *chstring1, const char *chstring2);
int wcscoll(const wchar_t *chstring1, const wchar_t *chstring2);
```

- **Return value.** The function has three possible return values, in which the result of the comparison is coded:

| | |
|---|---|
| < 0 | chstring1 <  chstring2 |
| 0 | chstring1 == chstring2 |
| > 0 | chstring1 >  chstring2 |

### Related function

strcmp()

## strcpy, wcscpy                                          <string.h><wchar.h>

Copies a character string

## Description

The function copies all the characters of the string source (including the zero termination character) into the memory area to which target points. The behaviour of the function has not been defined, if the memory area to which target points is overlapped by the memory area to which source points.

## Parameters

```
char *strcpy(char *target, const char *source);
wchar_t *wcscpy(wchar_t *target, const wchar_t *source);
```
• **Return value.** Pointer to the target string.

## Related function

strncpy()

See Practice section, category character strings, programming with C strings.

## strcspn, wcscspn                                        <string.h><wchar.h>

Prefix in string

## Description

The function determines the length of the preceding part string of chstring1, which does not contain characters from chstring2.

## Parameters

```
size_t strcspn(const char *chstring1,const char *chstring2);
size_t wcscspn(const wchar_t *chstring1, const wchar_t *chstring2);
```
• **Return value.** Length of the found prefix of chstring1.

## Related functions

strspn(), strncmp()

## strerror                                                <string.h>

Gets a system error message

## Description

The function strerror() is used for support when generating error messages. Usually it contains as the argument the global variable errno, which is set by a few functions of the runtime library, when an error has occurred during the processing of the corresponding function. The function `strerror()` writes the error message that belongs to the value of `errno` into a static buffer and returns a pointer to this buffer.

The error message is not output with this function.

## Parameters

`char *strerror(int errno);`

- **Return value.** Pointer to the error message that corresponds to the argument `errno`.

## Related function

`perror()`

**strftime, wcsftime**                                    **<time.h><wchar.h>**

Formats the time

## Description

The function adopts the time specification from the variable `time` of the structure `tm`, converts it according to the formatting statements contained in the parameter `format` and the local setting (`LC_TIME`) and outputs it in the string `str`.

The following formatting specifications are permitted for the parameter format:

```
%%        // percent sign %
%a        // abbreviated name of the day
%A        // full name of the day
%b        // abbreviated name of the month
%B        // full name of the month
%c        // date and time
%d        // day of the month (01 - 31)
%H        // hour (00 -23)
%I        // hour (01 - 12)
%j        // day of the year (001 - 366)
%m        // month (01 - 12)
%M        // minute (00 - 59)
%p        // AM or PM
%S        // second (00 - 59)
%U        // week number (00 - 53), week begings with Sunday
%w        // week day (0 - 6), Sunday == 0
%W        // week number (00 - 53), week begins with Monday
%x        // date
%X        // time
%y        // year without century (00 - 99)
%Y        // year with century
%Z        // name of time zone
```

## Parameters

```
size_t strftime(char *str, size_t maxsize,
                    const char *format, const struct tm *time);
size_t wcsftime(wchar_t *str, size_t maxsize,
                    const wchar_t *format, const struct tm *time);
```

- **str.** Output string in which the reformatted date/time specification is written.

- **maxsize.** Maximum number of characters which may be written into `str`.

- **format.** Formatting string which can consist of the formatting statements listed above.

- **time.** Date/time specification which is to be reformatted.

- **Return value.** The function returns the number of characters written to `str`. If more characters are required than specified by `maxsize`, zero is returned. The converted time specification is made available through the parameter `str`.

## Related functions

```
localtime(), time(), gmtime(), setlocale()
```

See Practice section, category internationalisation and localisation, local environment.

### strlen, wcslen                           <string.h><wchar.h>

Determines the length of a character string

## Description

The function determines the length of the passed string. The zero termination character which ends the string is not counted.

## Parameters

```
size_t strlen(const char *chstring);
size_t wcslen(const wchar_t *chstring);
```

- **Return value.** Length of the string (excluding the zero termination character).

## Related functions

```
strcpy(), sizeof-Operator
```

See Practice section, category character strings, programming with C strings.

### strncat, wcsncat                         <string.h><wchar.h>

Appends *n* characters to a string

## Description

The function copies the number of characters of the strings, to which source points, to the end of the string, to which target points. Copying is terminated when either number of characters have been transferred or the end of target has been reached.

## Parameters

```
char *strncat(char * target, const char *source, size_t number);
wchar_t *wcsncat(wchar_t * target, const wchar_t *source, size_t number);
```

- **Return value.** Pointer to target.

## Related functions

strcat(), strncpy()

### strncmp, wcsncmp  &lt;string.h&gt;&lt;wchar.h&gt;

Compares *n* characters in strings

## Description

The function compares the first number characters of the strings chstring1 and chstring2. The comparison is finished when either a zero termination character is read or a character pair has been found which is not identical.

## Parameters

```
int strncmp (const char *chstring1, const char *chstring2,
             size_t number);
int wcsncmp (const wchar_t *chstring1, const wchar_t *chstring2,
             size_t number);
```

- **Return value.** The function has three possible return values, in which the result of the comparison is coded:

| | |
|---|---|
| < 0 | chstring1 < chstring2 |
| 0 | chstring1 == chstring2 |
| > 0 | chstring1 > chstring2 |

## Related functions

strcmp(), strcoll()

## strncpy, wcsncpy                                        <string.h><wchar.h>
Copies *n* characters from a string

## Description
The function copies number characters from the memory area, to which source points, into the memory area, to which target points. If source possesses fewer characters than number characters, the zero termination character is copied until number characters have been written.

The memory area to which target points has to be number characters big, otherwise other data or code may be overwritten.

## Parameters
```
char *strncpy(char *target, const char *source, size_t number);
wchar_t *wcsncpy(wchar_t *target, const wchar_t *source, size_t number);
```
- **Return value.** Pointer to target.

## Related functions
```
strcat(), strncat(), strspn()
```

## strpbrk, wcspbrk                                        <string.h><wchar.h>
Searches for characters in a string

## Description
The function checks whether the the string chstring1 contains any character from the string chstring2.

## Parameters
```
C:
char *strpbrk(const char *chstring1, const char *chstring2);
wchar_t *wcspbrk(const wchar_t *chstring1, const wchar_t *chstring2);
C++:
const char *strpbrk(const char *chstring1, const char *chstring2);
const wchar_t *wcspbrk(const wchar_t *chstring1, const wchar_t
*chstring2);
char *strpbrk(char *chstring1, const char *chstring2);
wchar_t *wcspbrk(wchar_t *chstring1, const wchar_t *chstring2);
```
- **Return value.** The function returns a pointer to the first corresponding character in chstring1 or a zero pointer if no identical character has been found.

## Related functions

strchr(), strrchr(), strstr()

## strrchr, wcsrchr                                                    <string.h>

Search for the last occurrence of a character

## Description

The function searches the passed string for a particular character. The final zero termination character is included in the search and can be the searched for character.

## Parameters

```
C:
char *strrchr(const char *chstring, int charac);
wchar_t *wcsrchr(const wchar_t *chstring, wchar_t charac);
C++:
const char *strrchr(const char *chstring, int charac);
const wchar_T *wcsrchr(const wchar_t *chstring, wchar_t charac);
char *strrchr(char *chstring, int charac);
wchar_t *wcsrchr(wchar_t *chstring, wchar_t charac);
```

- **Return value.** The function returns a pointer to the last (that is the furthest to the right) occurrence of charac in chstring, if the character has been found. Otherwise a zero pointer is returned.

## Related functions

strcspn(), strpbrk(), strspn()

## strspn, wcsspn                                           <string.h><wchar.h>

Search for first non-identical character

## Description

The function examines up to which position chstring1 consists exclusively of characters contained in chstring2.

## Parameters

```
size_t strspn(const char *chstring1, const char *chstring2);
size_t wcsspn(const wchar_t *chstring1, const wchar_t *chstring2);
```

- **Return value.** Length of the prefix up to the first non-identical character.

## Related functions

strcspn(), strpbrk(), strrchr()

## strstr, wcsstr                 **\<string.h>\<wchar.h>**

Find a string in another string

## Description

The function searches for `chstring2` in `chstring1`.

## Parameters

```
C:
char *strstr(const char *chstring1,const char *chstring2);
wchar_t *strstr(const wchar_t *chstring1, const wchar_t *chstring2);
C++:
const char *strstr(const char *chstring1, const char *chstring2);
const wchar_t *wcsstr(const wchar_t *chstring1, const wchar_t
*chstring2);
char *strstr(const char *chstring1, const char *chstring2);
wchar_t *wcsstr(const wchar_t *chstring1, const wchar_t *chstring2);
```

- **Return value.** Pointer to the first occurrence of `chstring2` in `chstring1`, or a zero pointer if `chstring2` has not been found.

## Related functions

`memchr(), strchr(), strcspn(), strrchr()`

## strtod, wcstod                 **\<stdlib.h>\<wchar.h>**

Conversion of `string` to `double`

## Description

The function converts a string `chstring` into a floating-point number of double precision (type `double`). The conversion is terminated after the first character that is not recognised as part of the number any more, or when `**endptr` has been reached.

## Parameters

```
double strtod(const char *chstring, char **endptr);
double wcstod(const wchar_t *chstring, wchar_t **endptr);
```

- **Return value.** The function returns the converted value.

## Related functions

`strtol(), strtoul()`

## strtok, wcstok      <string.h><wchar.h>

Search for next basic symbol in a string

### Description

The function determines individual basic symbols in a string. To find the basic symbols, it searches for the separators that are contained in chstring2.

From the second call-up onwards, the argument zero can be passed for chstring1. The function then searches for the next basic symbol from the position which has been internally stored at the first call-up.

Through repeated call-ups of the function the string chstring1 can be split into a number of part strings, which are each terminated by a character from chstring2.

The wide-character version requires an additional pointer to wchar_t, to be able to deposit auxiliary information.

```
char *strtok(char *chstring1, const char *chstring2);
wchar_t *wcstok(wchar_t *chstring1, const wchar_t *chstring2,
                wchar_t ** pointer);
```

- **Return value.** Pointer to the found basic symbol or zero pointer if there are no tokens.

### Related functions

strpbrk(), strcspn(), strspn(), strstr()

See Practice section, category strings analysing (parsing) strings.

## strtol, wcstol      <stdlib.h><wchar.h>

Conversion of string to long

### Description

The function converts a string into a value of the type long. The conversion is terminated after the first character which is not recognised as a part of the number, or when **endptr has been reached.

### Parameters

```
long strtol(const char *chstring, char **endptr, int basis);
long int wcstol(const wchar_t *chstring, wchar_t **endptr, int basis);
```

- **Return value.** Returns the converted value.

## Related functions

strtod(), strtoul(), sprintf(), atof()

## strtoul, wcstoul                                    <stdlib.h><wchar.h>

Conversion of string to unsigned long

## Description

The function converts a string into a value of the type unsigned long. The conversion is terminated after the first character which is not recognised as a part of the number, or when
**endptr has been reached.

## Parameters

```
unsigned long int strtoul (const char *chstring, char **endptr, int basis);
unsigned long int wcstoul (const wchar_t *zk,wchar_t **endptr, int basis);
```

- **Return value.** When successful the converted value, otherwise zero.

## Related functions

strtod(), strtol()

## strxfrm, wcsxfrm                                    <string.h><wchar.h>

Conversion according to local setting

## Description

The function converts a maximum of num characters of the string source and writes the result
to target. In a successful transformation the call-ups return:

strcmp(target, x)

and

strcoll(source, x)

afterwards the same result.

## Parameters

```
size_t strxfrm (char *target, char *source, size_t num);
size_t wcsxfrm (wchar_T *target, wchar_t *source, size_t num);
```

- **Return value.** Number of the converted characters.

## Related functions

strcmp(), strcoll()

## system <stdlib.h>

Executes an operating system command

### Description

With the function system() another program can be carrried out from a C program. The currently running process is interrupted, and the passed system command transmitted to the command interpreter, if one exists.

### Parameters

```
int system(const char *prgname)
```

- *prgname. Implementation-specific.

## tan, tanh <math.h>

Calculates the tangent

### Description

The function tan() calculates the tangent and tanh() the hyperbolic tangent of its argument.

### Parameters

```
double tan(double x);
double tanh(double x);
```

- **Return value.** tan() returns the tangent of the argument in the range [–8, 8]. tanh() returns the hyperbolic tangent of the argument in the range [–1, 1].

### Warning

The tangent approaches the values –8 and 8 in the environment of the multiple of p /2.

### Related functions

```
acos(), asin(), atan(), atan2(), sinh()
```

See example for header file math.h

## time <time.h>

Determines current time

### Description

The function time() determines the current calendar time. The calendar time is the number of seconds that have passed since 1st January 1970, 00:00:00 hrs

If the argument p_time is not a zero pointer, the calendar time is written to the address to which p_time points.

## Parameters

```
time_t time(time_t *p_time);
```

- **Return value.** Number of seconds that have passed since 1st January 1970, 00:00:00 hrs.

## Related functions

```
asctime(), ctime(), gmtime(), localtime()
```

See example for header file `time.h`

## tmpfile <stdio.h>

Creates a temporary file

## Description

The function `tmpfile()` produces a temporary file. The file is opened in wb+ mode and automatically removed when the file is closed or the program ends.

## Parameters

```
FILE *tmpfile(void);
```

- **Return value.** Pointer to a FILE structure. If the file cannot be opened, a zero pointer is returned.

## Related functions

```
tmpnam()
```

## tmpnam <stdio.h>

Generates a temporary file name

## Description

The function `tmpnam()` produces a temporary file name. If the function has a zero pointer as argument, the name is written into an internal static buffer, which is overwritten by further call-ups of the function.

Otherwise, `chstring` points to a memory area in which the name is to be deposited. The memory area intended for the file name has to be at least `L_tmpnam` bytes big. Thus, you should use this constant in the definition of an array to `char`.

## Parameters

```
char *tmpnam(char *chstring);
```

- **Return value.** Pointer to a temporary name.

## Related functions

tmpfile()

### tolower, towlower                              <ctype.h><wctype.h>

Conversion of upper case to lower case

### Description

The function converts the passed character into a lower case letter. The function tolower() checks whether the passed letter is a upper case letter for which there exists a corresponding lower case letter, and only then carries out the conversion.

### Parameters

int tolower(int charac);
wint_t towlower(wchar_t charac);

- **Return value.** The function returns the converted character. If a lower case letter is passed, it is returned unchanged..

### Related functions

toupper(), towupper()

### toupper, towupper                             <ctype.h><wctype.h>

Conversion of lower case to upper case

### Description

The function converts the passed character into an upper case letter. The function toupper() checks whether the passed letter is a upper case letter for which there exists a corresponding lower case letter, and only then carries out the conversion.

### Parameters

int toupper(int charac);
wint_t towupper(wchar_t charac);

- **Return value.** The function returns the converted character. If an upper case letter is passed, it is returned unchanged.

### Related functions

tolower(), towlowerr()

## towctrans  <wctype.h>
Wide character mapping

## Description
Converts a wide character according to the diagram provided by the parameter description. Arguments for the parameter description can be produced with the function `wctrans()`.

## Parameters
```
wint_t towctrans(wint_t wc, wctrans_t description);
```
- **Return value.** Value to which the character has been formed.

## Related function
`wctrans()`

## ungetc, ungetwc  <stdio.h><wchar.h>
Sends a character back to the stream

## Description
The function writes the read character back to the stream. The function cannot be carried out indefinitely in sequence. In buffered input and output the character is written into the buffer and consequently gets lost in operations which delete the buffer ( such as `fseek()`, `rewind()`, `fflush()`, `fsetpos()`).

## Parameters
```
int ungetc(int charac, FILE *stream);
wint_t ungetwc(wchar_t charac, FILE *stream);
```
- **Return value.** The function returns the argument `charac`, when successful, otherwise it returns EOF (WEOF).

## Related functions
`getc()`, `getchar()`

## va_...  <stdarg.h>
Variable number of arguments

## Description
The macros `va_arg()`, `va_end()` and `va_start()` are used to implement functions which are called up with a variable number of arguments, such as `printf()` or `scanf()`.

## Parameters

```
type va_arg(va_list arg_ptr, type);
void va_end(va_list arg_ptr);
void va_start(va_list arg_ptr, last_param);
```

## Related functions

```
vfprintf(), vprintf(), vsprintf()
```

See Practice section, category functions, functions with an arbitrary number of arguments.

### v-,vf-,vs- (w)printf                           <stdio.h><wchar.h>

Outputs formatted data

## Description

These six functions output formatted data. They are almost identical to the functions `fprintf()`, `printf()` and `sprintf()`. The variable number of arguments is not passed as list, but as a pointer to a list of arguments.

The three functions are distinguished by the target of their output. `vfprintf()` writes to any stream, `vprintf()` to the stream `stdout` and `vsprintf()` to a memory area.

## Parameters

```
int vfprintf(FILE *stream, const char *format, va_list argptr);
int vfwprintf(FILE *stream, const wchar_t *format, va_list argptr);
int vprintf(const char *format, va_list argptr);
int vwprintf(const wchar_t *format, va_list argptr);
int vsprintf(char *buffer, const char *format, va_list argptr);
int vswprintf(wchar_t *buffer, size_t n, const wchar_t *format,
              va_list argptr);
```

- **Return value.** The three functions return the number of the written characters without the '\0' character. In case of an error a negative value is returned.

## Related functions

```
fprintf(), printf(), sprintf(), va_arg(), va_end(), va_start()
```

### wcstombs, wcsrtombs                           <stdlib.h><wchar.h>

`wchar_t` to multi-byte

## Description

Both functions convert the passed sequence of `wchar_t` characters into a multi-byte string. The conversion terminates if *n* bytes have been converted or a zero termination character or an invalid multi-byte character has occurred. If exactly *n* bytes without a final zero termination character are converted, the string is not zero-terminated. The conversion takes into account the local setting of the LC_TYPE category.

The function wcstomb() produces a sequence of multi-byte characters in the initial shift status (status in which the characters from the C character set are coded 1:1). The function wcsrtomb() produces a sequence of multi-byte characters through the conversion status specified in the mbstate_t argument.

## Parameters

```
size_t wcstombs(char *mb_str, const wchar_t *wc, size_t n);
size_t wcsrtombs(char *mb_str,const wchar_t *wc,size_t n,mbstate_t *ps);
```

- **Return value.** Number of the changed bytes (without zero termination character), or −1 in case of an error.

## Related functions

wctomb(), wcrtomb()

## wctob                                                        <wchar.h>

Determines character type

## Description

Determines whether the character c is a character of an extended character set, whose multibyte representation in the initial shift status (status in which the characters from the C character set are coded 1:1) is a single byte.

## Parameters

```
int wctob(wint_t c);
```

- **Return value.** 1 byte representation of the passed character. EOF, if the character does not correspond to a multi-byte character, which consists of a single byte in the initial conversion status.

## Related functions

btowc()

## wctomb, wcrtomb                                    <stdlib.h><wchar.h>

wchar_t to multi-byte

## Description

Both functions convert the passed wchar_t character into a multi-byte character. The conversion stops after MB_CUR_MAX characters at the latest. The conversion takes into account the local setting of the LC_TYPE category.

## Parameters

```
int wctomb(char *mb_ch, const wchar_t *wc);
size_t wcrtomb(char *mb_ch, const wchar_t *wc, mbstate_t *ps);
```

- **Return value.** Number of the changed bytes (without zero termination character), or −1 in case of an error.

## Related function

```
wcstombs()
```

### wctrans                                                          <wctype.h>
Wide character marking

## Description

Produces a value of the `wctrans_t` type, which identifies the representation of a wide-character character set described by the parameter `property` into another (according to `LC_TYPE`). Is used together with `towctrans()`.

## Parameters

```
wctrans_t wctrans(const char *property);
```

- **Return value.** Value which represents a wide-character representation that is valid according to `LC_TYPE` and can be passed as the second argument to `towctrans()`.

## Related function

```
towctrans()
```

### wctype                                                           <wctype.h>
Mark wide character class

## Description

Produces a `wctype_t` value which identifies the class of wide characters, which has been passed as an argument. Is used together with `iswctype()` and permits the identification of a class by means of a string.

## Parameters

```
type_t wctype(const char *property);
```

- **Return value.** Value which represents a wide-character class and can be passed as the second argument to `iswctype()`.

## Related function

```
iswctype()
```

# The C++ standard library

## Overview of the standard library

The classes and functions defined in the C++ standard library can be divided into various groups:

- The container classes implement the most common models for the handling and storage of data. The models allow data objects to be stored according to certain criteria, for example as a simple set (set) or as stack (stack).

- Iterators are used to access elements in containers conveniently and homogeneously.

- Algorithms. In the header file <algorithm> a range of practical functions are implemented, which manipulate elements in containers with the help of iterators.

- Stream classes form a small class hierarchy for controlling the buffered or non-buffered data stream between hard disk memory, temporary memory and screen.

- String classes offer a user-friendly and less error-prone alternative for handling strings.

- The locale class and the corresponding facet classes are used to adapt to local systems.

- The mathematical classes include the two classes valarray (designed for use on parallel processors) and complex (for treating complex numbers).

- Diagnostic classes permit type identifications at runtime (important for pointers to class instances) and object-oriented error handling.

- The remaining utility classes support, for example, dynamic memory allocation and programming with function objects.

# Header files

Just as in C many important and frequently used functions are a fixed part of the C runtime library, C++ encompasses by default a range of useful classes and class hierarchies. These classes are also part of the runtime library. To be able to access these classes, the corresponding header files in turn have to be integrated  by means of #include statements.

The C++ classes extend the runtime library with new functionalities and operational areas, and also implement existing concepts in an object-oriented way. This applies particularly to the stream classes, which are used to control the data stream between temporary memory, screen and hard drive memory and, thus, replace the functions from the header file stdio.h

However, this does not mean that the old C functions are not available or the systems cannot be mixed. Whether you use the C++ classes or the C functions, or both concepts side by side in a program, depends solely on you. After all, anything else would adversely affect the compatibility of C and C++. In places a mixture of the two is even supported by overloading standard C functions to be able to use them together with the classes of the runtime library.

The elements of the C++ runtime library are included into the namespace std. Therefore it is usual for the #include statements for the header files to be followed by the statement

```
using namespace std;
```

## Warning

Not all compilers support all elements of the C++ library. Some compilers do not support namespaces or have not declared all the classes of the runtime library in the namespace std. Some compilers offer parts of the runtime library in the old C headers, for example iostream.h instead of iostream.

# algorithms

## Description

Contains a whole range of function templates which implement the most common algorithms for use on container elements (copying, moving, sorting, searching and so on). However, 'containers' does not only refer to the containers defined in the  C++ runtime library here. Algorithms can in the same way also be applied to self-defined containers or even simple arrays – appropriate iterators are available to access the elements in the containers and the elements can be processed by the algorithms.

## Included function templates

```
adjacent_find()              // search for adjacent occurrences
binary_search()              // search for elements in a sorted sequence
copy()                       // copy a sequence (begin with first element)
copy_backward()              // copy a sequence (begin with last element)
count()                      // count elements in a sequence
count_if()                   // count specific elements in a sequence
equal()                      // pairwise compare elements in a sequence
equal_range()                // search for a uniform sequence
fill()                       // assign value to an element in a sequence
fill_n()                     // assign a value to the first n elements
                             // in a sequence
find()                       // search for a value in a sequence
find_end()                   // search for last occurrence of a subsequence
find_first_of()              // search for an element in a sequence
find_if()                    // search for a specific element
for_each()                   // apply a function to an element
generate()                   // assign a sequence a calculated value
generate_n()                 // assign the first n elements in a
                             // sequence a calculated value
includes()                   // sequence contained in another sequence
inplace_merge()              // merge two sequences
iter_swap()                  // swap two elements
lexicographical_compare()    // perform a lexicographical comparison
                             // of two sequences
lower_bound()                // insert an element in a sorted sequence
make_heap()                  // convert a sequence into a heap
max()                        // return the larger of two values
max_element()                // return the largest value in a sequence
merge()                      // merge two sequences
min()                        // return the smaller of two value
min_element()                // return the smallest value in a sequence
mismatch()                   // search for the first non-equal elements
                             // of a pair of sequences
next_permutation()           // execute the next permutation
nth_element()                // insert the nth element in sort order
partial_sort()               // sort a part of a sequence
partial_sort_copy()          // sorted copy of a partial sequence
partition()                  // copy selected elements to beginning
pop_heap()                   // remove an element from a heap
prev_permutation()           // create a preceding pemutation
push_heap()                  // insert an element in a heap
random_shuffle()             // reorder elements into a sequence
remove()                     // remove elements with specific values
remove_copy()                // copy only elements which are not equal
                             // to a specific value
remove_copy_if()             // copy a selected element
remove_if()                  // remove specific elements
replace()                    // replace elements with a specific value
```

```
replace_copy()                      // copy a sequence, replacing elements
                                    // specified with a value
replace_copy_if()                   // copy a sequence, replacing specific
                                    // copied elements with a value
replace_if()                        // replace spcified elements
reverse()                           // reverse the order of the elements
reverse_copy()                      // copy a sequence in reverse order
rotate()                            // rotate elements
rotate_copy()                       // copy a sequence in rotated order
search()                            // search for a part of the sequence
search_n()                          // search for a partial sequence with
                                    // identical values
set_difference()                    // difference of two sorted sequences
                                    // (for elements from a, but not b)
set_intersection()                  // intersection of two sorted sequences
set_symmetric_difference()          // difference of two sorted sequences
                                    // (for elements either in a or b)
set_union()                         // union of two sorted sequences
sort()                              // sort a sequence
sort_heap()                         // sort a heap
stable_partition()                  // copy selected elements to beginning
                                    // maintaining their relative order
stable_sort()                       // sort a sequence (relative order of
                                    // identical elements remains the same)
swap()                              // swap two elements
swap_ranges()                       // swap elements of two sequences
transform()                         // assign new values to elements
                                    // of a sequence
unique()                            // remove duplicate from a sequence
unique_copy()                       // copy a sequence without duplicate
upper_bound()                       // insert an element into a
                                    // sorted sequence
```

## References
See Practice section, category the STL, algorithms.

# bitset

## Description
Defines a class template and a few overloaded operators for the management and processing of bit series with a fixed size.

## Included class templates
```
bitset          // For bit sets with a fixed size
```

## Overloaded operators

```
&, |, ^, <<, >>
```

## Example

```cpp
#include <iostream>
#include <bitset>
using namespace std;

int main(int argc, char **argv)
  {
  enum options {op1, op2, op3, op4};

  bitset<4> options("0100"); // initialise bits

  options.set(op1);          // set last bit
  options.set(op3,0);        // set 3rd bit from the right to zero

  cout << "Options: " << options << endl;
  for(int loop = op1; loop <= op4; loop++)
     if(options[loop])
        cout << loop << "-te option set" << endl;
        else
        cout << loop << "-te option not set" << endl;
  return 0;
  }
```

# complex

## Description

Defines the class template complex, including specialisations of the class templates, for the data types float, double and long double, for programming with complex numbers. Several function templates and overloaded operators are defined for use with complex objects.

## Included class templates

```
complex                  // class for complex numbers
complex<double>          // specialisation for double data type
complex<float>           // specialisation for float data type
complex<long double>     // specialisation for long data type
```

## Included function templates

```
abs()                    // calculates the amount
arg()                    // determines an argument
```

```
conj()                    // determines conjugated complex numbers
cos()                     // calculates cosine
cosh()                    // calculates hyperbolic cosine
exp()                     // calculates exponential function
imag()                    // determines imaginary part
log()                     // calculates normal logarithm
log10()                   // calculates the logarith on base 10
norm()                    // determines norm
polar()                   // determines complex number from polar form
pow()                     // exponentiates a number
real()                    // determines the real part
sin()                     // calculates sine
sinh()                    // calculares hyperbolic sine
sqrt()                    // calculates square root
tan()                     // calculates tangent
tanh()                    // calculates hyperbolic tangent
```

## Overloaded operators

+, -, *, /, +, -, ==, !=, <<, >>

## Example

```
#include <complex>
using namespace std;

complex<double> number(32,6, -5.1);
```

# deque

## Description

The class template deque implements a container for the management of objects of any data type. Additionally, functions (swap()) and operators are defined to be applied to deque objects.

## Included templates

```
deque              // a data structure, which is optimized for
                   // insertion/removal at the beginning and the end
                   // and allows fast direct access to any position
swap()             // swaps the elements of two deque containers
```

## Overloaded operators

==, !=, <, >, >=, <=

## Example

```
#include <deque>
using namespace std;

class demo;
deque<int> container(5);    // deque container for int objects
deque<demo> container(5);   // deque container for demo objects
```

## References

See Practice section, category the STL, data management with containers.

# exception

## Description

Contains various classes, type definitions and functions which are connected to exception handling in C++.

## Included classes and type definitions

```
exception                          // base class of the
                                   //   exception classes
                                   // defined in the runtime library
bad_exception                      // for exception objects
                                   //   triggered
                                   // by the unexpected() function
typedef void (*terminate_handler)()   // type of function argument
                                   // to set_terminate()
typedef void (*unexpected_handler)()  // type of function argument
                                   // to set_unexpected()
```

## Included functions

```
terminate()           // calls a function for program termination
set_terminate()       // sets up a function for program termination
unexpected()          // calls a function for handling of
                      // unexpected exceptions
set_unexpected()      // sets up a fuction for handling
                      // unexpected exceptions
uncaught_exception()  // returns true if an exception not yet
                      // caught has been triggered
```

## References

See Reference section, category language concepts, exception handling.

See Practice section, category exceptions, defining exception classes.

# fstream

## Description

Contains class templates for file streams and the corresponding buffers. For the character types `char` and `wchar_t` corresponding classes have already been instanced from the templates, which can be used directly in programs.

## Included class templates

```
basic_fstream       // makes HighLevel routines available for
                    // input and output from and to files
basic_ifstream      // makes a HighLevel routines available for
                    // reading from a file
basic_ofstream      // makes HighLevel routines available for
                    // output to a file
basic_filebuf       // buffer derived from basic_streambuf, which
                    // connects input and output to a file
```

## Included classes

```
fstream             // typedef basic_fstream<char> fstream
wfstream            // typedef basic_fstream<wchar_t> wfstream
ifstream            // typedef basic_ifstream<char> ifstream
wifstream           // typedef basic_ifstream<wchar_t> wifstream
ofstream            // typedef basic_ofstream<char> ofstream
wofstream           // typedef basic_ofstream<wchar_t> wofstream
filebuf             // typedef basic_filebuf<wchar_t> filebuf
wfilebuf            // typedef basic_filebuf<wchar_t> wfilebuf
```

## References

See Practice section, category input and output, text files in C++; input and output, dividing stream buffers.

# functional

## Description

Function objects are class instances for which in many cases only the () operator has been defined. The operator allows objects of these classes to be used like function calls, since the application of the operator to an instance of the class looks the same as a function call. In the STL function objects are often used as parameters for algorithms.

To further support programming with function objects, numerous auxiliary data types, classes and functions are defined in the header file.

# Included function objects

```
divides            // function object for division
equal_to           // function object to test equality
greater            // function object, equivalent to >
greater_equal      // function object, equivalent to >=
less               // function object, equivalent to <
less_equal         // function object, equivalent to <=
logical_and        // function object, equivalent to &&
logical_not        // function object, equivalent to !
logical_or         // function object, equivalent to ||
minus              // function object for subtraction
modulus            // function object for modulus calculation
                   // (remainder of the division)
multiplies         // function object for multiplication
negate             // function object for negation
not_equal_to       // function object to test inequality
plus               // function object for addition
```

# Included auxiliary elements

```
binary_function    // base class for a function object
                   // with two arguments
binary_negate      // auxiliary class for negation of a statement
                   // with two arguments
bind1st()          // function which combines the first argument
                   // of a function object for two arguments with
                   // a constant value
bind2nd()          // function which combines the second argument
                   // of a function object for two arguments with
                   // a constant value
binder1st          // auxiliary class to bind a value to the first
                   // argument of a function object
binder2nd          // auxiliary class to bind a value to the
                   // second argument of a function object
mem_fun_t          // auxiliary class to pass methods without
                   // argument to a function object parameter
mem_fun1_t         // auxiliary class to pass methods with
                   // one argument to a function object parameter
mem_fun()          // auxiliary function to pass methods without
                   // arguments to a function object parameter
mem_fun1()         // auxiliary function to pass methods with
                   // one argument to a function object parameter
mem_fun_ref_t      // auxiliary class to pass methods without
                   // arguments to a function object parameter
mem_fun1_ref_t     // auxiliary class to pass methods with
                   // one argument to a function object parameter
mem_fun_ref()      // auxiliary function to pass methods without
                   // arguments to a function object parameter
mem_fun1_ref()     // auxiliary function to pass methods with one
                   // argument to a function object parameter
```

```
not1()              // negates a unary statement (function object
                    // of return type bool)
not2()              // negates a binary statement (function object
                    // of return type bool)
pointer_to_binary_function  // generation of function objects
                            // from pointers to functions
                            // with two arguments
pointer_to_unary_function   // generation of function objects
                            // from pointers to functions
                            // with one argument
ptr_fun()           // auxiliary function, which allows a function
                    // to be passed to a binder or a negator
unary_function      // base class for function objects with
                    // one argument
unary_negate        // auxiliary class for the negation of an
                    // assertion with one argument
```

## Example

```
// application of a function object
// sorting  values
stable_sort(container.begin(), container.end(), less<int>());

// application of a binder
// searching for the first value greater than 500
iter i = find_if(container.begin(), container.end(),
                    bind2nd(greater<int>(),500));
```

## References

See Practice section, category the STL, creating function objects; function adapters.

# iomanip

## Description

Contains manipulators for the configuration of streams (they are sent to streams like data).

## Included functions

```
resetiosflags      // resets format flags
setbase            // determines the base number systems
setfill            // determines filling characters
setiosflags        // sets format flags
setprecision       // determines precision
setw               // determines field width
```

## Example

```
#include <iomanip>
using namespace std;

cout << setw(7);
cout << 1.23;
cout << setw(7);
cout << "Hi!" << endl;   // output:   1.23    Hi!
```

## References

See Reference section, category input and output, streams in C++.


# ios

## Description

Contains type definitions and basic classes for stream class templates as well as a range of manipulators for the configuration of stream input and output.

## Included classes and type definitions

```
basic_ios      // base class of the stream classes
ios_base       // class which contains the enumeration types,
               // bit fields and functions used for stream
               // configuration and diagnosis; serves as base
               // class for basic_ios
fpos           // auxiliary class for stream status and file
               // positioning
streamoff      // auxiliary type for streams
streamsize     // integer type used as return type of writing
               // and reading methods (as far as these return
               // the number of characters read or written)
```

## Included manipulators

```
boolalpha      // considers a bool type
dec            // decimal representation
hex            // hexadecimal representation
fixed          // fixed number of digits
internal       // fixed positions with padding characters
left           // output ranged left
noboolalpha    // does not consider a bool type
noshowbase     // does not show the base of number system
noshowpoint    // floating point numbers without decimal point
noshowpos      // positive numbers without sign
noskipws       // read whitespace as well
nouppercase    // no conversion to upper case
```

```
oct                    // octal representation
right                  // output ranged right
scientific             // representation with mantissa and exponent
showbase               // shows the base of the number system
showpoint              // floating point number with decimal point
showpos                // positive numbers with sign
skipws                 // does not read white space
uppercase              // specific characters as upper case letters
```

## Example

```
cout.width(10);
cout << 1234.5 << endl;
cout.width(10);
cout << left << 1234.5 << endl;
```

output:

```
1234.5
    1234.5
```

## References

See Reference section, category input and output, streams in C++.

# iosfwd

## Description

Contains the following type definitions (stream classes from the templates of the stream library) and the forward declarations of the templates which are required for this.

## Included class definitions

```
typedef basic_ios<char>                ios;
typedef basic_ios<wchar_t>             wios;
typedef basic_streambuf<char>          streambuf;
typedef basic_istream<char>            istream;
typedef basic_ostream<char>            ostream;
typedef basic_iostream<char>           iostream;
typedef basic_stringbuf<char>          stringbuf;
typedef basic_istringstream<char>      istringstream;
typedef basic_ostringstream<char>      ostringstream;
typedef basic_stringstream<char>       stringstream;
typedef basic_filebuf<char>            filebuf;
typedef basic_ifstream<char>           ifstream;
typedef basic_ofstream<char>           ofstream;
typedef basic_fstream<char>            fstream;
typedef basic_streambuf<wchar_t>       wstreambuf;
```

```
typedef basic_istream<wchar_t>                  wistream;
typedef basic_ostream<wchar_t>                  wostream;
typedef basic_iostream<wchar_t>                 wiostream;
typedef basic_stringbuf<wchar_t>                wstringbuf;
typedef basic_istringstream<wchar_t>            wistringstream;
typedef basic_ostringstream<wchar_t>            wostringstream;
typedef basic_stringstream<wchar_t>             wstringstream;
typedef basic_filebuf<wchar_t>                  wfilebuf;
typedef basic_ifstream<wchar_t>                 wifstream;
typedef basic_ofstream<wchar_t>                 wofstream;
typedef basic_fstream<wchar_t>                  wfstream;
typedef fpos<char_traits<char>::state_type>     streampos;
typedef fpos<char_traits<wchar_t>::state_type>  wstreampos;
```

# iostream

## Description

Defines a range of stream objects which are automatically established and available at the start
of each program.

## Defined standard stream objects

```
istream cin         // standard input stream for char
ostream cout        // standard input stream for char
ostream cerr        // standard error output for char
ostream clog        // standard protocol output for char
wistream wcin       // standard input for wchar_t
wostream wcout;     // standard output stream for wchar_t
wostream wcerr      // standard error output for wchar_t
wostream wclog      // standard protocol output for wchar_t
```

## Example

```
#include <string>
#include <iostream>
int main(int argc, char **argv)
  {
  string str;
  int value;
  cout << "Enter a string and an int value" << endl;
  cin >> str >> value;
  cout << left;            // manipulator
  cout << setw(10) << "String =" << setw(10) << str << endl;
  cout << setw(10) << "Value  =" << setw(10) << value << endl;
  rcturn 0;
  }
```

## References

See Reference section, category input and output, streams in C++.


# istream

## Description

Contains the class template `basic_istream` for the support of read operations on streams, as well as two instances of the templates for the data types `char` and `wchar_t`, which can be used directly in programs.

## Included templates

```
basic_istream          // makes HighLevel routines available for
                       // reading from a stream
basic_iostream         // stream to read and write
ws                     // manipulator to skip whitespace
```

## Included classes

```
istream                // specialisation for char data type
wistream               // specialisation for wchar_t data type
```

## Example

```
filebuf file;
file.open("data.dat", ios_base::in | ios_base::out);
istream dat_in(&file);
ostream dat_out(&filei);
```

## References

See Practice section, category input and output, dividing stream buffers.


# iterators

## Description

Iterators are used to de-reference elements of containers. Their application is similar to the indexing of arrays. Most of the functions from `<algorithm>` work with iterators. A few iterators are predefined in the header file (in the form of templates). Furthermore, the file contains various structures for the definition of individual iterators and auxiliary functions for programming with iterators.

## Auxiliary functions

```
advance()            // shifts an iterator
distance()           // determines the distance between two iterators
back_inserter()      // returns a back inserter for a container
front_inserter()     // returns a front inserter for a container
inserter()           // returns an inserter for a container
```

## Iterator templates

```
back_insert_iterator    // iterator for insertion at the end
                        // of a data structure
front_insert_iterator   // iterator for insertion at the beginning
                        // of a data structure
insert_iterator         // iterator for insertion at a specific
                        // position in a data structure
istream_iterator        // iterator for reading from a stream
istreambuf_iterator     // iterator for reading from a stream buffer
ostream_iterator        // iterator for writing to a stream
ostreambuf_iterator     // iterator for writing to a stream buffer
reverse_iterator        // random access iterator which cycles through
                        // the data structure in reverse direction
```

## Auxiliary structures

```
bidirectional_iterator_tag   // predefined structure as aid for
                             // creating user-defined iterators
forward_iterator_tag         // predefined structure as aid for
                             // creating user-defined iterators
input_iterator_tag           // predefined structure as aid for
                             // creating user-defined iterators
iterator                     // base class to define iterators
iterator_traits              // structure with the characteristics
                             // of iterators
output_iterator_tag          // predefined structure as aid for
                             // creating user-defined iterators
random_access_iterator_tag   // predefined structure as aid for
                             // creating user-defined iterators
```

## Overloaded operators

```
for reverse_iterator:     // ==, <, !=, >, >=, <=, -, +
for istream_iterator:     // ==, !=
for istreambuf_iterator:  // ==, !=
```

## Example

```
deque<int> container(5);
typedef deque<int>::iterator iter;
...
```

```
for(iter i = container.begin(); i != container.end(); i++)  {
    cout << *i << endl;
    }
```

## References

See Practice section, category the STL, iterators.

# limits

## Description

Contains the `numeric_limits` class template and its specialisations for the various data types, which the programmer can use for querying implementation-specific characteristics of elementary data types.

## Included elements

```
float_round_style     // enumeration type with the following values:
                      // round_indeterminate (-1)
                      // round_toward_zero (0)
                      // round_to_nearest (1)
                      // round_toward_infinity(2)
                      // round_toward_neg_infinity(3)
numeric_limits        // template class with information on
                      // implementation-specific representation
                      // of numeric data types;
                      // with spacialization for:
                      // bool
                      // char, signed char, unsigned char, wchar_t
                      // short, int, long
                      // unsigned short, unsigned int, unsigned long
                      // float, double, long double
```

## Example

```
#include <limits>
using namespace std;
...
cout << "Int: "   << setw(14) << numeric_limits<int>::min()
                  << setw(14) << numeric_limits<int>::max() << endl;
```

## References

See Practice section, category variables and data types, value range of integer data types.

# list

## Description

Defines the class template `list`, which implements a container for the management of objects of any data type. Additionally, functions (`swap()`) and operators are defined for application on `list` objects.

## Included functions and classes

```
list            // data structure, with fast insert/delete
                // at all positions, no direct access
swap()          // for swapping the elements of two list containers
```

## Overloaded operators

```
==, !=, <, >, >=, <=
```

## Example

```
#include <list>
using namespace std;

class demo;
list<int> container(5);    // list container for int object
list<demo> container(5);   // list container for demo object
```

## References

See Practice section, category the STL, data management with containers.

# locale

## Description

In certain applications it is necessary to take into account local settings (representations of characters or date specifications or the representation of numeric values). The individual areas are referred to as categories, which in turn are subdivided into facets (specialisations of the corresponding template classes). With the help of the class `locale` and its methods different local settings and their categories can be created and selected.

## Included classes

```
locale          // class for management of local settings
codecvt         // category ctype; supports conversions
                // between coding forms
codecvt_base    // defines an enumeration type for result values
```

```
codecvt_byname        // selects specific implementations according to
                      // the name of the local setting
collate               // class for the category of the same name;
                      // supports comparison and splitting of
                      // character strings
collate_byname        // selects specific implementations according to
                      // the name of the local setting
ctype                 // class for the category of the same name;
                      // supports character recognition as well as
                      // reading and formatting of character strings
ctype<char>           // specialisation for the char data type
ctype_base            // defines bit field for character classification
ctype_byname          // selects specific implementations according to
                      // the name of the local setting
ctype_byname<char>    // specialisation for the char data type
messages              // class for the category of the same name;
                      // supports reading of strings from
                      // message catalogs
messages_base         // defines the catalog data type
messages_byname       // selects specific implementations according to
                      // the name of the local setting
money_base            // defines the part enumeration type for the
                      // formatting of currency specifications, plus
                      // the pattern return type
moneypunct            // category monetary; supports punctuation
                      // in currency specifications
moneypunct_byname     // selects specific implementations according to
                      // the name of the local setting
money_get             // category monetary; supports reading of
                      // currency specifications
money_put             // category monetary; supports fomatted output
                      // of currency specifications
numpunct              // category numeric; supports punctuation
                      // in numerical values
numpunct_byname       // selects specific implementations according to
                      // the name of the local setting
num_get               // category numeric. supports reading of
                      // numeric values
num_put               // category numeric; supports formatting
                      // during output of numeric values
time_base             // enumeration type for date sequences
time_get              // category time; supports reading of time
                      // specifications into a variable of type tm
time_get_byname       // selects specific implementations according to
                      // the name of the local setting
time_put              // category time; supports output of time
                      // specifications
time_put_byname       // selects specific implementations according to
                      // the name of the local setting
```

## Function templates

```
has_facet()      // tests whether a specific  facet is available
use_facet()      // selects a facet according to a locale setting
is...            // methods for character classification
                 // (see C header ctype.h)
tolower()        // conversion to lower case
toupper()        // conversion to upper case
```

## References

See Practice section, category internationalisation and localisation, local environment.

# map

## Description

Defines the class templates map and multimap which implement containers for the management of objects of any data type. Additionally, functions (swap()) and operators are defined for the application on map and multimap objects.

## Included functions and classes

```
map              // a data structure which accesses its element with
                 // the aid of unique keys (ideal hashing)
multimap         // a data structure which accesses its element with
                 // the aid of not necessarily unique keys
swap()           // for swapping the elements of two map or
                 // multimap containers
```

## Overloaded operators

```
==, <, !=, > , >=, <=
```

## Example

```
#include <map>
#include <string>
using namespace std;

class demo;
map<int, string> container;   // map container for string objects
                              //                  with int key
map<int, demo> container;     // map container for demo objects
                              //                  with int key
```

### References

See Practice section, category the STL, data management with containers.

# memory

## Description

Contains various class and function templates for memory management. Most of these elements are intended for the implementation of containers and algorithms.

## Included class templates

```
allocator            // class for implementation of memory managers
allocator<void>      // specialisation for void
auto_ptr             // pointer class for automatic clearance
                     // of dynamic memory
raw_storage_iterator // for storage in non-initialised memory areas
```

## Included function templates

```
get_temporary_buffer()     // request for temporary memory
return_temporary_buffer()  // access to temporary memory
uninitialized_copy()       // fill non-initialized memory
uninitialized_fill()       // fill non-initialized memory
uninitialized_fill_n()     // fill non-initialized memory
```

## Overloaded operaotrs for allocators

```
==, !=
```

## References

See Practice section, category pointers and dynamic memory management, auto_ptr.

# new

## Description

Contains the overloaded operator functions for new and delete, as well as various auxiliary elements.

## Overloaded operators

```
new        // reserve memory
new[]      // reserve memory for a field
```

```
delete              // clear memory
delete[]            // clear memory for a field
```

## Included auxiliary elements

```
bad_alloc           // for exception objects triggered by bad memory
                    // reservation
nothrow_t           // structure type to be passed to the new operator
nothrow             // auxiliary structure as argument for new
set_new_handler()   // registers an error handling routine for new
```

## References

See Reference section, category operators, the new and delete operators.

See Practice section, category pointers and dynamic memory management.

# numeric

## Description

Contains various function templates for the execution of numeric algorithms on container elements.

## Included functions and classes

```
accumulate()            // calculates the sum
adjacent_difference()   // assigns the difference
inner_product()         // calculates the scalar product
partial_sum()           // calculates the sum
```

## Example

```cpp
#include <numeric>
#include <vector>
#include <iostream>
using namespace std;

vector<int> container;

int main() {
    for(int i = 0; i < 7; i++)
        container.push_back(i);

    cout << "Sum of the value: "
         << accumulate(container.begin(), container.end(), 0)
         << endl;

    return 0;
}
```

## References

See Practice section, category the STL, algorithms.

# ostream

## Description

Contains the class template `basic_ostream` for the support of write operations on streams, two templates for the data types `char` and `wchar_t`, which can be used directly in programs, and various manipulators.

## Included templates

```
basic_ostream          // makes HighLevel routines available for
                       // writing to a stream
endl                   // manipulator: end of line
ends                   // manipulator: end of string
flush                  // clears a stream buffer
```

## Included classes

```
ostream                // specialisation for the char data type
wostream               // specialisation for the wchar_t data type
```

## Example

```
filebuf file;                          //opens a file for reading and writing
file.open("data.dat",ios_base::in | ios_base::out);
istream dat_in(&file);                 // connects a file to an input stream
ostream dat_out(&file);                // connects a file to an output stream
```

## References

See Reference section, category input and output, dividing stream buffers.

# queue

## Description

Defines the class templates `queue` and `priority_queue`, which implement containers for the management of objects of any data type. Additionally, operators have been defined for application on `queue` objects.

## Included functions and classes

```
queue              // queue: a data structure which allows insertion
                   // of elements only at the end and removal of
                   // elements only at the beginning
priority_queue     // a data structure which allows the insertion
                   // of new elements and always deletes the element
                   // of highest priority in pop accesses
                   // (for example the largest element)
```

## Overloaded operators

```
==, <, !=, > , >=, <=
```

## Example

```cpp
#include <queue>
using namespace std;

class demo;
queue<int> container(5);   // queue container for int objects
queue<demo> container(5);  // queue container for demo objects
```

## References

See Practice section, category the STL, data management with containers.


# set

## Description

Defines the class templates set and multiset, which implement containers for the management of objects of any data type. Additionally, functions (swap()) and operators have been defined for application on set and multiset objects.

## Included functions and classes

```
set            // a data structure in which elements are
               // automatically ordered by their values, which
               // allows quick retrieval of the elements
multiset       // a data structure which works with not
               // necessarily unique values, which
               // allows quick retrieval of the elements
swap()         // for swapping the elements of two set containers
```

## Overloaded operators

```
==, <, !=, > , >=, <=
```

## Example

```
#include <set>
using namespace std;

class demo;
// set container for int objects, sorted with the < operator
set<int> container(5);
// set container for demo objects, sorted by greater<demo>
set<demo, greater<demo> > container(5);
```

## References

See Practice section, category the STL, data management with containers.


# sstream

## Description

Contains class templates which create the connection between strings and streams, as well as templates for the character types char and wchar_t. String streams can be used like the C functions sprintf() and sscanf().

## Included class templates

```
basic_stringstream      // makes HighLevel routines available
                        // for reading and writing from and to
                        // basic_string objects
basic_istringstream     // makes HighLevel routines available for
                        // reading from basic_string objects
basic_ostringstream     // makes HighLevel routines available for
                        // writing to basic_string objects
basic_stringbuf         // buffer classs derived from basic_streambuf
                        // for objects of the basic_string class
```

## Included classes

```
stringstream    // typedef basic_stringstream<char> stringstream
wstringstream   // typedef basic_stringstream<wchar_t> wstringstream
istringstream   // typedef basic_istringstream<char> istringstream
wistringstream  // typedef basic_istringstream<wchar_t> wistringstream
ostringstream   // typedef basic_ostringstream<char> ostringstream
wostringstream  // typedef basic_ostringstream<wchar_t> wostringstream
stringbuf       // typedef basic_stringbuf<char> stringbuf
wstringbuf      // typedef basic_stringbuf<wchar_t> wstringbuf
```

## References

See Practice section, category in- and output, string streams.

# stack

## Description

Defines the class template `stack`, which implements a container for the management of objects of any data type. Additionally, operators are defined for application on `stack` objects.

## Included functions and classes

```
stack        // stack: a data structure which allows insertion
             // and deletion only at upper end
```

## Overloaded operators

```
==, !=, <, >, >=, <=
```

## Example

```
#include <stack>
using namespace std;

class demo;
stack<int>  container(5);    // stack container for int objects
stack<demo> container(5);    // stack container for demo objects
```

## References

See Practice section, category the STL, data management with containers.


# stdexcept

## Description

Defines a range of exceptions for error messages in C++ programs.

## Included exception classes

```
domain_error     // for exception objects triggered at the occurrence
                 // of illegal values
invalid_argument // for exception objects triggered at the passing
                 // of invalid arguments
length_error     // for exception objects triggered if the legal
                 // size of data structures or types is exceeded
logic_error      // for exception objects which regard logical errors
out_of_range     // for exception objects triggered if an
                 // argument is not within the allowed range
overflow_error   // for exception objects triggered by arithmetical
                 // overflows
```

```
range_error        // for exception objects triggered by the violation
                   // of validity ranges
runtime_error      // for exception objects which regard runtime errors
anderflow_error    // for exception objectstriggered by arithmetical
                   // underflows
```

## References

See Practice section, category exceptions.

# streambuf

## Description

Contains the template for the stream buffer classes, as well as two templates for the data types char and wchar_t. The stream classes use instances of the buffer classes for write and read operations (in which the input and output does not really have to be buffered; the internal buffer of the buffer classes can also be set to zero).

## Included class templates

```
basic_streambuf        // base class for buffered LowLevel operations
```

## Included classes

```
streambuf          // typedef basic_streambuf<char> streambuf
wstreambuf         // typedef basic_streambuf<wchar_t> wstreambuf
```

## References

See Practice section, category input and output, dividing stream buffers.

See Reference section, category input and output, buffering.

# string

## Description

Contains the class template basic_string, which provides all the important methods for programming with strings, templates for the character types char and wchar_t, and operators and functions for working with strings.

## Included elements

```
basic_string           // class template for string handling
char_traits            // class which describes the characteristics
                       // of a character type
```

```
char_traits<char>       // specialisation for the char data type
char_traits<wchar_t>    // specialisation for the wchar_t data type
getline()               // reads a line
swap()                  // swaps the characters of two strings
string                  // specialisation of basic_string
                        // for the char data type
wstring                 // specialisation of basic_string
                        // for the wchar_t data type
```

## Overloaded operators for basic_string

+, ==, !=, <, >, <=, >=

## Overloaded operators for basic_istream

>>, <<

## References

See Reference section, category strings, the class string.

See Practice section, category strings, programming with the class string.

# typeinfo

## Description

Contains the class type_info, with which RTTI information programs are made available in C++, as well as two exception classes for error handling.

## Included classes

```
type_info    // manages informations on data types(description
             // string, priority value)
bad_cast     // for exception objects triggered by failed
             // dynamic_cast operations
bad_typeid   // for exception objects triggered to indicate a null
             // pointer in typeid expressions
```

## References

See Reference section, category inheritance and polymorphy, RTTI (runtime type identification).

See Practice section, category inheritance and polymorphy, type identification at runtime.

# utility

## Description

Contains templates which facilitate working with value pairs and are used within the C++ runtime library.

## Included templates

```
pair          // template class for structures with two elements
              // of different data types
make_pair()   // function which creates a pair from its two arguments
```

## Overloaded operators

```
==, <, !=, >, >=, <=
```

# valarray

## Description

Defines the data structure valarray, which manages its elements as if in an array (however, the memory is dynamically managed). The class valarray permits a multitude of operations which are carried out on all the elements of the array, as well as the option to form subsets with the help of auxiliary classes.

## Included clas templates and classes

```
valarray        // one-dimensional dynamic array with a multitude
                // of operations which are simultaneously carried
                // out on all elements
gslice          // auxiliary class to define a multi-dimensional
                // subset from a one-dimensional valarray object
gslice_array    // auxiliary class to manipulate a multi-dimensional
                // subset from a one-dimensional valarray object;
                // the subset is created by means of gslice
indirect_array  // auxiliary class to manipulate a subset
                // of a valarray objects; the subset is created
                // by means of an index array
mask_array      // auxiliary class to manipulate a subset of a
                // valarray object; the subset is created by
                // means of a mask
slice           // auxiliary class to define a subset of constant
                // length of stride from a valarray object
slice_array     // auxiliary class to manipulate a subset of constant
                // length of stride from a valarray object;
                // the subset is created by means of slice
```

## Overloaded functions for valarray

| abs  | atan2 | log   | pow  | tan  |
|------|-------|-------|------|------|
| acos | cos   | log10 | sin  | tanh |
| asin | cosh  | min   | sinh |      |
| atan | exp   | max   | sqrt |      |

## Overloaded operators for valarray

```
*, /, %, +, -, ^, &, <<, >>, &&, ==, !=, <, >, <=, >=
```

## Example

```cpp
#include <iostream>
#include <string>
#include <valarray>
using namespace std;

int main()
  {
  valarray<int> va(20);
  for(int i = 0; i < 20; i++)
    {
    va[i] = i;
    cout << va[i] << endl;
    }

  valarray<int> part(5);
  valarray<size_t> size(2);
  size[0] = 3; size[1] = 4;
  valarray<size_t> stride(2);
  stride[0] = 5; stride[1] = 1;

  part = va[gslice(2,size,stride)];
  cout << "\nPartial array\n";
    for(int i = 0; i < size[0]*size[1]; i++)
      {
      cout << part[i] << endl;
      }
  return 0;
  }
```

# vector

## Description

Defines the class template `vector`, which implements a container for the management of objects of any data type. Additionally functions (`swap()`) and operators are defined for application on `vector` objects.

## Included functions and classes

```
vector          // standard data structure which is optimized to
                // insert/delete at the end and allows fast direct
                // access to arbitrary positions
vector<bool>    // predefined specialisation of the class template
                // vector which guarantees an optimized storage
                // management
swap()          // swaps the elements of two vector containers
```

## Overloaded operators

```
==, !=, <, >, >=, <=
```

## Example

```
#include <vector>
using namespace std;

class demo;
vector<int>  container(5);    // vector container for int objects
vector<demo> container(5);    // vector container for demo objects
```

## References

See Practice section, category the STL, data management with containers.

# The container classes

## General characteristics

### Description
The container classes are intended to facilitate the management of larger data quantities in programs for the programmer. Thus, they are a convenient alternative to arrays and dynamic fields and save the programmer the implementation of his own higher data structures.

- Containers can be established for objects of elementary or self-defined class types. One precondition is, however, that the copy constructor and assignment operator of the class type have not been made inaccessible through a `private` or `protected` declaration. Also, for certain actions on the elements of a container the corresponding operators for the class type of the objects have to be overloaded (for example the `compare` operators).

- It is only possible to store objects of a single data type in a container.

- The container allows access as well as the insertion and deletion of objects. Deleting the container implies the deletion of the objects contained in it (if they are pointers, of course only the pointers and not the objects to which the pointer refer are deleted).

- The container only defines methods for management of the object not for processing. Algorithms are used for the latter purpose.

- The various container types have been defined as templates, which have to be specialised for the data type of the objects which are to be accommodated.

- The size of a container (that is, the number of the objects which it can accommodate) is not determined statically. For this purpose each container implements its own dynamic memory management.

- The individual container types differ in the way in which they manage data (sorted–non-sorted; organised–unorganised); which access options they allow (access at the beginning or end of the data structure, indexed access, and so on); and which access options are particularly efficient.

### Basic characteristics of containers
Although the class templates of the various containers do not go back to a common basic class template, there is a range of characteristics, common to all container types.

## General container characteristics

In this and the following lists X identifies a container type, a and b are containers, and i and j are iterators.

| Characteristic | Description |
| --- | --- |
| X() | Produces an anonymous container of the size 0 |
| X a | Produces the container a of the size 0 |
| X a(b) | |
| X a = b; | Produces a as a copy of b |
| (&a)->~X() | Destructor is applied to all elements |
| a.begin() | Returns iterator to first element in container |
| a.end() | Returns iterator behind final element |
| a.size() | Returns the current number of elements |
| a.empty() | Specifies, whether the container is empty |
| a.swap(b) | Exchanges the elements of the containers a and b |
| a == b | True, if both containers contain the same number of elements, which are pairwise identical |
| a != b | !(a == b) |
| a < b | Lexicographic comparison of a and b |
| a > b | Lexicographic comparison of a and b |
| a <= b | !(a > b) |
| a >= b | !(a < b) |

## Sequential and associative containers

Each container type has its own specialities and qualities. Independent of these individual characteristics containers can be divided into two groups, which differ in the order of the objects stored in them: sequential and associative containers.

### Sequential containers

- In a sequential container the elements are ordered linearly (for example as an array, list or a combination of both).

- The order depends on the time or position of the insertion of the individual elements.

- The linear order allows operations like the insertion at a particular position or the deletion of a particular area of elements.

- Sequential containers work with forward iterators or higher.

Sequential containers are vector, list, deque, queue, priority_queue and stack.

| Characteristic | Description |
|---|---|
| X(n,t),<br>X a(n,t) | Produces containers with n copies of the value t |
| X(i,j),<br>X a(i,j) | Produces containers as copy of the sequence [i,j)    (with i, without j) |
| a.insert(p, ) | Inserts before a position p; either a value t, n copies of a value t or a copy of a sequence [i,j) |
| a.erase(p) | Deletes the element at the n of the position p |
| a.erase(i,j) | Deletes the elements in the area [i,j) |
| a.clear() | Deletes all the elements in the container |

The following operations are only supported by the seqential containers, for which they can be implemented in constant time:

| Operation | Description | for the containers |
|---|---|---|
| a.front() | *a.begin() | vector, list, deque |
| a.back() | *--a.end() | vector, list, deque |
| a.push_front(t) | a.insert(a.begin(),t) | list, deque |
| a.push_back(t) | a.insert(a.end(),t) | vector, list, deque |
| a.pop_front() | a.erase(a.begin()) | list, deque |
| a.pop_back() | a.erase(--a.end()) | vector, list, deque |
| a[n] | *(a.begin() + n) | vector, deque |
| a.at(n) | *(a.begin() + n) | vector, deque |

Corresponding to the internal memory management – as can be seen in the table – not all these operations can be implemented for all sequential containers. For a vector container, which is very close to a dynamic array, for example, the insertion at the start of the container (push_front()) would require that all elements in the container, beginning from the container end, are shifted backwards by one position. As this is only possible in linear and not constant time, this operation is not supported by vector.

**Associative containers**

- In an associative container the elements are stored sorted (the basic data structure can be a binary tree or a Hashing table).
- The sorting is carried out according to keys of the elements and according to a specific sorting criterion, the compare object.
- For set and multiset the value and key fall together; that is, the value is also the key, according to where the sorting occurs.

- For `map` and `multimap` a separate key is assigned to each element, and element and key are stored as a pair in the container.
- Sorting allows the quick finding of elements by their value or a corresponding key.
- Associative containers work with bi-directional iterators.
- Associative containers are `set`, `multiset`, `map` and `multimap`.

| Characteristic | Description |
|---|---|
| X(c)<br>X a(c)<br>X(i,j,c)<br>X a(i,j,c) | Pendants to the constructors of the sequential containers, which as additional argument adopt a compare object as comparison criterion.<br>Without a called compare object, the default compare object of the container (see template definition) is used. |
| a.insert(... ) | Various overloaded versions for the insertion of elements into the container |
| a.erase(... ) | Various overloaded versions for the removal of elements from the container |
| a.clear() | Deletes all the elements in the container |
| a.find(k) | Returns an iterator to the first element with the key k |
| a.count(k) | Returns the number of the elements with the key k |
| a.lower_bound(k) | Returns an iterator to the first element, whose key is smaller than k |
| a.upper_bound(k) | Returns an iterator to the first element, whose key is greater than k |
| a.equal_range(k) | Returns the iterators of lower_bound() and upper_bound() as pair (see make_pair() ) |

## References

See Practice section, category the STL, data management with containers.

# bitset

Managing flags (from header bitset)

## Description

The `bitset` class manages of a definite number of elements (bits), which only adapt values of one and zero.

## Application

Instances of the `bitset` class can be used for the management of diagnosis and switch variables (flags). In contrast to the use of the bit operators or bit fields that originate in C, the methods and operators that are available for `bitset` are more convenient.

The number of bits is invariable and is determined through the joker N in the specialised template. To manage a variable number of flags, use the `vector<bool>` container.

```
bitset<4> options; // Initializes bits
```

The individual bits in the bitset can be initialised at the creation of the bitset with the values from an integer or a string.

```
bitset<4> options("0100");
```

The functions `to_ulong()` and `to_string()` convert a bitset into an integer value or a string object. The functions `set()`, `reset()` and `flip()` can be used to set all bits or a particular bit. To query individual bits the `test()` function is employed. The index operator [ ] is used for the manipulation of individual bits. The operators &=, |= and ^= use a second bitset to manipulate their instance.

## Warning

The class `bitset` is deifferent from the other containers (it does not support iterators, does not possess the basic characteristics, and so on).

## Example

```
template<size_t N> class bitset {
  public:
  class reference {
      friend class bitset;
      reference();
    public:
     ~reference();
      reference& operator=(bool x);           // for b[i] = x;
      reference& operator=(const reference&); // for b[i] = b[j];
      bool operator~() const;                 // inverts the bit
      operator bool() const;                  // for x = b[i];
      reference& flip();                      // for b[i].flip();
    };
  // Constructors:
    bitset();
    bitset(unsigned long val);
    template<class charT, class traits, class Allocator>
      explicit bitset(
        const basic_string<charT,traits,Allocator>& str,
        typename basic_string<charT,traits,Allocator>::size_type pos = 0,
        typename basic_string<charT,traits,Allocator>::size_type n =
          basic_string<charT,traits,Allocator>::npos);
```

```
// Operators:
  bitset<N>& operator&=(const bitset<N>& rhs);
  bitset<N>& operator|=(const bitset<N>& rhs);
  bitset<N>& operator^=(const bitset<N>& rhs);
  bitset<N>& operator<<=(size_t pos);
  bitset<N>& operator>>=(size_t pos);
  bitset<N>& set();
  bitset<N>& set(size_t pos, int val = true);
  bitset<N>& reset();
  bitset<N>& reset(size_t pos);
  bitset<N>  operator~() const;
  bitset<N>& flip();
  bitset<N>& flip(size_t pos);
  reference operator[](size_t pos);    // for b[i];

  unsigned long  to_ulong() const;
  template <class charT, class traits, class Allocator>
    basic_string<charT, traits, Allocator> to_string() const;
  size_t count() const;
  size_t size()  const;
  bool operator==(const bitset<N>& rhs) const;
  bool operator!=(const bitset<N>& rhs) const;
  bool test(size_t pos) const;
  bool any() const;
  bool none() const;
  bitset<N> operator<<(size_t pos) const;
  bitset<N> operator>>(size_t pos) const;
};
```

## Reference

See header file bitset.

# deque

Sequential container (from header deque)

## Description

The abbreviation deque stands for double ended queue. It is a data structure, which is usually based on a string of array blocks, and arranges its elements in a sequential series.

The deque class is similar to the vector class and also offers quick, direct access to individual elements ([] operator, at() method) as well as the insertion and deletion of elements at any position (insert(), erase()). However, unlike access to existing elements, the insertion or deletion of elements is time-consuming, since these operations usually require internal recopying of the elements in the container. Only at the beginning or end of the data structure is it possible to insert or delete in constant time.

In comparison to `vector`, access to any position is slightly slower, but in return memory management is favourable.

Insertion and deletion is more time-intensive than with a `list` container. In return, however, `deque` permits convenient indexed access to particular positions (for reading or writing).

Iterators for `deque` containers should belong to the `forward_iterator` category; however, different functions require higher iterator categories. Insert or delete operations in the middle of the container always result in the invalidity of existing iterators and references to container elements.

## Application

Behind `deque` stands a class template from which a container class is created. In this the data type of the objects which are to be managed is passed to the template parameter T.

```
deque<int> container;
```

The overloaded forms of the constuctors allow the creation of empty containers or those which contain several copies of an element or the copy of a sequence of elements from another container.

New elements can be inserted with `insert()`, `push_front()`, `push_back()`, `resize()` or `assign()`, where the latter function empties the container first.

Existing elements can be deleted with `erase()`, `pop_front()`, `pop_back()`, `resize()` or `clear()`.

Individual elements can be accessed with returned iterators (`begin()`, `end()`, `rbegin()`, `rend()` and `insert()`) or through returned references (operator `[]`, `at()`, `front()`, `back()`).

Finally, it is possible to manipulate, sort and search the container through the global functions of the `<algorithm>` header file.

## Example
```
template <class T, class Allocator = allocator<T> >
  class deque {
  public:
    typedef typename Allocator::reference          reference;
    typedef typename Allocator::const_reference    const_reference;
    typedef implementation defined                 iterator;
    typedef implementation defined                 const_iterator;
    typedef typename Allocator::size_type          size_type;
    typedef typename Allocator::difference_type    difference_type;
```

```
            typedef T                                        value_type;
            typedef Allocator                                allocator_type;
            typedef typename Allocator::pointer              pointer;
            typedef typename Allocator::const_pointer        const_pointer;
            typedef std::reverse_iterator<iterator>          reverse_iterator;
            typedef std::reverse_iterator<const_iterator>
                                                  const_reverse_iterator;
// Constructors and allocation:
    explicit deque(const Allocator& = Allocator());
    explicit deque(size_type n, const T& value = T(),
        const Allocator& = Allocator());
    template <class InputIterator>
      deque(InputIterator first, InputIterator last,
            const Allocator& = Allocator());
    deque(const deque<T,Allocator>& x);
    ~deque();
    deque<T,Allocator>& operator=(const deque<T,Allocator>& x);
    template <class InputIterator>
      void assign(InputIterator first, InputIterator last);
    template <class Size, class T>
      void assign(Size n, const T& t = T());
    allocator_type get_allocator() const;
// Iterators:
    iterator               begin();
    const_iterator         begin() const;
    iterator               end();
    const_iterator         end() const;
    reverse_iterator       rbegin();
    const_reverse_iterator rbegin() const;
    reverse_iterator       rend();
    const_reverse_iterator rend() const;
// Size:
    size_type size() const;
    size_type max_size() const;
    void      resize(size_type sz, T c = T());
    bool      empty() const;
// Access to elements:
    reference       operator[](size_type n);
    const_reference operator[](size_type n) const;
    reference       at(size_type n);
    const_reference at(size_type n) const;
    reference       front();
    const_reference front() const;
    reference       back();
    const_reference back() const;
// Inserting, deleting:
    void push_front(const T& x);
    void push_back(const T& x);
    iterator insert(iterator position, const T& x = T());
    void     insert(iterator position, size_type n, const T& x);
```

```
      template <class InputIterator>
          void insert(iterator position,InputIterator first,
                      InputIterator last);
      void pop_front();
      void pop_back();
      iterator erase(iterator position);
      iterator erase(iterator first, iterator last);
      void     swap(deque<T,Allocator>&);
      void     clear();
  };
```

## References

See Practice section, category the STL, data management with containers.

# list
Sequential container (from header list)

## Description

The class template list represents, like deque and vector, a sequential container with direct access to the first and final element, as well as insertion and deletion of elements at any position.

The insertion and deletion of elements at any position within the container is carried out more quickly for list than for deque or vector, as these operations do not require the shifting of the following elements. However, list lacks indexed access to elements at a particular position.

Iterators for list containers should at least belong to the forward_iterator category; however, different functions require higher iterator categories. Insert and delete operations do not affect the validity of existing iterators and references to container elements.

## Application

Behind list stands a class template from which a container class is created. In this the data type of the objects which are to be managed is passed to the template parameter T.

list<int> container;

The overloaded forms of the constuctors allow the creation of empty containers or those which contain several copies of an element or the copy of a sequence of elements from another container.

New elements can be inserted with insert(), push_front(), push_back(), resize(), assign() or merge().

Existing elements can be deleted with `erase()`, `pop_front()`, `pop_back()`, `resize()`, `clear()`, `unique()` or `remove()`, `remove_if()`.

Individual elements can be accessed with returned iterators (`begin()`, `end()`, `rbegin()`, `rend()` as well as `insert()`) or through returned references (`front()`, `back()`).

With the function `sort()` the elements can be sorted, where the sorting type can be determined through the < operator or a self-defined compare function. The order can be inversed with `reverse()`.

Finally, it is possible to manipulate, sort and search the container with the global functions of the `<algorithm>` header file.

## Example

```
template <class T, class Allocator = allocator<T> >
  class list {
  public:
    typedef typename Allocator::reference           reference;
    typedef typename Allocator::const_reference     const_reference;
    typedef implementation defined                  iterator;
    typedef implementation defined                  const_iterator;
    typedef typename Allocator::size_type           size_type;
    typedef typename Allocator::difference_type     difference_type;
    typedef T                                       value_type;
    typedef Allocator                               allocator_type;
    typedef typename Allocator::pointer             pointer;
    typedef typename Allocator::const_pointer       const_pointer;
    typedef std::reverse_iterator<iterator>         reverse_iterator;
    typedef std::reverse_iterator<const_iterator>
                                           const_reverse_iterator;
    // Constructors and allocation:
    explicit list(const Allocator& = Allocator());
    explicit list(size_type n, const T& value = T(),
               const Allocator& = Allocator());
    template <class InputIterator>
      list(InputIterator first, InputIterator last,
          const Allocator& = Allocator());
    list(const list<T,Allocator>& x);
    ~list();
    list<T,Allocator>& operator=(const list<T,Allocator>& x);
    template <class InputIterator>
      void assign(InputIterator first, InputIterator last);
    template <class Size, class T>
      void assign(Size n, const T& t = T());
    allocator_type get_allocator() const;
  // Iterators:
    iterator              begin();
    const_iterator        begin() const;
```

```
  iterator              end();
  const_iterator        end() const;
  reverse_iterator      rbegin();
  const_reverse_iterator rbegin() const;
  reverse_iterator      rend();
  const_reverse_iterator rend() const;
// Size:
  bool      empty() const;
  size_type size() const;
  size_type max_size() const;
  void      resize(size_type sz, T c = T());
// Access to elements:
  reference       front();
  const_reference front() const;
  reference       back();
  const_reference back() const;
// Insertion and deletion:
  void push_front(const T& x);
  void pop_front();
  void push_back(const T& x);
  void pop_back();
  iterator insert(iterator position, const T& x = T());
  void     insert(iterator position, size_type n, const T& x);
  template <class InputIterator>
    void insert(iterator position, InputIterator first,
                InputIterator last);
  iterator erase(iterator position);
  iterator erase(iterator position, iterator last);
  void     swap(list<T,Allocator>&);
  void     clear();
// Operators:
  void splice(iterator position, list<T,Allocator>& x);
  void splice(iterator position, list<T,Allocator>& x, iterator i);
  void splice(iterator position, list<T,Allocator>& x, iterator first,
              iterator last);
  void remove(const T& value);
  template <class Predicate> void remove_if(Predicate pred);
  void unique();
  template <class BinaryPredicate> void unique(BinaryPredicate
                                               binary_pred);
  void merge(list<T,Allocator>& x);
  template <class Compare> void merge(list<T,Allocator>& x,
                                      Compare comp);
  void sort();
  template <class Compare> void sort(Compare comp);
  void reverse();
};
```

## References
See Practice section, category the STL, data management with containers.

# map and multimap
Associative container (from the header map)

## Description

The map and multimap containers use a key to allow quick access to its elements. The idea is that the objects to manage are assigned with a key (this is similar to arrays, for example, where single elements are bound with indices).

In the container, the elements are sorted according to their key. The value of a key of an inserted element should not be modified because this will destroy the sequence.

Iterators on map and multimap must be of bidirectional category.

While the map class allows only a particular key, in multimap more keys regarding the comparison function are identical. This means that a key refers to more different objects, which then must be searched to find a particular object. This means an extended runtime with a small storage requirements.

The multimap class does not control the index operator [ ].

## Application

Behind map and multimap stand a class template from which container classes are created. In this the data type of the keys is passed to the template parameter Key and the data type of the objects which are to be managed to the template parameter T.

```
map<int, string> container;
```

Additionally, it is possible to pass a function object, which determines how the elements in the container are to be sorted with the keys, to the third template parameter.

```
map<int, string, greater<int> > container;
```

The overloaded forms of the constuctors allow the creation of empty containers or those which contain several copies of an element or the copy of a sequence of elements from another container. The objects for allocation and comparison can be self-defined or adopted from the default.

New elements can be inserted with insert.

Existing elements can be deleted with `erase()` or `clear()`.

Individual elements can be accessed with returned iterators (`begin()`, `end()`, `rbegin()`, `rend()`, `find()`, `lower_bound()`, `upper_bound()` and `insert()`).

Finally, it is possible to manipulate, sort and search, the container with the global functions of the header file `<algorithm>`.

## map                                                              map>

```
template <class Key, class T, class Compare = less<Key>,
         class Allocator = allocator<T> >
  class map {
  public:
    typedef Key                                    key_type;
    typedef T                                      mapped_type;
    typedef pair<const Key, T>                     value_type;
    typedef Compare                                key_compare;
    typedef Allocator                              allocator_type;
    typedef typename Allocator::reference          reference;
    typedef typename Allocator::const_reference    const_reference;
    typedef implementation defined                 iterator;
    typedef implementation defined                 const_iterator;
    typedef typename Allocator::size_type          size_type;
    typedef typename Allocator::difference_type    difference_type;
    typedef Allocator::pointer                     pointer;
    typedef Allocator::const_pointer               const_pointer;
    typedef std::reverse_iterator<iterator>        reverse_iterator;
    typedef std::reverse_iterator<const_iterator>
                                              const_reverse_iterator;
    class value_compare
      : public binary_function<value_type,value_type,bool> {
    friend class map;
    protected:
      Compare comp;
      value_compare(Compare c) : comp(c) {}
    public:
      bool operator()(const value_type& x, const value_type& y) const {
        return comp(x.first, y.first);
      }
    };
  // Constructors and allocation:
    explicit map(const Compare& comp = Compare(), const Allocator& =
                                                Allocator());
    template <class InputIterator>
      map(InputIterator first, InputIterator last,
          const Compare& comp = Compare(), const Allocator& =
                                                Allocator());
    map(const map<Key,T,Compare,Allocator>& x);
  ~map();
    map<Key,T,Compare,Allocator>&
```

```
            operator=(const map<Key,T,Compare,Allocator>& x);
  // Iterators:
    iterator                begin();
    const_iterator          begin() const;
    iterator                end();
    const_iterator          end() const;
    reverse_iterator        rbegin();
    const_reverse_iterator  rbegin() const;
    reverse_iterator        rend();
    const_reverse_iterator  rend() const;
  // Size:
    bool      empty() const;
    size_type size() const;
    size_type max_size() const;
  // Access to elements:
    reference operator[](const key_type& x);
  // Insertion and deletion:
    pair<iterator, bool> insert(const value_type& x);
    iterator             insert(iterator position, const value_type& x);
    template <class InputIterator>
      void insert(InputIterator first, InputIterator last);
    void      erase(iterator position);
    size_type erase(const key_type& x);
    void      erase(iterator first, iterator last);
    void swap(map<Key,T,Compare,Allocator>&);
    void clear();
// Others:
    key_compare   key_comp() const;
    value_compare value_comp() const;
    iterator        find(const key_type& x);
    const_iterator find(const key_type& x) const;
    size_type      count(const key_type& x) const;
    iterator       lower_bound(const key_type& x);
    const_iterator lower_bound(const key_type& x) const;
    iterator       upper_bound(const key_type& x);
    const_iterator upper_bound(const key_type& x) const;
    pair<iterator,iterator>                  equal_range(const key_type& x);
    pair<const_iterator,const_iterator> equal_range(const key_type& x)
                                                                  const;

  };
```

## multimap                                                    <map>

```
template <class Key, class T, class Compare = less<Key>,
          class Allocator = allocator<T> >
  class multimap {
  public:
    typedef Key                                key_type;
    typedef T                                  mapped_type;
    typedef pair<const Key,T>                  value_type;
```

```
  typedef Compare                                key_compare;
  typedef Allocator                              allocator_type;
  typedef typename Allocator::reference          reference;
  typedef typename Allocator::const_reference    const_reference;
  typedef implementation defined                 iterator;
  typedef implementation defined                 const_iterator;
  typedef typename Allocator::size_type          size_type;
  typedef typename Allocator::difference_type    difference_type;
  typedef typename Allocator::pointer            pointer;
  typedef typename Allocator::const_pointer      const_pointer;
  typedef std::reverse_iterator<iterator>        reverse_iterator;
  typedef std::reverse_iterator<const_iterator>
                                        const_reverse_iterator;
  class value_compare
    : public binary_function<value_type,value_type,bool> {
  friend class multimap;
  protected:
    Compare comp;
    value_compare(Compare c) : comp(c) {}
  public:
    bool operator()(const value_type& x, const value_type& y) const {
      return comp(x.first, y.first);
    }
  };
// Constructors and allocation:
  explicit multimap(const Compare& comp = Compare(),
                    const Allocator& = Allocator());
  template <class InputIterator>
    multimap(InputIterator first, InputIterator last,
          const Compare& comp=Compare(),const Allocator&=Allocator());
  multimap(const multimap<Key,T,Compare,Allocator>& x);
 ~multimap();
  multimap<Key,T,Compare,Allocator>&
    operator=(const multimap<Key,T,Compare,Allocator>& x);
  allocator_type get_allocator() const;
// Iterators:
  iterator               begin();
  const_iterator         begin() const;
  iterator               end();
  const_iterator         end() const;
  reverse_iterator       rbegin();
  const_reverse_iterator rbegin() const;
  reverse_iterator       rend();
  const_reverse_iterator rend() const;
// Size:
  bool          empty() const;
  size_type     size() const;
  size_type     max_size() const;
// Insertion and deletion:
  iterator insert(const value_type& x);
```

```
      iterator insert(iterator position, const value_type& x);
      template <class InputIterator>
        void insert(InputIterator first, InputIterator last);
      void      erase(iterator position);
      size_type erase(const key_type& x);
      void      erase(iterator first, iterator last);
      void swap(multimap<Key,T,Compare,Allocator>&);
      void clear();
  // Others:
      key_compare     key_comp() const;
      value_compare   value_comp() const;
      iterator        find(const key_type& x);
      const_iterator find(const key_type& x) const;
      size_type       count(const key_type& x) const;
      iterator        lower_bound(const key_type& x);
      const_iterator lower_bound(const key_type& x) const;
      iterator        upper_bound(const key_type& x);
      const_iterator upper_bound(const key_type& x) const;
      pair<iterator,iterator>             equal_range(const key_type& x);
      pair<const_iterator,const_iterator> equal_range(const key_type& x)
                                                                  const;
  };
```

## References

See Practice section, category the STL, data management with containers.

# priority_queue

Sequential container (from the header queue)

## Description

A priority_queue is a waiting queue which ensures that read and delete access always goes to the element with the highest precedence.

Waiting queues are usually used for the differentiated processing of chronologically ordered entries/statements. The entries are assigned a priority on account of certain characteristics (size, value of a variable, and so on). During processing, entries with higher precedence skip all other entries, whereas entries with the same precedence are processed in the order of their appearance over time.

## Application

The class priority_queue does not implement a new container. Instead it uses a protected instance of a sequential container and only makes accessible those methods of this container class (through the definition of public methods, which call the corresponding methods of the container class), which are required for the implementation of a priority queue.

Behind `priority_queue` stands a class template. In this the data type of the objects which are to be managed is passed to the template parameter T.

```
priority_queue<int> container;
```

A container which is internally used for the storage of the elements, can be specified as a second template parameter. The passed container must possess the methods `empty()`, `size()`, `front()`, `back()`, `push_back()`, `pop_back()` and support random access iterators (for example, `vector` or `deque`, but not `list`). A `vector <T>` container is used by default.

```
priority_queue<int, deque<int> > container;
```

A function object can be passed as third template parameter which specifies the sorting criterion for the determination of precedence.

```
priority_queue<int, deque<int>, greater<int> > container;
```

## Example

```
template <class T, class Container = vector<T>,
         class Compare = less<Container::value_type> >
  class priority_queue {
  public:
    typedef typename Container::value_type          value_type;
    typedef typename Container::size_type           size_type;
    typedef typename Container                      container_type;
  protected:
    Container c;
    Compare comp;
  public:
    explicit priority_queue(const Compare& x = Compare(),
                            const Container& = Container());
    template <class InputIterator>
      priority_queue(InputIterator first, InputIterator last,
                     const Compare& x = Compare(),
                     const Container& = Container());
    bool      empty() const       { return c.empty(); }
    size_type size()  const       { return c.size(); }
    const value_type& top() const { return c.front(); }
    void push(const value_type& x);
    void pop();
  };
```

## References

See Practice section, category the STL, data management with containers.

# queue
Sequential container (from header queue)

## Description

A queue is a sequential data structure which only allows the insertion of new elements at its end, and the deletion of elements only at the beginning – just like a real queue.

Queues are usually used for the differentiated processing of chronologically ordered entries/ statements.

## Application

The class queue does not implement a new container. Instead it uses a protected instance of a sequential container and only makes accessible those methods of this container class (through the definition of public methods, which call the corresponding methods of the container class), which are required for the implementation of a waiting queue.

Behind queue stands a class template out of which a container class needs to be created. In this, the data type of the objects which are to be managed is passed to the template parameter T.

```
queue<int> container;
```

A container which is internally used for the storage of elements, can be specified as a second template parameter. The passed container must possess the methods empty(), size(), front(), back(), push_back(), pop_front() (for example, list or deque, but not vector). A deque <T> container is used by default.

```
queue<int, list<int> > container;
```

## Example

```
template <class T, class Container = deque<T> >
  class queue {
  public:
    typedef typename Container::value_type     value_type;
    typedef typename Container::size_type      size_type;
    typedef typename Container                 container_type;
  protected:
    Container c;
  public:
    explicit queue(const Container& = Container());
    bool      empty() const           { return c.empty(); }
    size_type size()  const           { return c.size(); }
    value_type&    front()            { return c.front(); }
```

```
  const value_type& front() const      { return c.front(); }
  value_type&        back()            { return c.back(); }
  const value_type& back() const       { return c.back(); }
  void push(const value_type& x)       { c.push_back(x); }
  void pop()                           { c.pop_front(); }
};
```

## Reference

See Practice section, category the STL, data management with containers.

# set and multiset

Associative container (from header set)

## Description

The classes set and multiset are practically identical to map and multimap, with the difference that map (multimap) use their keys to gurantee quick access to objects of a different type, whereas with set (multiset) the values (objects) themselves represent the keys.

For set and multiset, therefore, the following applies:

- value_type = key_type = Key.
- value_compare = key_compare = Vergl.
- Index operator [] has not been defined.

## Application

Behind set and multiset stand class templates from which container classes have to be created. In this the data type of the objects which are to be managed is passed to the template parameter T.

```
set<int> container;
```

A function object which determines how the elements in the container are to be sorted, can be passed as a second template parameter.

```
set<int, greater<int> > container;
```

**set**                                                                    **<set>**
```
template <class Key, class Compare = less<Key>,
          class Allocator = allocator<Key> >
  class set {
  public:
    typedef Key                                    key_type;
```

```
              typedef Key                              value_type;
              typedef Compare                          key_compare;
              typedef Compare                          value_compare;
              typedef Allocator                        allocator_type;
              typedef typename Allocator::reference    reference;
              typedef typename Allocator::const_reference const_reference;
              typedef implementation defined           iterator;
              typedef implementation defined           const_iterator;
              typedef typename Allocator::size_type    size_type;
              typedef typename Allocator::difference_type difference_type;
              typedef typename Allocator::pointer      pointer;
              typedef typename Allocator::const_pointer const_pointer;
              typedef std::reverse_iterator<iterator>  reverse_iterator;
              typedef std::reverse_iterator<const_iterator>
                                                       const_reverse_iterator;
    // Constructors and allocation:
      explicit set(const Compare& comp = Compare(), const Allocator& =
                                                   Allocator());
      template <class InputIterator>
        set(InputIterator first, InputIterator last,
            const Compare& comp = Compare(), const Allocator& =
                                                   Allocator());
      set(const set<Key,Compare,Allocator>& x);
     ~set();
      set<Key,Compare,Allocator>&
                         operator=(const set<Key,Compare,Allocator>& x);
      allocator_type get_allocator() const;
    // Iterators:
      iterator              begin();
      const_iterator        begin() const;
      iterator              end();
      const_iterator        end() const;
      reverse_iterator      rbegin();
      const_reverse_iterator rbegin() const;
      reverse_iterator      rend();
      const_reverse_iterator rend() const;
    // Größe:
      bool        empty() const;
      size_type   size() const;
      size_type   max_size() const;
    // Insertion and deletion:
      pair<iterator,bool> insert(const value_type& x);
      iterator            insert(iterator position, const value_type& x);
      template <class InputIterator>
          void insert(InputIterator first, InputIterator last);
      void    erase(iterator position);
      size_type erase(const key_type& x);
      void    erase(iterator first, iterator last);
      void swap(set<Key,Compare,Allocator>&);
      void clear();
```

```
// Others:
  key_compare    key_comp() const;
  value_compare value_comp() const;
  iterator  find(const key_type& x) const;
  size_type count(const key_type& x) const;
  iterator  lower_bound(const key_type& x) const;
  iterator  upper_bound(const key_type& x) const;
  pair<iterator,iterator> equal_range(const key_type& x) const;
};
```

## set                                                   <set>

```
template <class Key, class Compare = less<Key>,
          class Allocator = allocator<Key> >
  class multiset {
  public:
    typedef Key                                  key_type;
    typedef Key                                  value_type;
    typedef Compare                              key_compare;
    typedef Compare                              value_compare;
    typedef Allocator                            allocator_type;
    typedef typename Allocator::reference        reference;
    typedef typename Allocator::const_reference  const_reference;
    typedef implementation defined               iterator;
    typedef implementation defined               const_iterator;
    typedef typename Allocator::size_type        size_type;
    typedef typename Allocator::difference_type  difference_type;
    typedef typename Allocator::pointer          pointer;
    typedef typename Allocator::const_pointer    const_pointer;
    typedef std::reverse_iterator<iterator>      reverse_iterator;
  typedef std::reverse_iterator<const_iterator>
                                               const_reverse_iterator;
  // Constructors and allocation:
    explicit multiset(const Compare& comp = Compare(),
                      const Allocator& = Allocator());
    template <class InputIterator>
      multiset(InputIterator first, InputIterator last,
             const Compare& comp = Compare(), const Allocator& =
                                                Allocator());
    multiset(const multiset<Key,Compare,Allocator>& x);
   ~multiset();
    multiset<Key,Compare,Allocator>&
        operator=(const multiset<Key,Compare,Allocator>& x);
    allocator_type get_allocator() const;
  // Iterators:
    iterator              begin();
    const_iterator        begin() const;
    iterator              end();
    const_iterator        end() const;
    reverse_iterator      rbegin();
```

```
        const_reverse_iterator rbegin() const;
        reverse_iterator        rend();
        const_reverse_iterator rend() const;
    // Size:
        bool          empty() const;
        size_type     size() const;
        size_type     max_size() const;
    // Insertion and deletion:
        iterator insert(const value_type& x);
        iterator insert(iterator position, const value_type& x);
        template <class InputIterator>
          void insert(InputIterator first, InputIterator last);
        void      erase(iterator position);
        size_type erase(const key_type& x);
        void      erase(iterator first, iterator last);
        void swap(multiset<Key,Compare,Allocator>&);
        void clear();
    // Others:
        key_compare   key_comp() const;
        value_compare value_comp() const;
        iterator  find(const key_type& x) const;
        size_type count(const key_type& x) const;
        iterator  lower_bound(const key_type& x) const;
        iterator  upper_bound(const key_type& x) const;
        pair<iterator,iterator> equal_range(const key_type& x) const;
    };
```

## References

See Practice section, category the STL, data management with containers.

# stack

Sequential container (from header stack)

## Description

A stack is a sequential data structure, which only allows insertion or deletion at its end. It behaves like a stack of books, onto which further books can be put and whose topmost book can be removed, but adding or removing a book in the middle of the stack is forbidden. For the processing of entries this means that the last entry is processed first; that is, in the opposite order that they are processed in a queue.

## Application

The class `stack` does not implement a new container. Instead it uses a `protected` instance of a sequential container and only makes accessible those methods of this container class (through the definition of `public` methods, which call the corresponding methods of the container class), which are required for the implementation of a stack.

Behind `stack` stands a class template from which a container class has to be created. In this the data type of the objects which are to be managed is passed to the first template parameter `T`.

```
stack<int> container;
```

A container which is used internally for the storage of elements, can be specified as a second template parameter. The passed container must possess the methods `empty()`, `size()`, `back()`, `push_back()`, `pop_back()` (for example, `list`, `vector` or `deque`). A `deque <T>` container is used by default.

```
stack<int, list<int> > container;
```

## Example

```
template <class T, class Container = deque<T> >
  class stack {
  public:
    typedef typename Container::value_type      value_type;
    typedef typename Container::size_type        size_type;
    typedef typename Container                   container_type;
  protected:
    Container c;
  public:
    explicit stack(const Container& = Container());
    bool      empty() const            { return c.empty(); }
    size_type size()  const            { return c.size(); }
    value_type&      top()             { return c.back(); }
    const value_type& top() const      { return c.back(); }
    void push(const value_type& x)     { c.push_back(x); }
    void pop()                         { c.pop_back(); }
  };
```

## References

See Practice section, category the STL, data management with containers.

# vector

Sequential container (from header vector)

## Description

The class vector offers, like an array, quick direct access to individual elements ([] operator, at() method) as well as the insertion and deletion of elements at any position in linear time. It is only possibly to insert or delete more quickly, in constant time, at the end of the data structure.

In contrast to deque, vector is only optimised for insertion or deletion at the end of the data structure. In return access to specific positions is slightly quicker than with deque. In comparison to a list container, the insertion or deletion in middle positions is more time-consuming, however, vector permits convenient, indexed access to specific positions (for reading or writing).

Iterators for vector containers should belong to the forward_iterator category. However, various functions require higher iterator categories. Insert and delete operations may cause invalidity of existing interators and references to container elements.

## Application

Behind vector stands a class template from which a container class is created. In this the data type of the objects which are to be managed is passed to the first template parameter T.

vector<int> container;

The overloaded forms of the constructors allow the creation of empty containers or containers that contain several copies of an element or the copy of a sequence of elements from another container.

New elements can be inserted with insert(), push_back(), resize() or assign(), where the latter function empties the container first.

Existing elements can be deleted with erase(), pop_back(), resize() or clear().

Individual elements can be accessed with returned iterators (begin(), end(), rbegin(), rend() and insert() ) or with returned references ([]operator, at(), front(), back() ).

Finally, it is possible to manipiulate, sort and search containers through the global functions of the <algorithm> header file.

## Example

```
template <class T, class Allocator = allocator<T> >
  class vector {
  public:
    typedef typename Allocator::reference          reference;
    typedef typename Allocator::const_reference    const_reference;
```

```
  typedef implementation defined                        iterator;
  typedef implementation defined                        const_iterator;
  typedef typename Allocator::size_type                 size_type;
  typedef typename Allocator::difference_type           difference_type;
  typedef T                                             value_type;
  typedef Allocator                                     allocator_type;
  typedef typename Allocator::pointer                   pointer;
  typedef typename Allocator::const_pointer             const_pointer
  typedef std::reverse_iterator<iterator>               reverse_iterator;
  typedef std::reverse_iterator<const_iterator>
                                          const_reverse_iterator;
  // Constructors and allocation:
  explicit vector(const Allocator& = Allocator());
  explicit vector(size_type n, const T& value = T(),
      const Allocator& = Allocator());
  template <class InputIterator>
    vector(InputIterator first, InputIterator last,
      const Allocator& = Allocator());
  vector(const vector<T,Allocator>& x);
 ~vector();
  vector<T,Allocator>& operator=(const vector<T,Allocator>& x);
  template <class InputIterator>
    void assign(InputIterator first, InputIterator last);
  template <class Size, class U> void assign(Size n, const U& u = U());
  allocator_type get_allocator() const;
// Iterators:
  iterator               begin();
  const_iterator         begin() const;
  iterator               end();
  const_iterator         end() const;
  reverse_iterator       rbegin();
  const_reverse_iterator rbegin() const;
  reverse_iterator       rend();
  const_reverse_iterator rend() const;
// Size:
  size_type size() const;
  size_type max_size() const;
  void      resize(size_type sz, T c = T());
  size_type capacity() const;
  bool      empty() const;
  void      reserve(size_type n);
// Access to elements:
  reference       operator[](size_type n);
  const_reference operator[](size_type n) const;
  const_reference at(size_type n) const;
  reference       at(size_type n);
  reference       front();
  const_reference front() const;
  reference       back();
  const_reference back() const;
```

```
// Insertion and deletion:
  void push_back(const T& x);
  void pop_back();
  iterator insert(iterator position, const T& x = T());
  void    insert(iterator position, size_type n, const T& x);
  template <class InputIterator>
    void insert(iterator position, InputIterator first,
                InputIterator last);
  iterator erase(iterator position);
  iterator erase(iterator first, iterator last);
  void    swap(vector<T,Allocator>&);
  void    clear();
};
```

### References

See Practice section, category the STL, data management with containers.

# The iterator classes

## General points

### Description

Iterators are abstractions of pointers and are used to access elements of containers.

### Application

Iterators are used by algorithms to access the elements from various containers. The problem which arises here and which is why the STL works with iterators is that the algorithm wants to access the elements in the container through iterators and, if required, jump from element to element with a fixed syntax. On the other hand, the containers are based on different data structures (dynamic arrays, lists, trees, and so on), for which operations like jumping from element to element are carried out completely differently. Because of this the containers implement their iterators themselves and stick with the interface that is typical for iterators, so that these can be used by the algorithms.

According to the performance capacity of the iterators, different iterator categories are distinguished as follows.

# Iterator categories

The category of an iterator determines its performance capacity and, thus, its operational area.

## Category                                                           outpt_iterator

With output iterators it is possible to run through the elements of a container and change the value of the elements, but not read them. Furthermore, with an output iterator you can only move from the position of its initialisation into the direction of the container end; that is, you can increment (++) an output iterator, but not decrement (– –) it.

To insert new values into a container there are special adaptations – the insert iterators, which transform assignments to the element of the iterator into an insert operation.

### Requirements

- Copy constructor and destructor
- Assignment =
- De-referencing for writing *i = t
- Increment ++i, i++

## category                                                           input_iterator

With input iterators container elements can be accessed to read their values but their values cannot be changed. Furthermore, with an input iterator you can only move from the position of its initialisation into the direction of the container end; that is, you can increment (++) an input iterator, but not decrement (– –) it.

### Requirements

- Copy constructor and destructor
- Assignment =
- Comparison ==, where from i == j also follows *I == *j (however, not ++i == ++j)
- Comparison !=
- De-referencing for reading *i, j->m
- Increment ++i, i++

## category                                                         forward_iterator

Forward iterators can be used for reading and writing. With forward iterators it is only possible to move with the increment operator into the direction of the container end; however, with copies of a forward iterator you can run through a container several times.

**Requirements**

- Constructor for creation
- De-referencing for writing: *i = t

## category                                                    bidirectional_iterator

Bidirectional iterators possess all the characteristics of forward iterators, as well as the option to run through a container forwards and backwards.

**Requirements** (additional)

- Decrement – –i, i– –
- *i– –

## category                                                    random_access_iterator

Random access iterators possess all the characteristics of bidirectional iterators, as well as compare operations and the option to access elements directly, instead of running through all the elements in between.

**Requirements** (additional)

- Forward jumps    i += n, a + n
- Backward jumps  i –= n, a- n
- Distance  i – j
- Indexing  i[n]
- Comparisons i < j, i <= j, i > j, i >= j

## References

See Practice section, category the STL, iterators.

# reverse_iterator

From <iterator>

## Description

An instance of the reverse_iterator class is an adaptation of a bidirectional or random access iterator, with which it is possible to run through a container in the reverse direction, where:

```
&*(reverse_iterator(i)) == &*(i-1)
```

A `reverse_iterator` is, therefore, an iterator which transforms an increment into a decrement and a decrement into an increment. Thus it is possible to have a function which has an iterator run from front to back through a sequence of elements, run through the sequence in reverse order by passing a reverse iterator.

## Application

Reverse iterators can be returned, for example from the container methods `rbegin()` and `rend()`.

```
// Returning elements of a container
typedef vector<int>::reverse_iterator r_iter;
for(r_iter i = container.rbegin(); i != container.rend(); i++)
    cout << *i << endl;
```

## Reference

```
template <class Iterator>
  class reverse_iterator :
        public iterator<iterator_traits<Iterator>::iterator_category,
                        iterator_traits<Iterator>::value_type,
                        iterator_traits<Iterator>::difference_type,
                        iterator_traits<Iterator>::pointer,
                        iterator_traits<Iterator>::reference> {
  protected:
    Iterator current;
  public:
    typedef Iterator iterator_type;
    reverse_iterator();
    explicit reverse_iterator(Iterator x);
    Iterator base() const;
    Reference operator*() const;
    Pointer   operator->() const;
    reverse_iterator& operator++();
    reverse_iterator  operator++(int);
    reverse_iterator& operator--();
    reverse_iterator  operator--(int);
    reverse_iterator  operator+ (Distance n) const;
    reverse_iterator& operator+=(Distance n);
    reverse_iterator  operator- (Distance n) const;
    reverse_iterator& operator-=(Distance n);
    Reference operator[](Distance n) const;
  };
```

## References

See Practice section, category the STL, iterators.

# insert iterators

## Description

Insert iterators are iterator adapters which transform a copy syntax (overriding) into an insert operation.

## Application

In this way it is possible to use algorithms which copy elements with the help of iterators, through the passing of insert iterators for insertion.

Insert iterators are usually returned by one of the corresponding function templates back_inserter(), front_inserter() or inserter() (see below), to which the container class, on which the iterator is to operate is passed as a template parameter.

The iterators themselves use a reference to the associated container and operators to run through and insert into the container.

## Example

```
copy(container.begin(), container.end(),
     back_inserter(container));
```

or also

```
back_insert_iterator<vector<int> > b_iter(container);
b_iter = 333;  // Adds to a container end
```

### back_insert_iterator                                  <iterator>

The iterator is directly created for a container and allows the insertion of elements at the end of the container.

The implementation of back_insert_iterator uses the push_back method of the container for insertion. Consequently, a back_insert iterator can only be applied to containers for which this method has been defined (vector, deque, list).

```
template <class Container>
  class back_insert_iterator :
        public iterator<output_iterator_tag,void,void,void,void> {
  protected:
    Container& container;
  public:
    typedef Container container_type;
    explicit back_insert_iterator(Container& x);
    back_insert_iterator<Container>&
      operator=(const typename Container::value_type& value);
    back_insert_iterator<Container>& operator*();
    back_insert_iterator<Container>& operator++();
```

```
    back_insert_iterator<Container> operator++(int);
  };
template <class Container>
  back_insert_iterator<Container> back_inserter(Container& x);
```

## front_insert_iterator <iterator>

The iterator is created for a container and allows the convenient insertion of elements at the beginning of the container.

The implementation of front_insert_iterator uses the push_front method of the container for insertion. Consequently, a front_insert iterator can only be applied to containers for which this method has been defined (deque, list).

```
template <class Container>
  class front_insert_iterator :
          public iterator<output_iterator_tag,void,void,void,void> {
  protected:
    Container& container;
  public:
    typedef Container container_type;
    explicit front_insert_iterator(Container& x);
    front_insert_iterator<Container>&
      operator=(const typename Container::value_type& value);
    front_insert_iterator<Container>& operator*();
    front_insert_iterator<Container>& operator++();
    front_insert_iterator<Container> operator++(int);
  };
template <class Container>
    front_insert_iterator<Container> front_inserter(Container& x);
```

## insert_iterator <iterator>

The iterator is directly created for a container and allows the convenient insertion of elements at the beginning of the container.

```
template <class Container>
  class insert_iterator :
        public iterator<output_iterator_tag,void,void,void,void> {
  protected:
    Container& container;
    typename Container::iterator iter;
  public:
    typedef Container container_type;
    insert_iterator(Container& x, typename Container::iterator i);
    insert_iterator<Container>&
      operator=(const typename Container::value_type& value);
    insert_iterator<Container>& operator*();
    insert_iterator<Container>& operator++();
    insert_iterator<Container>& operator++(int);
  };
```

```
template <class Container, class Iterator>
    insert_iterator<Container> inserter(Container& x, Iterator i);
```

## References

See Practice section, category the STL, iterators.

# stream iterators

## Description

Stream iterators are adapters with which algorithms that are based on iterators (more general functions) can be used for reading and writing in files. The 'container elements', which are accessed by the iterator, are then the input and output.

## Application

At the instantiation of the iterator from its class template the data type of the 'container elements' is passed as a template parameter. The stream which is operated on can be passed as a constructor.

## Example

```
// Reading container elements over istream_iterator
copy(istream_iterator<int>(cin), istream_iterator<int>(),
    back_inserter(container));
    ostream_iterator<int, char> (cout,"\n"));
// Distributing container elements over ostream_iterator
copy(container.begin(), container.end(),
    ostream_iterator<int, char> (cout,"\n"));
```

### istream_iterator                                          <iterator>

The iterator is designed for the reading of data from a stream. As it is derived from the input_iterator class, it can only be used for a single pass.

The fact that it is an input iterator and not a forward iterator (the latter would permit several passes) should not restrict its use, since the read data are usually buffered in the working memory, where other operations can be carried out significantly more quickly.

It is not possible to assign data to an istream_iterator.

```
template <class T, class charT, class traits = char_traits<charT>,
        class Distance = ptrdiff_t>
  class istream_iterator
    : public iterator<input_iterator_tag,T,Distance,const T*,const T&> {
```

```
public:
    typedef charT char_type;
    typedef traits traits_type;
    typedef basic_istream<charT,traits> istream_type;
    istream_iterator();
    istream_iterator(istream_type& s);
    istream_iterator(const istream_iterator<T,charT,traits,Distance>&
x);
    ~istream_iterator();
    const T& operator*() const;
    const T* operator->() const;
    istream_iterator<T,charT,traits,Distance>& operator++();
    istream_iterator<T,charT,traits,Distance>  operator++(int);
};
```

## ostream_iterator                                          **<iterator>**

The iterator has been designed for the output of data in a stream. As it is derived from the output_iterator class, it can only be used for a single pass.

The fact that it is an output iterator and not a forward iterator (the latter would permit several passes) should not restrict its use, since the read data are usually buffered in the working memory, where other operations can be carried out significantly more quickly.

It is not possible to query the value of an ostream_iterator.

The de-referencing operator may only stand on the left-hand side of assignments.

```
template <class T, class charT, class traits = char_traits<charT> >
    class ostream_iterator
        : public iterator<output_iterator_tag,void,void,void,void> {
    public:
    typedef charT char_type;
    typedef traits traits_type;
    typedef basic_ostream<charT,traits> ostream_type;
    ostream_iterator(ostream_type& s);
    ostream_iterator(ostream_type& s, const charT* delimiter);
    ostream_iterator(const ostream_iterator<T,charT,traits>& x);
    ~ostream_iterator();
    ostream_iterator<T,charT,traits>& operator=(const T& value);
    ostream_iterator<T,charT,traits>& operator*();
    ostream_iterator<T,charT,traits>& operator++();
    ostream_iterator<T,charT,traits>& operator++(int);
};
```

## istreambuf_iterator                                       **<iterator>**

The iterator has been designed for reading the characters from a basic_streambuf object. The iterator can only be used for a single pass.

```
template<class charT, class traits = char_traits<charT> >
  class istreambuf_iterator
    : public iterator<input_iterator_tag, charT,
                      typename traits::off_type, charT*, charT&> {
  public:
    typedef charT                          char_type;
    typedef traits                         traits_type;
    typedef typename traits::int_type      int_type;
    typedef basic_streambuf<charT,traits> streambuf_type;
    typedef basic_istream<charT,traits>   istream_type;

    istreambuf_iterator() throw();
    istreambuf_iterator(istream_type& s) throw();
    istreambuf_iterator(streambuf_type* s) throw();
    istreambuf_iterator(const proxy& p) throw();
    charT operator*() const;
    istreambuf_iterator<charT,traits>& operator++();
    proxy operator++(int);
    bool equal(istreambuf_iterator& b);
};
```

## ostreambuf_iterator                                   <iterator>

The iterator has been designed for writing characters into a `basic_streambuf` object. It can only be used for a single pass.

The de-referencing operator may only stand on the left-hand side of assignments.

```
template <class charT, class traits = char_traits<charT> >
  class ostreambuf_iterator :
        iterator<output_iterator_tag,void,void,void,void>{
  public:
    typedef charT                          char_type;
    typedef traits                         traits_type;
    typedef basic_streambuf<charT,traits> streambuf_type;
    typedef basic_ostream<charT,traits>   ostream_type;
  public:
    ostreambuf_iterator(ostream_type& s) throw();
    ostreambuf_iterator(streambuf_type* s) throw();
    ostreambuf_iterator& operator=(charT c);
    ostreambuf_iterator& operator*();
    ostreambuf_iterator& operator++();
    ostreambuf_iterator& operator++(int);
    bool failed() const throw();
  };
```

# Supporting user-defined implementations

To be able to adapt functions through parameters to the various iterator categories, the C++ library defines the following structures.

## struct iterator_traits <iterator>

```
template<class Iterator> struct iterator_traits {
    typedef Iterator::difference_type difference_type;
    typedef Iterator::value_type value_type;
    typedef Iterator::pointer pointer;
    typedef Iterator::reference reference;
    typedef Iterator::iterator_category iterator_category;
    };
```

which is also available as a specialisation for normal pointers

```
template<class T> struct iterator_traits<T*> {
    typedef ptrdiff_t difference_type;      typedef T value_type;
    typedef T* pointer;        typedef T& reference;
    typedef random_access_iterator_tag iterator_category;
    };
```

## iterator tags <iterator>

```
struct input_iterator_tag {};
struct output_iterator_tag {};
struct forward_iterator_tag: public input_iterator_tag {};
struct bidirectional_iterator_tag: public forward_iterator_tag {};
struct random_access_iterator_tag: public bidirectional_iterator_tag {};
```

These structures are used to enable the adaptation of function or template parameters to the various iterator categories.

## Example

The following example contains two functions for bidirectional and random access iterators and an encapsulation function which, depending on the passed iterator type, calls the most suitable implementation:

```
template <class mindestensBDIter>
inline void tu_was(mindestensBDIter first, mindestensBDIter last) {
    tu_was(first, last,
        iterator_traits<mindestensBDIter>::iterator_category());
    }

template <class BDIter>
    void tu_was(BDIter first, BDIter last,
            bidirectional_iterator_tag)
                { // general, but not very efficient }
```

```
template <class RAIter>
    void tu_was(RAIter first, RAIter last,
            random_access_iterator_tag) {
            { // efficient, but less general }
```

### struct iterator                                                      <iterator>

User-defined iterators can be derived from the iterator class:

```
template<class Category, class T, class Distance = ptrdiff_t,
        class Pointer = T*, class Reference = T&>
    struct iterator {
        typedef T          value_type;
        typedef Distance   difference_type;
        typedef Pointer    pointer;
        typedef Reference  reference;
        typedef Category   iterator_category;
        }
```

Finally, there are two auxiliary functions, with which it is possible to shift iterators of any category by *n* positions or determine the distance between two iterators:

### advance()                                                            <iterator>

```
template <class InIter, class Distance>
    void advance(InIter& i, Distance n);
```

shifts the iterator by *n* positions (with +/– or ++/– –)

### distance()                                                           <iterator>

```
template <class InIter>
    iterator_traits<InIter>::difference_type distance(InIter& i,InIter& j);
```

returns the distance (number of increment/decrement operations) between i and j.

# The algorithms

## Description

The algorithms are a collection of function templates which can be specialised for any data type and be applied to the objects of containers through iterators.

## Application

Since algorithms are not implemented as methods of the container templates, but as independent templates, the connection to the elements in the container occurs through iterators. This has, for example, the advantage that algorithms do not have to be implemented individually for each container and can also be used for self-defined containers (including arrays and dynamic fields).

However, the precondition is that the interface between algorithm and container is correct. The interface are the iterators. In the following list you can, therefore, read the names of the iterator template parameters and which requirements the iterator, to which the algorithm is passed has to meet.

If the interface is correct, the application of the algorithms on the container elements is very easy:

```
deque<int> container(5);
...
fill(container.begin(), container.end(), 4);
or
int feld[30];
...
fill(&feld[0], &feld[30], 3);
```

Several of the algorithms require a further argument for the execution of their operation. This is usually:

- a value (for example fill(), which assigns the passed value to the elements), or

- a function object, which usually specifies a condition which has to be met so that the operation of the algorithm is applied to an element (for example make_heap() transforms an area into a heap. By passing a function object a compare function can be passed, which determines the sorting of the heap). Function objects which carry out comparisons are referred to as Compare in the following list of the algorithms, and function objects which are applied to one or two de-referenced iterators and then return a bool value are referred to as Predicate or BinaryPredicate.

Often the templates of the algorithms are overloaded, so that the same algorithm can be called with various arguments. Thus, the find() algorithm can search for an element which either contains a particular value or meets a specific condition.

From numeric:

```
template <class InputIter, class T>
  accumulate(InputIter first, InputIter last, T init);
template <class InputIter, class T, class BinaryOperation>
  accumulate(InputIter first, InputIter last, T init,
             BinaryOperation binary_op);
template <class InputIter, class OutputIter>
  OutputIter adjacent_difference(InputIter first, InputIter last,
                                 OutputIter result);
template <class InputIter, class OutputIter, class BinaryOperation>
  OutputIter adjacent_difference(InputIter first, InputIter last,
                                 OutputIter result,
                                 BinaryOperation binary_op);
```

```
template <class InputIter1, class InputIter2, class T>
  T inner_product(InputIter1 first1, InputIter1 last1,
                  InputIter2 first2, T init);
template <class InputIter1, class InputIter2, class T,
          class BinaryOperation1, class BinaryOperation2>
  T inner_product(InputIter1 first1, InputIter1 last1,
                  InputIter2 first2, T init,
                  BinaryOperation1 binary_op1, BinaryOperation2 binary_op2);
template <class InputIter, class OutputIter>
  OutputIter partial_sum(InputIter first, InputIter last,
                         OutputIter result);
template <class InputIter, class OutputIter, class BinaryOperation>
  OutputIter partial_sum(InputIter first, InputIter last,
                         OutputIter result, BinaryOperation binary_op);
```

From algorithm:

```
template<class ForwardIter>
  ForwardIter adjacent_find(ForwardIter first, ForwardIter last);
template<class ForwardIter, class BinaryPredicate>
  ForwardIter adjacent_find(ForwardIter first, ForwardIter last,
                            BinaryPredicate pred);
template<class ForwardIter, class T>
  bool binary_search(ForwardIter first,ForwardIter last,const T& value);
template<class ForwardIter, class T, class Compare>
  bool binary_search(ForwardIter first, ForwardIter last,
                     const T& value, Compare comp);
template<class InputIter, class T>
  Iter_traits<InputIter>::difference_type
  count(InputIter first, InputIter last, const T& value);
template<class InputIter, class Predicate>
  Iter_traits<InputIter>::difference_type
  count_if(InputIter first, InputIter last, Predicate pred);
template<class InputIter, class OutputIter>
  OutputIter copy(InputIter first, InputIter last, OutputIter result);
template<class BidirectionalIter1, class BidirectionalIter2>
  BidirectionalIter2 copy_backward(BidirectionalIter1 first,
                                   BidirectionalIter1 last,
                                   BidirectionalIter2 result);
template<class InputIter1, class InputIter2>
  bool equal(InputIter1 first1, InputIter1 last1, InputIter2 first2);
template<class InputIter1, class InputIter2, class BinaryPredicate>
  bool equal(InputIter1 first1, InputIter1 last1,
             InputIter2 first2, BinaryPredicate pred);
template<class ForwardIter, class T>
  pair<ForwardIter, ForwardIter>
      equal_range(ForwardIter first, ForwardIter last, const T& value);
template<class ForwardIter, class T, class Compare>
  pair<ForwardIter, ForwardIter>
      equal_range(ForwardIter first, ForwardIter last, const T& value,
                  Compare comp);
```

```
template<class ForwardIter, class T>
  void fill(ForwardIter first, ForwardIter last, const T& value);
template<class OutputIter, class Size, class T>
  void fill_n(OutputIter first, Size n, const T& value);
template<class InputIter, class T>
  InputIter find(InputIter first, InputIter last, const T& value);
template<class ForwardIter1, class ForwardIter2>
  ForwardIter1 find_end(ForwardIter1 first1, ForwardIter1 last1,
                        ForwardIter2 first2, ForwardIter2 last2);
template<class ForwardIter1, class ForwardIter2, class BinaryPredicate>
  ForwardIter1 find_end(ForwardIter1 first1, ForwardIter1 last1,
                        ForwardIter2 first2, ForwardIter2 last2,
                        BinaryPredicate pred);
template<class ForwardIter1, class ForwardIter2>
  ForwardIter1 find_first_of(ForwardIter1 first1, ForwardIter1 last1,
                             ForwardIter2 first2, ForwardIter2 last2);
template<class ForwardIter1, class ForwardIter2, class BinaryPredicate>
  ForwardIter1 find_first_of(ForwardIter1 first1, ForwardIter1 last1,
                             ForwardIter2 first2, ForwardIter2 last2,
                             BinaryPredicate pred);
template<class InputIter, class Predicate>
  InputIter find_if(InputIter first, InputIter last, Predicate pred);
template<class InputIter, class Function>
  Function for_each(InputIter first, InputIter last, Function f);
template<class ForwardIter, class Generator>
  void generate(ForwardIter first, ForwardIter last, Generator gen);
template<class OutputIter, class Size, class Generator>
  void generate_n(OutputIter first, Size n, Generator gen);
template<class InputIter1, class InputIter2>
  bool includes(InputIter1 first1, InputIter1 last1,
                InputIter2 first2, InputIter2 last2);
template<class InputIter1, class InputIter2, class Compare>
  bool includes(InputIter1 first1, InputIter1 last1,
                InputIter2 first2, InputIter2 last2, Compare comp);
template<class BidirectionalIter>
  void inplace_merge(BidirectionalIter first,
                     BidirectionalIter middle,
                     BidirectionalIter last);
template<class BidirectionalIter, class Compare>
  void inplace_merge(BidirectionalIter first,
                     BidirectionalIter middle,
                     BidirectionalIter last, Compare comp);
template<class ForwardIter1, class ForwardIter2>
  void iter_swap(ForwardIter1 a, ForwardIter2 b);
template<class InputIter1, class InputIter2>
  bool lexicographical_compare(InputIter1 first1, InputIter1 last1,
                               InputIter2 first2, InputIter2 last2);
template<class InputIter1, class InputIter2, class Compare>
  bool lexicographical_compare(InputIter1 first1, InputIter1 last1,
                               InputIter2 first2, InputIter2 last2,
                               Compare comp);
```

```
template<class ForwardIter, class T>
  ForwardIter lower_bound(ForwardIter first, ForwardIter last,
                          const T& value);
template<class ForwardIter, class T, class Compare>
  ForwardIter lower_bound(ForwardIter first, ForwardIter last,
                          const T& value, Compare comp);
template<class RandomAccessIter>
  void make_heap(RandomAccessIter first, RandomAccessIter last);
template<class RandomAccessIter, class Compare>
  void make_heap(RandomAccessIter first, RandomAccessIter last,
                 Compare comp);
template<class T> const T& max(const T& a, const T& b);
template<class T, class Compare>
  const T& max(const T& a, const T& b, Compare comp);
template<class ForwardIter>
  ForwardIter max_element(ForwardIter first, ForwardIter last);
template<class ForwardIter, class Compare>
  ForwardIter max_element(ForwardIter first, ForwardIter last,
                          Compare comp);
template<class InputIter1, class InputIter2, class OutputIter>
  OutputIter merge(InputIter1 first1, InputIter1 last1,
                   InputIter2 first2, InputIter2 last2,
                   OutputIter result);
template<class InputIter1, class InputIter2, class OutputIter,
         class Compare>
  OutputIter merge(InputIter1 first1, InputIter1 last1,
                   InputIter2 first2, InputIter2 last2,
                   OutputIter result, Compare comp);
template<class T> const T& min(const T& a, const T& b);
template<class T, class Compare>
  const T& min(const T& a, const T& b, Compare comp);
template<class ForwardIter>
  ForwardIter min_element(ForwardIter first, ForwardIter last);
template<class ForwardIter, class Compare>
  ForwardIter min_element(ForwardIter first, ForwardIter last,
                          Compare comp);
template<class InputIter1, class InputIter2>
  pair<InputIter1, InputIter2>
  mismatch(InputIter1 first1, InputIter1 last1, InputIter2 first2);
template<class InputIter1, class InputIter2, class BinaryPredicate>
  pair<InputIter1, InputIter2>
  mismatch(InputIter1 first1, InputIter1 last1,
           InputIter2 first2, BinaryPredicate pred);
template<class BidirectionalIter>
  bool next_permutation(BidirectionalIter first,
                        BidirectionalIter last);
template<class BidirectionalIter, class Compare>
  bool next_permutation(BidirectionalIter first,
                        BidirectionalIter last, Compare comp);
```

```
template<class RandomAccessIter>
  void nth_element(RandomAccessIter first, RandomAccessIter nth,
                   RandomAccessIter last);
template<class RandomAccessIter, class Compare>
  void nth_element(RandomAccessIter first, RandomAccessIter nth,
                   RandomAccessIter last, Compare comp);
template<class RandomAccessIter>
  void partial_sort(RandomAccessIter first, RandomAccessIter middle,
                    RandomAccessIter last);
template<class RandomAccessIter, class Compare>
  void partial_sort(RandomAccessIter first, RandomAccessIter middle,
                    RandomAccessIter last, Compare comp);
template<class InputIter, class RandomAccessIter>
  RandomAccessIter
        partial_sort_copy(InputIter first, InputIter last,
                          RandomAccessIter result_first,
                          RandomAccessIter result_last);
template<class InputIter, class RandomAccessIter, class Compare>
  RandomAccessIter
        partial_sort_copy(InputIter first, InputIter last,
                          RandomAccessIter result_first,
                          RandomAccessIter result_last,
                          Compare comp);
template<class BidirectionalIter, class Predicate>
  BidirectionalIter partition(BidirectionalIter first,
                              BidirectionalIter last, Predicate pred);
template<class RandomAccessIter>
  void pop_heap(RandomAccessIter first, RandomAccessIter last);
template<class RandomAccessIter, class Compare>
  void pop_heap(RandomAccessIter first, RandomAccessIter last,
                Compare comp);
template<class BidirectionalIter>
  bool prev_permutation(BidirectionalIter first,
                        BidirectionalIter last);
template<class BidirectionalIter, class Compare>
  bool prev_permutation(BidirectionalIter first,
                        BidirectionalIter last, Compare comp);
template<class RandomAccessIter>
  void push_heap(RandomAccessIter first, RandomAccessIter last);
template<class RandomAccessIter, class Compare>
  void push_heap(RandomAccessIter first, RandomAccessIter last,
                 Compare comp);
template<class RandomAccessIter>
  void random_shuffle(RandomAccessIter first, RandomAccessIter last);
template<class RandomAccessIter, class RandomNumberGenerator>
  void random_shuffle(RandomAccessIter first, RandomAccessIter last,
                      RandomNumberGenerator& rand);
template<class ForwardIter, class T>
  ForwardIter remove(ForwardIter first, ForwardIter last,
                     const T& value);
```

```
template<class InputIter, class OutputIter, class T>
  OutputIter remove_copy(InputIter first, InputIter last,
                         OutputIter result, const T& value);
template<class InputIter, class OutputIter, class Predicate>
  OutputIter remove_copy_if(InputIter first, InputIter last,
                            OutputIter result, Predicate pred);
template<class ForwardIter, class Predicate>
  ForwardIter remove_if(ForwardIter first, ForwardIter last,
                        Predicate pred);
template<class ForwardIter, class T>
  void replace(ForwardIter first, ForwardIter last,
               const T& old_value, const T& new_value);
template<class InputIter, class OutputIter, class T>
  OutputIter replace_copy(InputIter first, InputIter last,
                          OutputIter result,
                          const T& old_value, const T& new_value);
template<class Iter, class OutputIter, class Predicate, class T>
  OutputIter replace_copy_if(Iter first, Iter last,
                             OutputIter result,
                             Predicate pred, const T& new_value);
template<class ForwardIter, class Predicate, class T>
  void replace_if(ForwardIter first, ForwardIter last,
                  Predicate pred, const T& new_value);
template<class BidirectionalIter>
  void reverse(BidirectionalIter first, BidirectionalIter last);
template<class BidirectionalIter, class OutputIter>
  OutputIter reverse_copy(BidirectionalIter first,
                          BidirectionalIter last, OutputIter result);
template<class ForwardIter>
  void rotate(ForwardIter first, ForwardIter middle, ForwardIter last);
template<class ForwardIter, class OutputIter>
  OutputIter rotate_copy(ForwardIter first, ForwardIter middle,
                         ForwardIter last, OutputIter result);
template<class ForwardIter1, class ForwardIter2>
  ForwardIter1 search(ForwardIter1 first1, ForwardIter1 last1,
                      ForwardIter2 first2, ForwardIter2 last2);
template<class ForwardIter1, class ForwardIter2, class BinaryPredicate>
  ForwardIter1 search(ForwardIter1 first1, ForwardIter1 last1,
                      ForwardIter2 first2, ForwardIter2 last2,
                      BinaryPredicate pred);
template<class ForwardIter, class Size, class T>
  ForwardIter  search_n(ForwardIter first, ForwardIter last,
                        Size count, const T& value);
template<class ForwardIter, class Size, class T, class BinaryPredicate>
  ForwardIter1 search_n(ForwardIter first, ForwardIter last, Size count,
                        const T& value, BinaryPredicate pred);
template<class InputIter1, class InputIter2, class OutputIter>
  OutputIter set_difference(InputIter1 first1, InputIter1 last1,
                            InputIter2 first2, InputIter2 last2,
                            OutputIter result);
```

```
template<class InputIter1, class InputIter2, class OutputIter,
          class Compare>
  OutputIter set_difference(InputIter1 first1, InputIter1 last1,
                            InputIter2 first2, InputIter2 last2,
                            OutputIter result, Compare comp);
template<class InputIter1, class InputIter2, class OutputIter>
  OutputIter set_intersection(InputIter1 first1, InputIter1 last1,
                              InputIter2 first2, InputIter2 last2,
                              OutputIter result);
template<class InputIter1, class InputIter2, class OutputIter,
         class Compare>
  OutputIter set_intersection(InputIter1 first1, InputIter1 last1,
                              InputIter2 first2, InputIter2 last2,
                              OutputIter result, Compare comp);
template<class InputIter1, class InputIter2, class OutputIter>
  OutputIter set_symmetric_difference(InputIter1 first1,InputIter1
last1,
                                      InputIter2 first2,InputIter2 last2,
                                      OutputIter result);
template<class InputIter1, class InputIter2, class OutputIter,
          class Compare>
  OutputIter set_symmetric_difference(InputIter1 first1,
                                      InputIter1 last1,
                                      InputIter2 first2,InputIter2 last2,
                                      OutputIter result, Compare comp);
template<class InputIter1, class InputIter2, class OutputIter>
  OutputIter set_union(InputIter1 first1, InputIter1 last1,
                       InputIter2 first2, InputIter2 last2,
                       OutputIter result);
template<class InputIter1, class InputIter2, class OutputIter,
          class Compare>
  OutputIter set_union(InputIter1 first1, InputIter1 last1,
                       InputIter2 first2, InputIter2 last2,
                       OutputIter result, Compare comp);
template<class RandomAccessIter>
  void sort(RandomAccessIter first, RandomAccessIter last);
template<class RandomAccessIter, class Compare>
  void sort(RandomAccessIter first, RandomAccessIter last,
                                    Compare comp);
template<class BidirectionalIter, class Predicate>
  BidirectionalIter stable_partition(BidirectionalIter first,
                                     BidirectionalIter last,
                                     Predicate pred);
template<class RandomAccessIter>
  void stable_sort(RandomAccessIter first, RandomAccessIter last);
template<class RandomAccessIter, class Compare>
  void stable_sort(RandomAccessIter first, RandomAccessIter last,
                   Compare comp);
template<class T> void swap(T& a, T& b);
```

```
template<class ForwardIter1, class ForwardIter2>
  ForwardIter2 swap_ranges(ForwardIter1 first1, ForwardIter1 last1,
                           ForwardIter2 first2);
template<class InputIter, class OutputIter, class UnaryOperation>
  OutputIter transform(InputIter first, InputIter last,
                       OutputIter result, UnaryOperation op);
template<class InputIter1, class InputIter2, class OutputIter,
         class BinaryOperation>
  OutputIter transform(InputIter1 first1, InputIter1 last1,
                       InputIter2 first2, OutputIter result,
                       BinaryOperation binary_op);
template<class ForwardIter>
  ForwardIter unique(ForwardIter first, ForwardIter last);
template<class ForwardIter, class BinaryPredicate>
  ForwardIter unique(ForwardIter first, ForwardIter last,
                     BinaryPredicate pred);
template<class InputIter, class OutputIter>
  OutputIter unique_copy(InputIter first, InputIter last,
                         OutputIter result);
template<class InputIter, class OutputIter, class BinaryPredicate>
  OutputIter unique_copy(InputIter first, InputIter last,
                         OutputIter result, BinaryPredicate pred);
template<class ForwardIter, class T>
  ForwardIter upper_bound(ForwardIter first, ForwardIter last,
                          const T& value);
template<class ForwardIter, class T, class Compare>
  ForwardIter upper_bound(ForwardIter first, ForwardIter last,
                          const T& value, Compare comp);
template<class RandomAccessIter>
  void sort_heap(RandomAccessIter first, RandomAccessIter last);
template<class RandomAccessIter, class Compare>
  void sort_heap(RandomAccessIter first, RandomAccessIter last,
                 Compare comp);
```

## References

See Practice section, the STL, algorithms.

# The stream classes

## Overview

### Description

The stream classes represent the object-oriented alternative to the ANSI C functions from stdio.h. A stream can be thought of as a data stream between a source and a target where, depending on the used stream class, the instance of the stream class is either the source or the target. For an instance of the ifstream class the file linked to the instance is the source, and for an instance of the ofstream class it is the target.

According to the new ANSI standard the basic frame of the C++ stream classes looks as follows:

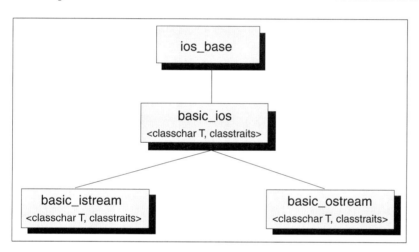

| Characteristic | Description |
|---|---|
| ios_base | The ios_base class contains information as well as type and constant definitions, which are used by all stream classes and do not depend on a special character type – for example format flags, status bits, opening modes for files. |
| | (Many elements which have been defined in ios_base used to be in ios.) |

| Characteristic | Description |
|---|---|
| basic_ios | The basic class. It is defined as a template in order to permit character-specific specialisations. As template arguments it expects the name of the character type and a char_traits<charT> specialisation that characterises the character type. |
| | basic_ios creates the connection to a buffer object (for the buffering of input and output) and a locale object (for the adaptation to national formats) by means of the definition of corresponding methods and constructors. |
| basic_istream and basic_ostream | Derived class templates which inherit basic_ios as virtual basis. |
| | The classes istream and ostream, which can be instanced for the establishment of input and output streams, are specialisations of these class templates for the char data type. The stream objects cin, cout, cerr and clog introduced in the previous paragraph are instances of the classes istream and ostream. |
| | The class templates istream and ostream in turn are used as basic classes by other stream class templates. |

The other auxiliary classes and derived classes that depend on this basic frame can be seen in the following diagram.

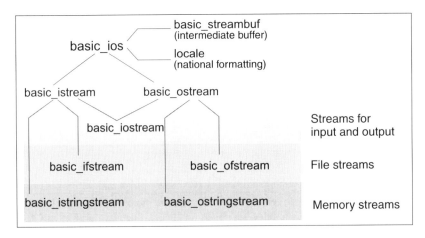

## Application

To be able to work with streams, stream objects are required. Stream objects are created by creating stream classes from the class templates of the C++ runtime library through specialisation in a character type.

Several stream classes have already been predefined in the C++ runtime library , for example:

```
typedef basic_istream<char>       istream;      // input stream class
typedef basic_ostream<char>       ostream;      // output strea class
typedef basic_fstream<char>       fstream;      // file stream class
typedef basic_stringstream<char>  stringstream; // string stream class
// for a complete list refer to the header file iosfwd
```

- by instantiation stream objects form the stream classes.

In the iostream header file the following stream objects have already been predefined:

```
istream cin      // standard input stream for char
ostream cout     // standard output stream for char
ostream cerr     // standard error output for char
ostream clog     // standard protocol output for char
wistream wcin    // standard input stream for wchar_t
wostream wcout   // standard output stream for wchar_t
wostream wcerr   // standard error output for wchar_t
wostream wclog   // standard protocol output for wchar_t
```

For further programming with streams the following are used:

- methods of the stream class templates,
- overloaded operators, and
- manipulators.

## References

See Reference section, category input and output.

See Practice section, category input and output.

# ios_base

aus <ios>

## Description

The class ios_base is the basic class of basic_ios. It does not contain routines for input and output, but encompasses a range of data types, constants and methods for exception handling, querying of stream status, and formatting of input and output.

## Example

```
class ios_base {
    public:
        class failure;
        typedef T1 fmtflags;
        static const fmtflags boolalpha;
```

```
              static const fmtflags dec;
              static const fmtflags fixed;
              static const fmtflags hex;
              static const fmtflags internal;
              static const fmtflags left;
              static const fmtflags oct;
              static const fmtflags right;
              static const fmtflags scientific;
              static const fmtflags showbase;
              static const fmtflags showpoint;
              static const fmtflags showpos;
              static const fmtflags skipws;
              static const fmtflags unitbuf;
              static const fmtflags uppercase;
              static const fmtflags adjustfield;
              static const fmtflags basefield;
              static const fmtflags floatfield;
              typedef T2 iostate;
              static const iostate badbit;
              static const iostate eofbit;
              static const iostate failbit;
              static const iostate goodbit;
              typedef T3 openmode;
              static const openmode app;
              static const openmode ate;
              static const openmode binary;
              static const openmode in;
              static const openmode out;
              static const openmode trunc;
              typedef T4 seekdir;
              static const seekdir beg;
              static const seekdir cur;
              static const seekdir end;
              class Init;
         // Formatting flags:
            fmtflags flags() const;
            fmtflags flags(fmtflags fmtfl);
            fmtflags setf(fmtflags fmtfl);
            fmtflags setf(fmtflags fmtfl, fmtflags mask);
            void unsetf(fmtflags mask);
            streamsize precision() const;
            streamsize precision(streamsize prec);
            streamsize width() const;
            streamsize width(streamsize wide);
         // Locale:
            locale imbue(const locale& loc);
            locale getloc() const;
         // Memory:
            static int xalloc();
            long&  iword(int index);
```

```
      void*& pword(int index);
      ~ios_base();
      enum event { erase_event, imbue_event, copyfmt_event };
      typedef void (*event_callback)(event, ios_base&, int index);
      void register_callback(event_call_back fn, int index);
      static bool sync_with_stdio(bool sync = true);
   protected:
      ios_base();
  };
```

## References

See Reference section, category input and output, streams in C++.

See Practice section, category input and output, error handling for streams.

# basic_ios

From <ios>

## Description

Basic class template for stream classes. Contains general routines for controlling the stream and its coordinated buffer object (of the basic_streambuf class template).

The basic_ios class template defines

- a few higher functions for querying the most important status information (good(), eof(), fail(), bad(), bool(), rdstate() and the ! operator).

- functions for accessing and exchanging the buffer object (rdbuf()) and linked output streams (tie()).

## Example

```
template <class charT, class traits = char_traits<charT> >
 class basic_ios : public ios_base {
 public:
   typedef charT                    char_type;
   typedef typename traits::int_type int_type;
   typedef typename traits::pos_type pos_type;
   typedef typename traits::off_type off_type;
   typedef traits                    traits_type;
   operator void*() const
   bool operator!() const
   iostate rdstate() const;
   void clear(iostate state = goodbit);
   void setstate(iostate state);
   bool good() const;
   bool eof()  const;
```

```
  bool fail() const;
  bool bad()  const;
  iostate exceptions() const;
  void exceptions(iostate except);
// Constructor:
  explicit basic_ios(basic_streambuf<charT,traits>* sb);
  virtual ~basic_ios();
  basic_ostream<charT,traits>* tie() const;
  basic_ostream<charT,traits>* tie(basic_ostream<charT,traits>*
                                                      tiestr);
  basic_streambuf<charT,traits>* rdbuf() const;
  basic_streambuf<charT,traits>*
                          rdbuf(basic_streambuf<charT,traits>* sb);
  basic_ios& copyfmt(const basic_ios& rhs);
  char_type fill() const;
  char_type fill(char_type ch);
// Locale:
  locale imbue(const locale& loc);
  char    narrow(char_type c, char dfault) const;
  char_type widen(char c) const;
protected:
  basic_ios();
  void init(basic_streambuf<charT,traits>* sb);
};
```

# basic_streambuf

From <streambuf>

## Description

The class template basic_streambuf is the basic template for all stream buffers (basic_filebuf, basic_stringbuf). The class template basic_streambuf and the derived stream buffers are used to control character sequences in the working memory. Each instance has available, when required, memory areas for character input and output. Three pointers refer to each of these character sequences:

− a pointer to the first element of the sequence,

− a pointer to the next address, from which is read or to which is written, and

− a pointer to the next element address after the end of the sequence.

Through the connection with a stream the buffer is linked to an input or output unit. To access characters in the buffer the high-level functions of the stream class use the low-level functions of the associated buffer object.

The insertion of buffer objects permits a buffered input and output. This means, that − for example when reading from a file − not every read call of the program requires access to the hard drive. Instead larger parts of the file are loaded into the buffer in the working memory, and the read operations of the program are carried out in this buffer, until it has been read completely and is filled again from the hard drive. Reduced access to the hard drive significantly improves the runtime, however it also means that data may get lost when in an unexpected program termination, for example, the buffer is not emptied. The synchronisation of buffer and in- or output unit can be achieved by calling pubsync().

## Application

The classes of the template cannot be instanced directly, because they do not contain a public constructor.

The buffer classes control the internal buffer and, thus, form an interface between stream and buffer. This also works if the streams set the size of the internal buffer of the buffer object to 0 (see pubsetbuf() ). In this case the result is an unbuffered input or output (which, however, still occurs through the instance of the buffer class).

## Example

```
template <class charT, class traits = char_traits<charT> >
  class basic_streambuf {
  public:
    typedef charT                    char_type;
    typedef typename traits::int_type int_type;
    typedef typename traits::pos_type pos_type;
    typedef typename traits::off_type off_type;
    typedef traits                   traits_type;
    virtual ~basic_streambuf();
  // Locale:
    locale   pubimbue(const locale &loc);
    locale   getloc() const;
  // Buffer:
    basic_streambuf<char_type,traits>* pubsetbuf(char_type* s,
                                          streamsize n);
    pos_type pubseekoff(off_type off, ios_base::seekdir way,
                 ios_base::openmode which=ios_base::in|ios_base::out);
    pos_type pubseekpos(pos_type sp,
                 ios_base::openmode which=ios_base::in| os_base::out);
    int      pubsync();

    streamsize in_avail();
    int_type snextc();
    int_type sbumpc();
    int_type sgetc();
    streamsize sgetn(char_type* s, streamsize n);
    int_type sputbackc(char_type c);
    int_type sungetc();
    int_type   sputc(char_type c);
    streamsize sputn(const char_type* s, streamsize n);
```

```
protected:
  basic_streambuf();
  char_type* eback() const;
  char_type* gptr()  const;
  char_type* egptr() const;
  void       gbump(int n);
  void       setg(char_type* gbeg, char_type* gnext, char_type* gend);
  char_type* pbase() const;
  char_type* pptr() const;
  char_type* epptr() const;
  void       pbump(int n);
  void       setp(char_type* pbeg, char_type* pend);
// Virtual functions:
  virtual void imbue(const locale &loc);
// Buffer management:
  virtual basic_streambuf<char_type,traits>*
                setbuf(char_type* s, streamsize n);
  virtual pos_type seekoff(off_type off, ios_base::seekdir way,
          ios_base::openmode which = ios_base::in | ios_base::out);
  virtual pos_type seekpos(pos_type sp,
          ios_base::openmode which = ios_base::in | ios_base::out);
  virtual int       sync();
  virtual int       showmanyc();
  virtual streamsize xsgetn(char_type* s, streamsize n);
  virtual int_type   anderflow();
  virtual int_type   uflow();
  virtual int_type   pbackfail(int_type c = traits::eof());
  virtual streamsize xsputn(const char_type* s, streamsize n);
  virtual int_type   overflow (int_type c = traits::eof());
};
```

## References

See Practice section, category input and output, dividing stream buffers.


# basic_istream

From <istream>

## Description

The basic_istream class template provides the higher functions and operators for reading from a buffer object. The buffer object itself is associated with the input unit (the source of the data stream). For cin this is by default the keyboard (stdin).

basic_istream is the basic class of basic_ifstream (reading from file) and basic_istringstream (reading from basic_string objects), and it can be instanced itself, to establish stream objects for convenient, formatted or unformatted reading. In this sense the instances `cin` and `win` are predefined in `iostream` for reading `char` or `wchar_t` characters from the keyboard.

## Application

The first step in the creation of an input stream is to specialise the `basic_istream` template for a character type. This has already been done for the character types `char` and `wchar_t` . The type definitions stand in `iostream`:

```
typedef basic_istream<char>                    istream;
typedef basic_istream<wchar_t>                 wistream;
```

The second step is to create an input stream object by instantiating the stream class. This requires the passing of a buffer object to the constructor:

```
filebuf file;
file.open("data.dat", ios_base::in | ios_base::out);
istream dat_in(&file);
```

The implementation through the compiler builder takes care of the instantiation of the `cin` input stream, which is to be linked to the default entry.

## Example

```
template <class charT, class traits = char_traits<charT> >
  class basic_istream : virtual public basic_ios<charT,traits> {
  public:
   // Constructors:
    explicit basic_istream(basic_streambuf<charT,traits>* sb);
    virtual ~basic_istream();
    class sentry;
  // Formatted input:
    basic_istream<charT,traits>& operator>>
       (basic_istream<charT,traits>&
(*pf)(basic_istream<charT,traits>&))
    basic_istream<charT,traits>& operator>>
       (basic_ios<charT,traits>& (*pf)(basic_ios<charT,traits>&))
    basic_istream<charT,traits>& operator>> (ios_base& (*pf)(ios_base&))
    basic_istream<charT,traits>& operator>>(bool& n);
    basic_istream<charT,traits>& operator>>(short& n);
    basic_istream<charT,traits>& operator>>(unsigned short& n);
    basic_istream<charT,traits>& operator>>(int& n);
    basic_istream<charT,traits>& operator>>(unsigned int& n);
    basic_istream<charT,traits>& operator>>(long& n);
    basic_istream<charT,traits>& operator>>(unsigned long& n);
    basic_istream<charT,traits>& operator>>(float& f);
    basic_istream<charT,traits>& operator>>(double& f);
    basic_istream<charT,traits>& operator>>(long double& f);
    basic_istream<charT,traits>& operator>>(void*& p);
    basic_istream<charT,traits>& operator>>
       (basic_streambuf<char_type,traits>* sb);
```

```
  // Unformatted input:
    streamsize gcount() const;
    int_type get();
    basic_istream<charT,traits>& get(char_type& c);
    basic_istream<charT,traits>& get(char_type* s, streamsize n);
    basic_istream<charT,traits>& get(char_type* s, streamsize n,
                                     char_type delim);
 basic_istream<charT,traits>& get(basic_streambuf<char_type,
                                  traits>& sb);
 basic_istream<charT,traits>& get(basic_streambuf<char_type,traits>& sb,
                                  char_type delim);
    basic_istream<charT,traits>& getline(char_type* s, streamsize n);
    basic_istream<charT,traits>& getline(char_type* s, streamsize n,
                                         char_type delim);
    basic_istream<charT,traits>& ignore
                    (streamsize n = 1, int_type delim = traits::eof());
    int_type                     peek();
    basic_istream<charT,traits>& read    (char_type* s, streamsize n);
    streamsize                   readsome(char_type* s, streamsize n);
    basic_istream<charT,traits>& putback(char_type c);
    basic_istream<charT,traits>& unget();
    int sync();
    pos_type tellg();
    basic_istream<charT,traits>& seekg(pos_type);
    basic_istream<charT,traits>& seekg(off_type, ios_base::seekdir);
  };
```

## References

See Practice section, category input and output, dividing stream buffers.

# basic_ostream

From <ostream>

## Description

The basic_ostream class template provides the higher functions and operators for writing into a buffer object. The buffer object itself is associated with the output unit (the target of the data stream). For cout this is by default the console screen (stdout).

basic_ostream is the basic class of basic_ofstream (writing into file) and basic_ostringstream (writing into basic_string objects), and it can be instanced to establish stream objects for convenient, formatted or unformatted output. In this sense the instances cout, cerr, clog and wout, werr, wlog are predefined in iostream for the output of char or wchar_t characters.

## Application

The first step in the creation of an output stream is to specialise the basic_ostream template for a character type. This has already been done for the character types char and wchar_t. The type definitions stand in iostream:

```
typedef basic_ostream<char>                    ostream;
typedef basic_ostream<wchar_t>                 wostream
```

The second step is to create an output stream object through instantiating the stream class. This requires the passing of a buffer object to the constructor:

```
filebuf file;
file.open("data.dat", ios_base::in | ios_base::out);
ostream dat_out(&file);
```

The implementation through the compiler builder takes care of the instantiation of the cout output stream, which is to be linked with the standard output.

## Example

```
template <class charT, class traits = char_traits<charT> >
  class basic_ostream : virtual public basic_ios<charT,traits> {
  public:
  // Constructors:
   explicit basic_ostream(basic_streambuf<char_type,traits>* sb);
   virtual ~basic_ostream();
   class sentry;
  // Formatted output:
    basic_ostream<charT,traits>& operator<<
      (basic_ostream<charT,traits>&
(*pf)(basic_ostream<charT,traits>&));
    basic_ostream<charT,traits>& operator<<
      (basic_ios<charT,traits>& (*pf)(basic_ios<charT,traits>&));
    basic_ostream<charT,traits>& operator<<
      (ios_base& (*pf)(ios_base&));
    basic_ostream<charT,traits>& operator<<(bool n);
    basic_ostream<charT,traits>& operator<<(short n);
    basic_ostream<charT,traits>& operator<<(unsigned short n);
    basic_ostream<charT,traits>& operator<<(int n);
    basic_ostream<charT,traits>& operator<<(unsigned int n);
    basic_ostream<charT,traits>& operator<<(long n);
    basic_ostream<charT,traits>& operator<<(unsigned long n);
    basic_ostream<charT,traits>& operator<<(float f);
    basic_ostream<charT,traits>& operator<<(double f);
    basic_ostream<charT,traits>& operator<<(long double f);
    basic_ostream<charT,traits>& operator<<(void* p);
    basic_ostream<charT,traits>& operator<<
        (basic_streambuf<char_type,traits>* sb);
  // Unformatted output:
    basic_ostream<charT,traits>& put(char_type c);
```

```
      basic_ostream<charT,traits>& write(const char_type* s,
                                   streamsize n);
      basic_ostream<charT,traits>& flush();
// Seek:
      pos_type tellp();
      basic_ostream<charT,traits>& seekp(pos_type);
      basic_ostream<charT,traits>& seekp(off_type, ios_base::seekdir);
   };
```

## References

See Practice section, category input and output, dividing stream buffers.


# basic_iostream

from <istream>

## Description

The template is derived from basic_istream and basic_ostream and does not define elements apart from constructor and destructor.

## Application

The class template is used for input and output in a fundamental buffer.

## Example

```
template <class charT, class traits = char_traits<charT> >
  class basic_iostream :
    public basic_istream<charT,traits>,
    public basic_ostream<charT,traits> {
  public:
    explicit basic_iostream(basic_streambuf<charT,traits>* sb);
    virtual ~basic_iostream();
  };
```


# basic_stringbuf

from <sstream>

## Description

The basic_stringbuf class template is derived from basic_streambuf to link the input or output sequence of a buffer object with a basic_string object. basic_stringbuf represents the buffer objects for string streams (basic_istringstream, basic_ostringstream and basic_stringstream).

## Application

Amongst the public methods of the basic_stringbuf class there are methods which create the connection between string and buffer:

- the constructors are used to establish the buffer object and possibly initialise the pointers of the in- or output sequence in accordance with a passed basic_string object,

- str() is used to create a basic_string object from the in- or output sequence, and

- str(const basic_string<char_type>&) is used to initialise the buffer with a basic_string object.

## Example

```
template <class charT, class traits = char_traits<charT>,
          class Allocator = allocator<charT> >
  class basic_stringbuf : public basic_streambuf<charT,traits> {
  public:
    typedef charT                      char_type;
    typedef typename traits::int_type int_type;
    typedef typename traits::pos_type pos_type;
    typedef typename traits::off_type off_type;
  // Constructors:
    explicit basic_stringbuf(ios_base::openmode which
                              = ios_base::in | ios_base::out);
    explicit basic_stringbuf(
              const basic_string<charT,traits,Allocator>& str,
              ios_base::openmode which = ios_base::in | ios_base::out);
  // Access to string:
    basic_string<charT,traits,Allocator> str() const;
    void str(const basic_string<charT,traits,Allocator>& s);
  protected:
    virtual int_type   underflow();
    virtual int_type   pbackfail(int_type c = traits::eof());
    virtual int_type   overflow (int_type c = traits::eof());
    virtual  basic_streambuf<charT,traits>* setbuf(charT*, streamsize);
    virtual pos_type   seekoff(off_type off, ios_base::seekdir way,
                          ios_base::openmode which
                          = ios_base::in | ios_base::out);
    virtual pos_type   seekpos(pos_type sp,
                          ios_base::openmode which
                          = ios_base::in | ios_base::out);
  };
```

# basic_istringstream

From <sstream>

## Description

Stream class for reading from `basic_string` objects. Uses an instance of the `basic_stringbuf` class as the buffer object.

## Application

The first step in the creation of a string stream is to specialise the `basic_istringstream` template for a character type. This has already been done for the character types char and `wchar_t`. The type definitions stand in `iosfwd`:

```
typedef basic_istringstream<char>                istringstream;
typedef basic_istringstream<wchar_t>             wistringstream;
```

The second step is to create a string stream object from the stream class:

```
istringstream str("Hello");
char s[10];
str >> s;
```

With the two `str()` methods the fundamental `basic_string` object can be set or returned. Otherwise the >> operator or the methods inherited from `basic_istream` are used for reading.

## Example

```
template <class charT, class traits = char_traits<charT>,
          class Allocator = allocator<charT> >
  class basic_istringstream : public basic_istream<charT,traits> {
  public:
    typedef charT                   char_type;
    typedef typename traits::int_type int_type;
    typedef typename traits::pos_type pos_type;
    typedef typename traits::off_type off_type;
    explicit basic_istringstream(ios_base::openmode which
=ios_base::in);
    explicit basic_istringstream(
                    const basic_string<charT,traits,Allocator>& str,
                    ios_base::openmode which = ios_base::in);
    basic_stringbuf<charT,traits,Allocator>* rdbuf() const;
    basic_string<charT,traits,Allocator> str() const;
    void str(const basic_string<charT,traits,Allocator>& s);
  };
```

## References

See Practice section, category input and output, string streams.

# basic_ostringstream

From <sstream>

## Description

Stream class for outputting in basic_string objects. Uses an instance of the basic_stringbuf class as the buffer object.

## Application

The first step in the creation of a string stream is to specialise the basic_ostringstream template for a character type. For the character types char and wchar_t this has already been done. The type definitions stand in iosfwd:

```
typedef basic_ostringstream<char>              ostringstream;
typedef basic_ostringstream<wchar_t>           wostringstream;
```

The second step is to create a string stream object from the stream class:

```
ostringstream str;
str << "Hello";
```

With the two str() methods the fundamental basic_string object can be set or returned. Otherwise the << operator or the methods inherited from basic_ostream are used for writing.

## Example

```
template <class charT, class traits = char_traits<charT>,
          class Allocator = allocator<charT> >
  class basic_ostringstream : public basic_ostream<charT,traits> {
  public:
    typedef charT             char_type;
    typedef typename traits::int_type int_type;
    typedef typename traits::pos_type pos_type;
    typedef typename traits::off_type off_type;
    explicit basic_ostringstream(ios_base::openmode
which=ios_base::out);
    explicit basic_ostringstream(
                    const basic_string<charT,traits,Allocator>& str,
                    ios_base::openmode which = ios_base::out);
    virtual ~basic_ostringstream();
    basic_stringbuf<charT,traits,Allocator>* rdbuf() const;
    basic_string<charT,traits,Allocator> str() const;
    void     str(const basic_string<charT,traits,Allocator>& s);
  };
```

## References

See Practice section, category input and output, string streams.

# basic_stringstream

From <sstream>

## Description

Stream class for input and output in basic_string objects. Uses an instance of the basic_stringbuf class as the buffer object.

## Application

With the two overloaded methods str() the fundamental basic_string object can be set or returned.

Otherwise the stream operators and the other methods inherited from basic_iostream are used.

## Example

```
template <class charT, class traits = char_traits<charT>,
          class Allocator = allocator<charT> >
  class basic_stringstream : public basic_iostream<charT,traits> {
  public:
    typedef charT                        char_type;
    typedef typename traits::int_type int_type;
    typedef typename traits::pos_type pos_type;
    typedef typename traits::off_type off_type;
  // Constructors
    explicit basic_stringstream(
        ios_base::openmode which = ios_base::out|ios_base::in);
    explicit basic_stringstream(
        const basic_string<charT,traits,Allocator>& str,
        ios_base::openmode which = ios_base::out|ios_base::in);
  // Access to buffer and string:
    basic_stringbuf<charT,traits,Allocator>* rdbuf() const;
    basic_string<charT,traits,Allocator> str() const;
    void str(const basic_string<charT,traits,Allocator>& str);
  };
```

## References

See Practice section, category input and output, string streams.

# basic_filebuf

From <fstream>

## Description

The `basic_filebuf` class template is derived from `basic_streambuf` to link the in- or output sequence of the buffer object with a file.

It specialises the `basic_streambuf` class for the creation of buffer objects, which are linked to files, and represents the buffer objects for objects of the class templates `basic_ifstream`, `basic_ofstream` and `basic_fstream`.

## Application

Aqmong the `public` methods of the `basic_filebuf` class, there are methods which create the connection between file and buffer:

- `open()` to open a file, and

- `close()` to close a file.

```
filebuf file;                    // filebuf is equal to basic_filebuf<char>
file.open("Data.dat", ios_base::in | ios_base::out);
file.close();
```

## Example

```
template <class charT, class traits = char_traits<charT> >
  class basic_filebuf : public basic_streambuf<charT,traits> {
  public:
    basic_filebuf();
    virtual ~basic_filebuf();
    bool is_open() const;
    basic_filebuf<charT,traits>* open(const char* s,
                                      ios_base::openmode mode);
    basic_filebuf<charT,traits>* close();
  protected:
    virtual int       showmanyc();
    virtual int_type underflow();
    virtual int_type uflow();
    virtual int_type pbackfail(int_type c = traits::eof());
    virtual int_type overflow (int_type c = traits::eof());
    virtual basic_streambuf<charT,traits>* setbuf(char_type* s,
                                                  streamsize n);
    virtual pos_type seekoff(off_type off, ios_base::seekdir way,
                             ios_base::openmode which
                             = ios_base::in | ios_base::out);
    virtual pos_type seekpos(pos_type sp, ios_base::openmode which
                             = ios_base::in | ios_base::out);
    virtual int       sync();
    virtual void      imbue(const locale& loc);
  };
```

## References

See Practice section, category input and output, dividing stream buffers.

# basic_ifstream

From <fstream>

## Description

The basic_ifstream class template provides the functions for opening and closing files.

## Application

The first step in the creation of an input stream for a file is to specialise the basic_ifstream template for a character type. For the character types char and wchar_t this has already been done. The type definitions stand in iostream:

```
typedef basic_ifstream<char>                    ifstream;
typedef basic_ifstream<wchar_t>                 wifstream;
```

The second step is to create a stream object through instantiation of the stream class. This requires that a buffer object is passed to the constructor:

```
ifstream dat_ein;
dat_in.open("filename", ios_base::in);
```

The actual read methods are inherited from basic_istream.

## Example

```
template <class charT, class traits = char_traits<charT> >
  class basic_ifstream : public basic_istream<charT,traits> {
  public:
    typedef charT                    char_type;
    typedef typename traits::int_type int_type;
    typedef typename traits::pos_type pos_type;
    typedef typename traits::off_type off_type;
    basic_ifstream();
    explicit basic_ifstream(const char* s,
                            ios_base::openmode mode = ios_base::in);
    basic_filebuf<charT,traits>* rdbuf() const;
    bool is_open();
    void open(const char* s, openmode mode = in);
    void close();
  };
```

## References

See Practice section, category input and output, text files in C++; binary files in C++.

# basic_ofstream

from <fstream>

## Description

The basic_ofstream class template provides functions for opening and closing files.

## Application

The first step in the creation of an output stream for a file is to specialise the basic_ofstream template for a character type. For the character types char and wchar_t this has already been done. The type definitions stand in iostream:

```
typedef basic_ofstream<char>                    ofstream;
typedef basic_ofstream<wchar_t>                 wofstream;
```

The second step is to create a stream object through instantiation of the stream class. This requires that a buffer object is passed to the constructor:

```
ofstream dat_out;
dat_out.open("filename", ios_base::out);
```

The actual write methods are inherited from basic_ostream.

## Example

```
template <class charT, class traits = char_traits<charT> >
  class basic_ofstream : public basic_ostream<charT,traits> {
  public:
    typedef charT                    char_type;
    typedef typename traits::int_type int_type;
    typedef typename traits::pos_type pos_type;
    typedef typename traits::off_type off_type;
    basic_ofstream();
    explicit basic_ofstream(const char* s,
              ios_base::openmode mode = ios_base::out|ios_base::trunc);
    basic_filebuf<charT,traits>* rdbuf() const;
    bool is_open();
    void open(const char* s, ios_base::openmode mode = out | trunc);
    void close();
  };
```

## References

See Practice section, category input and output, text files in C++; binary files in C++.

# basic_fstream

From <fstream>

## Description

Stream class for input and output in files. Uses an instance of the `basic_filebuf` class as buffer object.

## Application

Files can be opened and closed with `open()` and `close()`

For input and output, the stream operators and the other methods inherited from `basic_iostream` are used.

## Example

```
template <class charT, class traits=char_traits<charT> >
  class basic_fstream : public basic_iostream<charT,traits> {
  public:
    typedef charT                       char_type;
    typedef typename traits::int_type ins_type;
    typedef typename traits::pos_type pos_type;
    typedef typename traits::off_type off_type;
  // Constructors
    basic_fstream();
    explicit basic_fstream(const char* s,
                 ios_base::openmode mode = ios_base::in|ios_base::out);
  // Access to buffer and files:
    basic_filebuf<charT,traits>* rdbuf() const;
    bool is_open();
    void open(const char* s,
            ios_base::openmode mode = ios_base::in|ios_base::out);
    void close();
  };
```

## References

See Practice section, category input and output, text files in C++; binary files in C++.

# The string classes

## Overview

### Description

The `basic_string` class template represents the object-oriented alternative to the ANSI C functions from `string.h`. The implementation as template permits the creation of strings for any character type.

To be able to implement the class type independently, the fundamental routines that are independent of the used character type have been separated into a traits class — as in the `iostream` classes. The character type and its traits class are then passed to the template instances of `basic_string` as template parameters.

### Application

For the character types `char` and `wchar_t` specialisations of the traits template as well as type definitions of `basic_string` specialisations have already been defined in the runtime library. The latter are called `string` and `wstring`.

The most important string manipulations are implemented as methods and/or operators in `basic_string`.

Through global overloading of the operators + (concatenation), == , !=, <, <=, >, >= (for comparisons), as well as >> and << (input and output), the handling of strings is further facilitated.

### References

See Reference section, category, the class string.

See Practice section, category strings, programming with the class string.

## char_traits

From `<string>`

### Description

This is a template structure which contains methods and type definitions which depend on the passed `charT` character type and which are required for the implementation of the basic_string template. In this way the implementation of the basic_string template can be kept independent of the characters that are to be manipulated.

Specialisations of the template are used as template arguments for basic_string and the stream classes.

## Example

```
template<> struct char_traits<char> {
  typedef char        char_type;
  typedef int         int_type;
  typedef streamoff   off_type;
  typedef streampos   pos_type;
  typedef mbstate_t   state_type;

  static void assign(char_type& c1, const char_type& c2);
  static bool eq(const char_type& c1, const char_type& c2);
  static bool lt(const char_type& c1, const char_type& c2);
  static int compare(const char_type* s1, const char_type* s2, size_t
n);
  static size_t length(const char_type* s);
  static const char_type* find(const char_type* s, int n,
                                const char_type& a);
  static char_type* move(char_type* s1, const char_type* s2, size_t n);
  static char_type* copy(char_type* s1, const char_type* s2, size_t n);
  static char_type* assign(char_type* s, size_t n, char_type a);
  static int_type not_eof(const int_type& c);
  static char_type to_char_type(const int_type& c);
  static int_type to_int_type(const char_type& c);
  static bool eq_int_type(const int_type& c1, const int_type& c2);
  static state_type get_state(pos_type pos);
  static int_type eof();
  };
```

# basic_string

From <string>

## Description

The class supports the programming with strings and offers a wealth of functions for their creation and manipulation.

In particular there are template functions:

- for the creation of strings,
- for assignments, attachment and insertion,
- for deletion, removal and replacement,

- for the determination of size of strings,
- for indexed access to individual characters in the string,
- for the comparison of strings, and
- for searching for characters and sub-strings.

Where it is useful the functions are overloaded, usually to be able to accept, apart from strings, individual characters or basic_string objects as arguments, or to be able to work with iterators.

## Application

The use of the class occurs through the specialisation of the class template for the character type that is to be used. For char and wchar_t this has already been done. The corresponding string types are:

string and wstring.

For these classes objects can be created which then can be manipulated through their methods and operators.

## Example

```
template<class charT, class traits = char_traits<charT>,
        class Allocator = allocator<charT> >
  class basic_string {
  public:
    typedef            traits                      traits_type;
    typedef typename traits::char_type             value_type;
    typedef            Allocator                   allocator_type;
    typedef typename Allocator::size_type          size_type;
    typedef typename Allocator::difference_type    difference_type;
    typedef typename Allocator::reference          reference;
    typedef typename Allocator::const_reference    const_reference;
    typedef typename Allocator::pointer            pointer;
    typedef typename Allocator::const_pointer      const_pointer;
    typedef implementation defined                 iterator;
    typedef implementation defined                 const_iterator;
    typedef std::reverse_iterator<iterator> reverse_iterator;
    typedef std::reverse_iterator<const_iterator>
const_reverse_iterator;
    static const size_type npos = -1;
  // Constructors, copying:
    explicit basic_string(const Allocator& a = Allocator());
    basic_string(const basic_string& str, size_type pos = 0,
                 size_type n = npos, const Allocator& a = Allocator());
    basic_string(const charT* s, size_type n, const Allocator& a =
                                       Allocator());
    basic_string(const charT* s, const Allocator& a = Allocator());
    basic_string(size_type n, charT c, const Allocator& a = Allocator());
```

```
            template<class InputIterator>
                    basic_string(InputIterator begin, InputIterator end,
                                 const Allocator& a = Allocator());
            ~basic_string();
            basic_string& operator=(const basic_string& str);
            basic_string& operator=(const charT* s);
            basic_string& operator=(charT c);

        // Iterators:
            iterator          begin();
            const_iterator begin() const;
            iterator          end();
            const_iterator end() const;
            reverse_iterator          rbegin();
            const_reverse_iterator rbegin() const;
            reverse_iterator          rend();
            const_reverse_iterator rend() const;
        // Size:
            size_type size() const;
            size_type length() const;
            size_type max_size() const;
            void resize(size_type n, charT c);
            void resize(size_type n);
            size_type capacity() const;
            void reserve(size_type res_arg = 0);
            void clear();
            bool empty() const;
        // Access to characters:
            const_reference operator[](size_type pos) const;
            reference        operator[](size_type pos);
            const_reference at(size_type n) const;
            reference        at(size_type n);

        // Altering operations:
            basic_string& operator+=(const basic_string& str);
            basic_string& operator+=(const charT* s);
            basic_string& operator+=(charT c);
            basic_string& append(const basic_string& str);
            basic_string& append(const basic_string& str, size_type pos,
                                 size_type n);
            basic_string& append(const charT* s, size_type n);
            basic_string& append(const charT* s);
            basic_string& append(size_type n, charT c);
            template<class InputIterator>
                    basic_string& append(InputIterator first, InputIterator last);
            basic_string& assign(const basic_string&);
            basic_string& assign(const basic_string& str, size_type pos,
                                 size_type n);
            basic_string& assign(const charT* s, size_type n);
```

```
    basic_string& assign(const charT* s);
    basic_string& assign(size_type n, charT c);
    template<class InputIterator>
          basic_string& assign(InputIterator first, InputIterator last);

    basic_string& insert(size_type pos1, const basic_string& str);
    basic_string& insert(size_type pos1, const basic_string& str,
                              size_type pos2, size_type n);
    basic_string& insert(size_type pos, const charT* s, size_type n);
    basic_string& insert(size_type pos, const charT* s);
    basic_string& insert(size_type pos, size_type n, charT c);
    iterator insert(iterator p, charT c = charT());
    void      insert(iterator p, size_type n, charT c);
    template<class InputIterator>
    void insert(iterator p, InputIterator first, InputIterator last);
    basic_string& erase(size_type pos = 0, size_type n = npos);
    iterator erase(iterator position);
    iterator erase(iterator first, iterator last);
    basic_string& replace(size_type pos1, size_type n1,
                          const basic_string& str);
    basic_string& replace(size_type pos1, size_type n1,
                  const basic_string& str, size_type pos2, size_type n2);
    basic_string& replace(size_type pos, size_type n1, const charT* s,
                          size_type n2);
    basic_string& replace(size_type pos, size_type n1, const charT* s);
    basic_string& replace(size_type pos, size_type n1, size_type n2,
                          charT c);
    basic_string& replace(iterator i1, iterator i2,
                          const basic_string& str);
    basic_string& replace(iterator i1, iterator i2, const charT* s,
                          size_type n);
    basic_string& replace(iterator i1, iterator i2, const charT* s);
    basic_string& replace(iterator i1, iterator i2,
                          size_type n, charT c);
    template<class InputIterator>
        basic_string& replace(iterator i1, iterator i2,
                              InputIterator j1, InputIterator j2);
    size_type copy(charT* s, size_type n, size_type pos = 0) const;
    void swap(basic_string<charT,traits,Allocator>&);

// Non-altering operations:
  const charT* c_str() const;
  const charT* data() const;
  allocator_type get_allocator() const;
  size_type find (const basic_string& str, size_type pos = 0) const;
  size_type find (const charT* s, size_type pos, size_type n) const;
  size_type find (const charT* s, size_type pos = 0) const;
  size_type find (charT c, size_type pos = 0) const;
  size_type rfind(const basic_string& str, size_type pos = npos) const;
  size_type rfind(const charT* s, size_type pos, size_type n) const;
```

```
         size_type rfind(const charT* s, size_type pos = npos) const;
         size_type rfind(charT c, size_type pos = npos) const;
         size_type find_first_of(const basic_string& str, size_type pos = 0)
                                                                   const;
         size_type find_first_of(const charT* s, size_type pos, size_type n)
                                                                   const;
         size_type find_first_of(const charT* s, size_type pos = 0) const;
         size_type find_first_of(charT c, size_type pos = 0) const;
         size_type find_last_of (const basic_string& str,
                              size_type pos = npos) const;
         size_type find_last_of (const charT* s, size_type pos, size_type n)
                                                                   const;
         size_type find_last_of (const charT* s, size_type pos = npos) const;
         size_type find_last_of (charT c, size_type pos = npos) const;
         size_type find_first_not_of(const basic_string& str,
                                  size_type pos = 0) const;
         size_type find_first_not_of(const charT* s, size_type pos,
                                  size_type n) const;
         size_type find_first_not_of(const charT* s, size_type pos = 0) const;
         size_type find_first_not_of(charT c, size_type pos = 0) const;
         size_type find_last_not_of (const basic_string& str,
                                  size_type pos = npos) const;
         size_type find_last_not_of (const charT* s, size_type pos,
                                  size_type n) const;
         size_type find_last_not_of (const charT* s, size_type pos = npos)
                                                                   const;
         size_type find_last_not_of (charT c, size_type pos = npos) const;
         basic_string substr(size_type pos = 0, size_type n = npos) const;
         int compare(const basic_string& str) const;
         int compare(size_type pos1, size_type n1,
                  const basic_string& str) const;
         int compare(size_type pos1, size_type n1,
                  const basic_string& str,
                  size_type pos2, size_type n2) const;
         int compare(const charT* s) const;
         int compare(size_type pos1, size_type n1,
                  const charT* s, size_type n2 = npos) const;
      };
```

## References

See Reference section, category strings, the class string.

See Practice section, category strings, programming with the class string.

# Classes for local settings

## Overview

### Description

Date specifications, currency symbols, and the punctuation in floating-point numbers differ from country to country. In which way, then, should a date be formatted in a C++ program, which is supposed to be used internationally? The answer lies in the local setting. In it, sorted by categories, is the necessary information for country-specific handling. Each category in turn contains several aspects, as follows.

| Category | Aspect |
| --- | --- |

Classification and conversion of characters:

| | |
| --- | --- |
| ctype | ctype<char>, ctype<wchar_t> |
| | codecvt<char,char,mbstate_t> |
| | codecvt<wchar_t,char,mbstate_t> |

Comparison of characters:

| | |
| --- | --- |
| collate | collate<char>, collate<wchar_t> |

Message processing:

| | |
| --- | --- |
| messages | messages<char>, messages<wchar_t> |

Formatting currency:

| | |
| --- | --- |
| monetary | moneypunct<char>, moneypunct<wchar_t> |
| | moneypunct<char,true>, moneypunct<wchar_t,true> |
| | money_get<char>, money_get<wchar_t> |
| | money_put<char>, money_put<wchar_t> |

Punctuation in numerical specifications:

| | |
| --- | --- |
| numeric | numpunct<char>, numpunct<wchar_t> |
| | num_get<stream,InIter>, |
| | num_put<stream,OutputIter> |

Date specifications:

| | |
| --- | --- |
| time | time_get<char, InIter> |
| | time_get<wchar_t, InIter> |
| | time_put<char, OutputIterator> |
| | time_put<wchar_t, OutputIterator> |

## Application

In C++ the local setting and individual aspects are represented through classes. You can use these classes to implement your own settings, to modify existing settings, and to switch between local settings.

It makes sense to fall back on local settings, for example when input and outputting data. The stream classes, therefore, possess their own methods (imbue()) for the selection of a local setting.

Through corresponding implementations of the operators << and >> you can write programs which either adapt to local circumstances (that is, are adopted from the operating system) or whose formatting occurs independently of the national differences.

## References

See Practice section, category internationalisation and localisation, local environment.

# locale

From <locale>

## Description

Class for the representation and management of a locale setting.

The locale class defines:

- constructors for the creation of new locale settings, based on other locale settings,
- functions and operators for querying information about the locale setting (name(), ==(), !=() as well as the global function templates use_facet() and has_facet()),
- functions for global locale settings (global(), classic()), and
- compare function operator() for strings.

## Application

With the help of the class locale you can create your own locale settings which you can then assign, for example with the imbue() stream method, to a stream to carry out formatted input and output in accordance with your locale setting.

## Example

```
class locale {
  public:
    class facet;
    class id;
    typedef int category;
    static const category;
      /* none, collate, ctype,
         monetary, numeric,
         time, messages,
         all = collate | ctype | monetary | numeric | time  | messages;
         */
  // Constructors:
    locale() throw();
    locale(const locale& other) throw();,
    explicit locale(const char* std_name);
    locale(const locale& other, const char* std_name, category);
    template <class Facet> locale(const locale& other, Facet* f);
    template <class Facet> locale(const locale& other,
                                  const locale& one);
    locale(const locale& other, const locale& one, category);
   ~locale() throw();  // non-virtual
    const locale& operator=(const locale& other) throw();

    basic_string<char>                name() const;
    bool operator==(const locale& other) const;
    bool operator!=(const locale& other) const;
    template <class charT, class Traits, class Allocator>
      bool operator()(const basic_string<charT,Traits,Allocator>& s1,
              const basic_string<charT,Traits,Allocator>& s2) const;
  // global locale:
    static      locale  global(const locale&);
    static const locale& classic();
};
```

## References

See Practice section, category internationalisation and localisation, local environment.

# Auxiliary classes for individual categories

## Application

With the classes in the following list, you can create your own settings. These can, for example, be integrated into separate locales (instances of the class `locale`).

## Example

```
class de_Num : public numpunct_byname<char> {
  public:
    de_Num(const char* name) : numpunct_byname<char>(name) {}
  protected:
    virtual char_type do_decimal_point() const {
      return '.';
      }
  };

// Special locale with de_Num facet
locale myloc(locale("C"), new de_Num(""));
```

## ctype_base                                                        <locale>

Basic class of the ctype class template, which defines a list type that is used as a mask in character classification.

```
class ctype_base {
    public:
      enum mask {
          space,  // non-printable character
          print,  // printable character
          cntrl,  // control character
          upper,  // upper case letter
          lower,  // lower case letter
          alpha,  // letter
          digit,  // digit
          punct,  // punctuation character
          xdigit, // hexadecimal number
          alnum,  // alpha | digit
          graph   // alnum | punct
      };
    };
```

## ctype                                                             <locale>

A class template for the creation of ctype settings, for character classification and conversion.

Contains a set of public methods for character classification and conversion. For each function there is a corresponding virtual protected version, which calls it and which can be overridden in derived classes.

```
template <class charT>
 class ctype : public locale::facet, public ctype_base {
 public:
  typedef charT char_type;
  explicit ctype(size_t refs = 0);
  bool        is(mask m, charT c) const;
```

```
const charT* is(const charT* low, const charT* high, mask* vec) const;
const charT* scan_is(mask m,const charT* low,const charT* high) const;
const charT* scan_not(mask m,const charT* low,const charT* high)
                        const;
charT        toupper(charT) const;
const charT* toupper(charT* low, const charT* high) const;
charT        tolower(charT c) const;
const charT* tolower(charT* low, const charT* high) const;
charT        widen(char c) const;
const char*  widen(const char* low, const char* high, charT* to) const;
char         narrow(charT c, char dfault) const;
const charT* narrow(const charT* low, const charT*, char dfault,
                    char* to) const;
static locale::id id;
protected:
 ~ctype();  // virtual
 virtual bool        do_is(mask m, charT c) const;
 virtual const charT* do_is(const charT* low, const charT* high,
                        mask* vec) const;
 virtual const charT* do_scan_is(mask m,
                        const charT* low, const charT* high) const;
 virtual const charT* do_scan_not(mask m,
                        const charT* low, const charT* high) const;
 virtual charT        do_toupper(charT) const;
 virtual const charT* do_toupper(charT* low, const charT* high) const;
 virtual charT        do_tolower(charT) const;
 virtual const charT* do_tolower(charT* low, const charT* high) const;
 virtual charT        do_widen(char) const;
 virtual const char*  do_widen(const char* low, const char* high,
                        charT* dest) const;
 virtual char         do_narrow(charT, char dfault) const;
 virtual const charT* do_narrow(const charT* low, const charT* high,
                        char dfault, char* dest) const;
};
```

## ctype_byname                                            <locale>

This offers the option to create a setting which fits a locale setting that is specified through its name. For this the name of the locale setting is passed to the constructor.

```
template <class charT>
 class ctype_byname : public ctype<charT> {
 public:
   explicit ctype_byname(const char*, size_t refs = 0);
 protected:
  ~ctype_byname();  // virtual
  virtual bool        do_is(mask m, charT c) const;
  virtual const charT* do_is(const charT* low, const charT* high,
                        mask* vec) const;
```

```
virtual const char*  do_scan_is(mask m,
                          const charT* low, const charT* high) const;
virtual const char*  do_scan_not(mask m,
                          const charT* low, const charT* high) const;
virtual charT        do_toupper(charT) const;
virtual const charT* do_toupper(charT* low, const charT* high) const;
virtual charT        do_tolower(charT) const;
virtual const charT* do_tolower(charT* low, const charT* high) const;
virtual charT        do_widen(char) const;
virtual const char*  do_widen(const char* low, const char* high,
                          charT* dest) const;
virtual char         do_narrow(charT, char dfault) const;
virtual const charT* do_narrow(const charT* low, const charT* high,
                          char dfault, char* dest) const;
};
```

## codecvt_base                                              <locale>

The basic class of the codecvt class template, which defines a list types with the various result values of the conversion function codecvt::convert().

```
class codecvt_base {
    public:
      enum result {
            ok,      // complete conversion
            partial  // not enough memory
            error    // no conversion possible
            noconv   // no conversion required
            };
};
```

## codecvt                                                   <locale>

A class template for the creation of settings in the codecvt category, for the conversion of character sets.

The class contains public methods for the conversion of one character set into another. For each function there is a corresponding virtual protected version, which calls it and which can be overridden in derived classes.

```
template <class internT, class externT, class stateT>
class codecvt : public locale::facet, public codecvt_base {
public:
 typedef internT  intern_type;
 typedef externT  extern_type;
 typedef stateT state_type;
 explicit codecvt(size_t refs = 0);
 result out(stateT& state, const internT* from, const internT* from_end,
         const internT*& from_next, externT*    to,
         externT* to_limit, externT*& to_next) const;
```

```
result unshift(stateT& state, externT*   to,
               externT* to_limit,      externT*& to_next) const;
result in(stateT& state, const externT* from, const externT* from_end,
          const externT*& from_next, internT*   to,
          internT* to_limit, internT*& to_next) const;
int encoding() const throw();
bool always_noconv() const throw();
int length(const stateT&, const externT* from, const externT* end,
           size_t max) const;
int max_length() const throw();
static locale::id id;
protected:
~codecvt();   // virtual
virtual result do_out(stateT& state, const internT* from,
            const internT* from_end, const internT*& from_next,
            externT* to, externT* to_limit, externT*& to_next) const;
virtual result do_unshift(stateT& state, externT* to,
                          externT* to_limit, externT*& to_next) const;
virtual result do_in(stateT& state, const externT* from,
                const externT* from_end, const externT*& from_next,
                internT* to,           internT* to_limit,
                internT*& to_next) const;
virtual int do_encoding() const throw();
virtual bool do_always_noconv() const throw();
virtual int do_length(const stateT&, const externT* from,
                  const externT* end, size_t max) const;
virtual int do_max_length() const throw();
};
```

## codecvt_byname                                             <locale>

This offers the option to create new locale settings. For this the name of the locale
setting is passed to the constructor.

```
template <class internT, class externT, class stateT>
 class codecvt_byname : public codecvt<internT, externT, stateT> {
 public:
   explicit codecvt_byname(const char*, size_t refs = 0);
 protected:
  ~codecvt_byname();   // virtual
   virtual result do_out(stateT& state, const internT* from,
                const internT* from_end, const internT*& from_next,
                externT* to,           externT* to_limit,
                externT*& to_next) const;
   virtual result do_in(stateT& state, const externT* from,
                const externT* from_end, const externT*& from_next,
                internT* to,           internT* to_limit,
                internT*& to_next) const;
   virtual int do_encoding() const throw();
```

```
     virtual bool do_always_noconv() const throw();
     virtual int do_length(const stateT&, const externT* from,
                         const externT* end,size_t max) const;
     virtual int do_max_length() const throw();
 };
```

## collate                                                    <locale>

A class template for the creation settings in the collate category, for the comparison of strings.

Contains a set of public methods for the comparison of strings. For each method there is a corresponding virtual protected version, which calls it and which can be overridden in derived classes.

```
template <class charT>
 class collate : public locale::facet {
 public:
    typedef charT              char_type;
    typedef basic_string<charT> string_type;
    explicit collate(size_t refs = 0);
    int compare(const charT* low1, const charT* high1,
            const charT* low2, const charT* high2) const;
    string_type transform(const charT* low, const charT* high) const;
    long hash(const charT* low, const charT* high) const;
    static locale::id id;
 protected:
  ~collate();  // virtual
    virtual int    do_compare(const charT* low1, const charT* high1,
                          const charT* low2, const charT* high2) const;
    virtual string_type do_transform(const charT* low,
                                    const charT* high) const;
    virtual long   do_hash (const charT* low, const charT* high) const;
 };
```

## collate_byname                                             <locale>

Offers the option to create a locale setting that is specified through its name. For this the name of the locale setting is passed to the constructor.

```
template <class charT>
 class collate_byname : public collate<charT> {
 public:
    explicit collate_byname(const char*, size_t refs = 0);
 protected:
  ~collate_byname();  // virtual
    virtual int    do_compare(const charT* low1, const charT* high1,
                          const charT* low2, const charT* high2) const;
```

```
  virtual string_type do_transform(const charT* low,
                             const charT* high) const;
  virtual long   do_hash( const charT* low, const charT* high) const;
};
```

## messages_base                                          <locale>

A basic class in the `messages` class template, which defines an abbreviation for the type of the message catalogues.

```
class messages_base {
  public:
    typedef int catalog;
};
```

## messages                                               <locale>

A class template for the creation of settings in the `messages` category, for the selection of messages from catalogues.

Contains a set of `public` methods for the selection of messages from catalogues. For each function there is a corresponding virtual `protected` version, which calls it and which can be overridden in derived classes.

```
template <class charT>
 class messages : public locale::facet, public messages_base {
 public:
   typedef charT char_type;
   typedef basic_string<charT> string_type;
   explicit messages(size_t refs = 0);
   catalog open(const basic_string<char>& fn, const locale&) const;
   string_type  get(catalog c, int set, int msgid,
                    const string_type& dfault) const;
   void     close(catalog c) const;
   static locale::id id;
 protected:
  ~messages();  // virtual
   virtual catalog do_open(const basic_string<char>&,
                      const locale&) const;
   virtual string_type  do_get(catalog, int set, int msgid,
                          const string_type& dfault) const;
   virtual void    do_close(catalog) const;
};
```

## messages_byname                                        <locale>

This offers the option to create a `locale` setting that is specified through its name. For this the name of the `locale` setting is passed to the constructor.

```
template <class charT>
 class messages_byname : public messages<charT> {
 public:
   explicit messages_byname(const char*, size_t refs = 0);
 protected:
  ~messages_byname();  // virtual

   virtual catalog do_open(const basic_string<char>&,
                           const locale&) const;
   virtual string_type  do_get(catalog, int set, int msgid,
                               const string_type& dfault) const;
   virtual void    do_close(catalog) const;
 };
```

## money_get                                                    <locale>

A class template for the creation of settings in the monetary category, for reading currency specifications.

Contains public methods for reading currency specifications. For each method there is a corresponding virtual protected version, which calls it and which can be overridden in derived classes.

```
template <class charT, class InputIterator = istreambuf_iterator<charT>
>
 class money_get : public locale::facet {
 public:
   typedef charT            char_type;
   typedef InputIterator    iter_type;
   typedef basic_string<charT> string_type;
   explicit money_get(size_t refs = 0);
   iter_type get(iter_type s, iter_type end, bool intl,
                 ios_base& f, ios_base::iostate& err,
                 long double& units) const;
   iter_type get(iter_type s, iter_type end, bool intl,
                 ios_base& f, ios_base::iostate& err,
                 string_type& digits) const;
   static const bool intl = Intl;
   static locale::id id;
 protected:
  ~money_get();  // virtual
   virtual iter_type do_get(iter_type, bool, iter_type, ios_base&,
                       ios_base::iostate& err, long double& units) const;
   virtual iter_type do_get(iter_type, bool, iter_type, ios_base&,
                       ios_base::iostate& err, string_type& digits) const;
 };
```

## money_put <locale>

A class template for the creation of settings in the `monetary` category, for outputting currency specifications.

Contains `public` methods for outputting currency specifications. For each function there is a corresponding virtual `protected` version, which calls it and which can be overridden in derived classes.

```
template <class charT, bool Intl = false,
         class OutputIterator = ostreambuf_iterator<charT> >
 class money_put : public locale::facet {

 public:
   typedef charT             char_type;
   typedef OutputIterator    iter_type;
   typedef basic_string<charT> string_type;
   explicit money_put(size_t refs = 0);
   iter_type put(iter_type s, bool intl, ios_base& f,
                 char_type fill, long double units) const;
   iter_type put(iter_type s, bool intl, ios_base& f,
                 char_type fill, const string_type& digits) const;
   static locale::id id;
 protected:
  ~money_put();  // virtual
   virtual iter_type do_put(iter_type, bool, ios_base&, char_type fill,
                            long double units) const;
   virtual iter_type do_put(iter_type, bool, ios_base&, char_type fill,
                            const string_type& digits) const;
 };
```

## money_base <locale>

A basic class in the `moneypunct` class template, which defines a list type and a corresponding structure type used for the determination of the order of elements in currency specifications.

```
class money_base {
  public:
    enum part {
              none, // no instructions
              space, // non representable character
              symbol, // currency symbol
              sign, // signs
              value // value };
    struct pattern { char field[4]; };
 };
```

## moneypunct <locale>

A class template for the creation of settings in the `monetary` category, for punctuation in currency specifications.

Contains a set of `public` methods for punctuation in currency specifications. For each method there is a corresponding virtual `protected` version, which calls it and which can be overridden in derived classes.

```
template <class charT, bool International = false>
 class moneypunct : public locale::facet, public money_base {
 public:
   typedef charT char_type;
   typedef basic_string<charT> string_type;
   explicit moneypunct(size_t refs = 0);
   charT        decimal_point() const;
   charT        thousands_sep() const;
   string       grouping()      const;
   string_type  curr_symbol()   const;
   string_type  positive_sign() const;
   string_type  negative_sign() const;
   int          frac_digits()   const;
   pattern      pos_format()     const;
   pattern      neg_format()     const;
   static locale::id id;
   static const bool intl = International;
 protected:
  ~moneypunct();  // virtual
   virtual charT        do_decimal_point() const;
   virtual charT        do_thousands_sep() const;
   virtual string       do_grouping()      const;
   virtual string_type  do_curr_symbol()   const;
   virtual string_type  do_positive_sign() const;
   virtual string_type  do_negative_sign() const;
   virtual int          do_frac_digits()   const;
   virtual pattern      do_pos_format()     const;
   virtual pattern      do_neg_format()     const;
 };
```

## moneypunct_byname <locale>

This offers the option to create a `locale` setting that is specified through its name. For this the name of the `locale` setting is passed to the constructor.

```
template <class charT, bool Intl = false>
 class moneypunct_byname : public moneypunct<charT, Intl> {
 public:
   explicit moneypunct_byname(const char*, size_t refs = 0);
```

```
protected:
  ~moneypunct_byname();  // virtual
  virtual charT         do_decimal_point() const;
  virtual charT         do_thousands_sep() const;
  virtual string        do_grouping()      const;
  virtual string_type   do_curr_symbol()   const;
  virtual string_type   do_positive_sign() const;
  virtual string_type   do_negative_sign() const;
  virtual int           do_frac_digits()   const;
  virtual pattern       do_pos_format()    const;
  virtual pattern       do_neg_format()    const;
};
```

## num_get <locale>

A class template for the creation of settings in the numeric category, for reading numeric values.

Contains a set of public methods for reading numeric values. For each method there is a corresponding virtual protected version, which calls it and which can be overridden in derived classes.

```
template <class charT, class InputIterator = istreambuf_iterator<charT>
>
    class num_get : public locale::facet {
    public:
      typedef charT            char_type;
      typedef InputIterator    iter_type;
      explicit num_get(size_t refs = 0);
      iter_type get(iter_type in, iter_type end, ios_base&,
                  ios_base::iostate& err, bool& v)          const;
      iter_type get(iter_type in, iter_type end, ios_base& ,
                  ios_base::iostate& err, long& v)          const;
      iter_type get(iter_type in, iter_type end, ios_base&,
                  ios_base::iostate& err, unsigned short& v) const;
      iter_type get(iter_type in, iter_type end, ios_base&,
                  ios_base::iostate& err, unsigned int& v)  const;
      iter_type get(iter_type in, iter_type end, ios_base&,
                  ios_base::iostate& err, unsigned long& v) const;
      iter_type get(iter_type in, iter_type end, ios_base&,
                  ios_base::iostate& err, float& v)         const;
      iter_type get(iter_type in, iter_type end, ios_base&,
                  ios_base::iostate& err, double& v)        const;
      iter_type get(iter_type in, iter_type end, ios_base&,
                  ios_base::iostate& err, long double& v)   const;
      iter_type get(iter_type in, iter_type end, ios_base&,
                  ios_base::iostate& err, void*& v)   const;
      static locale::id id;
```

```
protected:
 ~num_get();  // virtual
  virtual iter_type do_get(iter_type, iter_type, ios_base&,
                           ios_base::iostate& err, bool& v) const;
  virtual iter_type do_get(iter_type, iter_type, ios_base&,
                           ios_base::iostate& err, long& v) const;
  virtual iter_type do_get(iter_type, iter_type, ios_base&,
                    ios_base::iostate& err, unsigned short& v) const;
  virtual iter_type do_get(iter_type, iter_type, ios_base&,
                      ios_base::iostate& err, unsigned int& v) const;
  virtual iter_type do_get(iter_type, iter_type, ios_base&,
                     ios_base::iostate& err, unsigned long& v) const;
  virtual iter_type do_get(iter_type, iter_type, ios_base&,
                             ios_base::iostate& err, float& v) const;
  virtual iter_type do_get(iter_type, iter_type, ios_base&,
                            ios_base::iostate& err, double& v) const;
  virtual iter_type do_get(iter_type, iter_type, ios_base&,
                       ios_base::iostate& err, long double& v) const;
  virtual iter_type do_get(iter_type, iter_type, ios_base&,
                             ios_base::iostate& err, void*& v) const;
};
```

## num_put                                                    <locale>

A class template for the creation of settings in the numeric category, for outputting numeric values.

Contains a set of public methods for outputting numeric values. For each method there is a corresponding virtual protected version, which calls it and which can be overridden in derived classes.

```
template <class charT, class OutputIterator =ostreambuf_iterator<charT>
>
 class num_put : public locale::facet {
 public:
   typedef charT            char_type;
   typedef OutputIterator   iter_type;
   explicit num_put(size_t refs = 0);
   iter_type put(iter_type s, ios_base& f, char_type fill, bool v) const;
   iter_type put(iter_type s, ios_base& f, char_type fill, long v) const;
   iter_type put(iter_type s, ios_base& f, char_type fill,
             unsigned long v) const;
   iter_type put(iter_type s, ios_base& f, char_type fill,
             double v) const;
   iter_type put(iter_type s, ios_base& f, char_type fill,
             long double v) const;
   iter_type put(iter_type s, ios_base& f, char_type fill,
             void* v) const;
   static locale::id id;
```

```
protected:
 ~num_put();  // virtual
  virtual iter_type do_put(iter_type, ios_base&, char_type fill,
                           bool v) const;
  virtual iter_type do_put(iter_type, ios_base&, char_type fill,
                           long v) const;
  virtual iter_type do_put(iter_type, ios_base&, char_type fill,
                           unsigned long) const;
  virtual iter_type do_put(iter_type, ios_base&, char_type fill,
                           double v) const;
  virtual iter_type do_put(iter_type, ios_base&, char_type fill,
                           long double v) const;
  virtual iter_type do_put(iter_type, ios_base&, char_type fill,
                           void* v) const;
};
```

## numpunct                                              <locale>

A class template for the creation of settings in the numeric category, for punctuation in numeric values.

Contains a set of public methods for punctuation. For each function there is a corresponding virtual protected version, which calls it and which can be overridden in derived classes.

```
template <class charT>
 class numpunct : public locale::facet {
 public:
     typedef charT             char_type;
     typedef basic_string<charT> string_type;
     explicit numpunct(size_t refs = 0);
     char_type    decimal_point()   const;
     char_type    thousands_sep()   const;
     string       grouping()        const;
     string_type  truename()        const;
     string_type  falsename()       const;
     static locale::id id;
   protected:
    ~numpunct();  // virtual
     virtual char_type    do_decimal_point() const;
     virtual char_type    do_thousands_sep() const;
     virtual string       do_grouping()      const;
     virtual string_type  do_truename()      const;  // for bool
     virtual string_type  do_falsename()     const;  // for bool
   };
```

## numpunct_byname                                       <locale>

This offers the option to create a locale setting that is specified through its name. For this the name of the locale setting is passed to the constructor.

```
template <class charT>
    class numpunct_byname : public numpunct<charT> {
    public:
      explicit numpunct_byname(const char*, size_t refs = 0);
    protected:
     ~numpunct_byname();   // virtual
      virtual char_type    do_decimal_point() const;
      virtual char_type    do_thousands_sep() const;
      virtual string       do_grouping()      const;
      virtual string_type  do_truename()      const;  // for bool
      virtual string_type  do_falsename()     const;  // for bool
    };
```

## time_base <locale>

A basic class in the `time_get` class template, which defines a list type that specifies the most important sequences of date specifications.

```
class time_base {
    public:
        enum dateorder { no_order,  // no favourite order
                         dmy,       // day - month - year
                         mdy,       // month - day - year
                         ymd,       // year - month - day
                         ydm        // year - day - month   };
    };
```

## time_get <locale>

A class template for the creation of settings in the `time` category, for reading time specifications.

Contains a set of `public` methods for reading time specifications. For each function there is a corresponding virtual `protected` version, which calls it and which can be overridden in derived classes.

```
template <class charT, class InputIterator = istreambuf_iterator<charT>
>
 class time_get : public locale::facet, public time_base {
 public:
    typedef charT          char_type;
    typedef InputIterator  iter_type;
    explicit time_get(size_t refs = 0);
    dateorder date_order()  const { return do_date_order(); }
    iter_type get_time(iter_type s, iter_type end, ios_base& f,
                  ios_base::iostate& err, tm* t)  const;
    iter_type get_date(iter_type s, iter_type end, ios_base& f,
                  ios_base::iostate& err, tm* t)  const;
    iter_type get_weekday(iter_type s, iter_type end, ios_base& f,
                     ios_base::iostate& err, tm* t) const;
```

```
  iter_type get_monthname(iter_type s, iter_type end, ios_base& f,
                       ios_base::iostate& err, tm* t) const;
  iter_type get_year(iter_type s, iter_type end, ios_base& f,
                    ios_base::iostate& err, tm* t\fP) const;
  static locale::id id;
protected:
 ~time_get();  // virtual
 virtual dateorder do_date_order()  const;
 virtual iter_type do_get_time(iter_type s, iter_type end, ios_base&,
                            ios_base::iostate& err, tm* t) const;
 virtual iter_type do_get_date(iter_type s, iter_type end, ios_base&,
                            ios_base::iostate& err, tm* t) const;
 virtual iter_type do_get_weekday(iter_type s, iter_type end,
ios_base&,
                              ios_base::iostate& err, tm* t) const;
 virtual iter_type do_get_monthname(iter_type s, ios_base&,
                              ios_base::iostate& err, tm* t) const;
 virtual iter_type do_get_year(iter_type s, iter_type end, ios_base&,
                            ios_base::iostate& err, tm* t) const;
 };
```

## time_get_byname                                      <locale>

This offers the option to create a locale setting that is specified through its name.
For this the name of the locale setting is passed to the constructor.

```
template <class charT, class InputIterator = istreambuf_iterator<charT>
>
 class time_get_byname : public time_get<charT, InputIterator> {
 public:
   explicit time_get_byname(const char*, size_t refs = 0);
 protected:
 ~time_get_byname();  // virtual
  virtual dateorder do_date_order()  const;
  virtual iter_type do_get_time(iter_type s, iter_type end, ios_base&,
                             ios_base::iostate& err, tm* t) const;
  virtual iter_type do_get_date(iter_type s, iter_type end, ios_base&,
                             ios_base::iostate& err, tm* t) const;
 virtual iter_type do_get_weekday(iter_type s, iter_type end,
                          ios_base&,
                               ios_base::iostate& err, tm* t) const;
 virtual iter_type do_get_monthname(iter_type s,iter_type end,
                          ios_base&,
                               ios_base::iostate& err, tm* t) const;
 virtual iter_type do_get_year(iter_type s, iter_type end, ios_base&,
                          ios_base::iostate& err, tm* t) const;
 };
```

## time_put <locale>

A class template for the creation of settings in time category, for outputting time specifications.

Contains a set of public methods for outputting time specifications. For each function there is a corresponding virtual protected version, which calls it and which can be overridden in derived classes.

```
template <class charT, class OutputIterator =ostreambuf_iterator<charT>
>
 class time_put : public locale::facet {
 public:
   typedef charT          char_type;
   typedef OutputIterator  iter_type;
   explicit time_put(size_t refs = 0);
   iter_type put(iter_type s, ios_base& f, char_type fill, const tm* tmb,
               const charT* pattern, const charT* pat_end) const;
   iter_type put(iter_type s, ios_base& f, char_type fill,
               const tm* tmb, char format, char modifier = 0) const;
   static locale::id id;
 protected:
  ~time_put();  // virtual
   virtual iter_type do_put(iter_type s,ios_base&,char_type,const tm* t,
                          char format, char modifier) const;
 };
```

## time_put_byname <locale>

This offers the option to create a locale setting that is specified through its name. For this the name of the locale setting is passed to the constructor.

```
template <class charT, class OutputIterator =ostreambuf_iterator<charT>
>
 class time_put_byname : public time_put<charT, OutputIterator> {
 public:
   explicit time_put_byname(const char*, size_t refs = 0);
 protected:
  ~time_put_byname();  // virtual
   virtual iter_type do_put(iter_type s,ios_base&,char_type,const tm* t,
                          char format, char modifier) const;
 };
```

# The numeric classes

## complex

aus <complex>

### Description

The complex template implements a representation of the complex numbers as well as the operations which are defined on them.

### Application

The complex class itself only defines the constructors for the creation of complex objects and overloaded versions of the arithmetic operators.

```
complex<float> c(12.3, 0.5);
```

The class itself may only define the arithmetic operators; however, globally, further functions for working with complex object have been defined:

- overloaded forms of the mathematical C functions,
- overloaded forms of the compare operators,
- overloaded forms of the operators for input and output, and
- special functions for complex numbers (real(), imag(), abs(), arg(), norm(), conj() and polar()).

Integers or floating-point values can be represented by complex numbers, whose real part corresponds to the integer/floating-point number and whose imaginary part is equal to zero.

For the datatypes float, double and long double corresponding template instances have already been specialised.

### Example

```
template<class T>
    class complex {
    public:
      typedef T value_type;

      complex(const T& re = T(), const T& im = T());
      complex(const complex&);
      template<class X> complex(const complex<X>&);

      T real() const;
      T imag() const;
```

```
complex<T>& operator= (const T&);
complex<T>& operator+=(const T&);
complex<T>& operator-=(const T&);
complex<T>& operator*=(const T&);
complex<T>& operator/=(const T&);

complex& operator=(const complex&);
template<class X> complex<T>& operator= (const complex<X>&);
template<class X> complex<T>& operator+=(const complex<X>&);
template<class X> complex<T>& operator-=(const complex<X>&);
template<class X> complex<T>& operator*=(const complex<X>&);
template<class X> complex<T>& operator/=(const complex<X>&);
};
```

# valarray

from <valarray>

## Description

The valarray template is used to represent sorted sets. It is possible to handle the sets as arrays or matrixes (or derive corresponding classes) through the various indexing options available.

The valarray class is completed by the globally overloaded mathematical functions and auxiliary classes for the creation of subsets (slice, slice_array, gslice, gslice_array, mask_array and indirect_array).

## Application

To create a valarray object the template has to be specialised for the data type of the set elements and an object of the class has to be defined:

```
valarray<int> va(20);
```

The class valarray defines – with the exception of the index operator [ ] – a range of functions for the manipulation of sets, which concern all elements of the class.

The most important operators and the mathematical functions for valarray<T> are overloaded; in doing so the operations are carried out on all elements in the valarray object.

The index operator is overloaded to access either individual elements or subsets.

```
for(int i = 0; i < 20; i++) {
    va[i] = i;                 // Access to a single element
    }
```

With the help of the index operator [ ] subsets can be extracted from a `valarray` object. As operand an object which specifies the indices of the `valarray` elements that are to be part of the subset is passed to the index operator. This can be an instance of the classes `slice`, `gslice`, `valarray<bool>` or `valar-ray<size_t>`.

```
valarray<int> part(5);
valarray<size_t> size(2);
size[0] = 3; size[1] = 4;
valarray<size_t> stride(2);
stride[0] = 5; stride[1] = 1;

teil = va[gslice(2,size,stride)];
cout << "\nTeilarray\n";
for(int i = 0; i < size[0]*size[1]; i++)   {
    cout << part[i] << endl;
    }
```

If an operand is applied to a constant `valarray` object, it returns a copy of the subset as a new `valarray` object. If the operand is applied to a non-constant `valarray` object, it returns a reference to the subset as an object of the types `slice_array`, `gslice_array`, `mask_array` or `indirect_array`. Accessing these references is equivalent to accessing the original valarray.

## Example

```
template<class T> class valarray {
    public:
        typedef T value_type;

        // Constructors:
        valarray();
        explicit valarray(size_t);
        valarray(const T&, size_t);
        valarray(const T*, size_t);
        valarray(const valarray&);
        valarray(const slice_array<T>&);
        valarray(const gslice_array<T>&);
        valarray(const mask_array<T>&);
        valarray(const indirect_array<T>&);
      ~valarray();
  // Allocation:
        valarray<T>& operator=(const valarray<T>&);
        valarray<T>& operator=(const T&);
        valarray<T>& operator=(const slice_array<T>&);
        valarray<T>& operator=(const gslice_array<T>&);
        valarray<T>& operator=(const mask_array<T>&);
        valarray<T>& operator=(const indirect_array<T>&);
    // Access to elements:
        T                  operator[](size_t) const;
        T&                 operator[](size_t);
```

```
          // Operations on subsets:
            valarray<T>       operator[](slice) const;
            slice_array<T>    operator[](slice);
            valarray<T>       operator[](const gslice&) const;
            gslice_array<T>   operator[](const gslice&);
            valarray<T>       operator[](const valarray<bool>&) const;
            mask_array<T>     operator[](const valarray<bool>&);
            valarray<T>       operator[](const valarray<size_t>&) const;
            indirect_array<T> operator[](const valarray<size_t>&);
          // Others:
            valarray<T> operator+() const;
            valarray<T> operator-() const;
            valarray<T> operator~() const;
            valarray<T> operator!() const;
            valarray<T>& operator*= (const T&);
            valarray<T>& operator/= (const T&);
            valarray<T>& operator%= (const T&);
            valarray<T>& operator+= (const T&);
            valarray<T>& operator-= (const T&);
            valarray<T>& operator^= (const T&);
            valarray<T>& operator&= (const T&);
            valarray<T>& operator|= (const T&);
            valarray<T>& operator<<=(const T&);
            valarray<T>& operator>>=(const T&);
            valarray<T>& operator*= (const valarray<T>&);
            valarray<T>& operator/= (const valarray<T>&);
            valarray<T>& operator%= (const valarray<T>&);
            valarray<T>& operator+= (const valarray<T>&);
            valarray<T>& operator-= (const valarray<T>&);
            valarray<T>& operator^= (const valarray<T>&);
            valarray<T>& operator|= (const valarray<T>&);
            valarray<T>& operator&= (const valarray<T>&);
            valarray<T>& operator<<=(const valarray<T>&);
            valarray<T>& operator>>=(const valarray<T>&);

            size_t size() const;
            T    sum() const;

            valarray<T> shift (int) const;
            valarray<T> cshift(int) const;
            valarray<T> apply(T func(T)) const;
            valarray<T> apply(T func(const T&)) const;
            void resize(size_t sz, T c = T());
          };
```

## Reference

See example for header file valarray.

# Subsets of valarray objects

## Description
A range of auxiliary classes are used to select a specific set of elements from a `valarray` object. Instances of these classes correspond to a list of indices of subsets which are to be selected and passed as operands to the index operator.

## slice <valarray>

An instance of the class defines a number of indices, each of which corresponds to a subset of a `valarray` object. The indices are specified as

- first index,
- number of indices, and
- distance between the indices.

## Examples
```
slice(3,5,2)
```

selects the elements with the indexes

```
3, 5, 7, 9, 11
```

from an array.

To be able to access the subset, the index operator [ ] of the `valarray` class is used, for example:

```
valarr[slice(3,5,2)]
class slice {
    public:
      slice();
      slice(size_t, size_t, size_t);

      size_t start() const;
      size_t size() const;
      size_t stride() const;
    };
```

## Reference
See example for header file `valarray`.

## gslice <valarray>

An instance of the class defines a number of indices, each of which corresponds to a subset of a valarray object. The indices are specified as

- first index (start),
- number of indices per dimension (size), and
- distance between the indices for each dimension (stride).

The dimension is given by the number of elements for size and stride.

## Examples

An instance with

```
start = 2;
size = {3,4};
stride = {5,1};
```

selects, for example the following 3x4 matrix from a valarray object:

```
2,   3, 4, 5
7, 8, 9, 10
12, 13, 14, 15
```

The calculation of the indices k of the selected elements in the valarray object is represented as

```
for(i=0;i<size[0];i++)
    for(j=0;j<size[1];j++)
        k = start + i*stride[i] + j*stride[j];
```

To be able to access the subset, the index operator [ ] of the valarray class is used, for example:

```
valarray<size_t> size(2);
size[0] = 3;  size[1] = 4;
valarray<size_t> stride(2);
stride[0] = 5;  stride[1] = 1;

part = va[gslice(2,size,stride)];
```

## Example

```
class gslice {
 public:
  gslice();
  gslice(size_t s, const valarray<size_t>& l, const valarray<size_t>&
d);

  size_t          start() const;
  valarray<size_t> size() const;
  valarray<size_t> stride() const;
};
```

## Subsets of valarray

The classes `slice_array`, `gslice_array`, `mask_array` and `indirect_array` are used as the return type by the index operator of `valarray`, if applied to a non-constant `valarray` object. The returned objects are used as references to the subsets of a `valarray` objects, which have been selected by means of `slice`, `gslice`, `valarray<bool>`, or `valarray<size_t>`. Operations on these subsets (for example the use of the `fill()` method, thus, concern the original `valarray` object. However, the `valarray` class also defines constructors to create own `valarrays` from these reference objects.

The classes should not be initialised explicitly, which is why only `private` constructors have been defined. Besides, the various forms of assignment operators and the `fill()` function have been defined to change the elements of the `valarray` object, to which the `xxx_array` object refers.

## slice_array                                                    <valarray>

The class is used to select a subset – defined by a `slice` instance – of a `valarray` object (index operator [ ] of the `valarray` class), operate on it or transform it into an independent `valarray` object (the latter with the help of the corresponding constructor of the `valarray` class).

# Examples
```
valarr[slice(3,8,2)].fill(3);
template <class T> class slice_array {
    public:
      typedef T value_type;

      void operator=  (const valarray<T>&) const;
      void operator*= (const valarray<T>&) const;
      void operator/= (const valarray<T>&) const;
      void operator%= (const valarray<T>&) const;
      void operator+= (const valarray<T>&) const;
      void operator-= (const valarray<T>&) const;
      void operator^= (const valarray<T>&) const;
      void operator&= (const valarray<T>&) const;
      void operator|= (const valarray<T>&) const;
      void operator<<=(const valarray<T>&) const;
      void operator>>=(const valarray<T>&) const;
      void fill(const T&);
     ~slice_array();
    private:
      slice_array();
      slice_array(const slice_array&);
      slice_array& operator=(const slice_array&);
    };
```

## gslice_array <valarray>

The class is used to select a subset – defined by a `gslice` instance – of a `valarray` object (index operator [ ] of the `valarray` class), operate on it or transform it into an independent `valarray` object (the latter with the help of the corresponding constructor of the `valarray` class)

```
template <class T> class gslice_array {
    public:
      typedef T value_type;

      void operator=  (const valarray<T>&) const;
      void operator*= (const valarray<T>&) const;
      void operator/= (const valarray<T>&) const;
      void operator%= (const valarray<T>&) const;
      void operator+= (const valarray<T>&) const;
      void operator-= (const valarray<T>&) const;
      void operator^= (const valarray<T>&) const;
      void operator&= (const valarray<T>&) const;
      void operator|= (const valarray<T>&) const;
      void operator<<=(const valarray<T>&) const;
      void operator>>=(const valarray<T>&) const;
      void fill(const T&);
     ~gslice_array();
    private:
      gslice_array();
      gslice_array(const gslice_array&);
      gslice_array& operator=(const gslice_array&);
    };
```

## mask_array <valarray>

The class is used to select a subset – defined by a `valarray<bool>` instance – of a `valarray` object (index operator [ ] of the `valarray` class), operate on it or transform it into an independent valarray object (the latter with the help of the corresponding constructor of the `valarray` class).

```
template <class T> class mask_array {
    public:
      typedef T value_type;

      void operator=  (const valarray<T>&) const;
      void operator*= (const valarray<T>&) const;
      void operator/= (const valarray<T>&) const;
      void operator%= (const valarray<T>&) const;
      void operator+= (const valarray<T>&) const;
      void operator-= (const valarray<T>&) const;
      void operator^= (const valarray<T>&) const;
      void operator&= (const valarray<T>&) const;
      void operator|= (const valarray<T>&) const;
```

```
   void operator<<=(const valarray<T>&) const;
   void operator>>=(const valarray<T>&) const;
   void fill(const T&);
  ~mask_array();
private:
  mask_array();
  mask_array(const mask_array&);
  mask_array& operator=(const mask_array&);
};
```

## indirect_array                                    <valarray>

The class is used to select a subset – defined by a `valarray<size_t>` instance – of a `valarray` object (index operator [ ] of the `valarray` class), operate on it or transform it into an independent `valarray` object (the latter with the help of the corresponding constructor of the `valarray` class).

```
template <class T> class indirect_array {
   public:
     typedef T value_type;

     void operator=  (const valarray<T>&) const;
     void operator*= (const valarray<T>&) const;
     void operator/= (const valarray<T>&) const;
     void operator%= (const valarray<T>&) const;
     void operator+= (const valarray<T>&) const;
     void operator-= (const valarray<T>&) const;
     void operator^= (const valarray<T>&) const;
     void operator&= (const valarray<T>&) const;
     void operator|= (const valarray<T>&) const;
     void operator<<=(const valarray<T>&) const;
     void operator>>=(const valarray<T>&) const;
     void fill(const T&);
    ~indirect_array();
   private:
     indirect_array();
     indirect_array(const indirect_array&);
     indirect_array& operator=(const indirect_array&);
   };
```

# numeric_limits

from <limits>

## Description

The class `numeric_limits` encapsulates information about the implementation-specific representation of numeric data types. Various elements of the class can only be defined usefully for particular data types. Data elements which do not contribute to the characterisation of a data type are set to zero or false. Apart from the template, specialisations for elementary data types have also been defined in the runtime library.

## Example

```
template<class T> class numeric_limits {
    public:
        static const bool is_specialized = false;
        static T min() throw();
        static T max() throw();
        static const int  digits = 0;
        static const int  digits10 = 0;
        static const bool is_signed = false;
        static const bool is_integer = false;
        static const bool is_exact = false;
        static const int  radix = 0;
        static T epsilon() throw();
        static T round_error() throw();

        static const int  min_exponent = 0;
        static const int  min_exponent10 = 0;
        static const int  max_exponent = 0;
        static const int  max_exponent10 = 0;

        static const bool has_infinity = false;
        static const bool has_quiet_NaN = false;
        static const bool has_signaling_NaN = false;
        static const bool has_denorm = false;
        static const bool has_denorm_loss = false;
        static T infinity() throw();
        static T quiet_NaN() throw();
        static T signaling_NaN() throw();
        static T denorm_min() throw();

        static const bool is_iec559 = false;
        static const bool is_bounded = false;
        static const bool is_modulo = false;

        static const bool traps = false;
        static const bool tinyness_before = false;
        static const float_round_style round_style = round_toward_zero;
    };
```

## References

See Practice section, category variables and data types, value range and precision of floating-point numbers.

# Classes and functions for exception handling

## exception

from <exception>

### Description

A basic class for the exception objects which are triggered from the language and the components of the C++ standard libraries (or are predefined for the convenience of the programmer). Directly derived from this are the exceptions (bad_...) used by the language, as well as the classes logic_error and runtime_error, from which in turn the remaining exception classes are derived.

### Application

Apart from constructor and destructor, it contains also a copy constructor and a separate version of the assignment operator, as well as a method for issuing a message string.

Since all elements of the class have been declared with throw(), the class cannot trigger exceptions itself.

Exception objects are not usually formed from the exception class itself. It is only used as a basic class.

### Example

```
class exception {
    public:
        exception() throw();
        exception(const exception&) throw();
        exception& operator=(const exception&) throw();
        virtual ~exception() throw();
        virtual const char* what() const throw();
```

## Derived exception classes

aus <exception>, <stdexcept> und <typeinfo>

A class type for exceptions which are triggered by the methods of the runtime library in the event of an error in memory reservation.

```
class bad_alloc : public exception {
    public:
      bad_alloc() throw();
      bad_alloc(const bad_alloc&) throw();
      bad_alloc& operator=(const bad_alloc&) throw();
      virtual ~bad_alloc() throw();
      virtual const char* what() const throw();
};
```

Class type for exceptions which are triggered by dynamic_cast in a failed type conversion.

```
class bad_cast : public exception {
    public:
      bad_cast() throw();
      bad_cast(const bad_cast&) throw();
      bad_cast& operator=(const bad_cast&) throw();
      virtual ~bad_cast() throw();
      virtual const char* what() const throw();
};
```

Class type for exceptions which are triggered by errors in exception handling (triggering of an exception in a class, for which the exception has not been declared, occurrence of an exception that has not been handled, and so on).

```
class bad_exception : public exception {
    public:
      bad_exception() throw();
      bad_exception(const bad_exception&) throw();
      bad_exception& operator=(const bad_exception&) throw();
      virtual ~bad_exception() throw();
      virtual const char* what() const throw();
};
```

Class type for exceptions which are triggered if a zero pointer occurs in a typeid term.

```
class bad_typeid : public exception {
    public:
      bad_typeid() throw();
      bad_typeid(const bad_typeid&) throw();
      bad_typeid& operator=(const bad_typeid&) throw();
      virtual ~bad_typeid() throw();
      virtual const char* what() const throw();
};
```

Class type for exceptions which are triggered if inadmissable values occur.

```
class domain_error : public logic_error {
    public:
      domain_error(const string& what_arg);
};
```

Class type for exceptions which are triggered if inadmissable arguments are passed.

```
class invalid_argument : public logic_error {
    public:
        invalid_argument(const string& what_arg);
    };
```

Class type for exceptions which are triggered if the admissable size of data structures is exceeded.

```
class length_error : public logic_error {
    public:
        length_error(const string& what_arg);
    };
```

Class type for exceptions which are triggered if logic errors – that is, errors which could be detected before program execution – occur.

```
class logic_error : public exception {
    public:
        logic_error(const string& what_arg);
    };
```

Class type for exceptions which are triggered if a passed argument does not lie within the specified value range.

```
class out_of_range : public logic_error {
    public:
        out_of_range(const string& what_arg);
    };
```

Class type for exceptions which are triggered if arithmetic variables overflow.

```
class overflow_error : public runtime_error {
    public:
        overflow_error(const string& what_arg);
    };
```

Class type for exceptions which are triggered if a validity range is exceeded.

```
class range_error : public runtime_error {
    public:
        range_error(const string& what_arg);
    };
```

Class type for exceptions which are triggered if runtime errors – that is, errors which could only be detected during program execution – occur.

```
class runtime_error : public exception {
    public:
        runtime_error(const string& what_arg);
    };
```

Class type for exceptions which are triggered if arithmetic values are underrun.

```
class underflow_error : public runtime_error {
    public:
        underflow_error(const string& what_arg);
    };
```

# Functions for exception handling

### set_new_handler()                                       \<new\>

This establishes the function which is called by the new operator for error handling. For this a pointer to the error handling function, which has to have the type

```
new_handler (typedef void (*new_handler)() )
```

is passed.

```
new_handler set_new_handler(new_handler new_p) throw();
```

- **Return value:** Pointer to the old error handling function.

### set_terminate()                                   \<exception\>

This establishes the function which is called in the event of premature program termination, for example because of exceptions that have not been handled. For this a pointer to the program termination function, which has to have the type

```
terminate_handler (typedef void (*terminate_handler)() )
```

is passed.

```
terminate_handler set_terminate(terminate_handler t_func) throw();
```

- **Return value:** Pointer to the old program termination function.

### set_unexpected()                                 \<exception\>

This establishes the function which is called if an exception is triggered within a function for which the function has not been declared. The established function either has to:

- trigger an exception for which the function has been declared,
- trigger a bad_exception exception,
- call the terminate() function, or
- call abort() or exit().

For this a pointer to the error handling function, which has to have the type

```
unexpected_handler(typedef void (*unexpected_handler)() )
```

is passed.

```
unexpected_handler set_unexpected(unexpected_handler unexp_func);
```

- **Return value:** Pointer to the old function.

## terminate() **&lt;exception&gt;**

The terminate() function is called to prematurely terminate the program if an error occurs, for example if a handling function for a triggered exception cannot be found (therefore usually by unexpected() ). The terminate() function in turn calls the function for program termination that has been established by set_terminate().

```
void terminate();
```

## uncaught_exception() **&lt;exception&gt;**

This indicates that an exception has been triggered for which a handler has not yet been found. Can be used, for example in destructors.

```
bool uncaught_exception();
```
• **Return value:** True, if there is an exception which has not yet been handled.

## unexpected() **&lt;exception&gt;**

The unexpected() function is called if an exception is triggered in a function for which the function has not been declared. The function unexpected() in turn calls the function for handling which has been established by set_unexpected().

```
void unexpected();
```

# Runtime type identification

# type_info

From &lt;typeinfo&gt;

### Description

Every instance of a derived class in C++ can also be understood as an instance of its basic classes. On the one hand this broadens the possibilities of dynamic type conversion, however, on the other hand it also impedes the overview of the current data types of pointers and references to class instances. The type_info class provides an option to query information about the data type of an object at program runtime.

## Application

The `type_info` class only defines private constructors. Therefore, it cannot be initialised explicitly. Instead the class is used in connection with the `typeid` operator, which creates references of the class.

## Example

```
class type_info {
    public:
      virtual ~type_info();
      bool operator==(const type_info& rhs) const;
      bool operator!=(const type_info& rhs) const;
      bool before(const type_info& rhs) const;
      const char* name() const;
    private:
      type_info(const type_info& rhs);
      type_info& operator=(const type_info& rhs);
    };
  }
```

## References

See Practice section, category inheritance and polymorphy, type identification at runtime.

# Utilities

## The pair structure

From `<utility>`

The class template represents a pair of objects with different data types. Apart from the constructor, it is also possible to call the global function template `make_pair()`.

```
template <class T1, class T2>
  struct pair {
    typedef T1 first_type;
    typedef T2 second_type;

    T1 first;
    T2 second;
    pair();
```

```
    pair(const T1& x, const T2& y);
    template<class U, class V> pair(const pair<U, V> &p);
  };
template <class T1, class T2>
    pair<T1, T2> make_pair(const T1& x, const T2& y);
```

# Function objects

From <functional>

## Description

The implementation of generic functions is often based on the passing of functions as parameters (compare qsort() ). The STL extends this concept by encapsulating functions in classes. All these classes have in common is that the () operator has been overloaded for them, so that the instances of the class (the function objects) can be called like functions.

Function objects are more powerful than functions, since they can fall back on the internal data and methods of their class. Moreover, all function objects of the STL have been implemented as templates to be able to work with any data type.

The STL distinguishes:

- arithmetic function objects which carry out arithmetic operations (divides, and so on),

- predicates, which carry out a comparison (equal_to, etc.), have bool as result type, and are frequently used in the algorithms of the STL to define a condition which the elements on which the algorithm function operates have to meet,

- negators, which negate a predicate,

- binders, which permit the use of binary function objects (two arguments) like a function object with one argument, and

- adapters, which enable the passing of methods or pointers to functions as arguments to algorithms.

## References

See Practice section, category the STL, creating function objects; function adapters.

## Basic structures

The function objects are derived from the structures unary_function and binary_function, depending on whether their () operator expects one or two arguments.

```
template <class Arg, class Result>
struct unary_function {
```

```
        typedef Arg      argument_type;
        typedef Result result_type;
        };
template <class Arg1, class Arg2, class Result>
struct binary_function {
        typedef Arg1    first_argument_type;
        typedef Arg2    second_argument_type;
        typedef Result result_type;
        };
```

## Arithmetic function objects

All function objects define the () operator so that they can be called like functions.

```
template <class T> struct divides : public binary_function<T,T,T>
    T operator()(const T& x, const T& y) const;
template <class T> struct minus : public binary_function<T,T,T>
    T operator()(const T& x, const T& y) const;
template <class T> struct modulus : public binary_function<T,T,T>
    T operator()(const T& x, const T& y) const;
template <class T> struct multiplies : public binary_function<T,T,T>
    T operator()(const T& x, const T& y) const;
template <class T> struct negate : public unary_function<T,T>
    T operator()(const T& x) const;
template <class T> struct plus : public binary_function<T,T,T>
    T operator()(const T& x, const T& y) const;
```

## Predicates

The predefined predicates also only define the () operator.

```
template <class T> struct equal_to : public binary_function<T,T,bool>
    bool operator()(const T& x, const T& y) const;
template <class T> struct greater : public binary_function<T,T,bool>
    bool operator()(const T& x, const T& y) const;
template <class T> struct greater_equal:public binary_function<T,T,bool>
    bool operator()(const T& x, const T& y) const;
template <class T> struct less : public binary_function<T,T,bool>
    bool operator()(const T& x, const T& y) const;
template <class T> struct less_equal : public binary_function<T,T,bool>
    bool operator()(const T& x, const T& y) const;
template <class T> struct logical_and : public binary_function<T,T,bool>
    bool operator()(const T& x, const T& y) const;
template <class T> struct logical_or: public binary_function<T,T,bool>
    bool operator()(const T& x, const T& y) const;
template <class T> struct logical_not: public unary_function<T,bool>
    bool operator()(const T& x) const;
template <class T> struct not_equal_to: public
binary_function<T,T,bool>
    bool operator()(const T& x, const T& y) const;
```

## Negators

```
template <class Predicate>
    class unary_negate
       : public unary_function<Predicate::argument_type,bool> {
  public:
    explicit unary_negate(const Predicate& pred);
    bool operator()(const argument_type& x) const;
  };
```

The function class for the negation of a statement object. The template parameter `Predicate` refers to a unary function object, whose statement is to be negated. Usually the global function template `not1()` is used to form a `unary_negate` object.

```
template <class Predicate>
    class binary_negate
       : public binary_function<Predicate::first_argument_type,
                                 Predicate::second_argument_type, bool> {
    public:
      explicit binary_negate(const Predicate& pred);
      bool operator()(const first_argument_type&  x,
                      const second_argument_type& y) const;
    };
```

Function class for the negation of a statement object. The template parameter `Predicate` refers to a unary function object, whose statement is to be negated. Usually the global function template `not2()` is used to form a `binary_negate` object.

```
template <class Predicate>
    unary_negate<Predicate> not1(const Predicate& pred);
template <class Predicate>
    binary_negate<Predicate> not2(const Predicate& pred);
```

The `not1()` function adopts a unary statement, the `not2()` function a binary statement. Both return the negated statements as instances of the template classes `unary_negate` or `binary_negate`.

## Binders

```
template <class Operation>
 class binder1st
       : public unary_function<Operation::second_argument_type,
                               Operation::result_type> {
```

```
protected:
   Operation                                op;
   Operation::first_argument_type value;
public:
   binder1st(const Operation& x,const Operation::first_argument_type&
y);
   result_type operator()(const argument_type& x) const;
};
```

The above converts a binary function object into a unary function object by assigning a fixed value to the first argument. Usually the global function template bind1st is used to form a binder1st object.

```
template <class Operation>
 class binder2nd
       : public unary_function<Operation::first_argument_type,
                                Operation::result_type> {
protected:
   Operation                                op;
   Operation::second_argument_type value;
public:
  binder2nd(const Operation& x,const Operation::second_argument_type& y);
  result_type operator()(const argument_type& x) const;
 };
```

The above converts a binary function object into a unary function object by assigning a fixed value to the first argument. Usually the global function template bind2nd()is used to form a binder2nd object.

```
template <class Operation, class T>
    binder1st<Operation> bind1st(const Operation& op, const T& x);
template <class Operation, class T>
    binder2nd<Operation> bind2nd(const Operation& op, const T& x);
```

Both functions are used to convert a function object with two arguments into a function argument with one object. To do this an argument is 'bound' to a constant value. bind1st() binds the first argument, bind2nd() the second.

## Adapters

To be able to pass function pointers to binders, the C++ library provides the adapter classes pointer_to_unary_function and pointer_to_binary_function:

```
template <class Arg, class Result>
class pointer_to_unary_function
  : public unary_function<Arg,Result>
  {
  public:
      explicit pointer_to_unary_function(Result (*f)(Arg));
      Result operator()(Arg x) const;
  };
```

```
template <class Arg1, class Arg2, class Result>
class pointer_to_binary_function
  : public binary_function<Arg1,Arg2,Result>
  {
  public:
  explicit pointer_to_binary_function(Result (*f)(Arg1,Arg2));
  Result operator()(Arg1 x, Arg2 y) const;
  };
```

as well as the overloaded global function `ptr_fun()`:

```
template <class Arg, class Result>
pointer_to_unary_function<Arg, Result>
       ptr_fun(Result (*f)(Arg));
template <class Arg1, class Arg2, class Result>
pointer_to_binary_function<Arg1,Arg2,Result>
       ptr_fun(Result (*f)(Arg1, Arg2));
```

To be able also to pass methods as arguments to function object parameters of algorithms (methods must be called through instances), the classes `mem_fun_t`, `mem_fun1_t`, `mem_fun_ref_t` and `mem_fun1_ref_t` have been defined for methods with and without arguments:

```
template <class S, class T> class mem_fun_t
          : public unary_function<T*, S>  {
    public:
      explicit mem_fun_t(S (T::*p)());
      S operator()(T* p);
    };
template <class S, class T, class A> class mem_fun1_t
          : public binary_function<T*, A, S> {
    public:
      explicit mem_fun1_t(S (T::*p)(A));
      S operator()(T* p, A x);
    };
template <class S, class T> class mem_fun_ref_t
          : public unary_function<T, S> {
    public:
      explicit mem_fun_ref_t(S (T::*p)());
      S operator()(T& p);
    };
template <class S, class T, class A> class mem_fun1_ref_t
          : public binary_function<T, A, S> {
    public:
      explicit mem_fun1_ref_t(S (T::*p)(A));
      S operator()(T& p, A x);
  };
```

as well as the global functions `mem_fun()`, `mem_fun1()`, `mem_fun_ref()` and `mem_fun1_ref()`, to which a method pointer (or method reference) can be passed as an argument and whose return value can be passed as an argument to a function object parameter.

```
template<class S, class T> mem_fun_t<S,T>
      mem_fun(S (T::*f)());
template<class S, class T, class A> mem_fun1_t<S,T,A>
      mem_fun1(S (T::*f)(A));
template<class S, class T> mem_fun_ref_t<S,T>
      mem_fun_ref(S (T::*f)());
template<class S, class T, class A> mem_fun1_ref_t<S,T,A>
      mem_fun1_ref(S (T::*f)(A));
```

# Memory allocation

## allocator

from <memory>

### Description

The allocator class defines methods for requesting and allocating physical memory. An instance of the class takes on the task of a memory manager. The implementation provided by ANSI is based on the customary use of the operators new and delete.

The STL containers use allocators to request memory; that is, the methods of the containers internally fall back on the methods of the allocator objects to request and manage memory. By default the containers use an instance of the parameter class allocator, which is intended as a default argument for the corresponding template.

Through the implementation and passing of allocators with the same interface a programmer can adapt the memory management of a container to various memory models (for example, DOS, 16-bit Windows, etc.).

### Reference

```
template <class T> class allocator {
    public:
      typedef size_t     size_type;
      typedef ptrdiff_t  difference_type;
      typedef T*         pointer;
      typedef const T*   const_pointer;
      typedef T&         reference;
      typedef const T&   const_reference;
      typedef T          value_type;
      template <class U> struct rebind { typedef allocator<U> other; };
      allocator() throw();
      allocator(const allocator&) throw();
```

```
    template <class U> allocator(const allocator<U>&) throw();
   ~allocator() throw();
    pointer address(reference x) const;
    const_pointer address(const_reference x) const;
    pointer allocate(
      size_type, typename allocator<void>::const_pointer hint = 0);
    void deallocate(pointer p, size_type n);
    size_type max_size() const throw();
    void construct(pointer p, const T& val);
    void destroy(pointer p);
  };
```

# auto_ptr

from <memory>

This is used to automatically free the memory area of an object that has been established with new after the pointer to the memory area has been deleted (for example by leaving its validity range).

```
template<class X> class auto_ptr {
    public:
      typedef X element_type;
      explicit auto_ptr(X* p =0) throw();
      auto_ptr(const auto_ptr&) throw();
      template<class Y> auto_ptr(const auto_ptr<Y>&) throw();
      auto_ptr& operator=(const auto_ptr&) throw();
      template<class Y> auto_ptr& operator=(const auto_ptr<Y>&) throw();
    ~auto_ptr();
      X& operator*() const throw();
      X* operator->() const throw();
      X* get() const throw();
      X* release() const throw();
  };
```

## References

See Practice section, category pointers and dynamic memory management.

# Functions and iterators

## raw_storage_iterator                                          <memory>

This is used to deposit objects in non-initialised memory areas.

```
template <class OutputIterator, class T>
  class raw_storage_iterator
       : public iterator<output_iterator_tag,void,void> {
```

```
public:
    explicit raw_storage_iterator(OutputIterator x);
    raw_storage_iterator<OutputIterator,T>& operator*();
    raw_storage_iterator<OutputIterator,T>& operator=(const T& element);
    raw_storage_iterator<OutputIterator,T>& operator++();
    raw_storage_iterator<OutputIterator,T>  operator++(int);
};
```

## get_temporary_buffer()                                          <memory>

This returns the buffer address and capacity of the buffer in units of T as instances of the pair class.

```
template <class T> pair<T*, ptrdiff_t> get_temporary_buffer(ptrdiff_t n);
```

## return_temporary_buffer()                                       <memory>

This returns the buffer to which ptr points and which has been allocated with get_temporary_buffer().

```
template <class T> void return_temporary_buffer(T* ptr);
```

## uninitialized_...                                               <memory>

The function uninitialized_copy() calls new in a loop to initialise the range from result to result + last with the values from (first, last).

The function uninitialized_fill() calls new in a loop to initialise the range from first to last with wert.

The function uninitialized_fill_n() calls new in a loop to initialise the range from first to first+n with wert.

```
template <class InIter, class FWIter>
    FWIter uninitialized_copy(InIter first, InIter last, FWIter result);
template <class FWIter, class T>
    void uninitialized_fill(FWIter first,FWIter last, const T& wert);
template <class FWIter, class Size, class T>
    void uninitialized_fill_n(FWIter first, Size n, const T& wert);
```

# Practice

# Category: variables and data types

# Value ranges of integer data types

int, short, long, char

## Application

The value range of a data type depends on how many bytes the compiler reserves for variables of this data type and how the compiler codes the values of the data type in binary representation. Here the ANSI standard only defines the general conditions, so that the value ranges of the elementary data types can vary depending on the compiler used and the platform intended (Win32, UNIX, etc.).

Fortunately, the ANSI standard envisages that compiler developers store all the relevant data for the implementation of the data types in the ANSI runtime libraries.

Programmers can use this to get information about the specific implementation of the data types for their compiler or even in critical cases – such as in the development of platform-independent programs – to query and evaluate the implementation characteristics within the program.

## Implementation in C

In C all the relevant data are grouped together in the limits.h header file:

| Constant | Description | According to ANSI, at least |
| --- | --- | --- |
| CHAR_BIT | Number of bits reserved for the smallest object that is not a bit field. | 8 bits |
| SCHAR_MIN | Smallest value for an object of the signed char type | −127 |
| SCHAR_MAX | Greatest value for an object of the signed char type | +127 |
| UCHAR_MAX | Greatest value for an object of the unsigned char type | 255 |
| CHAR_MIN | Smallest value for an object of the char type | 0 or SCHAR_MIN |
| CHAR_MAX | Greatest value for an object of the char type | UCHAR_MAX or SCHAR_MAX |
| MB_LEN_MAX | Number of bytes in a multi-byte character | 1 |
| SHRT_MIN | Smallest value for an object of the short int type | −32767 |
| SHRT_MAX | Greatest value for an object of the short int type | +32767 |
| USHRT_MAX | Greatest value for an object of the unsigned short int type | +65535 |

| Constant | Description | According to ANSI, at least |
|----------|-------------|----------------------------|
| INT_MIN | Smallest value for an object of the int type | –32767 |
| INT_MAX | Greatest value for an object of th int type | +32767 |
| UINT_MAX | Greatest value for an object of th unsigned int type | +65535 |
| LONG_MIN | Smallest value for an object of the long int type | –2147483647 |
| LONG_MAX | Greatest value for an object of the long int type | +2147483647 |
| ULONG_MAX | Greatest value for an object of the unsigned long int type | 4294967295 |

## Example

```
#include <stdio.h>
#include <limits.h>

int main()
  {
  char c;
  int i_c;

  printf("\nLimits of different integer types:\n\n");
  printf("Type\t BYTES\t\t MIN\t\t MAX\n");
  printf("Char: \t %5d\t%12d\t%12d\n",
                          sizeof(char),CHAR_MIN, CHAR_MAX);
  printf("Short:\t %5d\t%12d\t%12d\n",
                          sizeof(short),SHRT_MIN, SHRT_MAX);
  printf("Int:  \t %5d\t%12d\t%12d\n",
                          sizeof(int),INT_MIN, INT_MAX);
  printf("Long: \t %5d\t%12d\t%12d\n",
                          sizeof(long),LONG_MIN, LONG_MAX);
  printf("\n\n");

  printf("Other limits of char characters:\n\n");
  printf("Number of bits:  \t %11d\n",CHAR_BIT);
  printf("Bytes in MB:  \t %11d\n",MB_LEN_MAX);
  c = 'A' - 100;
  i_c = c;
  printf("Char is signed?\t %s\n", (i_c < 0 ? "true" : "false"));
  return 0;
  }
```

Output:

```
Limits of different integer types:

Type       BYTES        MIN          MAX
Char:        1         -128          127
Short:       2        -32768        32767
```

```
Int:      4  -2147483648   2147483647
Long:     4  -2147483648   2147483647

Other limits of char characters:

Number of bits:        8
Bytes in MB:           1
Char is signed?       true
```

## Implementation in C++

In C++ the characteristics of the elementary data types are recorded in specialisations of the numeric_limits template. To query them you need to integrate the limits header file, use the std namespace, and access the methods of the template specialisations.

For example, to query the greatest value for the int data type, you need to call the max() method of the numeric_limits<int> specialisation:

```
numeric_limits<int>::max()
```

## Example

```cpp
#include <iostream>
#include <iomanip>
#include <limits>
using namespace std;

int main()
  {
  char c;
  int i_c;

  cout << "Limits of different elementary data types:" << endl << endl;
  cout << "Typ       BYTES          MIN             MAX\n" << endl;
  cout << "Char:  " << setw(8) << sizeof(char)
          << setw(14) << (int) numeric_limits<char>::min()
          << setw(14) << (int) numeric_limits<char>::max() << endl;

  cout << "Short: " << setw(8) << sizeof(short)
          << setw(14) << numeric_limits<short>::min()
          << setw(14) << numeric_limits<short>::max() << endl;

  cout << "Int:   " << setw(8) << sizeof(int)
          << setw(14) << numeric_limits<int>::min()
          << setw(14) << numeric_limits<int>::max() << endl;
  cout << "Long:  " << setw(8) << sizeof(long)
          << setw(14) << numeric_limits<long>::min()
          << setw(14) << numeric_limits<long>::max() << endl;
  cout << endl;
```

```
if(numeric_limits<char>::is_signed)
  cout << "Data type char is signed" << endl;
  else
  cout << "Data type char is unsigned" << endl;

return 0;
}
```

## References

See value range and precision of floating point numbers.

See Reference section, category variables and data types.

# Value range and precision of floating point numbers

`float`, `double`, `long double`

## Application

When programming with floating point numbers, the size of the value range is important, but so is with what degree of precision numbers with decimals can be reproduced.

## Implementation

The relevant data that tells the programmer the value ranges of the floating point types of his compiler and the degree of precision with which real numbers can be represented, for C, are grouped together in the constants of the `float.h` header file and for C++ are in the specialisations of the `numeric_limits` template from the `limits` header file.

| Constant | Meaning |
|---|---|
| FLT_RADIX numeric_limits<>::radix | Basis of the exponent (b) Also applies to double and long double numbers. Usually calculations are carried out with binary numbers, so that b = 2 |
| FLT_MANT_DIG numeric_limits<>::digits | Number of digits in the mantissa, if represented to the base FLT_RADIX (p) |
| FLT_DIG numeric_limits<>::digits10 | Number of the significant digits in the mantissa, if represented to the base 10. This value is important for estimating the precision of floating point numbers. |

| Constant | Meaning |
|---|---|
| FLT_MIN_EXP<br>numeric_limits<>::min_exponent | Smallest negative number for the exponent to the base FLT_RADIX (emin) |
| FLT_MIN_10_EXP<br>numeric_limits<>::min_exponent 10 | Smallest negative number for the exponent to the base 10. |
| FLT_MAX_EXP<br>numeric_limits<>::max_exponent | Greatest positive number for the exponent to the base FLT_RADIX (emax) |
| FLT_MAX_10_EXP<br>numeric_limits<>::max_exponent 10 | Greatest positive number for the exponent to the base 10. |
| FLT_MAX<br>numeric_limits<>::max() | Greatest positive number.<br>The smallest negative number is: -FLT_MAX |
| FLT_MIN<br>numeric_limits<>::min() | Smallest negative number<br>(How close to 0 you can get) |
| FLT_EPSILON<br>numeric_limits<>::epsilon() | Difference between 1 and the next greater number that can be represented. |
| FLT_ROUNDS<br>numeric_limits<>::round_style | Mode, according to which numbers are rounded:<br>-1 undefined<br>0 to zero<br>1 to the next value<br>2 to +infinite<br>3 to −infinite<br>Applies also to double and long double numbers. |

## References

See value ranges of integer data types.

See Reference section, category variables and data types.

# The std namespace of the runtime library

```
using namespace std
```

## Application

Namespaces are one option for dividing the global validity range. The aim of this concept, which was only integrated into the language with the ANSI C++ standard, is to enable software developers to avoid name conflicts caused by identical identifiers in the global validity range.

Developers of software libraries can also help to avoid name conflicts by defining the elements of their library in a separate namespace – as has been done, for example, for the elements of the C++ runtime library.

In accordance with the ANSI C++ standard all the elements of the C++ runtime library should be declared in the std namespace. The same applies to the elements of the C runtime library, if the programmer uses the C++ header with the C runtime library (thus, for example #include <cstdio> instead of #include <stdio.h>).

## Implementation

The usual and simplest way to work with the elements of the C++ runtime library in a program is to introduce the std namespace into the global validity range by the using directive.

Subsequently all the elements declared in the namespace are also available in the global validity range of the program (and, thus, of course also in all subordinate validity ranges – unless they are hidden) and can be used through their identifier without prefixing the namespace.

## Example

Without introducing the namespace, you need to address each element of the default library with its complete qualifier:

```
#include <iostream>
#include <cmath>

int main()
  {
  std::cout << std::cos(0) << std::endl;
  return 0;
  }
```

After the introduction of the namespace, you only need to specify the identifiers under which the elements have been declared in the namespace.

```
#include <iostream>
#include <cmath>
using namespace std;

int main()
  {
  cout << cos(0) << endl;

  return 0;
  }
```

## Warning

Whether you really have to introduce the `std` namespace depends on whether the elements of the runtime library have been declared in the `std` namespace in the header files of your compiler.

At the moment, only newer compilers follow the ANSI standard in this. If you use older versions, you can presumably do without the `using` statement; perhaps your compiler is not even familiar with the namespace concept.

If you use the old C header files with the .h extension or pre-ANSI C++ headers (for example `iostream.h`), you will not require a `using` statement.

## References

See basics section, using the default libraries.

See Reference section, category variables and data types, validity ranges; namespaces.

# Using elements from namespaces

`using`

## Application

Elements which have been declared in namespaces cannot be simply called by the name under which they have been declared in the namespace, from outside the namespace.

Therefore, if you use libraries whose elements have all been declared in a particular namespace or if you are working with colleagues on a joint software project in which each programmer uses their own namespace, and you want to access elements from a colleague's code, you need to know how to access elements that have been declared in namespaces.

## Implementation

To access elements from namespaces:

- the complete identifier (including the name of the namespace) must be used,
- the identifier may be introduced through a `using` statement. This is equivalent to a new declaration. After the new declaration the element of the namespace

can be accessed without prefixing the namespace. However, if there is already an identical identifier in the surrounding validity range, the new declaration fails, or

- the namespace and all declarations contained in it are introduced through a using statement. Afterwards, elements of the namespace can be accessed without prefixing the namespace. However, this is not a new declaration. If identical identifiers are used in the surrounding validity range and in the namespace, the identifiers of the surrounding validity range hide the elements from the namespace. By means of complete qualification (prefixing the namespace to the identifier), however, the hidden elements can also be accessed.

## Example

You are using a library for which the following header file is available:

```
/* Header file bib.h */
namespace SpecLib {
    int var1, var2;
    int func(int param);
    }
```

The following options are available to access the elements in the header file:

```
#include <iostream>
#include "bib.h"
using namespace std;

int main() {
    //cout << var1 << endl;     // error: var1 not defined

    // access to the complete qualifier
    cout << SpecLib::var1 << endl;
    cout << SpecLib::func(SpecLib::var1) << endl;

    // redeclaration  of var1
    using SpecLib::var1;
    cout << var1 << endl;
    cout << SpecLib::func(var1) << endl;

    // insertion of the complete namespace
    using namespace SpecLib;
    cout << var2 << endl;
    cout << func(var2) << endl;

    return 1;
    }
```

### References

See basics section, using the default libraries.

See Reference section, category variables and data types, validity ranges; namespaces.

# Introducing namespaces into local validity ranges

```
using namespace
```

## Application

Declarations from namespaces can be introduced into particular validity ranges.

## Implementation

Suppose you are using a special library whose elements have all been declared in one namespace 'SpecLib'. However, you only require these elements in a specific function or method. In this case, it makes sense to introduce the namespace of the library specifically into this function.

## Example

```cpp
#include <iostream>
#include "bib.h"      // includes namespace SpecLib with int var1;
using namespace std;
...
int func() {
  using namespace SpecLib;
  var1 = 13;
  return var1;
  }

int main()
{
  // cout << "Value = " << var1 << endl;  // error: var1 unknown here
  cout << "Value = " << func() << endl;
  return 0;
}
```

## References

See using elements from namespaces.

See Reference section, category variables and data types, validity ranges; namespaces.

# Namespaces in extensive software projects

```
namespace
```

## Application

With the help of the keyword namespace it is possible to divide the global validity range (file range) into sub-ranges. In this way name conflicts caused by identical identifiers in the global validity range can be avoided.

## Implementation

Imagine you are working together with several colleagues on a large software project. Each programmer works at a sub-area and produces different source text files, which are later linked to a single program. During linking, the global validity ranges are merged to a single global validity range. If two programmers have declared two global variables, classes, data types or functions with the same name, this results in a name conflict. In C++ this can be prevented by the individual programmers declaring their global variables in a separate namespace.

Therefore, if you work on such a project or implement a software library which is later integrated into the programs of other programmers, you should declare all global elements in a separate namespace.

## Example

The header file for your library could look as follows:

```
/* StatLib.h */
#ifndef StatistH
#define StatistH
namespace StatLib {
  double arm_Mean(double *value, int number);
  double harm_Mean(double *value, int number);
  }
#endif
```

### References

See categories multiple files programs and libraries.

See Reference section, category variables and data types, validity ranges; namespaces.

# Enumeration types in switch statements

enum, switch

## Application

Lists can be easily used in connection with switch statements, since they represent a scalar data type, and the individual values can be used as case constants.

## Implementation

With the help of the switch statement, it is possible to carry out different, alternative statement blocks subject to the value of a variable. Often it is convenient – if not for the efficiency of the program, then at least for the legibility of the source text – to use enum variables in the switch condition and to use the individual constants from the list type as case constants.

## Example

```
#include <stdio.h>

enum Days {Monday = 1, Tuesday, Wednesday, Thursday,
           Friday, Saturday, Sunday};

int main()
  {
  char line[100];
  enum Days weekday;

  printf("Enter a week-day (1 - 7): ");
  fgets(line, sizeof(line), stdin);
  sscanf(line,"%d\n",&weekday);

  switch(weekday)
    {
    case Monday:
    case Tuesday:
```

```
      case Wednesday:
      case Thursday:
      case Friday:
              printf("Working day\n");
              break;
      case Saturday:
      case Sunday:
              printf("Week-end\n");
              break;
      default:
          printf("You have entered an incorrect value\n");
          break;
      }

    return 0;
    }
```

## References

See Reference section, category combined data types, list types.

# Enumeration types as sets

`enum`

## Application

In C a variable of a list type is essentially equivalent to a variable of an integer type (`short`, `int`, and so on). Assignments of `int` values to `enum` variables are, thus, possible without any problems (provided that the value range of the integer type on which the list type is based is not left).

```
enum Value {Minimum = 1, Maximum = 10};
enum Value var = 1;    // okay
          var = 100;  // okay
```

However, list types are separate data types in C++. Without explicit type conversion variables of a list type can only be assigned values from that list type. However, the assignment of `enum` values to integer variables is possible (default conversion).

```
enum Values {Minimum = 1, Maximum = 10};
enum Values var = 1;       // error
          var = Minimum; // okay
```

Also in C++ the `enum` type is based on an integer type, and the ANSI standard ensures that you can assign all integer values to an `enum` variable that lies between the smallest and the greatest value of the enum constant. However, when assigning a value for which no constant has been defined in the list type, you need to carry out an explicit type conversion:

```
enum Values {Minimum = 1, Maximum = 10};
enum Values var = (Values) 4;
```

The fact that an enum type not only introduces a group of constants into a validity range, but also permits the definition of variables which in principle can adopt all integer values between the smallest and the greatest constant, makes it possible to understand enum types as rudimentary set types.

## Implementation

Enum sets can be specified by explicitly listing all elements or by identifying the minimum and the maximum.

If all elements of the set are represented by successive integer values, you can run through the set in for loops.

## Warning

Note that incrementing (or decrementing) an enum variable results in increasing (decreasing) the integer value of the enum variable by 1, and not in setting the enum variable to the value of the next constant on the list.

## Example

```
// definition through explicit list
enum days {Monday = 1, Tuesday, Wednesday, Thursday,
           Friday, Saturday, Sunday};
// Definition through samll and large value
enum Values {Minimum = 1, Maximum = 10};

// running in loop
enum Values var;
for(Values loop = Minimum; loop <= Maximum; loop++)
    {
    printf("loop = %d\n", loop);
    }
```

## Tip

List types are not real set types. A real set type is understood as a data type whose variables do not only represent one value from a predefined set, but are themselves sets. Moreover, certain operations such as union and intersection should be defined with a set type.

Set types can be implemented in form of classes in C++. In the STL this has already been done. For example, `set` or `multiset` containers could be used to realise sets (depending on whether the elements may be unambiguous or a set may contain an element several times),. Alternatively, you could derive your own classes from these container classes and further adapt the given functionality to your own ideas.

## References

See Reference section, category combined data types, list types.

# Arrays and dynamic fields

## Application

Arrays are a useful device when trying to manage a larger amount of data of a shared data type, such as a group of read measured values. Arrays are distinguished by the fact that the elements of an array are stored one after the other in a connected block in the memory.

The great advantages of arrays are indexed access with the index operator [ ] and efficient searching in sorted arrays.

One disadvantage is that the size of the array must be determined in the declaration and cannot be changed later.

Dynamic fields are closely related to arrays: these are dynamically reserved memory blocks for a group of elements with the same data type. Fields and arrays can generally be handled in the same way. However, dynamic fields have the advantage that their size only needs to be determined at runtime.

## Implementation

Arrays and dynamic fields can be handled in the same way in C and C++, because the memory representation for arrays and dynamic fields is identical.

The compiler reserves a connected memory block in which the elements are stored successively and without gaps. The array name or pointer which is returned by the functions for memory reservation (`malloc`, `new`) indicates the initial address of the memory block.

With the help of the index operator [ ] it is possible to specify the element in the array/field that you want to access. The call of the index operator is internally converted into a pointer term by the compiler. The access

```
array[n] =
```

therefore corresponds to the pointer term

```
*(array + n) =
```

Thus, the array name is interpreted as a pointer to the start of the array. This pointer is incremented by n (that is, set to an address, which is greater by

n * sizeof(Datentyp_des_Zeigers)). Then the address is accessed (* operator).

Due to the equivalence of array name and field pointer, it is possible to use either the index operator or the pointer syntax for an array as well as a field.

## Warning

An array name is not a pointer! The compiler only interprets the array name as a pointer in statements (this also applies to the passing of arrays to function parameters).

## Example

```c
#include <stdio.h>
#include <stdlib.h>
#define ARRAY_SIZE5

int main()
  {
  // Declaring array and field
  int array[ARRAY_SIZE];

  int number = 5;
  int *field;
  field = (int*) malloc( number * sizeof(int));

  // Initialising elements in array and field
  int i;
  for(i=0; i < ARRAY_SIZE; i++)
      array[i] = i;    // *(array+i) = i;

  for(i=0; i < number; i++)
      field[i] = i;     // *(field+i) = i;

  // Outputting array and field
  puts("\nElements in array: \n");
  for(i=0; i < ARRAY_SIZE; i++)
      printf("\t%d\n",*(array+i));

  puts("\nElements in field: \n");
  for(i=0; i < number; i++)
      printf("\t%d\n",*(field+i));
```

```
return 0;
}
```

## References

See sorting arrays and searching arrays; category pointers and dynamic memory management.

See Reference section, category variables and data types, arrays.

# Sorting arrays

## Application

One of the great advantages of arrays and dynamic fields is that it is possible to search efficiently in sorted arrays or fields.

However, the condition is that the elements in the array/field are sorted. For this purpose, there are a range of algorithms, which are distinguished by efficiency, operational area and complexity. Two of the most common sorting algorithms are BubbleSort and QuickSort.

## Implementation

BubbleSort

| BubbleSort | | | | | | | | | | |
|---|---|---|---|---|---|---|---|---|---|---|
| 1. pass | 30 | 46 | 82 | 56 | 17 | 90 | 15 | 48 | 26 | 95 |
| 2. pass | 30 | 46 | 56 | 17 | 82 | 15 | 48 | 26 | 90 | 95 |
| 3. pass | 30 | 46 | 17 | 56 | 15 | 48 | 26 | 82 | 90 | 95 |
| 4. pass | 30 | 17 | 46 | 15 | 48 | 26 | 56 | 82 | 90 | 95 |
| 5. pass | 17 | 30 | 15 | 46 | 26 | 48 | 56 | 82 | 90 | 95 |
| 6. pass | 17 | 15 | 30 | 26 | 46 | 48 | 56 | 82 | 90 | 95 |
| 7. pass | 15 | 17 | 26 | 30 | 46 | 48 | 56 | 82 | 90 | 95 |
| 8. pass | 15 | 17 | 26 | 30 | 46 | 48 | 56 | 82 | 90 | 95 |
| 9. pass | 15 | 17 | 26 | 30 | 46 | 48 | 56 | 82 | 90 | 95 |
| 10. pass | 15 | 17 | 26 | 30 | 46 | 48 | 56 | 82 | 90 | 95 |

BubbleSort is a simple algorithm for sorting data. The data is stored in an array and then compared pair by pair. If the data in the array is to be sorted in ascending order, it checks for each pair whether the first element is greater than the second. If this is the case, the positions of the two elements are switched. If an array with *n* elements has been gone through in this way *n*–1 times, it is sorted afterwards.

QuickSort

QuickSort is more powerful and usually faster than BubbleSort. However, it is also more difficult to implement. Fortunately, in the C runtime library, there is the function qsort() that sorts any array according to the QuickSort algorithm.

# Example
## Sorting with BubbleSort

```c
#include <stdio.h>
#include <stdlib.h>

#define MAX 40

void bubbleSort(int field[], int num)  {
  int tmp;
  int loop1, loop2;

  for(loop1=1; loop1 < num; loop1++)
    for (loop2=0; loop2 < num 1; loop2++)
      {
      if(field[loop2] > field[loop2+1])
        {
        tmp = field[loop2];
        field[loop2] = field[loop2+1];
        field[loop2+1] = tmp;
        }
      }
  }

int main()  {
  int data[MAX];
  int loop;

  for (loop=0; loop < MAX; loop++)
    data[loop] = rand()%100;

  bubbleSort(data,MAX);

  for (loop=0; loop < MAX; loop++)
    printf("%d\t",data[loop]);

  return 0;
  }
```

## References

See searching arrays; arrays of structures.

See reference of the C runtime library, qsort().

# Searching arrays

## Application

It is possible to search efficiently in sorted arrays by halving the search area at each comparison. This is called binary search.

## Implementation

To illustrate the concept of binary search, let us look at the following array:

1  1  3  3  5  6  6  8  9

and search for the value 2.

The algorithm determines the approximate middle of the array and queries the value of the middle element. In the example this is the 5th element, which has the value 5.

According to the value of this element, the algorithm then determines whether the search should continue in the lower or the upper half of the array. In the example, we have an array that is sorted in ascending order. Since the searched for value (2) is smaller than the value of the middle element (5), the searched for value can only be found in the lower half. Therefore, the new search area is now the lower half of the array.

Now the algorithm determines the middle of the new search area, thus the middle of the lower half of the array. In the example, this is the element 2, whose value is 1. As the middle element has a smaller value than the search value, the new search area is the upper half of the present search area.

Therefore the algorithm consists of three steps:

1.  Determining the middle of the current search area.

2.  Comparing the middle value to the search value.

3.  Determining the new search area and continuing with step 1.

The algorithm ends when the searched for element has been found, or the search area only consists of an initial and a final element.

Since the search area is halved in each step, the number of iterations can be calculated easily from the number of elements. For $n$ elements the algorithm ends after a maximum of log2 $(n + 1)$ comparisons.

### Example

```
/* binary search */
int binarysearch(int field[], int anf, int end, int found)  {
  int centre;

  while(anf <= end     {
    centre = (beg+end)/2;

    if(field[centre] == found)
      return centre;
    else if (field[centre] < found)
      anf = centre + 1;
      else
      end = centre - 1;
    }
  return -1;  // not found
  }
```

### Tip

The function bsearch() of the C runtime library carries out a binary search on a sorted array.

### References

See sorting arrays.

See reference of the C runtime library, bsearch().

# Arrays as function parameters

### Application

The use of arrays would be quite restricted without the option to pass arrays as parameters to functions, thus it is possible to write generic functions which operate on arrays.

## Implementation

When passing an array to a function, the address of the first element is passed. Thus, the array is not copied and cannot be changed by the function (call by reference).

At the function declaration, the array parameter is specified by the square brackets. A value for the array size is not specified in the brackets, since this depends on the array that is to be passed. To provide the function with the size of the array, it is possible to pass the number of elements as an additional parameter.

```
void init(int field[], int max);
```

The specification of the array size may be missing, since arrays are not copied but are passed as pointers when they are passed to parameters. As the passed array does not need to be copied for the function, memory does not need to be reserved for an array copy, and therefore the size specification is not required. Instead, the function receives a pointer to the original array and accesses the array elements directly.

Since the function expects a pointer, a pointer needs to be passed to it:

```
#define MAX 100
int measurevalues[MAX];
...
init(measurevalues, MAX);
```

As you can see, only the array name is passed which, to the compiler, is equivalent to the first element of the array, namely the initial address of the array.

If you want to pass a sub-array only to the function, simply pass the address of the first element of the sub-array.

```
init(&measurevalues[20], MAX - 20);
```

## Warning

The number of elements of an array can usually be determined at runtime with the sizeof operator:

```
(sizeof(x) / sizeof(x[0]) )
```

In this case, you benefit from the fact that sizeof recognises x as an array variable and returns the size of the whole field.

However, after passing to an array, you use a pointer to access the array. Thus, for

```
(sizeof(field) / sizeof(field[0]) )
```

sizeof(field) returns the size of the pointer, and the calculation of the number of elements in the array fails. Because of this, it is customary to pass the number of elements as a separate parameter.

The passing of multidimensional arrays requires a type conversion into pointers, unless the array parameters are defined with size specifications.

## Example

```
#include <iostream.h>
#define NUMBER 10

// Definition of an array parameter
void init( int field[], int max) {
   for(int i=0; i<max; i++)
       field[i] = 2*i;
   }

int main() {
   int x[NUMBER];

   init(x,     NUMBER);     // passing an array
   init(&x[5],NUMBER-5);    // passing a partial array

   for(int i=0; i<NUMBER; i++)
      cout << x[i] << endl;

   return 0;
   }
```

## References

See category functions, pointers and references as parameters.

See Reference section, category combined data types, arrays; category functions, parameters.

# Arrays with elements of different data types

## Application

All the elements of an array must belong to the same data type. However, it is possible to relax this restriction by storing generic pointers in the array, which point to objects with different data types.

Such generic pointers may be `void` pointers or base class pointers.

## Implementation

Programming with `void` pointers is inconvenient and prone to errors, because of the required explicit type conversions (see `compare` function for `qsort()`, section on arrays of structures).

In contrast, the use of base class pointers, which can point to objects of various derived classes, is common in C++ and is a powerful programming device, not simply for the storing of objects in arrays.

Imagine that for a drawing program you have defined two classes `Rectangle` and `Circle`, which are both derived from the base class `CharacterObject`, for a drawing program. When the user draws rectangles and circles, the program produces instances of the derived class. All these instances (rectangles as well as circles) are to be stored in a single array.

The point is that objects of derived classes can be understood as objects of the base class. Therefore, you define pointers to the base class and assign the addresses of the objects of the derived class to them. These pointers can be managed in a single array. To be able to access the derived objects through the base class pointers later on, you will use the various options for runtime identification: virtual methods, `dynamic_cast` or `typeid`.

## Example

```
#include <iostream>
#include <cstdlib>
using namespace std;

class CharacterObject {                   // base class
  public:
    CharacterObject() {}
    virtual int character() = 0;          // abstract method
};

class rectangle : public CharacterObject {
  public:
    rectangle() {}

    virtual int character() {             // draw rectangle
      cout << "#";
      }
};
class circle : public CharacterObject {
  public:
    circle() {}
```

```
        virtual int character() {              // draw circle
           cout << "O";
           }
        };

int main()  {
  class CharacterObject  *geomFig[10];

  int wichObject;
  for(int loop = 0; loop < 10; loop++)
     {
       whichObjegt = rand() % 2;
       switch (whichObject)
         {
         case 0  :  geomFig[loop] = new Rectangle();
                    break;
         case 1  :  geomFig[loop] = new Circle();
                    break;

         }
      }

  for(int loop = 0; loop < 10; loop++)  {
    geomFig[loop]->character();
    }

  return 0;
  }
```

Possible output:

*###OO###O###*

## Warning

You must always store pointers to objects of derived classes in an array. You could also directly deposit objects of a derived class in an array for base class objects; however, you then lose the advantages of polymorphism. Furthermore, you should not handle arrays of derived objects as arrays of base class objects (for example by passing them to a corresponding function parameter).

## References

See category inheritance and polymorphism, base class pointers and arrays; RTTI.

See Reference section, category inheritance and polymorphism, base class pointers.

# Arrays of structures

## Application

In an array, you can not only deposit objects of simple data types, but also structures or objects of classes. The disadvantage of static field size is offset by the advantages of indexed access and efficient searching.

## Implementation

The declaration of arrays with structures as elements, as well as indexed access to structures in arrays, follows the array-typical syntax.

- Declaration of a structure :

```
struct person{
    char   first_name[20];
    char   name[20];
    int    zip;
    };
```

- Declaration of an array for the storage of up to 100 addresses (variables of the structure person):

```
struct person    address[100];
```

- Access to the name of the third person:

```
address[2].name
```

The sorting of arrays with structures as elements is more complicated. Before a group of elements can be sorted, they must be comparable. Elements of simple data types such as int can be directly compared with the help of the compare operators. For structures (or more general classes) this is not directly possible. In C++, the required compare operators would need to be overloaded first; in C, a compare function would be defined:

```
// Compare two addresses according to names
// for qsort
int vgl(const void* p1,const void* p2)
  {
  struct person* adr1,*adr2;
  adr1=(struct person*)p1;
  adr2=(struct person*)p2;
  return strcmp(adr1->name,adr2->name);
  }
```

Furthermore, a function would be required which runs through the field of the structure objects and sorts it with the help of the compare function. In C++, the objects would be stored in a container and a suitable STL algorithm would be called. In C, the qsort() function would be used:

```
qsort(addresses,              // beginning of the field
      n,                      // number of field elements
                              // to be sorted
      sizeof (struct person), // element size
      cmp                     // comparison function
      );
```

## Tips

To manage objects of elementary data types, structures or classes in dynamic data structures, it is best to use the containers in the C++ runtime library. To manipulate and process the elements in the containers – for example, for sorting – numerous functions can be used, which are also part of the C++ runtime library and have been declared in the `algorithms` header file (which can also be applied to arrays).

## References

See arrays and dynamic fields.

See sorting arrays.

See category operators, overloading operators.

See Reference section, category combined data types, arrays and structures.

See reference of the C runtime library, `qsort`.

# Recursive structures

## Application

An interesting feature of structures is that as well as containing elements of the type of other structures, they may also contain pointers to elements of their own structure type and pointers to declared, but not yet defined, structures.

```
struct s_type {
  int value;
  struct s_type *next;};
```

However, without the option to incorporate pointers into incompletely declared structures as elements of a structure, the implementation of lists and trees or alternate references between structures would not be possible.

# Implementation

All that C/C++ demands of the definition of a structure is that the size of the structure elements are known, so that the size and memory requirements of the declared structure can also be determined. A pointer always has the same size (under 32-bit systems it is 4 bytes), independent of whether it points to an `int` value, a structure, or a function. Therefore, pointers to elements of incompletely declared structures are allowed.

# Example

```
struct s_type1;
struct s_type2 {
  int elem1;
  struct s_type1 *elem2;
  };
struct s_type1 {
  int elem1;
  struct s_type2 *elem2;
  };
```

# Tip

This also allows recursive data types to be realised with classes.

# References

See Reference section, category combined data types, structures.

# Category:
# pointers and
# dynamic memory
# management

# Memory allocation with malloc()

## Application

Dynamic memory management is an important operational area of pointers. By means of the `malloc()` and `free()` functions memory can be requested and freed in C when necessary. In C++, the use of the operators `new` and `delete` is preferable.

## Implementation

Pointers refer to addresses in the working memory. These addresses can be the addresses of objects stored in the memory (the addresses of variables or functions), but it is also possible to reserve new memory and link it with the pointer. In this case, you need to call the function `malloc()`.

```
int *p_int;
p_int1 = (int*) malloc(n*sizeof(int));
```

The size of the memory area that is to be reserved in bytes is passed to the function `malloc()` as an argument. Usually, the size is calculated as the product of the number of elements which are to be deposited in the memory block, and the size of the individual element. The size of an individual element in bytes is usually returned by the `sizeof` operator.

If the function cannot reserve the requested memory, it returns a `NULL` pointer, otherwise it returns a `void` pointer to the initial address of the memory. This return value is converted and assigned to a pointer.

If the memory area is no longer required, it is freed with the `free()` function.

```
free(p_int);
```

Only the dynamically reserved memory to which the pointer refers, is resolved. The pointer itself remains and can be reinitialised when required with a new address.

## Warning

The fact that, to free dynamic memory, a pointer to the start of the memory area is required (argument to `free()`), means that the memory area cannot be freed if such a pointer no longer exists. This can happen for two reasons:

- if the address has been assigned to a local pointer variable, it expires when its validity range is left. The dynamically allocated memory area remains,

• if another address is assigned to the pointer and the address of the memory area is not stored in another pointer, the memory area may not be addressed.

Do not confuse the concepts `malloc/free` and `new/delete`. A memory area which has been reserved with `malloc()` should only be freed with `free()`. Conversely, a memory area which has been reserved with `new` should only be freed with `delete`.

Pointers that do not refer to a correct address in the memory, should be assigned the value zero (zero pointer), as an indicator that the pointer does not point to a valid object. Prior to de-referencing a pointer, you should always check whether it is a zero pointer. The de-referencing of a pointer which does not refer to a correctly allocated memory address can result in serious runtime errors.

## Example

```
#include <stdio.h>
#include <stdlib.h>
#define NUMBER 7

int main() {
  int *p_int = NULL;      // define pointer and initialise with NULL
  int loop;

  // allocate memory for NUMBER int values
  p_int = (int*) malloc(NUMBER * sizeof(int));

  if(p_int)    // does pointer point to valid memory ??
    {
    for(loop=0; loop < NUMBER; loop++) {   // write values in field
      *(p_int+loop) = loop;
      printf("p_int[%d] = %d\n",loop,*(p_int+loop));
      }
    }
  free(p_int);   // p_int = NULL can be omitted because the function is
  return 0;      // left here and the locale p_int pointer is cancelled
```

## Reference

See Reference section, category pointers and references.

# Memory allocation with new

## Application

Dynamic memory management is an important operational area of pointers. By means of the `new` and `delete` functions, memory can be requested and freed in C when necessary.

## Implementation

Pointers refer to addresses in the working memory. These addresses can be the addresses of objects stored in the memory (the addresses of variables or functions), but it is also possible to reserve new memory and link it with the pointer.

To reserve memory for a single object, you need to call the operator `new` with the data type of the object.

```
int *p_int;
p_int = new int;
```

The operator `new` can also be used to establish pointers to fields. The dimensions of the field are as usual specified in square brackets. In C++, the first size specification does not need to be a constant.

```
int n = 7;
int *p_int1, *p_int2;
p_int1 = new int[n];        // field of n int values
p_int2 = new int[n][100];   // returns a field of n pointers
                            // to 100 int values each
```

When successful, the `new` operator returns the initial address of the memory. This address is assigned to a self-defined pointer.

If the `new` operator is unable to reserve the requested memory, it triggers a `bad_alloc` exception. However, there is also an overloaded version of the operator, which returns a zero pointer instead of an exception:

```
p_int = new(nothrow) int;
```

If the memory area is no longer required, it is freed with the `delete` operator.

```
delete(p_int);
```

Only the dynamically reserved memory to which the pointer refers is resolved. The pointer itself remains and can be reinitialised, when required, with a new address.

The `delete` operator may not, in contrast to the `new` operator, recognise independently whether a pointer or an array of pointers is to be deleted. In the latter case `delete[]` has to be called.

The delete operator can be applied to zero pointers.

## Warning

The fact that, to free dynamic memory, a pointer to the start of the memory area is required (argument to delete), means that the memory area cannot be freed if such a pointer no longer exists. This can happen for two reasons:

- if the address has been assigned to a local pointer variable, it expires, when its validity range is left. The dynamically allocated memory area remains,
- if another address is assigned to the pointer and the address of the memory area is not stored in another pointer, the memory area may not be addressed.

Do not confuse the concepts malloc/free and new/delete. A memory area which has been reserved with malloc() should only be freed with free(). Conversely, a memory area which has been reserved with new should only be freed with delete.

Pointers that do not refer to a correct address in the memory should be assigned the value zero (zero pointer), as an indicator that the pointer does not point to a valid object. Prior to de-referencing of a pointer, you should always check whether it is a zero pointer. The de-referencing of a pointer which does not refer to a correctly allocated memory address can result in serious runtime errors.

## Example

```
#include <iostream>
#include <new>
#include <stdio.h>
using namespace std;

#define NUMBER 7

int main() {
  int *p_int = NULL;      // define pointer and initialise with NULL
  int loop;

  // allocate memory for NUMBER int values
  // copy beginning of address to pointer p_int
  try {
    p_int = new int[NUMBER];
    }
  catch (bad_alloc &ba) {
    cout << "Exception caught\n";
    cout << ba.what() << endl;
    exit(1);
    }
```

```
   if(p_int)
     {
     // Writes and submits values field
     for(loop=0; loop < NUMBER; loop++)
       {
       *(p_int+loop) = loop;
       printf("p_int[%d] = %d\n",loop,*(p_int+loop));
       }
     }

   delete[] p_int;   // p_int=NULL can be omitted as the function is left
   return 0;         // here and the local p_int pointer is cancelled
}
```

## References

See error handling for new.

See paragraphs on the reservation of dynamic memory.

See Reference section, category pointers and references.

# Error handling for new

new

## Application

The requested memory area cannot always be allocated by the new operator (for example, if more memory has been requested than is available). In such cases the operator must be able to report the failure of the memory reservation to the program.

## Implementation

C++ has three possible ways of doing this:

### bad_alloc exception

By default, the new operator triggers an exception of the bad_alloc class in the event of a memory allocation that cannot be carried out (defined in the header file <new>). It can be caught and processed, for example, by issuing an error message and terminating the program (see Reference section on exception handling).

```
try {
  ptr = new long int[2580000L];
  }
```

```
catch (bad_alloc &ba) {
    cout << "Exception caught\n";
    cout << ba.what() << endl;
    exit(1);
    }
```

## Return value

Another option is to have the `new` operator return a return value of zero and check the value of the pointer after the allocation. This is equivalent to the usual error handling in C programs (C does not recognise exceptions) and is still implemented as the default procedure by some compilers.

To deactivate exception handling and to return a return value of zero, the `new` operator must be called with the argument `nothrow`.

```
ptr = new(nothrow) long int[2580000L];

if (ptr == 0)       // compare with Null pointer (in C++ 0)
    {
    cout << "Memory allocation failed\n";
    exit(1);
    }
```

## Handler function

Finally, it is possible to define a special handler function which is called by the `new` operator in case of an error.

This function may not define either a return value or parameters, and should be registered with the C++ function `set_new_handler()`.

It is important to be aware of the fact that after the calling the handler function, the `new` operator attempts to allocate the requested memory. If that attempt also fails, the handler function is called again, and so on.

The handler function can, thus, attempt to free memory (under Windows, for example, also by prompting the user to close programs). However, if this fails, it must prevent the `new` operator from being further executed by triggering an exception itself or by terminating the program (`exit(1)`).

```
void my_new_handler() {
  char c;
  cout << "Not enough memory available!\n";
  cout << "Have you freed memory? \n";
  cin >> c;

  if( (c != 'j') && (c != 'J'))
    throw bad_alloc();
  }
...
```

```
set_new_handler(my_new_handler);
try {
  ptr = new long int[2580000L];
  }
catch (bad_alloc &ba) {
    cout << "Exception caught\n";
    cout << ba.what() << endl;
    exit(1);
    }
```

## Tip

The default in earlier compiler versions is that new returns a zero pointer in the event of a failed allocation, instead of triggering an exception.

## References

See memory allocation with new.

See Reference section, category exception handling.

# Pointer arithmetic

## Application

It is also possible, within certain limits, to calculate with pointers. Increment and decrement are permitted, as well as addition and subtraction of integers. Incrementing and decrementing of pointers is useful if data objects have been deposited in the form of a field, for example, as is the case for allocation with new[] or malloc().

## Implementation

In this case, the individual elements are stored without gaps in the memory. If the address of the pointer to this memory area is changed, this occurs in units of the referenced objects. For this reason, when incrementing, 1 is not simply added, but the address is increased by the size of the data object to which the pointer points. The same applies to decrementing. It is also possible for pointers to add or subtract an integer value. The compiler multiplies the size of the data object with this integer to determine the correct address.

## Example

```
#define MAX 50
int loop;
int* ptr = NULL;

ptr = (int*) malloc(MAX*sizeof(int));

for(loop=0; loop < MAX; loop++)
    *(ptr+loop) = loop;
```

## References

See category variables and data types, arrays and dynamic fields.

See Reference section, category pointers and references, pointers.

# Dynamic memory in functions

## Application

Of course, pointers can also be defined as local variables, for example in the statement block of a function. Here you must note that the memory for the pointer and the memory to which the pointer refers may be handled differently.

The memory for a locally defined pointer is reserved, the same as for all local variables, on the stack and automatically freed up by the compiler at the end of the block. The memory area to which the pointer refers may be memory on the stack (the pointer refers to another local variable) as well as memory on the heap (memory has been dynamically reserved and linked to the pointer). In the latter case, there may be problems because the memory reserved on the heap is automatically freed up at the end of the block.

## Implementation

### Scenario 1

Youwant to reserve dynamic memory, which is no longer required after the function has been executed, within a function.

Here, you must define a local pointer in the function. Then, you reserve the dynamic memory with `malloc()` or `new` and make the pointer refer to the memory area. Before the function is finished and left, you must ensure that the dynamically reserved memory is freed up (with `free()` or `delete`).

### Scenario 2

You want to use dynamic memory, which is also required outside of the function, within a function.

Usually, you can reserve the dynamic memory within the function and link it to a local pointer. However, before leaving the function, you must ensure that the function returns a pointer to the memory area to the caller: for example, as a return value or assignment to a global pointer. If this does not happen, the dynamically reserved memory still exists after the function has been terminated. However, the program can no longer access the memory because there is no pointer which refers to the initial address of the memory area.

However, it is recommended to reserve globally dynamic memory which is needed globally (for example in main() and then link it to a global pointer).

### Scenario 3

You require dynamic memory for objects in a class.

In this case, the constructor of the class is available for memory allocation. You reserve the memory in the constructor and link it to a pointer which has been defined as a data element of the class. You free up dynamically reserved memory in the destructor of the class.

## Example

```
#include <stdio.h>
#include <stdlib.h>

void func() {
   int *p_int = NULL;                          // define pointer
   p_int = (int*) malloc(NUMBER * sizeof(int));   // reserve memory

   ...

   free(p_int);            // free memory
   return 0;               // the local p_int pointer is cancelled
}
```

## References

See dynamic memory in classes.

See dynamic memory and exception handling.

# Dynamic memory in classes

## Application

Dynamic memory is not only required for global data or local use in functions. Often dynamic memory is also needed for the individual instances of a class.

## Implementation

In this case, the constructor of the class is available for memory allocation. You reserve the memory in the constructor and link it to a pointer, which has been defined as a data element of the class. You free up dynamically reserved memory in the destructor of the class.

If a class defines pointers as instance variables, depending on the use of the class, there are two further points to be noted, apart from the reservation and freeing up of the dynamic memory:

- If you use or define yourself the copy constructor or the assignment operator to copy objects of the class, you must think about what is to be copied for the pointers: the address to which the pointer refers (in this case pointer and copy refer to the same object in the memory), or the object to which the pointer refers (so that the original pointer and its copy point to two different objects, which contain identical values, in the memory). For more details, see section classes, copying class objects.
- If you store an instance of the class on the hard drive, you are faced with the same problem as in copying. Should you store the address or the object to which the pointer refers for a pointer? For more details, see section classes, persistent classes.

## Example

```
class Demo {
    int *field;
    int num_elements;
  public:
    Demo(int num) {
       num_elements = num;
       field = new int[num_elements];   // error handling is
       }                                // left to the program
    ~Demo() {
       delete field;                    // free memory at
       }                                // deletion of instance
    };
```

# Dynamic memory and exception handling

## Application

A constant potential source of danger in dynamic memory reservation with `new` or `malloc()` is the connection of a dynamically reserved memory area with a local pointer variable.

When the function in which the pointer variable has been defined is left, the pointer variable is resolved, but the dynamically reserved memory area to which the pointer used to point is not. A memory gap has been created.

This can be easily prevented by freeing up the reserved memory area before leaving the function with `delete` or `free()` (or pointing a global pointer to the memory area if the memory area is still required).

If there are several potential positions where the function can be left by calling the `return` statement, you must make sure that the freeing up of the memory area is ensured at each of these positions.

The whole business becomes even more complicated in C++, if the advantages of exception handling are used within the function. Depending on the implementation, this may mean that the function is directly left in reply to an error. In such cases you must make sure, during exception handling, that the memory is freed up.

## Implementation

To ensure, even in the event of an exception, that the dynamic memory is freed up, it is possible to encapsulate the statement part of the function into a `try` block in order to catch triggered exceptions in the statements (especially the sub-function called in these), free up the reserved memory area, and pass on the exception.

## Example

```
int func()
  {
  int *ptr = new int;    // reserve memory

  try {
     ...                 // instruction part
     }
  catch (...) {          // catch all exceptions
```

```
   delete(ptr);        // free memory
   throw;              // pass exception
   }

 free(ptr);
 return 0;
 }
```

### References

See auto_ptr.

See Reference section, category exception handling.

# auto_ptr

## Application

The auto_ptr template class offers an option to circumvent all the problems with locally reserved dynamic memory.

## Implementation

Instead of working with a local pointer, you now work with a local instance of a specialisation of the auto_ptr template class. (The specialisation occurs through passing the data type, to which the autopointer is to refer.)

The advantage of the autopointer in comparison to a simple local pointer is that the autopointer ensures by itself that the memory area to which it points is freed up as soon as it is resolved (when, for example the block or class area it belongs to is terminated).

This sounds like the solution to all problems. Why, then, do you not always use an autopointer when a dynamically reserved memory area is to be resolved together with the pointer that references it?

## Warning

Apart from the fact that the encapsulation of a pointer into an autopointer is unnecessary in many cases, autopointers are subject to separate rules and restrictions which have to be met:

- An autopointer cannot be used together with the array version of new (new[]).
- An autopointer completely takes over a pointer that has been assigned to it. This means that when an autopointer A is assigned to an autopointer B the

pointer contained in A is not only copied to B, but is transferred wholly to B and afterwards resolved together with the autopointer B and not with A.

```
int* ptr = new int;
auto_ptr<int> a_ptr1(ptr);
auto_ptr<int> a_ptr2(a_ptr1);          // a_ptr1 takes over ptr
```

- If two autopointers lead to the same pointer, their behaviour has not been defined. In any case, you can expect errors.

```
int* ptr = new int;
auto_ptr<int> a_ptr1(ptr);
auto_ptr<int> a_ptr2(ptr);      // permitted, but error prone
```

## Example

```
#include <memory>
using namespace std;

int func()
  {
  auto_ptr<int> ptr  = new int;

  ...

  return 0;
  }
```

## Tips

Smart pointers offer a higher level of convenience and security than `auto_ptr`. They are classes which have been defined in such a way that their objects can be used like normal pointers (requiring, for example, overloading of de-referencing operators). However, by internal implementation, they ensure that memory gaps are not created, that memory is automatically freed up when the last smart pointer to the memory is resolved, and so on.

## References

See dynamic memory in functions.

See dynamic memory and exception handling.

# Pointers versus references

## Description

In contrast to pointers

– references cannot refer successively to different objects

– references have to be initialised with the objects to which they are to point

– references can only refer to existing variables (and not, for example, to functions)

– references are addressed like normal variables (no de-referencing syntax)

– it is only possible to access the corresponding variable with references. The reference itself cannot be manipulated (there is no pendant to the pointer arithmetic).

Summing up, a reference is equivalent to a `const` pointer, which is automatically de-referenced when accessed. This has the advantages that:

– references are addressed like normal variables (no pointer-typical de-referencing syntax), and

– the use of references is more secure than that of pointers (since they always refer to one precisely defined object).

## Implementation

In principle, references are preferable to pointers, because of their simpler syntax and greater security, if

• you want to refer to an existing object (unlike pointers, references cannot remain uninitialised or refer to zero), or

• you only want to refer to a single object (unlike pointers, references cannot be diverted to other objects).

The main operational areas for references are

• passing parameters to functions, and

• returning results of overloaded operator functions.

## References

See references as parameters and as return value of operators.

See Reference section, category pointers and references.

# References as parameters

## Application

References are often used as parameters of functions, because

- for references, as well as for pointers, arguments are passed as calls by reference. Thus, time-consuming copy operations are avoided,
- the syntax for references is simpler than the pointer syntax,
- the use of references is more secure than the use of pointers, and
- parameters are always initialised at generation (this occurs at function call, when an argument is passed to the parameter) and are not usually diverted to other objects. This corresponds exactly to the specification for references.

## Implementation

In the function definition a reference parameter is marked by the & operator:

```
class People { ... };
...
void pass_reference(People& par)
```

If you want to prevent the function from changing the state of the passed object, you simply need to declare the reference parameter as `const`:

```
void pass_reference(const People& par)
```

At function call the arguments are passed as objects (not as addresses):

```
class People dennis(30);
...
pass_reference(dennis);
```

## Warning

Arguments and parameters must pertain to the same type. Earlier compilers, which are not fully ANSI compatible, generate a temporary object, in the event of not quite identical data types, which has the type of the reference parameter and is initialised with the values from the argument. The reference parameter is then a reference to this temporary object. According to the ANSI standard, the creation of temporary objects by the compiler is only allowed for `const` parameters, where it ensures that the function does not intend to change the state of the argument.

## Example

```
#include <iostream>
using namespace std;
```

```
class People {
   int ageing;
  public:
   People(int age)  {ageing = age;}
   void grow_older()   {ageing++;}
   int get_ageing() {return ageing;}
  };

// function with reference parameter
void pass_reference(People& par)  {
  par.grow_older();
  }

int main()  {
  People dennis(30);
  cout << "Dennis ist " << dennis.get_ageing()
       << " years old\n";

  // pass class object to reference parameter
  pass_reference(dennis);
  cout << "Dennis is " << dennis.get_ageing()
       << " years old\n";
  return 0;
  }
```

Output

```
Dennis is 30 years old
Dennis is 31 years old
```

## References

See references as return values of operators.

See Reference section, category pointers and references.

# References as return values of operators

## Application

For return values, as for parameters, you should try to pass larger objects as references (that is references or pointers) and not as copy.

With regard to the return values of self-defined operator functions, two questions arise:

- When can I return a return value as a pointer or a reference?
- Is it better to define the return value as a pointer or as a reference?

## Implementation

If the return value is to be returned as a pointer or a reference, you must make sure that the object to which it is referred still exists after calling the operator function.

This is the case, for example, if the operator function adopts a reference as an argument, whose value is changed in the operator function. Then the changed object can be returned, without danger, as a reference. This is usually used when overloading the combined operators (+=, -=, ...).

```
Vector& Vector::operator+=(const Vector & v)  {
   x += v.x;   y += v.y;   z += v.z;
   return *this;
   }
```

However, if the result of the operator is deposited in a local object, it cannot be returned with a reference, but only as a direct copy.

```
Vector Vector::operator+(const Vector & v)  {
   return Vector(x+v.x, y+v.y, z+v.z);
   }
```

If it is usually possible to return the return value as a reference (that is, a reference or pointer), the question arises as to whether to define the return value as a pointer or a reference. In principle, both are possible; however, in practice, the reference is used. The reason for this is that the return values of the concerned operators are usually used like objects and you will probably want to circumvent the de-referencing syntax required for pointers.

```
v1 += v2 += v3;
```

instead of

```
v1 += *(v2 += v3);
```

or

```
v[3] =
```

instead of

```
*v[3] =  // for overloaded [ ] operator
```

## Example

```
#include <iostream>
using namespace std;
```

```
class Vector {
   double x, y, z;
 public:
  Vector(double a, double b, double c) {
     x = a; y = b; z = c;
     }
  Vector& operator+=(const Vector & v);
  Vector operator+(const Vector & v);
 };

Vector& Vector::operator+=(const Vector & v)  {
  x += v.x;
  y += v.y;
  z += v.z;
  return *this;
  }

Vector Vector::operator+(const Vector & v)  {
  return Vector(x+v.x, y+v.y, z+v.z);
  }

int main()  {
  Vector v1(1,0,0), v2(0,0,1), v3(3,3,3);

  v1 += v3;
  v1 += v2 += v3;

  return 0;
  }
```

## References

See references as parameters.

See category operators, overloading the various operators.

# Category: operators

# The efficient use of operators

## Application

For the execution of algebraic operations such as addition, subtraction, etc., there may be several options in C/C++.

You can carry out the calculation and assignment with your own operators:

```
int a, b, c;
...
a = a + c;
```

or with a combined assignment operator:

```
a += c;
```

If you want to increase or decrease by a value, the post- and prefix versions of the increment and decrement operators are also available to you.

```
a++;
++a;
```

What is recommended?

## Implementation

Whenever possible, you should use the combined assignment operators (+=, -=, ...), since these usually work more efficiently than the purely arithmetic operators (the latter usually create temporary internal objects).

Post- and prefix versions of the increment and decrement operators are distinguished by when the value of the operand is returned and when it is increased. However, this is only important if the value of the operand is directly used again (for example in a term: a + ++b returns a different result than a + b++). If this is not the case, for example when the operator is used on its own in a term (a++; or ++a;), the prefix version is preferable, since it usually works more efficiently (the postfix operator is usually internally implemented in such a way that it generates a temporary object).

## Warning

Operators can also be overloaded for user-defined class types in C++. Whether in this case

```
obj1 = obj1 + obj2
```

is equivalent to

```
obj1 += obj2
```

and

```
++obj1
```

is equivalent to

```
obj1 +=1
```

depends on the respective implementation of the overloaded operators, as well as on the efficiency of the operators.

Programmers should take care when overloading operators that the functionality and efficiency considerations, known from the elementary data types, are adopted for the operators whenever possible.

### References

See Reference section, category operators.

See overloading of operators.

# Overloading of operators

## Application

With overloading, a great number of the C++ operators can be adapted to be used with operands of self-defined class types. For example, if you have created a class `Vector` to represent three-dimensional vectors, you can overload the arithmetic operators (+, -, ...) for operands of the `Vector` class type, in order to be able to manipulate objects of the class with the help of the operators.

## Implementation

The following considerations play an important part in the overloading of an operator:

- Should the operator function be defined in the class or in the global file space (or in a namespace)?

When overloading within the class, the first operand is automatically the current object of the class for which the operator function is called. The operator function, as a method of the class, has access to the `private` and `protected` elements of the class. The following operators can only be defined within classes:

```
=, (), [], ->
```

When overloading outside the class, both operators are passed as parameters. To be able to access `private` or `protected` elements of the class, the operator function must be declared as `friend` in the class (see overloading of stream operators).

- Which type should the return type of the operator function be?

The type of the return value depends on the operator. Compare operators return, for example `int` or `bool` values, arithmetic operators an object of the type of the class for which they have been overloaded.

- What quality should the return value of the operator function have?

If the operator function defines a local object as its result and wants to return it, a copy of the object must be returned.

If the operator function manipulates an object which also exists outside the operator function it can return a reference.

### Referencese

See following paragraphs.

See category pointers and dynamic memory management, references as return values of operators.

# Overloading the increment operator ++

## Application

When overloading the increment operator (as well as the decrement operator) it should be noted that there is a prefix and a postfix version.

```
++object;        // prefix
object++;        // postfix
```

## Implementation

To distinguish the operator function for prefix and postfix, the postfix has an additional `int` parameter. The declaration of the `int` parameter for the postfix increment operator does not specify a real second operand, but merely serves to distinguish it from the prefix increment operator.

The prefix operator usually returns a reference, the postfix operator a copy of its local object, where the return type is additionally defined as `const`, in order to prevent sequences such as `obj++++`.

## Example

```
class Thresholdvalue {
public:
   int value;
  public:
  Thresholdvalue() {value= 0;}

  // value should only be increased by steps of ten
  Thresholdvalue& operator ++ () {          // prefix increment
    this->value += 10;
    return *this;
    }
  const Thresholdvalue operator ++ (int) {  // postfix increment
    Thresholdvalue tmp = *this;
    this->value=10;
    return tmp;
    }
  };
...
class Thresholdvalue max;
max++;
```

## Reference

See operators, efficient use of the operators.

# Overloading the arithmetic operators +, +=

## Application

The application of the algebraic operations on any data types.

## Implementation

The simple arithmetic operators (+, −, ...) usually create a new object from two objects that have been passed as operands. The new object is created as a local object in the operator function and, thus, must be returned as a copy. The combined arithmetic operators (+=, −=, ...) manipulate the first operand, which is returned as a reference.

In principle, it is recommended that the simple and combined operators are overloaded pairwise, where the simple operator should be defined on the basis of the combined operator, to guarantee the equivalence of the terms

```
a = a + b;
```

and

```
a += b;
```

## Example

```
class Vector {
   double x, y, z;
 public:
  Vector(double a, double b, double c) {
     x = a; y = b; z = c;
     }
  Vector& operator+=(const Vector & v);
  Vector  operator+ (const Vector & v);
  };

Vector& Vector::operator+=(const Vector & v)  {
  x += v.x;   y += v.y;   z += v.z;
  return *this;
  }

Vector Vector::operator+(const Vector & v)  {
  Vector tmp(x, y, z);
  return tmp += v;
  }
```

## Reference

See operators, efficient use of the operators.

# Overloading the [] operator

## Application

The [ ] operator is usually overloaded to access an element of a set by means of an index. Here the set of the elements does not necessarily need to have been deposited en masse in the memory, as is the case with arrays.

## Implementation

The operator should in any case return a reference (for smaller objects a copy is sufficient), so that the operator can be used without pointer syntax.

The operator can only be defined within classes.

## Example

```
class person { .. };
class addressbook {
    /* contains a quantity of person entries as data elements
        which are not managed as a static array but as a dynamic
        list or tree */
    ...
  public:
    person& operator[] (int);
    };

person& addressbook:operator[] (int i) {
    class person *found
    /* search dynamic structure */
    ...
    return *found;
    };

int main() {
    class addressbook personal;
    class person entry;
    ...
    entry = personal[3];
    return 0;
    }
```

## References

See category pointers and dynamic memory management, references as return values of operators.

# Overloading the () operator

## Application

The () operator is usually overloaded to be able to use objects such as functions. Often the operator is also overloaded to access elements of multidimensional arrays.

## Implementation

The operator can only be defined within classes. The first operand is automatically the class instance that is calling and the second operand is the list of parameters.

## Example

```
class demo {
    ...
    public;
    int operator() (int a, int b) {return (a+b);};
    };

int main() {
    class demo demoobject;
    int sum;
    sum = demoobject(3,2);
    return 0;
    }
```

## References

See category the STL, creating function objects.

See reference of the C++ runtime library, utilities.

# Overloading the assignment operator =

## Application

The assignment operator = has three main features:

- it cannot be inherited,
- it can only be declared in the class space and,
- it has already been defined by default for each class as an elementwise assignment.

However, the use of the pre-defined assignment operator usually results in errors if it is used for classes which contain pointers as data elements. This is because the copied pointers still refer to the same address as the original ones. There are two options for preventing errors:

- overloading the operator, and
- declaring the operator as private.

## Implementation

When overloading the assignment operator, the following points should be noted:

- The operator can only be overloaded in the class space. This ensures that its first argument is a class object (and not an elementary data type).

- The operator should return a reference to its instance, for example, to allow linked assignments such as `a = b = c;`.

- Assignment operators of derived classes should use the base class version of the assignment operator to copy inherited data elements.

- The operator should check whether an object should be assigned to itself. First, it is usually possible to handle this case more efficiently than by complete copying. Second, self-assignment for pointer elements usually results in errors. This is because for pointer elements, the memory in the object on the left-hand side of the assignment is usually freed up, reallocated and then initialised with the memory contents of the object on the right-hand side. In case of a self-assignment, however, the memory for both objects is deleted in a single step.

## Example

```
class Demo
    {
    int    value1;
    double value2;
public:
    char * text;

    Demo& Demo::operator=(const Demo& op)
        {
        if (this != &op)
            {
            value1 = op.value1;
            value2 = op.value2;

            delete text;
            text = new char[strlen(op.text)+1];
            strcpy(text,op.text);
            }
        return *this;
        }
    };
```

## References

See category pointers and dynamic memory management, references as return values of operators.

See category classes, copying class objects.

# Overloading new and delete

## Application

C++ permits you to write your own versions of new and delete for individual memory management of class types, as well as to override globally the following predefined new and delete operators:

```
void* operator new(size_t size) throw(bad_alloc);
void* operator new(size_t size, const nothrow&) throw();
void* operator new[](size_t size) throw(bad_alloc);
void* operator new[](size_t size,const nothrow&) throw();
void operator delete(void* ptr) throw();
void operator delete(void* ptr, const nothrow&) throw();
void operator delete[](void* ptr) throw();
void operator delete[](void* ptr, const nothrow&) throw();
```

## Implementation

When you override the global versions, these are irretrievably replaced by your definitions. Thus, this is not a normal overriding, where you are usually still able to access the overridden version with the validity range operator, but for the current program the compiler replaces its definitions with yours.

Less drastic is the definition of own operator functions for special classes. If you want to adapt the memory allocation for a class by defining class-internal new and delete operators, note the following points:

- new operators always expect size_t as the first operand and void* as the return type,
- delete operators have void* as the first operand and void as the return type,
- if you define your own new operator for a class, you should also define a corresponding delete operator and ensure that the delete operator frees as much space as the new operator has reserved for the object, and
- you should, if possible, ensure that error handling and functionality of the operator agree with ANSI.

## Example

One reason for the definition of your own new and delete operators may be the deliberate rejection of the security mechanisms of the new operator. For this purpose, it would be possible to trace back the operators to their C pendants. (This corresponds to the use of the nothrow versions of the operators.)

```
class demo {
  public:
```

```
    int value;
    void* operator new(size_t);
    void operator delete(void *);
    };
void* demo::operator new(size_t size)  {
    return malloc(size);
    }
void demo::operator delete(void* p)     {
    if (p)  free(p);
    }
```

To write your own ANSI-conforming new operator, you must:

- return a correct address for requests of 0 byte memory, and
- call the new_handler function for error handling in the event of a failed memory reservation and afterwards reattempt the memory reservation or – if a error handling function has not been registered – trigger a bad_alloc exception.

Note that the delete operator can also be called for zero pointers.

```
void* operator new (size_t size)  {
    if(size == 0)                   // for requests of 0 bytes
       size = 1;                    // return pointer to 1 byte

    for(;;) {                       // endless loop for allocation
      if( void* ptr= malloc(size) ) // reserve memory
        return ptr;

      if(_new_handler == 0) throw bad_alloc();
        _new_handler();
      }
    }
```

Where new_handler stands for a global compiler-defined pointer which points to the last registered error handling function, this should usually be implemented in such a way that it attempts to free up memory or triggers a bad_alloc exception.

## References

See category pointers and memory management, error handling for new.

See Reference section, category operators, the operators new and delete.

# Overloading the stream operators << >>

## Application

Often the stream operators >> and << are overloaded to be able to read and output the data of objects of self-defined classes (sometimes this is done simply for debugging).

## Implementation

The stream operators expect a reference to a stream as the left-hand operator (first parameter of the operator function). Therefore, they can only be defined in the file space (otherwise the first operand would automatically be an instance of the class).

In order for the stream operators to be able to access `private` and `protected` data elements, in spite of the definition in the file space, they are usually declared as `friends` in the classes for which they are overloaded.

## Example

```
class Vector {
    double x, y, z;
public:
    ...
  // friend declaration
  friend ostream & operator<<(ostream & os, const Vector & v);
};

// overloading in file area
ostream & operator<<(ostream & os, const Vector & v)
  {
  os << v.x << " " << v.y << " " << v.z << endl;
  return os;
  }
```

## References

See Reference section, category classes, access specifiers.

See Reference section, category classes, access from outside the class.

See category input and output.

# Category: program control

# Infinite loops

```
for(;;)
while (1)
```

## Description

A deliberate infinite loop is present when the loop is to be continued until a certain condition is met. The loop condition no longer ensures the termination of the loop, but has a special code within the statement section of the loop, which leaves the loop with the help of a break or return statement.

## Implementation

To implement an infinite loop with the keyword while, you must specify, instead of the loop condition, the value 1 (which corresponds to true).

```
while(1) {
   ...
if(condition)
    break;   // quit loop
  ...
  }
```

To implement an infinite loop with the keyword for, you must use a special syntax:

```
for(;;)  {
   ...
  if(condition)
    break;   // quit loop
  ...
  }
```

## Example

The following program reads numbers in an infinite loop and outputs their roots. Since the roots of numbers smaller than zero are not defined, the program uses this as the break condition. The user can, therefore, terminate the program by entering a number smaller than or equal to zero. However, to check the value of the input in the loop condition would be fatal, as in that case the function sqrt() would be called with an invalid value. That is why the program checks the input directly in the loop and, if required, terminates it before sqrt() is called.

```
#include <stdio.h>
#include <math.h>
```

```
int main()
  {
  int value;

  while(1)
    {
    printf("Enter a number\t");
    scanf("%d",& value);
    fflush(stdin);

    if(value<=0)
      break;    // quit loop

    printf("The root of %d is %lf\n\n",value, sqrt(value));
    }

  return 0;
  }
```

## Tip
Always make sure that the infinite loop is exited correctly.

## Reference
See Reference section, category program control, loops.

# Menus with switch

## Description
More extensive programs usually make their commands available for selection in the form of menus. This also applies to Windows programs (whose description lies outside the scope of this book) as well as for console applications without a graphic user interface.

## Implementation
It is possible to equip console applications in a simple way with a (non-graphic) menu by outputting the list of menu commands on screen and stipulating various keys (digits or letters) to select the commands. If the user presses one of the suggested keys, the value of the key is read, analysed and answered with the calling of a corresponding function. The assignment of keys to the functions that are to be called occurs in a switch statement.

## Example

The menu:

```
vvoid menu()
  {
  printf("\n Menu \n\n");
  printf("Enter new addresses      <1> \n");
  printf("Search for address       <2> \n");
  printf("Output address list      <3> \n");
  printf("Finish program           <4> \n\n");
  }
```

Calling of the menu and evaluation:

```
int main()
  {
  int command;

  do  {
    menu();                          // display menu

    command = 0;                     // query user input
    while (command<1 || command>4)
      {
      printf("Your application : ");
      scanf("%d",&command);
      }

    switch(command)                  // process command
      {
      case '1': input();
              break;
      case '2': search();
              break;
      case '3': output();
              break;
      }

    } while (command!=4);            // do not abort

  return 0;
  }
```

## Reference

See Reference section, category program control, loops.

# Category: functions

# Pointers and references as parameters

call by reference

## Application

There can be several reasons for the definition of pointer types as parameters:

- avoiding the time-consuming and memory-intensive copying of larger arguments,
- making it possible to change the object which has been passed as an argument to the parameter, within the function, and
- you have no other choice but to pass a pointer.

## Implementation

### Reducing the amount of copying

At function call, suitable arguments, variables of the same or convertible data types, are passed to the parameters of the function. Memory is reserved for the parameter in the stack frame of the function and the value of the argument is copied into the parameter. If objects of classes with extensive data elements are passed as arguments, the copying required can be very labour-intensive. This can be reduced by passing a reference (or pointer) to the object instead of the object itself. Traditionally, a pointer is used. In C++, it is more secure and easier to use a reference, provided you only want to reduce the amount of copying needed.

A possible disadvantage when passing references is that the function can change the argument itself (see below). If this is undesirable, you must define the pointer or reference parameter as a reference (or pointer) to a const object.

The const declaration also has the advantage that it is possible to pass const arguments, which otherwise would not be the case. The reason is simply that the passing of parameters is like an assignment and, for assignments, the types of the terms to the left and right of the assignment must be compatible and the left-hand term must have all or more type qualifiers (const, volatile) that the right-hand term has.

### Access to argument

At function call, the parameter is installed as a copy of its argument. If the value of a parameter is changed within the function, this only concerns the parateter and not the object which has been passed as argument at function call.

However, if you want the function to be able to change the object, which has been passed as an argument, you must define the parameter as a reference (or pointer) and pass the address of the object as an argument.

## Elements that must be passed as pointers

Arrays and functions can only be passed as pointers. It is also possible to use pointers (base class pointers, pointers to void) for the implementation of generic functions which can adopt elements of different data types (apart from the option as function template).

## Example

The following example illustrates the use of pointer and reference parameters.

The first parameter of the function func() has been defined as a pointer for the function to change the passed argument (in the example int var;) through the parameter. The second parameter adopts arguments of one class type and, thus, has been defined as a reference, in order to reduce the amount of copying. To ensure that the function cannot change the passed object through the parameter (and also to accept const objects), the parameter has been defined as a reference to const objects.

```
#include <iostream>
using namespace std;

class demo {
  public:
    int value;
    demo(): value(3) {}
  };

void func(int *param1, const demo& param2)
  {
  *param1 = 33;          // also modifies the argument
  // param2.value = 33;  // error: const parameter
  }

int main()
  {
  int var = 10;
  const demo obj;
  cout << "var before function call: " << var << endl;

  func(&var, obj);

  cout << "var after function call: " << var << endl;

  return 0;
  }
```

Output:

```
var before function call: 10
var after function call: 33
```

## References

See Reference section, category functions, parameters; functions and the stack.

# Local static variables

## Application

The keyword static implies local validity and a single allocation (the latter means that static elements are not created on the stack).

## Implementation

Local variables of functions are reallocated at function call and deleted when the function is left. If such a variable has been declared as static, memory is only reserved at the first call of the function and, if required, initialised. Additionally, the lifespan of local variables ends with the program and not the function.

## Warning

Declarations of function parameters and function declarations in a block area cannot be specified as static.

Classes cannot be declared as static.

## Example

```
#include <stdio.h>

void func()
{
  static int callcounter = 0;
  callcounter++;

  printf("%d. call\n", callcounter);
}


int main (auto int argc, char **argv)
{
```

```
int loop;
for (loop = 0; loop < 12; loop++)
  func();

return 0;
}
```

## References

See category multi-file programs, restricting elements to one module.

See Reference section, category classes, static data elements.

# Recursive functions

## Application

Recursion is when a function calls itself up again.

## Implementation

Various problems, for example the calculation of faculty, can be elegantly solved by means of recursion.

Mathematically, faculty is defined as:

```
n! = 1,                    if n = 0
n! = 1 * 2 * 3 ... * n-1 * n,    for n = 1, ..
```

or to formulate it recursively:

```
fac(0) = 1;
fac(n) = n * fac(n-1);
```

The recursive formula can easily be transformed into a recursive function (see example below).

## Warning

Note that, for recursive functions, the recursion must be ended at some point and cannot continue ad infinitum.

Recursion also involves a further problem, and this is connected with the function calls. Function calls result in a function overhead and occupy memory on the stack. At a high recursion depth, this can become a problem.

### Example

Recursive function for the calculation of faculty:

```
int fac(int number) {
   if (number == 0)
      return 1;
   return (number * fac(number-1));
   }
```

# Functions with any number of arguments

### Application

C/C++ also allows the definition of functions with an unknown number of parameters.

### Implementation

The implementation of functions with any number of arguments is based on two elements:

```
double middle(int number, ...)
```

- **Ellipse.** The ellipse in the parameter list ... indicates that any number of arguments may follow the call. The ellipse must stand at the end of the parameter definition and it must be preceded by a proper parameter which indicates, within the function, the number of parameters that will follow.

The va_Macros from <stdarg.h>. These are used to adopt and evaluate arguments.

| Macro | Description |
|---|---|
| va_list | va_list is the array type which stores the information required by va_arg and va_end. When a called-up function adopts a variable argument list, it declares a variable ap of the type va_list. |
| va_start | va_start is a macro which sets ap as the first variable parameter that is passed to the function. va_start must be called before va_arg and va_end. |
| va_arg | The macro va_arg expects a pointer ap to one of the variable parameters and the data type of the parameter. The first call of va_arg returns the value of the first variable parameter and increases ap accordingly, so that afterwards ap points to the next parameter. Further calls of va_arg – again with ap – return the following parameter. |
| va_end | The macro va_end helps the called-up function to carry out a normal return. va_end should be called after va_arg has processed all arguments. |

## Processing variable parameters

You must declare an `ap` object of the `var_list` type.

```
va_list ap;
```

Then you must call `va_start` with `ap` and the last normal parameter.

```
va_start(ap, number);
```

Now you can run through and evaluate the list of parameters by means of `va_arg`

```
va_arg(ap,int);
```

At the end of the function you must call `va_end`

```
va_end(ap);
```

## Example

The following program defines a function `middle()`, which calculates the mean for any number of arguments.

```
#include <stdio.h>
#include <stdarg.h>

double middle(int number, ...)
  {
  double sum = 0;
  va_list ap;
  int loop;

  va_start(ap, number);
  for(loop=1;loop<= number;loop++)
    sum += va_arg(ap,int);

  va_end(ap);
  return sum/number;
  }

int main(void)
  {
  printf("the arithmetical average of 1+2+3+4 is %lf\n",
         average(4,1,2,3,4));
  return 0;
  }
```

## Reference

Compare to function `printf()` of the C runtime library.

# Overloading

## Application

C++ allows you to define several functions with the same name – as long as the functions are different with regard to their parameters.

How can this concept be usefully employed?

## Implementation

In principle, overloading functions only makes sense if it improves the clarity of the program. This is surely not the case if you assign identical names to functions that carry out different tasks.

To rephrase overloading functions makes sense when there is a task has to be carried out in a different manner according to the passed parameter types.

For example, the following functions are present in the ANSI C runtime library for the calculation of powers:

```
double pow10(int p);
double pow(double x, double y);
```

Instead of memorising two different names, you can write two overloaded functions which call the corresponding RTL functions subject to the parameter list:

```
double power(int p) {
    return pow10(p);
    }

double power(double x, double y) {
    return pow(x, y);
    }
```

However, may be you only require a range of functions to determine the maximum number of object pairs of different data types:

```
int max(int a, int b) {
    return ( a > b ? a : b);
    }

char* max(const char* s1, const char* s2) {
    return (strcmp(s1,s2) ? s1 : s2);
    }

 int max(int a, char* s) {
    return ( a > strlen(s) ? a : strlen(s));
    }
```

Thus, it is possible to write type-independent functions by overloading, like the above max() function, which can be called with integer values as well as with strings. To implement type-independent functions, you should also consider the use of templates or the combination of templates and overloaded functions.

Constructors of classes are a good operational area for overloading, because they make it possible for an object of a class to be determined on the basis of different data. With the help of overloaded constructors, it is possible to create new objects of the class on the basis of different arguments. Since constructors carry the same name as their class, it follows that several constructors for one class can only be established through overloading.

## Example

The following Vector class defines several overloaded constructors, that allow the creation of three-dimensional vectors on the basis of individual double coordinates, points or without specifications.

```
struct Punct {
  double x,y;
  };

class Vector {
  public:
   double x, y, z;
  public:
   Vector() {
      x = y = z = 0;
      }
   Vector(double a, double b, double c) {
      x = a; y = b; z = c;
      }
   Vector(Punct p) {
      x = p.x; y = p.y; z = 0;
      }
   Vector(Punct p, double c) {
      x = p.x; y = p.y; z = c;
      }
  };
```

## References

See category classes, default constructor.

See Reference section, category functions, overloading.

# Category: classes

# Class definition

## Application

By defining classes, the programmer can introduce new data types. Here classes have the advantage that they can gather data elements and methods that you can control by access specifiers; class elements are available from outside, and that you can create classes through inheritance on the basis of existing classes and construct complex class hierarchies. But, how should an individual class be constructed?

## Implementation

The most important thing in the conception of a class is that the class is self-contained. This means that

- a class should define all the elements (data elements and methods), which are required for working efficiently with the class, and
- a class should not contain unnecessary elements.

These two guidelines are very important, but they are also vague. The following technical guidelines, which are listed here in brief and discussed in detail on the following pages, are more practical.

- If you are in doubt, a class should possess a default constructor, since there are several restrictions for the use of classes without a default constructor.
- As a rule classes should declare data elements as `private` and only permit their manipulation through `public` methods. This adds to the internal security of the class.
- Classes should define a copy constructor and an assignment operator if they contain data elements which cannot be copied 1:1. This is done by the default versions of copy constructor and assignment operator.
- Classes with pointers as instance variables should always define a copy constructor and an assignment operator and carry out dynamic memory management in the class constructor and the destructor.
- Use the advantages of operator overloading.
- Base classes should define a virtual destructor. (See Reference section, category inheritance and polymorphism, inheritance and destructor.)
- Classes which are used together with STL containers and STL algorithms must meet certain requirements. (See the STL, preparing classes for containers and algorithms.)

# Default constructor

classname() {...}

## Application
A default constructor is a constructor which can be called without arguments.

Since the establishment of class objects is always linked with the calling of a suitable constructor, all classes must have a constructor. Therefore, the C++ compiler automatically assigns a default constructor with an empty statement section to classes which do not have their own constructor. If, on the other hand, the class defines its own constructor, the compiler does not produce a default constructor – thus, the class does not possess a default constructor unless has explicitly been defined in the class.

## Disadvantages of default constructors
Constructors are not only used to create objects in classes, but also have the task of correctly initialising the data elements of the created objects. This can be of crucial importance for the secure use of the class (just imagine what would happen if a class defines a pointer as an instance variable, and a method of the class which de-references this pointer is called before the pointer has been linked to a valid address).

- In order to ensure that objects in classes are initialised correctly, you can define your own default constructor. Like the default constructor of the compiler, it can be called without arguments. However, it does not have an empty statement section, but uses the statement section to initialise data elements.

- Sometimes a useful initialisation is only possible by passing arguments to the constructor during the creation of an object. In such a case, it is possible to define further constructors which can be called with arguments in addition to the default constructor.

- If you want to ensure that objects in a class are only created by passing values to the constructor, you must define your own constructors with parameters (which also stop the provision of the compiler default constructor) and do not define your own default constructor.

The rejection of the default constructor ensures the secure use of the class.

## Advantages of default constructors

If a class does not possess a default constructor, this means that corresponding arguments must be passed at each instance formation of objects of that class.

This is not a problem in normal instance formation. Instead of

```
class demo obj;
```

you simply write:

```
class demo obj(3);
```

However, there are also cases when instance formation runs in the background and the compiler automatically tries to involve the default constructor in instance formation. If it does not succeed, because a default constructor has not been defined, automatic instance formation cannot be carried out, and the compiler terminates with an error. The cases with instance formation in the background concern the following.

### Establishing inherited elements

When you create an object of a derived class, the compiler automatically calls up the default constructor of the base class (or the default constructors, if there are several base classes) to establish the inherited elements.

If the base class does not possess a default constructor, the constructor of the base class must be extended by a constructor list in which a suitable constructor of the base class is explicitly called.

### Establishing embedded objects

The same applies here as for establishing the inherited elements of a derived class.

### Establishing array elements

When you create an array of class objects, a constructor must be called for each element in the array. If a default constructor has been defined in the class of array elements, the compiler can automatically call a constructor for each array element.

If the class does not possess a default constructor, the array elements must be initialised that specifies a constructor call for each array element. For large arrays this is a very inconvenient task.

## Implementation

The constructor assigned by the compiler is a default constructor, because it can be called without arguments, but it is not really the default constructor. Every constructor which you define yourself and which does not define parameters or only defines parameters with default arguments, is also a default constructor.

Each of the three constructors mentioned below is a default constructor, and each can be used by the compiler for automatic initialisation.

```
demo()
demo(int i = 3)
demo(int i = 4, double d = 2.0)
```

However, it is not possible to define all three of these constructors in a single class:

```
class demo
  {
    int value;

  public:
    demo()                                    {value = 0;}
    demo(int i = 3)                           {value = i;}
    demo(int i = 4, double d = 2.0)           {value = i*d;}
    int distribute() {cout << "value = " << value << endl;}
  };
```

If you now attempt to establish an instance with one of the default constructors (if you do not pass any arguments), the compiler cannot resolve the call, since it has three constructors available which all are equally suitable. (Remember that the compiler considers the types of the arguments when resolving a call. This is a call without arguments, and there are three constructors at once which can be called without argument.)

## Example

Class with default constructor assigned by the compile;

```
class demo
  {
    int value;

  public:
    int distribute() {cout << "value = " << value << endl;}
  };
```

The following example defines its own default constructor in order to initialise its data element with a defined value.

```
class demo
  {
    int value;

  public:
    demo()        {value = 0;}
    int output() {cout << "value = " << value << endl;}
  };
```

In the last example, the class allows initialisations with and without arguments. By the definition of default arguments, the default constructor and argument constructor have been joined.

```
class demo
  {
    int value;

  public:
    demo(int i = 3)      {value = i;}
};
```

## References

See Reference section, category classes, the constructor; class instances as data elements; category inheritance and polymorphism, inheritance and constructors.

# Private data – public methods

## Application

The data elements of a class always pose a certain security problem. The class methods work with the data elements and often assume that these such data contain meaningful values. Insofar as the data elements have been initialised in the constructor and are only processed by class methods, this is correct, provided the class has carefully been implemented. However, if it is also possible to access the data elements, and if their value can be changed from outside the class, the functionality of the class may be impaired or even destroyed.

This is simple because the programmer who has written the class and the programmer who uses the class, are not necessarily the same person. The latter often lacks insight into the internal workings of the class.

Suppose the following class is given:

```
class demo {
class demo {
 public:
    int data[10];          // array for data storage
    int maximum;           // maximum value in array
    int number;            // number of values in array
    ...
  };
```

The methods defined in the class ensure that when values are inserted or deleted in the data array, the data elements maximum and number are always updated. If a programmer directly accesses the data array to store a new value in it, for example

```
demo obj;
obj.data[5] = 312;
```

we may forget to update the data elements maximum and number. This may lead to errors in future.

The user of the class cannot be blamed for this, since it is the responsibility of the class to protect its data.

## Implementation

If you want to ensure that a data element can only adopt certain values, or that the querying and assigning of values is linked to certain operations (such as the updating of the data elements maximum and number above), you must declare the data element as private (to prevent access through instances: obj.data element).

- If you want to give the option to query the value of the data element or to assign a value to the data element to the user of the class, you must define public methods for this purpose to ensure that queries and assignments are executed correctly.

- If you want to allow direct access to the data element to programmers who derive their own classes from the class, you must define the data element as protected.

## Example

```
#include <iostream>
using namespace std;

class demo {
    int data[10];          // array for data storage
    int maximum;           // maximum value in array
    int number;            // number of values in array
```

```
public:
  demo() {
    for (int i = 0; i < 5; i++)
      data[i] = i;
    maximum = 4;
    number = 5;
    }

  int value_insert(int value) {
    if (number < 10)                    // any space left in array?
      {
      if (value > maximum)              // update maximum
        maximum = value;
      data[number] = value;            // insert value
      number++;                         // update number
      return 1;
      }
    else
      return 0;
    }

  int value_ask(int pos) throw (char*) {
    if(pos < number)
      return data[pos];
     else {
      throw "Invalid Index";
      return 0;
      }
    }

  int get_number()  {return number;}
  int get_maximum() {return maximum;}
};

int main() {
  try {
    demo obj;

    obj.value_insert(12);
    for (int i = 0; i < obj.get_number(); i++)
      cout << i << " = " << obj.value_insert(i) << endl;
    }
  catch(char* str) {
    cout << str;
    }

  return 0;
  }
```

## References

See Reference section, category classes, access specifiers; category inheritance and polymorphism, access restriction in inheritance.

# Copying class objects: copy constructor and assignment operator

## Application

The copy constructor is called when you initialise a class instance with the values of another class instance. The copy constructor is also implicitly called when passing class objects to functions/methods and when returning class objects as return values of functions/methods (unless pointers or references are used).

However, to make an existing instance the copy of another instance, you must use the assignment operator.

Each class automatically possesses a copy instructor and an assignment operator which both copy 1:1. This results in errors if the class contains pointers. This is simply because the addressees contained in that pointer are copied, so that after copy initialisation, the two pointers of the original and the copy both point to the same object. However, what is usually desired 'deep copying' in which not the addresses in the pointer elements, but the objects to which the pointers refer, are copied.

## Implementation

If your classes contain pointers, you should define your own implementations of the copy constructor and the assignment operator.

## Warning

If you want to prevent objects in a class from being created on the basis of other objects of that class (copy constructor), or objects being assigned to one another (assignment operator), you must declare the copy constructor and the assignment operator in the class as `private`.

## Example

In the following example the pointer refers to another instance variable of the class. Therefore, there is no dynamic memory reservation. In the following

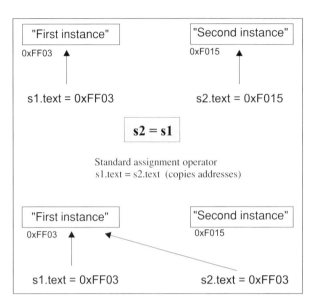

paragraph, Pointers as instance variables you will find an example with dynamic memory reservation.

```
class demo {
    int  i;
    int* p;
  public:
    demo(int value)   {i = value; p= &i;}

    demo(const demo& obj) {                    // copy constructor
       i = obj.i; p = &i;
       }
    demo& operator=(const demo &obj)    // allocation operator
      {
      if(this != &obj) {
        i = obj.i;
        p = &i;
        }
      return *this;
      }
  };
...
demo a1(3), a2(7);

demo b(a1);     // call copy constructor
b = a2;         // call assignment operator
```

## Reference

See pointers as instance variables (on p. 542).

# Pointers as instance variables

## Application

If you define pointers as instance variables, you should note three points:

- they are responsible for correct memory management,
- they are responsible for correct copying, and
- they are responsible for correct reading and writing.

## Implementation

The proper place for allocating memory and assigning memory to a pointer is the constructor. The memory is freed up in the destructor.

With regard to copying, please read the preceding section about the copy constructor and the assignment operator.

There are even more problems than with copying if you want to save objects of a class persistently in a file and, if required, reconstruct them. See the section on persistent classes.

## Example

```cpp
#include <iostream>
using namespace std;

class demo {
public:
    int  num_values;
    int* p;
  public:
    demo(int number);                  // constructor
    ~demo();                           // destructor
    demo(const demo& obj);             // copy constructor
    demo& operator=(const demo &obj);  // assignment operator
  };

// definition of the destructor
demo::~demo()   {
      delete p;                        // delete field
      }

// definition of the constructor
demo::demo(int number)   {
      num_values = number;             // store number of elements
      p = new int[number];             // allocate memory
      for(int i=0; i < num_values; i++) // initialise field elements
        p[i] = i;
```

```
      }

// definition of the copy constructor
demo::demo(const demo& obj) {
     num_values = obj.num_values;       // store number of elements
     p = new int[num_values];           // allocate memory
     for(int i=0; i < num_values; i++)  // copy field elements
       p[i] = obj.p[i];
     }

// definition of the assignment operator
demo& demo::operator=(const demo &obj) {
     if(this != &obj) {                 // avoid self-assigment
       num_values = obj.num_values;     // store number of elements
       delete[] p;                      // free old memory
       p = new int[num_values];         // reallocate memory
       for(int i=0; i < num_values; i++) // copy field elements
         p[i] = obj.p[i];
       }
     return *this;
     }

int main() {
  demo a1(3), a2(7);

  demo b(a1);            // call copy constructor
  b = a2;                // call assignment operator
  return 0;
  }
```

## References

See copying class objects.

See persistent classes.

# Overloading operators: +, <<

## Application

Wherever it makes sense and it is possible, you should use overloading operators instead of defining your own methods (or at least offer both).

## Implementation

If you, for example, write a class for three-dimensional vectors, you should implement algebraic operations such as addition, subtraction, scalar multiplication and vector multiplication through overloading of the suitable C++ operators.

The use (not the implementation) of operators is easier, quicker and produces a clearer source text, provided that it is easy to understand which operations the operator should carry out for the data types of its operands.

Thus, it is more natural to write

```
class Vector v1, v2, v3;
...
v1 = v2 + v3;
```

than

```
v1.add(v2, v3);
```

Often it is also appropriate to override the stream operators for reading and outputting objects of the class. The output stream operator << is very useful for debugging purposes.

## Example

```
#include <iostream>
using namespace std;

class Vector {
   double x, y, z;
 public:
  Vector(double a, double b, double c) {
     x = a; y = b; z = c;
     }
  Vector& operator+=(const Vector & v);
  Vector  operator+ (const Vector & v);
  friend ostream & operator<<(ostream & os, const Vector & v);
 };

Vector& Vector::operator+=(const Vector & v)  {
  x += v.x;
  y += v.y;
```

```
    z += v.z;
    return *this;
    }

Vector Vector::operator+(const Vector & v)  {
    return Vector(x+v.x, y+v.y, z+v.z);
    }

// overloading in file area
ostream & operator<<(ostream & os, const Vector & v)  {
    os << v.x << " " << v.y << " " << v.z << endl;
    return os;
    }

int main()  {
    Vector v1(1,0,0), v2(0,0,1), v3(3,3,3);

    cout << "v1 = " << v1 << endl;
    cout << "v2 = " << v2 << endl;
    cout << "v3 = " << v3 << endl;

    cout << "v1 + v2 = " << v1+v2 << endl;
    cout << "v1 + v2 + v3 = " << v1+(v2+v3) << endl;

    v1 += v3;
    cout << "v1 + v3 = " << v1 << endl;

    v1 += v2 += v3;
    cout << "v1 + v2 + v3 = " << v1 << endl;

    return 0;
    }
```

## Reference

See category operators, overloading operators.

# Conversion methods

## Example of a vector class

### Application

A constructor that can be called with only one argument is a conversion constructor of the type of its argument into the type of its class. Unless such a constructor has been declared as explicit, it is included in the default conversions of the compiler.

In many cases, however, the reverse conversion (from the type of class into another type) would also be desirable.

## Implementation

To convert an object of a class into an object of a different type, you can:

- define a method which returns the converted object as the return type, or
- overload the cast operator, so that this conversion is also included in the repertoire of default conversions.

## Example

The following program uses the conversion constructor and the cast operator.

```
#include <iostream>
using namespace std;

class complex   {
    double  value1;
    double  value2;
  public:
    // can be used as conversion constructor
    complex(const double par1, const double par2 = 0) {
      value1 = par1;
      value2 = par2;
      }
    // overload cast operator
    operator double() {
      return value1;
      }
   };

int main()  {
  double d;
  complex obj = 3;   // call conversion constructor
  d = obj;           // call conversion method

  return 0;
  }
```

## References

See copying class objects.

See category operators, overloading operators.

# Persistent classes

## Application

Occasionally, you may need to save objects in classes to a file (whether it is a simple text file or a database) and, if required, reconstruct them again (probably when calling the program again).

## Implementation

Problems arise when persistently saving and reconstructing classes if the classes contain pointers, especially pointers to class objects.

The first rule for persistent saving of objects is that you must be careful to save the objects to which they point ('deep copying').

Furthermore, there are additional problems:

- **Several pointers can refer to the same object.** In such cases, it would be convenient to save the object which is referred to only once. However, in any case you must rebuild the old reference structure, when reconstructing the object. This can be achieved by ensuring that the classes of the objects all go back to one base class, which defines a data element in which an object marker can be stored. If a reference (or pointer) to a new object is to be written into the file, the object is saved with a marker and recorded in a table. By using this table, it can be determined if a further reference to this object is to be saved. In this case, only the object ID is stored.

- **Should objects be saved by means of embedded or sequential saving?** In embedded saving, objects which are referred to are saved at the position of the reference (that is, within the object that contains a pointer or a reference to the object). In sequential saving, only the object marker is saved for references and the object itself is entered into a table under its marker.

- **Which type is an object?** When reconstructing an object, its data type has to be known. If objects of different data types are stored in a file, this may mean that the information about the data type must be saved together with the object, for example, by saving the class name.

- **In which sequence is the reconstruction carried out?** When reconstructing several objects which contain references to other objects, it must be noted that a reference can only be established correctly when the object which is to be referred to has been created correctly beforehand.

## References

See copying class objects.

A detailed description of the implementation of a class hierarchy which supports the saving and reconstruction of objects in your class is not possible within the scope of this book. Interested readers should have a look at <u>Object-oriented Programming in C++</u> by Nicolai Josuttis, published by Addison-Wesley.

# Category: inheritance and polymorphism

# Inheritance as an extension of existing classes

## Application

Inheritance is usually used for two reasons:

- You may want to extend an existing class and adapt it to your special requirements, use the functionality of an existing class in a class that is to be redefined.

- You may want to construct a class hierarchy and use polymorphism (see next paragraph).

## Implementation

If you only want to make available the functionality of a class to another class (grant access to data elements and methods), this can be done, apart from through inheritance, through `friend` declaration or embedding (objects as data elements).

- **Inheritance versus friend declaration.** The `friend` declaration is a drastic form of granting a class (or individual methods of the class) access to the elements of another class, since it circumvents the security mechanisms of that class (`friend` classes and methods have access to all, even `private`, elements of the class. Secondly, the `friend` declaration can only be used in a limited way, since the `friend` declaration must occur within the class whose elements are to be accessed. Therefore, you must have the source text of the class available, and be able to recompile it, which is not necessarily the case for classes of bought libraries. Third, the `friend` declaration does not offer you the specific advantages of inheritance and polymorphism).

- **Inheritance versus embedding.** Unless you are interested in the special options of polymorphism, and only want to use the functionality of another class in your class, you have a choice between inheritance (deriving a class from another class) and embedding (declaration of an instance variable of the type of the other class). You would choose inheritance if the object in your class is also an object in the other class (for example an object of the class `Sportscar` is also an object of the class `Car`). The basic condition is usually that all elements of the other class (the future base class) are also meaningful in your (derived) class. You would choose embedding if you can claim that an object of the other class is contained in all elements of your class (for example each object of the class `Sportscar` also contains an object of the class `Motor` and four objects of the class `Wheel`).

## References

See inheritance and polymorphism.

See guidelines for inheritance.

See Reference section, category inheritance and polymorphism, inheritance versus embedding; polymorphism; base class pointers.

# Inheritance and polymorphism

## Application

Polymorphism, which means 'varied in form', refers to a phenomenon which for the programmer means that he can handle different objects (which react differently) in the same way.

The different objects are objects of the various classes of a common class hierarchy (see below). Objects of different classes can be handled in the same way because they possess identical interfaces (identical `public` data elements and methods). The objects react differently because methods which have the same name in all classes can be implemented differently in each class.

## Implementation

To implement polymorphous behaviour for objects of different classes, inheritance, the overriding of methods and the keyword `virtual` are required. A typical example for the implementation of polymorphous objects is a class hierarchy for the management of graphic objects in a graphics program.

The program supports lines, rectangles and circles, for which separate classes are implemented. The polymorphism manifests itself in that objects of these classes can be output through the method `draw()` which is identical in all classes.

- **Inheritance.** Polymorphism only works for classes of a common class hierarchy. Therefore, the classes `Line`, `Rectangle` and `Circle` are derived from a common derived class `DrawingObject`. It is important that the shared interface of the derived classes (in this example the method `draw()`) has already been defined in the base class and is inherited from it.

- **Overriding.** Because the method draw() has been defined in the base class, it is inherited to all derived classes and can be called for line, rectangle or circle objects. However, for the method to show polymorphous behaviour, it must be overridden in the derived classes and be equipped with its own definition section with class-specific statements.

- **virtual.** To ensure that at the call of an overridden method for a derived class the overridden version and not the version of the base class is always called, the methods that are to be overridden must be declared as virtual in the base class. This is not necessary, but it is customary, to mark the overridden methods as virtual in the derived classes, too.

## Example

```
class DrawingObject {                    // base class
  ...
  public:
    virtual ~DrawingObject() {}
    virtual void draw() const {
      cout << "X";
      }
  };

class Line : public DrawingObject {
  ...
  public:
    virtual void draw() const {
      cout << "I";
      }
  };

class Rectangle : public DrawingObject {
  ...
  public:
    virtual void draw() const {
      cout << "#";
      }
  };

class Circle : public DrawingObject {
  ...
  public:
    virtual void draw() const {
      cout << "O";
      }
  };
```

## References

See guidelines for inheritance.

See base class pointers and arrays.

See base class pointers as parameters.

See sections on RTTI.

# Guidelines for inheritance

## Application

There are a few basic rules for inheritance which can help you to avoid errors, but which are not written in store. C++ is a language in which it is important not to restrict the freedom of the programmer, even if this means that security is impaired. Following the rules described below, security will remain a priority, which in most cases is desirable.

## Implementation

### When writing a base class, note that:

- all elements that are common to the derived classes should be assembled in the base class,
- elements which are also to be available through instances of the derived classes (interface) should be declared as `public`: elements which are only there for the implementation of the derived classes (thus, they are used in their methods), should be declared as `protected`; and elements which are only important for the implementation of the base class should be declared as `private`,
- methods which can or should be overridden in the derived classes should be declared as `virtual`. Otherwise the version of the method which is suitable for the type of the pointer and not the type of the object is called for pointers to objects. (Remember: objects of derived classes can be assigned to a pointer to a base class type.),
- base classes should define a virtual destructor (for the above reason), and
- methods which must be overridden in the derived classes are declared as virtual. (This implies that it is not possible to form instances of the class.)

### When writing a derived class, note that:

- you should only override methods which have been declared as `virtual` in the base classes, and

- inherited methods cannot be overloaded, but they can be overridden (i.e. the base class version is hidden) and then overloaded.

## Reference

See Reference section, category inheritance and polymorphism, inheritance versus embedding.

# Base class pointers and arrays

## Application

A base class pointer is a pointer which refers to objects of the type of a base class. A special characteristic of the base class pointer is that it is also possible to assign to it objects of classes that have been derived from the base class. This can be used to:

- manage objects of different derived classes in a single array or dynamic field, and

- define parameters which can adopt objects of the base class as well as of the various derived classes as arguments, in methods (see next section).

## Implementation

First, an array or a dynamic field which has base class pointers as elements is defined.

Then, you enter the addresses of objects of the base class or the derived class into the array/field.

Insofar as you only have to call virtual methods for objects, you can do this directly through the base class pointers (for more about this topic, see paragraphs on runtime type identification, RTTI).

## Warning

Only store pointers to objects of derived classes in an array. Usually, you could also directly deposit objects of a derived class in an array for base class objects; however, you then lose the advantages of polymorphism. Furthermore, you should not treat arrays of derived objects as arrays of base class objects (for example by passing them to a corresponding function parameter).

# Example

```
#include <iostream>
using namespace std;

// class hierarchy as in section inheritance and polymorphism
class DrawingObject { ... };
class Line      : public DrawingObject { ... };
class Rectangle : public DrawingObject { ... };
class Circle    : public DrawingObject { ... };

int main()  {
  class DrawingObject  *geomFig[10];      // array of base class pointers

  int wehichObject;
  for(int loop = 0; loop < 10; loop++)
     {
     whichObject = rand() % 3;
     switch (whichObject)   {
       case 0  :  geomFig[loop] = new Line();     // store objects
                  break;                          // in array
       case 1  :  geomFig[loop] = new Rectangle();
                  break;
       case 2  :  geomFig[loop] = new Circle();
                  break;

       }
     }

  for(int loop = 0; loop < 10; loop++)  {       // draw objects
    geomFig[loop]->draw();                      // call virtual
    }                                           // method

  return 0;
  }
```

# References

See inheritance and polymorphism.

See base class pointers as parameters.

See paragraphs on RTTI.

See Reference section, category inheritance and polymorphism, base class pointers.

# Base class pointers as parameters

## Application

A base class pointer is a pointer which refers to objects of the type of a base class. The special characteristic of the base class pointer is that it is also possible to assign to it objects of classes that have been derived from the base class. This can be used to:

- manage objects of different derived classes in a single array or dynamic field, or
- define parameters to adopt objects of the base class as well as of the various derived classes as arguments, in methods (see next section).

## Implementation

First, an array or a dynamic field is defined with base class pointers as elements.

Next, it is possible to enter the addresses of objects of the base class or the derived class into the array/field.

Since you only have to call virtual methods for objects, you can do this directly through the base class pointers (for more information on this topic, see paragraphs on runtime type identification, RTTI).

## Example

```
#include <iostream>
using namespace std;

// class hierarchy as in section inheritance and polymorphism
class DrawingObject { ... };
class Line      : public DrawingObject { ... };
class Rectangle : public DrawingObject { ... };
class Circle    : public DrawingObject { ... };

// funktion which takes over base class objects
void mark(const DrawingObject& object) {
    cout << " -----" << endl;
    cout << "|   ";
    object.draw();
    cout << "   |" << endl;
    cout << " -----" << endl;
    }

int main() {
  class DrawingObject  *geomFig[10];       // array of base class pointers
```

```
    int whichObject;
    for(int loop = 0; loop < 10; loop++)
        {
        whichObject = rand() % 3;
        switch (wewhichObject)   {
          case 0  :  geomFig[loop] = new Line();     // store objects
                     break;                           // in array
          case 1  :  geomFig[loop] = new Rectangle();
                     break;
          case 2  :  geomFig[loop] = new Circle();
                     break;
          }
        }

    for(int loop = 0; loop < 10; loop++)  {
      mark(*geomFig[loop]);                    // call function
      }                                        // pass objects via
                                               // base class pinters
    return 0;
    }
```

## References

See inheritance and polymorphism.

See base class pointers and arrays.

See paragraphs on RTTI.

See Reference section, category inheritance and polymorphism, base class pointers.

# RTTI with virtual methods

virtual

## Application

To be able to work efficiently with base class pointers to derived objects, there must be an option to access the full functionality of the derived object. The main problem of reconversion is type identification: to which derived class type does the object belong, to which the base class pointer refers? To determine this, there are various options in C++:

- virtual methods,
- dynamic_cast, and
- typeid.

## Implementation

For a derived object a virtual method which has been overridden in the derived class is called through a base class pointer:

```
base_ptr = &abg_obj;
base_ptr->overriddenMethod();
```

Type identification is automatically carried out by the compiler. As far as possible, this form of type identification should be used.

## Example

```
#include <iostream>
using namespace std;

class Basis {
   public:
      virtual void identify()      // version of base class
            {cout << "This is the base class\n";};
   };
class Derived : public Basis {
   public:
      virtual void identify()      // version of derived class
            {cout << "This is the derived class\n";};
   };

int main() {
  Derived derived_class;
  Basis *pointer = new Basis;      // pointer of type "pointer to Basis"
  pointer = &derived_class;        // points to object of derived class
  pointer->identify();             // method of object is called
  }
```

Output:

```
»This is the derived class«
```

## Warning

In C++ RTTI runtime identification depends on the existence of virtual methods in the classes. This is because RTTI is only feasible when the compiler stores type information in the classes. In order to avoid making programs unnecessarily complex and keeping costs low, RTTI has been linked to classes with virtual methods in C++, since additional internal code must be created for virtual methods, which can also be used for RTTI, and the existence of virtual methods often means that RTTI will also need to be used.

## References

See RTTI with `dynamic_cast`.

See type identification at runtime.

# RTTI with dynamic_cast

dynamic_cast

## Application

To be able to work efficiently with base class pointers to derived objects, there must be an option to access the full functionality of the derived object. The main problem of reconversion is type identification: to which derived class type does the object belong, to which the base class pointer refers? To determine this, there are various options in C++:

- virtual methods,
- dynamic_cast, and
- typeid.

## Implementation

For a derived object a method which has been redefined in the derived class, or a redefined data element, is to be called through a base class pointer:

```
base_ptr = &abg_obj;
if(abg_ptr = dynamic_cast<Derived *>(base_ptr))  {
  abg_ptr->newMethod();
  abg_ptr->Dataelement();
  }
```

The programmer uses the dynamic_cast operator to convert the base class pointer into a pointer to objects of a derived class and leaves the task of ensuring that the conversion is correct to the operator. The operator is used when virtual methods are inefficient.

## Example

```
#include <iostream>
using namespace std;

class Basis {
   public:
      virtual void identify() {cout << "Basis\n";}
   };

class Derived : public Basis {
   public:
      virtual void identify() {cout << "derived class\n";}
      void own_Method()      {cout << "own method\n";}
   };
```

561

```
int main() {
  Derived der_obj, *der_ptr;
  Basis *base_ptr;                  // base class pointer
  base_ptr = &der_obj;              // points to derived object

  // Rückverwandlung
  if(der_ptr = dynamic_cast<Derived *>(base_ptr)) {
    der_ptr->own_Method();
    }
  return 0;
  }
```

## Tips

The `dynamic_cast` operator can also be used for other pointer conversions and is not dependent on the existence of virtual methods in the classes of the object to be converted. However, downcasts (conversion of a base class pointer (or reference) into a pointer to a derived class) or crosscasts (conversion of a pointer to a base class into a pointer to a second base class (through a common derived class)) are only possible for polymorphous classes; that is, classes that contain virtual methods.

## References

See RTTI with virtual methods.

See type identification at runtime.

# Type identification at runtime: RTTI with typeid

`typeid`

## Application

To be able to work efficiently with base class pointers to derived objects, there must be an option to access the full functionality of the derived object. The main problem of reconversion is type identification: to which derived class type does the object belong, to which the base class pointer refers? To determine this, there are various options in C++:

• virtual methods,

- dynamic_cast, and
- typeid.

## Implementation

The typeid operator creates a corresponding instance of the type_info class (defined in <typeinfo>) for the object passed to it. In this instance, which is returned as a reference by the operator, information about the data type of the passed object is stored. type_info objects can be compared directly with the operators == and !=. The name() method, which returns a string that identifies the type of the typeid operand, can also be called.

## Warning

According to the ANSI standard, types that are only distinguished by the CV qualifiers (const, volatile) are identical. However, some compilers distinguish between these.

For some compilers, you must explicitly activate support for RTTI (runtime type identification) when using typeid.

## Examples

Comparison of two data types:

```
#include <iostream>
#include <typeinfo>
using namespace std;

class demo {int value;};

int main() {
  demo d1();
  const demo d2();

  if(typeid(d1) == typeid(d2))
     cout << "equals" << endl;
  cout << typeid(d1).name() << endl;
  return 0;
  }
```

Comparison of an object which is referred to by a base class pointer, of derived class type:

```
base_ptr = &der_obj;
if(typeid(*base_ptr) == typeid(Derived))  {
   cout << "Object is of Derived type";
   }
```

## Tips

The `typeid()` operator can also be applied to pointers to objects of non-polymorphous classes (classes that do not contain a virtual method) as well as to normal variables. In these cases, the operator simply returns the data type of its operand. Therefore, for a pointer `Basis *ptr`, which refers to an object of the non-polymorphous class `Derived`, it would return the type `Basis *`, and for the de-referencing of the pointer (`*ptr`) the type `Basis`.

## References

See RTTI with virtual methods.

See RTTI with `dynamic_cast`.

# Category: templates

# Type-independent functions

```
template<class T> int func(T a, T b)
```

## Application

A very old problem, which programmers face all the time, is the implementation of type-independent functions. In practice, this usually takes the form of the programmer wanting to write a function for a particular operation, such as the calculation of the maximum of two values. However, the programmer does not only want to calculate the value of `int` values, but also of floating point numbers, strings or even self-defined data types.

For very similar data types, for example `int` and `long`, you simply use the default conversions; that is, you leave it to the compiler to reformat the arguments, so that they are suitable for the type of the parameter.

However, what can you do if there is no default conversion?

## Implementation

In C, you can try to implement the function as a macro. Thus, for example, the function `max()` of the C default library is usually implemented as a macro:

```
#define max(a, b) ((a) > (b) ? (a) : (b))
```

Macros, however, have several shortcomings They:

* are unsuitable for larger functions,

* suspend type checking by the compiler, and

* these are extremely prone to errors.

Therefore, in C++, overloading and definition of templates are used instead of macros.

Function templates and function overloading should not be viewed as competing, but rather as complementing, techniques.

| Strengths of templates | Strengths of overloading |
|---|---|
| The implementation as function template has the advantage that there is only one definition in the source text. This facilitates maintenance, correction and extension of the code. | However, the fact that each overloaded function has its own statement section can be advantageous, namely, when the implementations of the functions are to be different, subject to the type of the parameters. |

| Strengths of templates | Strengths of overloading |
|---|---|
| When translating the program, the compiler independently generates from the template suitable function definitions for the desired function calls. Thus, you do not need to write code for each set of arguments, as is required for overloading. | When overloading, it is possible to vary not only the types of the parameters, but also their number. |

## Tips

The advantages and disadvantages of templates are listed below.

- It is possible to overload templates, through other function templates, through explicit specialisations for particular data types, and through normal functions.

- In many cases it is convenient to use templates by means of overloaded functions or operators. If you, for example, use the > operator in the max function template to determine the maximum, you can not only pass arguments of elementary data types for which the > operator is defined by default to the template, but also arguments of every data type for which the > operator has been overloaded (including self-defined class types).

## Example

Template definition:

```
template<class T> int func(T a, T b)
    {
    if (a == b)
      return 1;
    else
      return 0;
    }
```

Adaptation of a class to use with the template through overloading of the compare operator:

```
class demo {
  public:
    int value;
    demo(int w) { value = w;}

    int operator == (demo& obj) {
      return (value == obj.value) ? 1 : 0;
      }
  };
```

Specialisations of the template:

```
int var = 3;
int *ptr1, *ptr2;
ptr1 = ptr2 = &var;

cout << func(3, var);                    // output: 1
cout << func(3.14, -3.14);               // output: 0
cout << func(ptr1, ptr2);                // output: 1

class demo obj1(1), obj2(2), *p_obj;
p_obj = &obj1;

cout << func(obj1, obj2);                // output: 0
cout << func(obj1, *p_obj);              // output: 1
```

### References

See type-independent classes.

See Reference section, category templates.

# Type-independent classes

```
template<class T> class name {}
```

### Application

Apart from functions (and methods), it is also possible to define classes as templates. The classic example for this is the container classes of the C++ runtime library.

### Implementation

The container classes implement dynamic data structures in which the programmer can store and manage data (the values of elementary data types, objects of classes) in a similar way as in an array. How the data are ultimately stored in the container (whether in the form of a dynamic field, a list, a binary tree or a Hashing table) remains concealed from the programmer. Which methods a container makes available for the management of the data and how efficient the individual insert, delete, and access operations are.

The implementation of such a container class is naturally quite labour-intensive because of the internal memory management. It would take a long time if a separate container class had to be implemented for each data type. The logical consequence is, thus, to define the container class as a template, where a template parameter specifies the data type of the elements, which can be managed in the container.

When implementing the class template, remember that the class template should be used with as many data types as possible, and that the class types of objects which are to be managed in the container can be adapted to the container with as little work as possible.

Thus, the containers of the C++ runtime library only demand the following requirements of the data types of elements that are to be managed:

- copyable (for classes: accessible copy constructor and assignment operator)
- deleteable (for classes: accessible destructor)

as well as for particular operations:

- produceable (for classes: accessible default constructor)
- comparable (for classes: accessible == operator)
- sortable (for classes: accessible < operator)

## References

See category the STL, data management with containers.

See category the STL, preparing classes for containers and algorithms.

# Category: preprocessor directives

# Compiler switches

```
#define PPSwitch
```

## Application

Compiler switches are 'switches' set in a program by means of the `#define` preprocessor directive or passed to the compiler as a command line option.

In the program source text, the compiler switch can be used to exclude specific code blocks from compilation or, conversely, to include them into the program.

## Implementation

To set a compiler switch, you can:

- directly set the switch in the program source text using the #define directive, or
- pass the switch as an option to the compiler. (Check in the compiler manuals what the options are for the definition of compiler switches. Compilers with IDE (integrated drive electronics) usually allow the specification of preprocessor switches through special dialogues for the setting of the project options.)

To temporarily switch off a compiler switch, use the preprocessor directive `#undef`. To switch the compiler switch on again, use the preprocessor directive `#define`.

To query in a program whether a particular compiler switch has been set or not, use the operator `defined()` or the directive `#ifdef`.

To exclude or include code blocks from/in the compilation subject to a compiler switch, use `#if`, `#ifdef`, `#else`, `#elif`, and `#endif`.

## Example

```
#include <iostream>
using namespace std;

int main()
  {
  #if defined(PPSwitch)
    cout << "The switch is set" << endl;
  #else
    cout << "DThe switch is not set" << endl;
  #endif

  return 0;
  }
```

## References

See debugging with conditional compilation.

See Reference section, category preprocessor, directives for conditional compilation.

# Debugging with conditional compilation

```
#if defined(DEBUG_SWITCH)
```

## Application

Compiler switches and the directives for conditional compilation are also suitable, amongst other things, for debugging programs.

## Implementation

For this purpose bracket the debug code (for example, messages about the state of the program, the output of subtotals of calculations, and so on) into an `#if defined` / `#endif` block. Check with the `defined` operator whether the compiler switch has been set for activating the debug output.

You can set the compiler switch directly in the program with `#define` or pass it as an option to the compiler (see compiler documentation).

By defining several compiler switches for debugging you can establish and control debug outputs for special functions or different levels.

## Example

```cpp
#include <iostream>
using namespace std;

#define DEBUG1          // function calls
#define DEBUG2          // calculation of interest

void func1(int param) {
  #if defined(DEBUG1)
    cout << "in func1" << endl;
    cout << "   param = " << param << endl << endl;
  #endif
  ...
  }
```

```
// capital development without compound interest
double interest_gain(double starting_capital,
                     double interest, double runtime) {
  #if defined(DEBUG1)
    cout << "in interest_gain" << endl;
    cout << "   starting_capital = " << starting_capital << endl;
    cout << "   interest         = " << interest << endl;
    cout << "   runtime          = " << runtime << endl << endl;
  #endif

  #if defined(DEBUG2)
    double tmp;
    tmp = zins/100.0;
    cout << "Calculation of ineterest: " << tmp << endl;
    tmp = 1 + tmp * runtime;
    cout << "                   " << tmp << endl;
    tmp = starting_capital * tmp;
    cout << "                   " << tmp << endl;
  #endif
  return starting_capital * (1 + interest/100.0 * runtime);
  }

int main()
  {
  func1(3);
  cout << interest_gain(1000, 3, 10);
  return 0;
  }
```

## References

See compiler switche.s

See Reference section, category preprocessor, directives for conditional compilation.

# Portability with conditional compilation

```
#if defined(DEBUG_SWITCH)
```

## Application

Compiler switches and the directives for conditional compilation are also suitable for creating portable programs, amongst other things.

## Implementation

If you want a program to be compilable for, and able to run on, different platforms and operating systems, you might need to consider operating system-specific features.

Thus, for example Win16 and MS-DOS only permit file names with a maximum length of eight letters and a file extention (i.e. .doc) of three letters. whereas UNIX and Win95/NT support longer file names.

To cope with such situations, it is usual practice to write two alternative code blocks. The code block to be considered at compilation is determined through a compiler switch, which is set directly in the program with #define or passed as an option to the compiler (see compiler documentation).

## Example

```
#include <stdio.h>
#include <string.h>

#define DOS
#undef DOS

union  filetype
    {
    char filename_dos[12];
    char filename_unix[50];
    } file;

int main(int argc, char **argv)
  {
  #ifdef DOS
    strcpy(file.filename_dos,"12345678.txt");
    #else
    strcpy(file.filename_unix,"abcdefghijk.txt");
  #endif

  #ifdef DOS
    printf("In union   : %s\n",file.filename_dos);
    #else
    printf("In union   : %s\n",file.filename_unix);
  #endif

  printf("\nGSize of union   : %d bytes", sizeof(file));

  return 0;
  }
```

Output:

```
In union   : 12345678.txt
Size of union   : 50 bytes
```

## References

See compiler switches.

See Reference section, category preprocessor, directives for conditional compilation.

# Category: exceptions

# Catching exceptions

`try` / `catch`

## Application

Many C++ libraries are implemented in such a way that the functions and methods of the library trigger exceptions in in the event of serious errors. If you want to catch these (or self-defined and -triggered) exceptions, you must contain the statements which can trigger the exceptions in a `try` block and attach one or several `catch` handlers to the `try` block.

## Implementation

With the keyword `catch` you can catch exceptions which have been triggered in a previous `try` block. The type of exception triggered must be identical to the type of the `catch` handler.

The keyword `catch` is followed by the exception type that is caught in brackets. The type of the triggered exception must be identical to the type of the handler). The statement `catch (...)` catches all exceptions.

## Examples

```
try {
    float bruch;
    bruch = division(12,0);      // this library function triggers
                                 // an exception when a division
                                 // by 0 is about to occur

    }
catch (...) {                    // all exceptions caught
    cout << "Exception occurred!" << endl;
    }
```

## Tips

It is possible to set many compilers to react to exceptions of the operating system or the program (usually by terminating the program or by executing exception handling).

## References

See triggering exceptions.

See Reference section, category exception handling.

# Triggering exceptions

```
throw
```

## Application

Exceptions are an object-oriented form of error handling. If you write a function or method in which serious errors, for example due to an inappropriate call, might occur, which cannot properly be caught and repaired in the function, you have the option to pass on the occurred error to the functions that are calling, in the form of an exception.

## Implementation

To trigger an exception in a function, you must use the keyword `throw` followed by an exception object.

## Example

```
float division(int counter, int fact1, int fact2)
{
    if(fact1*fact2 == 0) {                   // division by zero
        throw string("Division by ZERO");    // triggers exception
        }                                    // of string type
    return counter/(fact1*fact2);
}
```

## References

See passing exceptions; catching exceptions.

See Reference section, category exception handling.

# Passing exceptions

```
throw
```

## Application

Occasionally, you may want to catch an exception and pass it immediately.

This may be the case, for example, if you reserve memory in a function which is to be freed up again at the end of the function. If an exception is triggered in the function (or in a subordinate function) this would result in the dynamically reserved memory not being freed up, as the exception handling prematurely breaks off the called-up functions one after the other, until the exception is caught in a function. This can be prevented by catching the exception directly in the function concerned and then freeing up the memory in the catch handler. However, what should you do with the exception? If you do not want to react to the exception, simply pass it with `throw`.

## Implementation

To re-trigger caught exceptions within a `catch` block, or a function, which is called in a `try` block, and pass it to the next `catch` handler, call the keyword `throw` without an object.

## Example

```
void func() {
  int *ptr = new int;

  try {
    ...  // statement part
    }
  catch (...) {
    delete(ptr);
    throw;
    }

  free(ptr);
  }
```

## References

See triggering exceptions.

See category pointers and dynamic memory management, dynamic memory and exception handling.

See Reference section, category exception handling.

# Defining exception classes

## Application

Because of the separation of error cause and error handling, the `catch` handler relies on the information which is transmitted to it by the exception when processing an error:

- this is the data type of the exception which determines the most suitable `catch` handler for processing the exception,
- an exception is an object, and every object contains data. An exception of the `int` type could, for example, transmit an error code, and an exception of the `char *` type an error message.

Therefore, class instances are best suited for exceptions, since these can contain several data and even suitable methods for error handling, and it is possible to define your own exception classes for different error types.

## Implementation

You can derive your own exceptions from the `exception` class of the C++ runtime library or define completely new exceptions.

## Example

```
#include <iostream>
using namespace std;

class my_exception                    // definition of an exception class
{
    int fact1, fact2;
  public:
    my_exception(int i, int j){fact1=i; fact2=j;}
    void output() {
              cout << "fact1 = " << fact1 << endl;
              cout << "fact2 = " << fact2 << endl;
              }
    };

float division(int counter, int fact1, int fact2)
{
    if(fact1*fact2 == 0) {                // division by zero
        throw my_exception(fact1,fact2); // triggers exception
        }                                // of type my_exception
    return counter/(fact1*fact2);
}
```

```
int main() {
  try {
      division(15,3,0);
      }
  catch(my_exception e) {
      cout << "Division by zero" << endl;
      e.output();
      }

  return 0;
  }
```

## References

See catching exceptions; triggering exceptions.

See Reference section, category exception handling.

# Category: strings

# Programming with C strings

```
char *str
```

## Application

In C, strings are defined as pointers to characters (`char`, `wchar_t`) or as arrays of characters. For other programming with strings, usually the string functions of the C runtime library only are only. The only point when programming with strings that is not covered by the string functions of the C runtime library is memory reservation for strings. This remains the responsibility of the programmer.

## Implementation

```
char str1[25];
```

When declaring a character array, you specify in the declaration how much memory (in bytes) is to be reserved. Since each character occupies one byte (for `char`), you determine at the same time the upper limit for the length of the strings, which can be stored in the array (minus one for the zero termination character). The disadvantage of this is that, for many strings, this memory can be too large and for others it may be too small.

```
char *p_str;
p_str = (char*) malloc(100);
```

By declaring a pointer to `char` you have not yet reserved memory. Therefore, if you forget to link the pointer variable to memory in the sequence, this will result in runtime errors when you later de-reference the pointer. To reserve a new memory area for the pointer, use the `malloc()` function. If you no longer require the pointer, free it up again with the `free()` function. In this way, you can adapt the memory area at runtime to the respective size of the string that needs to be accommodated. However, if you should forget this once, as for character arrays, you may try to write strings into a memory area that is too small. Furthermore, you are in danger of allocating memory areas which you will then not free up later.

A further option to link memory to a pointer is simply to assign the address of a reserved memory area to it:

- this may be a string literal

```
char *ptr;
ptr = "This is a test";
```

(Caution: string literals are the only constants for which memory is provided.)

- or the memory area of another character array or pointer to `char`.

```
char str1[25];
char *str2;
str2 = str1;
```

## Example

```
#include <stdio.h>
#include <stdlib.h>
#include <string.h>

int main()  {
  char str[3][21] = {"String1", "String2", "String3"};
  char *p_str;
  int bytes;

  // str[0] to str[2] are now associated with memory areas
  // of 21 bytes each (20 char characters + \0)
  // p_str is defined, but not associated to any memory area
  // we now remedy this and let str_p point to
  // the second array element

  p_str = str[1];

  strcpy(p_str,"Assign 20 characters!");    // copy string

  for(int loop = 0; loop < 3; loop++)       // output strings
    {
    printf("str[%d]= %s\n",loop, str[loop]);
    }
  puts("\n\n");

  // if we want to assign more than 20 characters, we need
  // more memory; now we copy str[0] to str[2] to p_str
  //
  // first we calculate the memory needed
  bytes = (strlen(str[0]) + strlen(str[1]) +
          strlen(str[2]) + 1)*sizeof(char);

  // then we allocate the memory
  p_str = (char*) malloc(bytes);

  // then we copy the strings
  strcpy(p_str,str[0]);
  strcat(p_str,str[1]);
  strcat(p_str,str[2]);
  printf("String = %s contains %d bytes\n",p_str,bytes);

  free(p_str);
  return 0;
  }
```

Output:
```
str[0]= String1
str[1]= Assign 20 characters!
str[2]= String3

String = String1Assign 20 characters!String3 contains 35 bytes
```

### References

See programming with the string class.

See analysing (parsing) strings.

# Programming with the string class

```
class string
```

## Application

In C++ it is possible to fall back on the class string (wstring for wide character strings), which takes over the task of memory management from the programmer.

## Implementation

Programming with strings which are defined as objects of the class string, is as easy as programming with any class. All you need to do is to get some information about the methods and operators available (see reference of the C++ runtime library). With their help, the strings in C++ can be manipulated conveniently and without considering memory management (which is taken care of internally by the class).

To support existing C code, the class string possesses a c_str() method which returns the text encapsulated into a string object as a C string.

## Example

The example shows the handling of string instances for a small selection of methods and operators:

```
#include <iostream>
#include <string>
using namespace std;

int main() {
  int res;
  size_type pos;
```

```
// declaration of string variables
   string text1;
   string text2;
   string message;

// read strings
   cout << "Please enter two strings\n";
   cin >> text1 >> text2;

// lexicographic comparison
   res = text1.compare(text2);                   // or if(text1 == text2)

   if (res == 0)
      message = "The strings are identical!";
      else if (res > 0)
        message = "The first string is greater!";
        else
        message = "The second string is greater!";

   cout << "\t" << message << "\n\n";

// copy
   cout <<"Text2 is copied to the \"message\" string" <<endl;
   message.assign(text2);                      // or message = text2
   cout << "\tMessage = " << message << endl << endl;

// pattern matching
   cout << "Text1 is checked for occurence of the "
                                      letter i" << endl;
   pos = message.find("i");
   pos++;
    cout << "\t";
   if(pos) {
    cout << "i was found in string " << message
        << " at position " << pos << endl << endl;
    }
   else
    cout << "i does not occur in " << message << "\n\n";

// concatenation
   cout << "Text1 is appended to text2" << endl;
   text2.append(text1);   // or text2 += text1
   cout << "\tResult = " << text2 << "\n\n";
   return 0;
   }
```

Output:

```
Please enter two strings
House Tree
        The second string is greater!
```

```
Text2 is copied to the "message" string
       Message = House
Text1 is checked for occurrence of the letter i
       i does not occur in House
Text1 is appended to text2
       Result = TreeHouse
```

### References

See programming with C strings.

See analysing (parsing) strings.

# Analysing (parsing) strings

```
strtok()
```

### Application

Occasionally, you may need to parse strings yourself that is; dissect a string into individual parts. An example would be that a keyboard entry is read and you want to split this into individual words. If you know how many words the entry contains, this is not a problem: you can carry out the split directly while reading with `scanf/cin` or later with `sscanf()`. If you do not know how many words the entry contains, you must go through the string character by character and identify the individual words. This is done by the `strtok()` function.

### Implementation

The `strtok()` function makes it possible for you to dissect a string into sub-strings (or tokens) with the help of a specified set of boundary characters.

```
char* strtok(char* source, const char* boundary character);
```

The function dissects the string `source` into tokens, each of which is specified by the characters from the parameter `boundary character`. The set of boundary characters is passed as a string. The `strtok()` function changes the source string by inserting the zero termination character '\0' after every token.

At the first call of the `strtok()` function, the string which is to be dissected is passed to it, as well as a second string with the separator characters (in the following example simply a space). Then the function returns the first sub-string as a result.

To parse the string further, and so that the first sub-string is not returned again at the next call, the next time you must call strtok() with zero as the first argument. Use a while condition, to check whether another sub-string has been found, or whether the string has already been completely parsed.

## Example

```
#include <stdio.h>
#include <string.h>

int main()
  {
  char *text = "Divide me into words";
  char *token;

  token = strtok(text," ");
  printf("%s\n",token);

  while(token = strtok(0," "))
    {
    printf("%s\n",token);
    }

  return 0;
  }
```

Output:

```
Divide
me
into
words
```

## Reference

Programming with C strings.

# Category: input and output

# Formatted input and output in C

scanf / printf

## Application
C uses the appropriate functions of the runtime library for outputting data on screen and inputting data through the keyboard.

## Implementation: outputting data
The following functions are mainly used to output data:

### puts()

Pure text, for example for instructions or messages, is easiest to output with puts(). To format the output, special characters such as

- \n, new line, and
- \t, tab

can be integrated into the string that is to be output.

### printf()

Values of elementary data types must be converted into string representations before they are output. The printf() function is usually used for this, to which a formatting string can be passed, into which wildcards for the values of variables listed afterwards can be passed (see reference of the C runtime library). The function replaces the wildcards with the reformatted values of the variables and outputs the resulting string.

To output individual characters, the following two functions can be used:

- putc(). Outputs a single character into a stream.
- putchar(). Like putc(), but the output automatically occurs on stdout.

## Implementation: reading data
To read data you usually use the scanf() function, which is the pendant to the output function printf(). The most important difference is that you must specify the addresses of variables as arguments for the wildcards specified in the format string for the function to be able to store the read values at these addresses.

The use of the scanf() function is, however, precarious, since it reacts sensitively to inappropriate entries and does not read final space characters (space characters, line breaks, and so on), but leaves them in the input stream. It is, thus, recommended that the input stream is emptied with fflush(stdin) after every call of scanf().

As an alternative to scanf() the keyboard entry can be read line by line with fgets()and be parsed with sscanf().

## Warning

Input and output are operating system-specific procedures. For this reason, they are not rooted in the language in form of keywords, but are implemented through functions/classes of the runtime library. However, these only support input and output for console programs. For Windows programs (under UNIX X Windows/ OSF Motif) these functions cannot be used, but you must resort to special functions from the APIs of the Windows systems.

## Example

The following program illustrates input and output in C. The first part reads data with scanf(), the second with fgets():

```c
#include <stdio.h>
#include <stdlib.h>
#include <string.h>

int main()  {
  char line[100];
  char first_name[40]= "";
  int age=0;

  printf("Please enter your first name and your age: \n\n\t");
  fgets(line, sizeof(line), stdin);
  sscanf(line,"%s %d\n", first_name, &age);
  printf("Your name is %s and you are %d\n\n", first_name, age);

  printf("Please enter your first name and your age: \n\n\t");
  scanf("%s %d",first_name, &age);
  printf("Your name is %s and you are %d\n\n", first_name, age);
  fflush(stdin);
  return 0;
  }
```

## References

See formatted input and output in C++.

See reference of the C runtime library.

See Reference section, category input and output.

# Formatted input and output in C++

cin / cout

## Application

For outputting data on screen and inputting data through the keyboard, the streams cout and cin, in connection with the overloaded stream operators << und >>, are used in C++.

## Implementation

The stream operators have been defined for outputting all elementary data types. The operators can be overloaded for the input and output of objects of self-defined class types.

## Example

```
#include <iostream>
#include <string>
using namespace std;

int main() {
  string first_name;
  int age=0;

  cout << "Please enter your first name and your age: " << endl;
  cin >> first_name >> age;

  cout << "Your name is " << first_name
       << " and you are "<< age << endl;
  return 0;
  }
```

## Warning

Input and output are operating system-specific procedures. For this reason they are not anchored in the language in form of keywords, but are implemented through functions/classes of the runtime library. However, these only support input and output for console programs. For Windows programs you must resort to special functions from the APIs of the Windows systems.

## References

See formatted in-and output in C.

See category operators, overloading stream operators.

See reference of the stream classes.

# Using manipulators

endl, left, ...

## Description

Manipulators are elements which can be passed as operands to stream operators. With their help, input and output through C++ streams can be appropriately formatted.

## Application

A range of manipulators have already been predefined (for a complete list see Reference section, input and output). Most manipulators permanently change the stream status and are therefore valid until their effect is cancelled by another manipulator (the only exception to this is the determination of the field width for the next input or output with setw()).

| Manipulator | E/A | Effect |
|---|---|---|
| boolalpha, noboolalpha | e/a | Boolean values as numbers or words |
| left | a | left-aligned output |
| right | a | right-aligned output |
| scientific | | exponential notation |
| showpoint, noshowpoint | a | show or hide decimal point |
| showpos, noshowpos | a | show or hide plus character |
| skipws, noskipws | e | read or skip whitespace characters when inputting |
| endl | a | new line and empty stream |
| ends | a | output zero termination character ('\0') |
| setfill(charT c) | e/a | as fill(c) |
| setprecision(int n) | e/a | as precision(n) |
| setw(int n) | e/a | as width(n) |
| ws | e | skip space characters |

To define your own manipulator you must define it as a function which adopts a stream object as an argument, manipulates it and returns it to the stream (the return type is a reference to the stream).

Second, the corresponding stream operator should be overloaded, so that it accepts a function as the operand.

## Example

Determination of the field width and orientation:

```
#include <iomanip>
cout << setw(10) << right << 1234.5 << endl;
```

Advanced formatting:

```
ios_base::fmtflags old_flags = cout.flags();   // storage of current
                                               // format flags of stream
cout.setf(ios_base::left,ios_base::adjustfield);   // output ranged
cout.width(20);                                    // left or right
cout << "left" << "right" << endl;

cout.unsetf(ios_base::adjustfield);                // output ranged left
cout.width(20);
cout << "links" << "rechts" << endl;

cout.precision(2);                                     // precision
cout.setf(ios_base::uppercase|ios_base::scientific);   // exponential
cout << 123.4567 << endl;                              // notation

cout.flags(old_flags);                                 // restore old flag
```

Output:

```
left               right
leftright
1.23E+02
```

## References

See formatted input and output in C++.

See reference of the C++ header files iomanip and ios.

See Reference section, category input and output, streams in C++.

# Error handling for streams

## Description

Input and output operations are relatively prone to errors since they are dependent on circumstances and conditions not controlled by the program. Professional programmers should thus control the execution of their I/O operations.

## Application

In C, error handling mainly occurs through checking the return values of the functions for input and output.

In C++, error handling is based on status bits, which every stream inherits from its base class `ios_base`. If there is an error during input and output the corresponding status bit is set to 1.

| Status bit | Error |
| --- | --- |
| ios_base::goodbit | No error occurred, everything is in order. |
| ios_base::eofbit | During reading the EOF character has been reached (can be simulated by Ctrl+D or Ctrl+Z when inputting through keyboard, if necessary). |
| ios_base::failbit | When inputting, the expected character could not be read (for example, because it was wrongly formatted). |
| | When outputting, the desired character could not be output. |
| ios_base::badbit | The stream cannot work correctly for some reason (usually this is the case when there are problems with the basic buffer (`basic_streambuf` objects)). |

As soon as one of these bits is set for a stream, the stream is blocked, that is, subsequent input and output operations are no longer carried out.

Therefore, if you do not want to depend on everything working out fine when input and output, you must query the stream status at crucial points. There are various methods to do this:

| Method | Description |
| --- | --- |
| bool good() | `true`, if no statusbit has been set |
| bool eof() | `true`, if `eofbit` has been set |
| bool fail() | `true`, if `failbit` or `badbit` have been set |
| bool bad() | `true`, if `badbit` has been set |
| bool operator!() | `true`, if `failbit` or `badbit` have been set |
| iostate rdstate() | Returns the complete stream status |

## Example

The following example reads entries in an infinite loop. After the desired values have been read, the status of the input stream is checked by calling the `good()` method.

- If everything is in order, the infinite loop is terminated with `break`.

- If not, the reading is repeated in the next loop iteration. However, for this, the input stream must be reactivated.

- The first step is to delete the status bits of the stream. This is done by the `clear()` method.

- The second step is to delete the characters which remain in the stream. To do so, simply output the characters up to the next new line character.

```
while(1)
    {
    cout << "Please enter two integer values\n";
    cin >> d1 >> d2;

    if(cin.good())
        break;
      else
        {
        cin.clear();
        while(cin.get() != '\n')
            ;
        }
    }

  cout << "d1 = " << d1 << endl;
  cout << "d2 = " << d2 << endl;
```

## Tips

By default, C++ streams do not trigger exceptions. However, exceptions of the ios_base::failure can be triggered if required. Call the method exceptions() for the stream and pass to it as an argument the status bits which are to be met with an exception:

```
try {
   cin.exceptions(ios_base::badbit);
   in >> x;
   }
catch(ios_base::failure& exc) {
   cerr << exc.what() << endl;
   throw;
   }
```

## References

See formatted input and output in C++.

See Reference section, category input and output, streams in C++.

# Text files in C

## Application

A frequent problem is the reading and writing of text files. For example, you may need to process the contents of the files directly (in a text editor), to read or store measuring data (in a program for analysing measuring data); so the program stores configuration data in an external file.

## Implementation

To be able to access a file, a pointer to a FILE structure is required:

```
FILE *file_in;
```

The file pointer is initialised by the fopen() function:

```
file_in = fopen("TEST.DAT", "wt");
```

- The first argument for fopen() is the file name.
- The second argument is also a string, which specifies which operations are permitted on the file (mode).

Mode argument for fopen():

| Value | Meaning |
|-------|---------|
| r | Read only |
| w | Write only, existing files are overwritten, non-existing files are created |
| a | Write only, attaches to existing files, non-existing files are created |
| r+ | Read and write, file has to exist |
| w+ | As w, however, also permits reading |
| a+ | As a, however, also permits reading |

For text or binary mode it is also possible to attach 't' or 'b' to these specifications.

- In text mode ('t') the program converts the new line character '\n' into the representation which conforms with the platform for which it has been compiled when outputting. Correspondingly, when reading, it converts line breaks into its new line character '\n'.
- In binary mode, the program does not carry out these conversions.

## Example

The following program opens a text file and outputs the contents on screen:

```
#include <stdio.h>

int main() {
  FILE *file_in;
  char filename[50];

  puts("Please enter the name of the file to be opened: \n\n\t");
  scanf("%s",filename);
  fflush(stdin);
  puts("\n");
```

```
if ((file_in = fopen(filename, "rb")) == NULL)
  {
  fprintf(stderr, "File could not be opened!\n");
  return 1;
  }

while (!feof(file_in))
  putchar(fgetc(file_in));

fclose(file_in);

return 0;
}
```

## References

See binary files in C.

See optional access in C.

See text files in C++.

# Binary files in C

## Application

A binary file is a file whose contents are not coded according to ASCII or another character set.

## Implementationg

In the following program, objects of the structure

```
struct Demo {
  int value;
  char text[30];
  };
```

are written unformatted into the file Output.dat.

To write unformatted data, the fwrite() function is used, to which the following parameters are passed:

- the address at which the files to be output can be found,

- the size of the individual objects (here the size of the structure),

- the number of objects to be output (since the structures are stored in an array, we can output all elements in the array at once), and

- the output stream.

The `fwrite()` function then writes the bit sequence found in the memory unchanged into the file, which means that the structure element `value` is always written ASCII-coded into the output file after the element `text`. When you open the `Output.dat` file with a text editor after executing the program, you can only read the `text` elements:

□□□□□□□□□□□□□□□□□0. Structurevariable□□□□□□□□□□□□□□□□□0.

Structurevar...

# Example

```c
#include <stdio.h>

struct Demo {
  int value;
  char text[30];
  } structures[10];

int main() {
  FILE *file_in, *file_out;

  // initialise array with structures
  int loop;
  for(loop=0; loop < 10; loop++) {
    structures[loop].value = loop;
    sprintf(structures[loop].text,"%d. Structurevariable",loop);
    }

  // open output file
  if ((file_out = fopen("Output.dat", "wb")) == NULL) {
    fprintf(stderr, "File could not be opened!\n");
    return 1;
    }

  // write array with structures to file
  fwrite(structures,sizeof(struct Demo),10,file_out);
  fclose(file_out);

  // open input file
  if ((file_in = fopen("Output.dat", "rb")) == NULL) {
    fprintf(stderr, "File could not be opened!\n");
    return 1;
    }

  // read structures
  loop = 0;
  while (!feof(file_in)) {
```

```
      fread(&structures[loop],sizeof(struct Demo),1,file_in);
      loop++;
      }

  // display read structures on screen
  for(loop=0; loop < 10; loop++)    {
    printf("%s\n\t",structures[loop].text);
    printf("%d\n\n",structures[loop].value);
    }
  fclose(file_in);
  return 0;
  }
```

## References

See text files in C.

See optional access in C.

See binary files in C++.

# Random access in C

## Application

In binary files it is possible to jump to particular positions in the stream with the stream pointer and read from or write to this position.

## Implementation

The function

```
int fseek(FILE *fp, long offset, int origin);
```

moves the stream pointer, to determine from which position it is read next (or to which position it is written).

The position is specified by

- selecting one of the following constants for origin:

```
SEEK_SET          // stands for beginning of file
SEEK_CUR          // stands for current position of stream pointer
SEEK_END          // stands for end of file
```

- and specifying the number of bytes for offset by which the stream pointer is to be moved from origin.

# Example

```c
#include <stdio.h>

struct Demo {
  int value;
  char text[30];
  } structures[10];

int main() {
  FILE *file_in, *file_out;
  int element;
  struct Demo read_obj;

  // initialise array with structures
  int loop;
  for(loop=0; loop < 10; loop++)    {
    structures[loop].value = loop;
    sprintf(structures[loop].text,"%d. Structure variable",loop);
    }

  // open output file
  if ((file_out = fopen("Output.dat", "wb")) == NULL)  {
    fprintf(stderr, "File could not be opened!\n");
    return 1;
    }

  // write array with structures to file
  fwrite(structures,sizeof(struct Demo),10,file_out);

  fclose(file_out);

  // open input file
  if ((file_in = fopen("Output.dat", "rb")) == NULL)     {
    fprintf(stderr, "File could not be opened!\n");
    return 1;
    }

  // which structure is to be read?
  printf("Which element is to be read <0 - 9> : ");
  scanf("%d",&element);
  fflush(stdin);

  // position file pointer
  fseek(file_in, element*sizeof(struct Demo),SEEK_SET);

  // read structure
  fread(&read_obj,sizeof(struct Demo),1,file_in);
```

```
// display read structures on screen
printf("%s\n\t",read_obj.text);
printf("%d\n\n",read_obj.value);

fclose(file_in);

return 0;
}
```

## References

See text files in C.

See binary files in C.

See optional access in C++.


# Text files in C++


## Application

A frequent problem is the reading and writing of text files. For example, you may need to directly process the contents of the files (in a text editor), to read or store measuring data (in a program for analysing measuring data); or so that the program stores configuration data in an external file.


## Implementation

For input and output from and to files using streams, use `ifstream`, `ofstream` or `fstream`.

To open a file, use `open()`, and, to close it, the `close()` method.

The `open()` method has the following syntax:

```
void open( const char* filename,
           openmode mode = in
           );
```

- The first parameter specifies the file name.

    The second parameter specifies the mode in which the file is to be opened. You can use the following modes:

| Mode | (in C) | Meaning |
|---|---|---|
| in | r | Read only |
| out \| trunc<br>out | w | Write only, existing files are overwritten, non-existing files are created |
| out \| app | a | Write only, attaches to existing files, non-existing files are created |
| in \| out | r+ | Read and write, file has to exist |
| in \| out \| trunc | w+ | Read and write, existing files are overwritten, non-existing files are created |
| in \| out \| app | a+ | Read and write, attaches to existing files, non-existing files are created |

You can switch from text to binary mode, by attaching '| binary'

- In text mode ('t') the program converts the new line character '\n' into the representation which conforms with the platform for which it has been compiled when outputting. Correspondingly, when reading, it converts line breaks into its new line character '\n'.

- In binary mode, the program does not carry out these conversions.

## Example

```
#include <iostream>
#include <fstream>
#include <string>
using namespace std;

int main()
  {
  ifstream file_in;
  string filename;

  cout << "Please enter the name of the file to be opened: \n\n\t";
  cin >> filename;
  cout << endl;

  file_in.open(filename.c_str(), ios_base::in);
  if(!file_in)
    {
    cerr << "File could not be opened!\n";
    return 1;
    }

  char charac;
  while (!file_in.eof())
```

```
    {
    file_in.get(charac);
    cout << charac;
    }

  file_in.close();

  return 0;
  }
```

## References

See binary files in C++.

See random access in C++.

See text files in C.

# Binary files in C++

## Application

A binary file is a file whose contents are not coded according to ASCII or another character set.

## Implementation

In the following program, objects of the structure

```
struct Demo {
  int value;
  char text[30];
  };
```

are written unformatted into a file Output.dat.

To write unformatted data, the fwrite() function is used, to which the following parameters are passed:

- the address at which the files to be output can be found,

- the size of the individual objects (here the size of the structure), and

- the number of objects to be output (since the structures are stored in an array, we can output all elements in the array at once).

The fwrite() function then writes the bit sequence found in the memory unchanged into the file, which means that the structure element value is always written ASCII-coded into the output file after the element text. When you open the

Output.dat file with a text editor after executing the program, you can only read the text elements:

□□□□□□□□□□□□□□□□0. Structurevariable□□□□□□□□□□□□□□□□□□0. Structurevar...

## Example

```cpp
#include <iostream>
#include <fstream>
#include <string>
#include <stdio.h>
using namespace std;

struct Demo {
  int value;
  char text[30];
  } structures[10];

int main() {
  ifstream file_in;
  ofstream file_out;

  // initialise array with structures
  int loop;
  for(loop=0; loop < 10; loop++) {
    structures[loop].value = loop;
    sprintf(structures[loop].text,"%d. Structure variable",loop);
    }

  // open output file
  file_out.open("Output.dat", ios_base::out);
  if (!file_out) {
    cerr << "File could not be opened!\n";
    return 1;
    }

  // write array with structures to file
  file_out.write((char *)structures, sizeof(struct Demo)*10);
  file_out.close();

  // open input file
  file_in.open("Output.dat", ios_base::in);
  if (!file_in) {
    cerr << "File could not be opened!\n";
    return 1;
    }

  // read structures
  loop = 0;
```

```
while(!file_in.eof()) {
  file_in.read((char *) &structures[loop],sizeof(struct Demo));
  loop++;
  }

// display read structures on screen
for(loop=0; loop < 10; loop++) {
  cout << structures[loop].text << endl;
  cout << "\t" << structures[loop].value << endl;
  }

file_in.close();
return 0;
}
```

## References

See text files in C++.

See random access in C++.

See binary files in C.

# Random access in C++

## Application

In binary files it is possible to jump to arbitrary positions in the stream with the stream pointer and read from or write to this position.

## Implementation

With the function

```
// for ifstream
seekg(off_type offset, ios_base::seekdir origin);

// for ofstream
seekp(off_type offset, ios_base::seekdir origin);
```

it is possible to move the stream pointer to the position it is to be read next (or to which position it is written).

The position is specified by

- selecting one of the following constants for origin

```
ios_base::beg      // stands for beginning of file
```

```
ios_base::cur          // stands for current position
                       // of the stream pointer
ios_base::end          // stands for end of file
```

- and specifying the number of bytes for offset by which the stream pointer is to be moved from origin.

## Example

```cpp
#include <iostream>
#include <fstream>
#include <string>
#include <stdio.h>
using namespace std;

struct Demo {
  int value;
  char text[30];
  } structures[10];

int main()  {
  ifstream file_in;
  ofstream file_out;
  int element;
  struct Demo read_obj;

  // initialise array with structures
  int loop;
  for(loop=0; loop < 10; loop++)  {
    structures[loop].value = loop;
    sprintf(structures[loop].text,"%d. Structure Variable",loop);
    }

  // open output file
  file_out.open("Output.dat", ios_base::out);
  if (!file_out)  {
    cerr << "File could not be opened!\n";
    return 1;
    }

  // write array with structures to file
  file_out.write((char *)structures, sizeof(struct Demo)*10);
  file_out.close();

  // open input file
  file_in.open("Output.dat", ios_base::in);
  if (!file_in)  {
    cerr << "File could not be opened!\n";
    return 1;
    }
```

```
// which structure is to be read
cout << "Which element is to be read <0 - 9> : ";
cin >> element;

// position file pointer
file_in.seekg(element*sizeof(struct Demo),ios_base::beg);

// read structure
file_in.read((char *) &read_obj,sizeof(struct Demo));

// display read structures on screen
cout << read_obj.text << endl;;
cout << read_obj.value << endl;

file_in.close();
return 0;
}
```

## References

See text files in C++.

See binary files in C++.

See random access in C.

# Dividing stream buffers

## Application

As input and output through C++ streams are always carried out through buffer objects (basic_streambuf), it is possible to couple the streams by linking them with the same buffer.

## Implementation

An option to use the coupling of streams through buffers is the opening of a file for reading and writing.

Here you first establish a buffer object of the filebuf type. Use open() to open the corresponding file and link it with the buffer object.

Then you must create the input and output streams and pass the buffer object to the constructors.

It is important to reposition the file pointer, if necessary, when switching between reading and writing (seekg() method).

## Example

```cpp
#include <iostream>
#include <fstream>
#include <string>
using namespace std;

struct Demo {
  int value;
  char text[30];
  };

int main()
  {
  filebuf file;
  file.open("Data.dat", ios_base::in | ios_base::out);
  istream file_in(&file);
  ostream file_out(&file);
  struct Demo read_obj[12];

  // read structures
  for(int i=0; i < 10; i++)
    file_in.read((char *) &read_obj[i],sizeof(struct Demo));

  // process data
  for(int i=0; i < 10; i++)  {
    cout << read_obj[i].text << endl;
    cout << read_obj[i].value << endl;
    }

  // write data back to file
  file_in.seekg(0);
  file_out.write((char *)read_obj, sizeof(struct Demo)*10);
  file.close();

  return 0;
  }
```

## References

See binary files in C++.

See random access in C++.

# String streams

## Application

A frequent problem when working with data is the conversion of data from elementary data types into strings and vice versa.

## Implementation

The C library provides the functions `sprintf()` and `ssc-anf()` for these conversions, unlike the C++ library, which uses the concept of string streams; that is, streams which use a string as an internal buffer.

String streams have the advantage that the stream operators can be used for input and output, and the stream operator can be overloaded for any data types.

The `str()` method can be used to directly access the internal string of the string stream.

## Example

```
#include <sstream>
#include <iostream>
using namespace std;

int main()
  {
  ostringstream str;                      // create string stream for output
  int value1 = 14, value2 = 0;

  str << value1;                          // write value1 to string
  cout << str.str() << endl;

  istringstream(str.str()) >> value2; // create string stream for input
                                      // and read content of the string
                                      // into value2

  cout << value2 << endl;

  return 0;
  }
```

## References

See Reference section, category input and output, streams in C++.

See reference of the C++ runtime library on the string stream classes.

# Category:
# the STL (Standard
# Template Library)

# Data management with containers

## Application

The container classes are there to facilitate the management of larger amounts of data. They are a convenient alternative to arrays and dynamic fields and save the programmer from having to the implement his own higher data structures.

## Implementation

When you decide to manage data or objects in a container, you then need to decide which container is the right one for you. Here the crucial point is the way in which the elements are stored in the container, and which access options the container provides and for which it is optimised.

| Container | Description |
|-----------|-------------|
| bitset | For bit sequences with a fixed size. It is slightly different from other containers. |
| deque | Linear data structure optimised for insertion and deletion at the beginning and end of the data structure, as well as for quickly accessing any position (dynamic array consisting of several linked blocks). |
| | Use deque if you prefer to insert or delete elements at the beginning and end and otherwise want to use indexed access with [] or at() (at() checks for a valid index). |
| list | Sequential data structure optimised for quick insertion and deletion at any position. However, it is slower with regard to access than vector and deque (doubly linked list). |
| | Use list if you want to insert or delete elements at any position, and otherwise run quickly through the elements. (No indexed access with [] or at() .) |
| map | Associative data structure, the elements of which consist of key/value pairs and are sorted by their keys. Each key may only occur once in the data structure. A map is equivalent to a list with quicker access to the individual elements (binary tree, hashing). |
| multimap | Data structure which is identical to map; however, may also contain several elements with identical keys (binary tree, hashing). |
| multiset | Data structure which is identical with set; however, may also contain several elements with identical values (binary tree, hashing). |
| queue | Adapter class which is based on a sequential data structure (for example deque) and which equips it with an interface typical for waiting queues: insertion of elements can only occur at the end, deletion of elements only at the beginning (first in, first out). |

| Container | Description |
|---|---|
| priority_queue | Adapter class which is based on a sequential data structure (for example vector) and which equips it with an interface typical for priority queues it: always returns the element with the highest priority in accessing (the priority is defined by a compare object). |
| set | Associative data structure which sorts its elements by their values. Each value may only occur once in the data structure. A set is equivalent to a list with quick access to the individual elements (binary tree). |
| stack | Adapter class which is based on a sequential data structure (for example vector) and which equips it with an interface typical for stacks: insertion and deletion is only permitted at the upper end (last in, first out). |
| vector | Linear data stricture which is optimised for quick insertion and deletion at the end of the data structure, as well as for quickly accessing any position (dynamic array). |
| | Use vector if you prefer to insert or delete elements at the beginning and end and otherwise want to use indexed access with [] or at() (at() checks for valid index). |

When you have chosen a container, you must include the header file

```
#include <vector>
```

and create a container object for elements of the desired data type from the template of the container class

```
vector<int> myData;  // specialisation for int
```

# Example

Programming with a sequential container:

```
#include <iostream>
#include <deque>
using namespace std;

int main()
  {
  deque<int> number_container(5);

  // initialise container
  for(int i = 0; i < number_container.size(); i++)
    {
    number_container[i] = i;
    }

  // add elements
  for(int i=0; i < 6; i++)
    {
    number_container.push_front(i + 10);
    }
```

```
  // delete elements
  number_container.pop_front();
  number_container.pop_back();

  // output elements
  for(int i = 0; i < number_container.size(); i++)
    {
    cout << i << ": " << number_container[i] << endl;
    }
  return 0;
  }
```

Output:

```
0: 14
1: 13
2: 12
3: 11
4: 10
5: 0
6: 1
7: 2
8: 3
```

Example for an associative container

```
#include <iostream>
#include <utility>
#include <map>
using namespace std;

int main()
  {
  map<int,string> container;

  // insert elements
  // the index operator adds the element when the key is new
  container[10] = "Message: file is being loaded";
  container[11] = "Message: please wait";
  container[21] = "Error: no correct datum";
  container[20] = "Error: incorrect input";
  container[30] = "Warning: memory is getting low";
  container.insert(make_pair(22,"Error: value is less than zero"));

  // delete elements for a specific key
  container.erase(11);

  // output elements
  // iterator i returns elements as pair objects
  typedef map<int, string>::const_iterator iter;
  for(iter i = container.begin(); i != container.end(); ++i)
```

```
    {
    cout << "Key:      " << i->first << ";   ";
    cout << "Value:    " << i->second << endl;
    }
  return 0;
  }
```

Output:

```
Key: 10;  Value:     Message: file is being loaded
Key: 20;  Value:     Error: incorrect input
Key: 21;  Value:     Error: no correct datum
Key: 22;  Value:     Error: value is less than zero
Key: 30;  Value:     Warning: memory is getting low
```

## Tip

Do not store pointers as elements in containers. The containers shift and copy elements, which can result in errors with pointer elements.

## References

See reference of the C++ runtime library, container classes.

See iterators.

See algorithms.

See preparing classes for containers and algorithms.

# Iterators

## Application

Iterators are abstractions of pointers and are used to access elements of containers.

## Why iterators?

The various container types have been defined as templates to include objects of any data type. Functions, which manipulate the elements of a container, therefore must also be implemented as templates, so that they can be specialised, like the container, for the various data objects.

However, this approach is not efficient when you want to write a function that is to be applied to different container types, for example a search function with which it is possible to find an element in a vector as well as in a list or map container.

Therefore, the STL introduces the model of the iterators. Five categories of iterators are defined, which are distinguished by increasing efficiency in the ANSI standard: the container of the STL defined methods, which returns iterators and uses iterators for insertion or deletion of elements; the algorithms of the header file algorithm, finally are completely designed for iterators, so that they can as far as possible be applied to all containers.

## Implementation

For all containers, access to individual elements occurs through iterators, a kind of intelligent pointer. Usually, this means that you have an iterator returned by a container method, and then access the element/s through it.

```
deque<int> meineDaten(5);          // Container definieren
typedef deque<int>::iterator iter; // Iterator definieren

for(iter i=meineDaten.begin(); i!=meineDaten.end(); i++)   {
    *i = rand()%5000;
    }
```

## Warning

- Access by means of iterators (which in principle are pointers) and internal dynamic memory management results in problems if the memory area of a container needs to be reallocated. In this case, addresses change and the pointers become invalid. deque and vector are affected especially by this.

- Note that the container methods end() and rend() return iterators which point behind the last element (or in front of the first element) in the container and, thus, must not be de-referenced. They are mostly used for break conditions of loops.

## Example

```
#include <cstdlib>
#include <iostream>
#include <deque>
using namespace std;

// generator for odd random numbers
int get_odd()  {
  int randomnumber;
  randomnumber = rand() % 10000;
  if (! (randomnumber & 1L))
      return randomnumber + 1;
```

```
      else
         return randomnumber;
   }

typedef deque<int>::iterator iter;

int main(int argc, char **argv)  {
   deque<int> container(5);
// initialise values
   for(iter i = container.begin(); i != container.end(); i++)    {
      *i = get_odd();
      }
// add values
   container.insert(container.end(),6,get_odd());
// delete values
   container.erase(container.begin(),container.begin()+3);
// output values
   int count = 1;
   for(iter i = container.begin(); i != container.end(); i++)    {
      cout << count++ << ": " << *i << endl;
      }
   return 0;
   }
```

## References

See reference of the C++ runtime library, iterators.

See containers.

See algorithms.

# Algorithms

## Application

Algorithms are a collection of function templates which can be specialised for any data type and applied to container objects by means of iterators.

Algorithms can be subdivided by their functionality in the following

### Non-changing algorithms for sequences

| | |
|---|---|
| adjacent_find | find_first_of |
| count | find_if |
| count_if | for_each |

| | |
|---|---|
| equal | mismatch |
| find | search |
| find_end | search_n |

## Changing algorithms for sequences

| | |
|---|---|
| copy | replace |
| copy_backward | replace_copy |
| fill | replace_copy_if |
| fill_n | replace_if |
| generate | reverse |
| generate_n | reverse_copy |
| iter_swap | rotate |
| random_shuffle | rotate_copy |
| remove | swap |
| remove_copy | swap_ranges |
| remove_copy_if | transfomr |
| remove_if | unique |
| | unique_copy |

## Sorting algorithms

| | |
|---|---|
| binary_search | partial_sort |
| equal_range | partial_sort_copy |
| inplace_merge | partition |
| lower_bound | sort |
| merge | stable_partition |
| nth_element | stable_sort |
| | upper_bound |

## Set algorithms

For application to sorted containers.

| | |
|---|---|
| includes | set_symmetric_difference |
| set_difference | set_union |
| set_intersection | |

## Heap algorithms

A heap is a sequence of elements between two random access iterators, whose 'greatest' element stands at the beginning and can be deleted with `pop_heap()`.

| | |
|---|---|
| make_heap | push_heap |
| pop_heap | sort_heap |

## Minimum and maximum

| | |
|---|---|
| lexicographical_compare | |
| max | min |
| max_element | min_element |

## Permutations

| | |
|---|---|
| next_permutation | prev_permutation |

## Numeric algorithms

| | |
|---|---|
| accumulate | adjacent_find |
| inner_product | partial_sum |

# Implementation

The algorithms of the STL are mainly used to manipulate container elements. For this purpose, most algorithms expect an iterator as argument, which points to the element that is to be manipulated, or adopt two iterators that specify the beginning and the end of a sequence of elements in a container.

Some of the algorithms return an iterator to the manipulated element (or an iterator pair, which indicates the beginning and the end of the manipulated elements).

Several of the algorithms require a further element to carry out their operation, usually:

- a value (for example `fill()`, which assigns the passed value to the elements), or

- a function object (see below), which usually specifies a condition which must be met for the operation of the algorithm to be carried out on an element (`make_heap()` converts an area into a heap. By passing a function object, a `compare` function can be passed, which determines the sorting of the heap.)

Often the templates of the algorithms are overloaded, so that the same algorithm can be called with different arguments. Thus, the find() algorithm can search for an element which either contains a particular value or meets a particular condition.

## Example

```
#include <cstdlib>
#include <iostream>
#include <functional>
#include <deque>
using namespace std;

// Generator for odd random numbers
int get_odd()  {
  int randomnumber;
  randomnumber = rand() % 10000;
  if (! (randomnumber & 1L))
    return randomnumber + 1;
    else
    return randomnumber;
  }

typedef deque<int>::iterator iter;
int main(int argc, char **argv)  {
  deque<int> container(5);

  // initialise values
  generate(container.begin(), container.end(),get_odd);

  // sort values
  stable_sort(container.begin(), container.end(),
            less<int>());
  // output values
  int count = 1;
  for(iter i = container.begin(); i != container.end(); i++)      {
    cout << count++ << ": " << *i << endl;
    }
  return 0;
  }
```

### Application to arrays

```
#include <algorithm>
#include <iostream>
using namespace std;

int field[30];

int main() {
    int *ptr1 = &field[28];
    int *ptr2 = &field[30];
```

```
fill(&field[0], &field[30], 3);
fill(ptr1, ptr2, 15);

for(int i = 0; i < 30; i++)
  cout << i << "\t" << field[i] << endl;

return 0;
}
```

## References

See reference of the C++ runtime library, algorithms; header file algorithm.

See container.s

See iterators.

See preparing classes for containers and algorithms.

# Preparing classes for containers and algorithms

## Application

Since the containers and algorithms have been implemented as templates and the data type of the elements has been declared as a template parameter, containers and algorithms can be used together with elements of any data type. In fact, containers and algorithms also have certain requirements.

## Implementation

To be stored in containers, it must be possible to copy, assign and delete the elements. For class types this means that a copy constructor (also for const arguments), a destructor and an assignment operator must be defined for the elements. This is usually the case, since these class elements are either defined in the class or are provided by the compiler. Only if the class elements have been declared as protected or private are the requirements not met.

For certain container methods and algorithms, it is possible to create, compare and/or sort the elements. For class types this means that a default constructor, the == operator and the < operator must be defined for the elements.

## Tips

If possible, manage objects and not pointers in containers, since the containers internally manage copies and even copy objects themselves, if necessary. This may result in errors if pointers are saved as elements in the container.

## References

See containers.

See classes.

See category operators, overloading.

# Creating function objects

## Application

The implementation of generic functions is based on the passing of functions as parameters (compare qsort()). The STL extends this concept by encapsulating functions in classes. All these classes have in common is that the () operator has been overloaded for them, for it to be possible to call the instances of the classes (the function objects) like functions.

Function objects are more powerful than functions, as they can fall back on the internal data and methods of their class. All function objects of the STL have been implemented as templates to be able to work with any data type.

## Implementation

Function objects are mostly used when you want to pass another function with parameters to a function (or method).

Suppose you had a field

```
int field[10];
```

and you want to write a function which runs through and manipulates all elements in the field (this is a simplified analogy for the algorithm for_each(), with which a sequence of container elements can be run through and manipulated).

How can you determine how the function manipulates the field elements? A second function is passed to the function as a parameter and applies this second function to all elements in the field

```
void for_all(void (*func)(int&)) {
  for(int i=0; i < 10; i++)
    func(field[i]);
  }
```

For example, the second function could add the value 13 to each element:

```
void add_13(int& elem) {
  elem += 13;
  }
```

The corresponding call would look as follows:

```
for_all(add_13);
```

Suppose you wanted to add the value 14. In this case, you would need to define your own function add_14(). You may want to rewrite the add() function in such a way that it accepts the value that is to be added as the second parameter. However, unfortunately, this does not work because, apart from the fact that you would need to change the declaration of for_all() so that this function adopts a function with two parameters, there is no option to pass the second parameter:

```
for_all(add_13(value));  // error: function cannot be passed
                         // with argument
```

If you wanted to do this, you would need to pass the value that is to be added as a parameter to the for_all() function and implement the function in such a way that it passes the parameter to the second function. However, this restricts the applicability of the for_all() function.

So, how is it possible to pass functions with parameters? The simple answer is that it is not possible. Instead, you must pass a class object for which the () operator has been overloaded. When you call the () operator for the class object, use the same syntax as for a function call. They are called function objects, because these objects can be used like functions. The value you want to pass as an argument to a function parameter is passed to the constructor of the class.

```
class addiere {
  int value;
 public:
  add(int w) {value = w;}
  void operator() (int& elem) {elem += value;}
  };
```

When calling

```
for_all(add(-26));
```

an object of the addiere class is created, whose data element value is set to −26. For this object the () operator function is carried out in each iteration in the for loop of the for_all() function and the current field element is passed as a parameter. The operator function adds the value of the data element value to the field element.

However, there is one more problem. The above definition of the for_all() function does not permit the passing of objects of the addiere class as arguments. If you want the for_all() function to accept real functions as well as function objects, it has to be defined as the function template.

## Example

Defining your own function object:

```
#include <iostream>
#include <string>
#include <algorithm>
using namespace std;

int field[10];

void add_13(int& elem) {
  elem += 13;
  }

class add {
  int value;
 public:
  add(int w) {value = w;}
  void operator() (int& elem) {elem += value;}
  };

template <class Function>
void for_all(Function func) {
  for(int i=0; i < 10; i++)
    func(field[i]);
  }

int main()
  {
  for(int i=0; i < 10; i++) {
    field[i] = i;
    cout << field[i] << endl;
    }
```

```
for_all(add_13);

for(int i=0; i < 10; i++)
  cout << field[i] << endl;

for_all(add(-26));

for(int i=0; i < 10; i++)
  cout << field[i] << endl;

return 0;
}
```

Using predefined function objects of the STL:

```
// for a vector container
typedef vector<int>::iterator iter;
...
// use of a function object
// sort values; cf. example for <algorithm>
stable_sort(container.begin(), container.end(), less<int>());

// use of a binder
// find first value greater than 500
iter i = find_if(container.begin(), container.end(),
                    bind2nd(greater<int>(),500));
if(i==container.end())
    cout << "Element not found" << endl;
    else
    cout << "Element found: " << *i << endl;
  }
```

## Tips

If you define your own function objects, you should derive them from either the `unary_function` class (for function objects with one parameter) or `binary_function` class (for function objects with two parameters), so that your function objects can be used together with function adapters.

## References

See function adapters.

See reference of the C++ runtime library, category utilities, function objects; header file functional.

See category operators, overloading the () operator.

# Function adapters

## Application

The concept of function objects and algorithms which adopt function objects as arguments is made even more variable by the definition of function adapters (defined in `<functional>`)

Function adapters are used to make certain objects appear to be function objects, so that they can be passed to algorithms.

## Implementation

### Binders

It is usually not possible to pass a function object with two parameters to an algorithm, which expects a function object with one parameter (such as `multiplies`). However, it is possible to assign a fixed value as a second argument and then use it like a function object with one parameter.

- To tie the first parameter of a binary function object to a fixed argument, use the `bind1st()` function.
- To tie the second parameter of a binary function object to a fixed argument, use the `bind2nd()` function.

### Negators

To negate the statement of a predicate (a function object with `bool` as the return type), use the functions `not1()` (for unary function objects) and `not2()` (for binary function objects).

### Function and method adapters

Methods cannot be passed as alternatives to functions and function objects, because they must be called through instances (different call syntax).

The functions `mem_fun()` and `mem_fun_ref()` make the passing of methods possible with or without an argument.

Although functions can be passed instead of function objects, arguments cannot be passed for binders. In this case, the insertion of one of the overloaded `ptr_fun()` functions helps.

## Example

```
#include <algorithm>
#include <functional>
#include <iostream>
```

```
#include <deque>
using namespace std;

// function to be applied later to th elements in the container
int mean_value(int a, int b) {
  return (int) (a + b) / 2;
  }

int main()  {
  typedef deque<int>::iterator iter;
  deque<int> container(5);                    // container

  int value = 0;
  for(iter i = container.begin(); i != container.end(); ++i)
    {
    *i = -(++value);                          // initialise elements
    }

  // apply a function to all elements in the container
  // transform only allows function with one parameter
  // transform passes the elements one after the other to this parameter
  // negate all elements: negate is a unary function object
  transform(container.begin(), container.end(),
            container.begin(), negate<int>());

  // multiply all elements by 2: multiplies is a binary
  // function object; therefore the factor with which the
  // individual elements are to be multiplied is written as 2nd
  // argument --thus bind2nd turns the function object multiplies
  // into a unary function
  transform(container.begin(), container.end(),
            container.begin(), bind2nd(multiplies<int>(),2));

  cout << "After negation and multiplication" << endl;
  for(iter i = container.begin(); i != container.end(); ++i)
    {
    cout << *i << endl;
    }

  // apply the mean_value function to all elements
  // since mean_value is a binary function, but transform
  // expects a unary function, the second argument must be bound
  // with the aid of the binder bind2nd. In order to apply
  // bind2nd to a function, however, the adapter ptr_fun
  // must be inserted in between
  transform(container.begin(), container.end(),
            container.begin(), bind2nd(ptr_fun(average),10));
```

```
cout << "After mean value" << endl;
for(iter i = container.begin(); i != container.end(); ++i)
   {
   cout << *i << endl;
   }
cout << endl;

cout << "First element greater than 7" << endl;
// find the 1st element whose value is greater than 7
iter i = find_if(container.begin(), container.end(),
                  bind2nd(greater<int>(),7));
cout << *i << endl;
cout << endl;

cout << "First element not gretaer than 7" << endl;
// negator: find the 1st element whose value is not greater than 7
i = find_if(container.begin(), container.end(),
            not1(bind2nd(greater<int>(),7)));
cout << *i << endl;
cout << endl;
return 0;
}
```

Output:

```
After negation and nultiplication
2
4
6
8
10
After mean value
6
7
8
9
10

First element greater than 7
8

First element not gretaer than 7
6
```

## References

See creating function objects.

See reference of the C++ runtime library, category utilities, function objects; header file functional.

# Category: multiple file programs

# Modularisation

## Application

Larger programs should not be written as an endless string of statements to be processed in sequence. Instead, the source code is organised by identifying sub-problems and solving these separately in the form of functions or classes.

To achieve a better code organisation and with a view to possible application in other programs, functions and classes of general interest are relocated to separate source text files.

## Implementation

To ensure that a function contributes in a useful way to the modularisation of a program, the following criteria must be observed:

- a function should have a precisely formulated and clearly defined task,
- task and function in turn must be formulated as general terms, since this will permit the function to be used in other programs. Therefore, it is important to carefully plan the interface of the function.
- interfaces should not be too complicated and should not have too many parameters.
- if several arguments are to be passed to modify the behaviour of the function, it makes sense to assign default arguments for the default setting (this is only possible in C++), and
- functions which are to be collected in libraries should be as independent as possible from the rest of the program; that is, global variables should be avoided. Where global elements are required, they must be declared in a common header file.

The same considerations apply to the definition of classes.

If elements (functions, classes, variables and so on) are relocated to separate source text files, it is customary

- to write the declaration into a separate header file (.h, .hpp), and
- to write the definition into the corresponding implementation file (.c, .cpp).

This division is not a requirement of the language, but it is a general custom and it contributes greatly to the uncomplicated use of program elements across file boundaries.

## References

See category libraries, creating own libraries.

See constructing a header and an implementation file.

See Reference section, category functions; category classes.

# Constructing a header and an implementation file

## Application

Relocating the code of classes and/or functions into separate source text files makes it easier to reuse these classes and functions in other programs.

Alternatively, you can

- simply adopt the source text files into the new program and recompile them with the program,

- compile the source text once (for the obj file) and then integrate the compiled file into other programs (this saves unnecessary recompilation), and

- convert the object file with an appropriate tool into a LIB file (static library) and use it like a library.

## Implementation

When you relocate elements to separate source text files, you should consider how you want to integrate these elements into programs to use them in other source text files.

It is important that:

- all source text files are bound together into a program. If the code is still a source text, the source text file first needs to be compiled together with the other source text files of the program. Then the resulting obj file can be linked with the other obj files. If the code is already a compiled obj file, you save compilation time and you only need to make sure that the linker integrates the obj file. (How this works depends on the compiler used. Usually a compiler with project management is used, otherwise you must specify, in the statement line, which source files are to be bound together.), and

- elements which are to be used in several files have been declared in all modules (translation unit, usually consisting of implementation file .cpp and header files .h, .hpp) in which they are to be used (so that the compiler knows what to do with the identifiers), but have only been defined once in the program (thus, only one memory area is reserved for these identifiers).

To ensure this, the customary procedure is as follows:

- All declarations of elements which you want to use in other modules are written into the header file. These are mostly function declarations (without a statement section), class declarations with inline method definitions, type definitions (not connected with memory reservation), and extern declarations of variables.
- All definitions are written into the implementation file (.c, .cpp). These are function definitions for the function declarations, non-inline method definitions for the class declarations, and variable definitions for the extern variables.
- All auxiliary elements (functions, classes, variables, and so on) which are required for the implementation of the elements listed in the header file are written into the implementation file. Thus, the implementation file can contain more functions, classes and variables than are listed in the header file. In this case, the header file also works like a filter that determines which elements of the implementation file are made publicly available (on the interface).
- The implementation file integrates a separate header file with an #include statement.

To be able to access elements in another module, you must

- make known to the compiler the elements that are to be used. This is not a problem thanks to the header file, as it contains all the required declarations. Therefore, you only need to integrate the header file with an #include statement, and
- ensure that the linker finds the definitions. For this you have the implementation file which, as described above, is either integrated into the program project as a source text file and compiled with it or is compiled beforehand and then integrated as an object module.

## Example

The MyClass.h header file:

```
#ifndef MyClassH
#define MyClassH
```

```
class MyClass                  // definition of the class
{
    int pValue;
 public:
    MyClass(int i) {           // inline function can be
      pValue = i;              // defined in header file!
      }

    int value();    // non-inline functions
                    // are defined in the implementation file
};

// declaration of variablen
extern MyClass myobj;
extern int global_value;

// declaration of a function
void func();
#endif
```

The `MyClass.cpp` implementation file:

```
#include <math.h>
#include <iostream>
#include "MyClass.h"
using namespace std;

int MyClass::value() {
  return pValue;
}

// definition of variables
MyClass myobj(4);
int global_value = 5;

// definition of the functions
void func()
{
  cout << "Hello from function" << endl;
}
```

The `Main.cpp` file, which accesses the elements of `MyClass.cpp`.

```
#include <iostream>
#include "MyClass.h"
using namespace std;
int main(int argc, char **argv) {
    // use of the class definition
    MyClass neuobj(3);
    cout << neuobj.value() << endl;
```

```
// use of the variables
cout << myobj.value() << endl;
cout << global_value << endl;

// use of the function
func();

return 0;
}
```

## Tips

Whereas you must make sure that normal functions are only defined once in the program, `inline` functions must be defined (identically) in every module in which they are used. This allows the definition of smaller methods directly in the class (which is automatically equivalent to an `inline` declaration).

## References

See modularisation.

See preventing multiple calls of header files.

See category libraries, creating own libraries.

See cross-module use of elements.

# Preventing multiple calls of header files

## Application

A header file may be called several times in a module. The reason for this is usually that header files in turn call other header files.

If you use, for example, an implementation file of two header files A1 and A2, which both call the header file B, B is unnecessarily called twice in the translation unit for the implementation file.

## Implementation

You can use conditional compilation to prevent the unnecessary multiple calls of header files.

To do this you use a compiler switch whose definition determines whether the contents of the header file are to be compiled or not. Usually this compiler switch runs in the same way as the header file.

It is important that, at the start, the compiler switch is not defined anywhere.

Check in the header file whether the switch is defined. If this is not the case, the switch is defined here and then the contents of the header file are specified. In later calls of the header files the switch is defined, and the declarations of the header file are skipped.

## Example

```
/* Statist.h */
#ifndef StatistH
#define StatistH
double arm_Mean(double *values, int number);
double harm_Mean(double *values, int number);
#endif
```

## Tips

The header files of the runtime library also use this technique. It is useful to take a look at the corresponding code.

## References

See constructing a header and an implementation file.

See Reference section, category preprocessor, directives for conditional compilation.

# Cross-module use of elements

## Application

If a program is divided into several translation units, how can program elements (type definitions, functions, variables) be exchanged between these units?

In the previous paragraphs, we discussed what needs to be considered in the code organisation of implementation and header files. This paragraph outlines what you must consider with regard to the various elements. Remember that you must distinguish between the declaration (header file) and definition (implementation file) of the elements, since the linker demands that each element should only be defined once in a program (insofar as the definition is connected with the reservation of memory), but must be declared in each module in which it is used so that the compiler knows what to do with the element.

## Implementation

### Classes

- Classes are type definitions for which memory does not usually need to be reserved. Thus, the class definition can be written into the header file without any problems.

- According to the ANSI standard, inline functions must be defined identically in each module in which they are used. Therefore, inline functions (functions which are explicitly declared as inline or which are defined as methods directly in the class definition) should be defined in the header file.

- Static data elements must be defined outside of the class, but in the same validity range as their class. This is done in the implementation file.

### Functions

- Function definitions are written into the implementation file.

- The header file contains the pure function declaration.

- Inline functions must be defined identically in each module in which they are used. Therefore, they are defined in the header file.

### Variables

For variables, the declaration is written into the header file, and the definition into the implementation file. The main feature here is the distinction between declaration and definition, since the usual declaration

```
type variable_identifier;
```

is both declaration and definition.

To indicate that memory is not to be reserved with such a declaration, prefix the keyword extern.

```
extern type variable_identifier;
```

## Warning

If in the course of an extern declaration, the variable is initialised, this cancels the effect of the extern declaration, since memory needs to be defined for the variable when assigning the value.

Therefore, variables must never be initialised in header files.

## Example

The above principles for separating definition and declaration are not tied to the concept of header files. The header file ultimately only introduces declarations for an implementation file into another implementation conveniently. Where there is no header file or where you want to save time and effort, you can also write the declarations directly into a source text file.

The following example illustrates two source text files of a program. In the first file a class, a function and a variable have been defined. The second file shows the declarations which are required to use the elements of the first file.

```
/* source text1.cpp */          /* source text2.cpp */
class demo {                     class demo {      // definition is
   ...                              ...            // repeated
   };                               };

int func(int par) {              int func(int par); // declaration without
   ...                                              // statement part
   };

int i;                           extern int i;     // extern declaration
```

### References

See constructing a header and an implementation file.

See restricting elements to one module.

# Restricting elements to one module

## Application

Occasionally you may want to define global elements whose validity is to be restricted to their own data range; for example, a global variable through which all functions in the current file can exchange data (which is to be distinguished from identical global variables of other translation units of the program).

## Implementation

Traditionally the keyword static is used to define global functions and variables, but which are otherwise restricted to their file. In C++, this is equivalent to the declaration in an unnamed namespace.

Alternatively, it is also possible to declare the elements in a named namespace in C++. This has the advantage that you can still decide later on whether to access the elements through the introduction of the namespace or through qualified identifiers in other translation units.

## Example

If you want to use your own definitions for func() and i in a second source text file, you must assign internal linkage to the identifier. This is done through a declaration as static.

```
/* source text1.cpp */          /* source text2.cpp */
int func(int par) {...}         static int func(int par) {...}
int i;                          static int i;
```

## References

See cross-module use of elements.

See Reference section, category variables and data types, namespaces.

# Category: libraries

# Using libraries

## Application

To avoid having to program everything yourself, you often fall back on libraries and the elements defined in these libraries (functions, classes, and so on). Apart from the runtime library, which is provided with every C++ compiler, and compiler-specific libraries (for example the MFC by Microsoft or the VCL by Delphi and the C++ Builder – both supporting Windows), you will occasionally buy further libraries for specific task areas (statistics, recording of measuring data, accounting, and so on).

## Implementation

To be able to access and use the elements of a library, the following conditions must be met:

- The linker must know where the definitions of the library elements can be found. You need to tell the linker where the library files (for example xxx.lib) can be found. Usually, it is possible to specify a directory path for the library files for this purpose. Secondly, you must specify that the current project uses the library. For compilers with integrated development environment, this is usually done through the project settings, where there is usually an entry field for specifying additional libraries. For statement line compilers, the libraries that are to be integrated can be specified through MAKE files or directly through the statement line call of the linker. (Incidentally, the C/C++ runtime library is automatically integrated.)

- If you wish to use an element from one of the libraries in a translation unit, this must be made known to the compiler beforehand. For this purpose, there are a few header files provided with the library. Check in which header file the desired element/s have been declared, and integrate the header file with an #include statement at the beginning of the source text file. For the compiler to find the header file/s, you must enter the path to the header files into the header directory path of the compiler or specify the path directly in the #include statement.

| | |
|---|---|
| #include <bib.h> | Compiler searches for file in its header directory path |
| #include "bib.h" | Compiler searches for file in the directory of the source text files |
| #include "c:\\list\\bib.h" | Compiler searches for file in the specified directory |

## Tips

To be able to call library functions which have been created by a C compiler in a C++ program, the function has to be declared as

```
extern "C"
```

in the corresponding header file.

## References

See Reference section, category preprocessor, inserting and replacing source code.

See basics section, using default libraries.

# Creating user-defined libraries

## Application

Apart from the use of ready-made libraries, there is also the option to create your own libraries. Libraries have three essential advantages:

- they have already been compiled,
- when creating a program, the complete code of the library is not integrated into the program, but only those parts (functions, classes) that are actually required, and
- for programmers who produce commercial libraries, there is the additional advantage that the source code does not need to be provided, which means that their know-how remains hidden from the user.

## Implementation

The creation of a library usually occurs in several steps.

- It becomes apparent that certain functions or classes are of general importance and can thus be used by various programs.
- After the source text has been carefully checked, cleared of possible bugs errors, and the interface of the functions or classes has been optimised for general use, connected functions, classes, global variables and so on, can be collected into separate source files. Collections of functions and classes are created in this way.
- It is possible to construct new libraries or to extend or change existing ones from the individual source files, by means of compilation and the calling of special library programs. The corresponding programs for creating and

managing libraries are provided with the compilers. Compilers with integrated development environment and project management often also have a separate project type for creating libraries

## Overview: comparison of libraries

We can distinguish between three types of collections of functions or classes:

- Collections of functions or classes are simple files in which the source text has been made up, containing function definitions, class declarations, global data types and so on. Such source text collections must be recompiled when creating a program. However, you can save the compilation by compiling the module separately and integrating the resulting object file into the programs. The disadvantage is that the whole object program is adopted each time.

- Static libraries (LIB) are constructed of object files. During creation, a directory of the symbols (names of the defined functions, classes, and so on) contained in the library is created, which enables the linker to extract only the code required.

- Dynamic libraries (DLL), as used by Windows, are not integrated into programs. Instead, programs contain references to the dynamic library. Only when the program is executed and a DLL function is called is the library loaded into the working memory. If several simultaneously running programs call the same DLL, only one copy, which is used by all programs, is loaded into the working memory.

| Library | Compiled | In .exe | In memory |
|---------|----------|---------|-----------|
| collection | yes/no | complete | several times |
| static | yes | according to requirements | several times |
| dynamic | yes | no | once |

## References

See category multiple file programs, modularisation; constructing a header and an implementation file.

See using libraries.

# Category: internationalisation and localisation

# Special characters in MS-DOS

## Application

Currently, most Windows applications use the Windows ANSI code to characterise code. This also applies to most compilers, which are used under Windows (C++ Builder, Visual C++).

This may lead to problems if you write strings for outputting on the Windows console (MS-DOS entry prompt) with such a compiler (or generally with an editor that uses the ANSI character code), since the Windows console uses the ASCII/ OEM character set. This is identical to the ANSI character set for the characters with the coding 32 to 127, however, from 128 onwards, the character sets diverge.

Therefore, if you write a program in an ANSI editor, which outputs 'ä'

```
puts("ä");
```

the editor codes the character in the source text file according to ANSI with the decimal code 228 (hexadecimal E4).

If the program is subsequently executed on the console, a character with the hexadecimal code E4 is output, however, it will be coded according to the OEM character table. It is difficult to predict which character is now output, as different code pages can be used for the ASCII characters from 128 to 255 (non-US Windows versions commonly use pages containing fewer graphic characters and more accented letters). In any case, the desired character will not have the same code in ANSI and ASCII and will not be represented correctly in the editor and the console (ANSI and ASCII are identical only for the characters up to 128).

## Implementation

To be able to correctly represent umlauts or other accents from the OEM character set above 127 on the console, you must circumvent the ANSI coding when writing the source text.

You enter the OEM code of the character, instead of entering the actual character.

Instead of

```
puts("Wählen Sie eine Option [select an option]: ");
```

you would write

```
puts("W\x84hlen Sie eine Option [select an option]: ");
```

## Example

```
#include <iostream>
using namespace std;

int main()
  {
  cout << "Umlauts and special characters:" << endl;

        // ä     ö     ü
  cout << "\x84 \x94 \x81" << endl;

        // ‡     ·     ,    Ë    È
  cout << "\x85 \xa0 \x83 \x8a \x82" << endl;

        //      Ê     Á
  cout << "\x86 \x91 \x87" << endl;

  return 0;
  }
```

## Tips

Characters which are not on the keyboard can be entered using the ALT key through the numeric keypad, provided that Num Lock is activated (press the NUM key).

To type in a special character, (whose ANSI code you know) in an ANSI editor press the ALT key, and then type the ANSI code on the numeric keypad (starting with 0).

To test how individual characters are coded on the console, press the ALT key, and then type the ASCII code on the numeric keypad.

## References

See ASCII and ANSI tables in the appendix.

# Wide characters

## Application

Gradually, the software industry is converting to larger, 16- or 32-bit character sets as default character sets. The most important 16-bit character set is UNICODE.

## Implementation

To work with 16-bit character sets in your program, you must work with wide characters; thus, instead of using the char type, use wchar_t.

If you work with C strings,

- declare the strings as pointers to wchar_t or arrays of the wchar_t type,
- prefix L to string and character literals, and
- use the wc functions of the runtime library for programming with the strings.

If you work with C++ strings,

- declare the strings as objects of the wstring type,
- prefix L to string and character literals, and
- use the methods of the wstring class for programming with the strings.

## Example

Using wide character strings in C:

```
#include <stdio.h>
#include <string.h>

int main()
  {
  wchar_t wc_str1[100] = {L"Hello"};
  wchar_t *wc_str2 = L" World!";

  wcscat(wc_str1, wc_str2);

  wprintf(L"Gruss: %s\n", wc_str1);

  return 0;
  }
```

Using wide character strings in C++:

```
#include <iostream>
#include <string>
using namespace std;

int main()
  {
  wstring wc_str3(L"Hello");
  wstring wc_str4(L" World!");

  wc_str3.append(wc_str4);

  wcout << wc_str3 << endl;

  return 0;
  }
```

## Reference

See Reference section, category strings, wide characters and multi-byte characters.

# Localising output

## Application

Programs use text output at many positions:

- for menus,
- for entry prompts, and
- for warnings and other messages.

These text passages are distributed as string literals all over the program, and it is very inconvenient to localise them, when necessary, for example for sale in another country and to translate the literals into another language.

## Implementation

The localisation of literals can be carried out through various concepts, which are more or less difficult to implement.

- All strings can be defined in the form of a string table at the start of the program. If localisation is required, you only need to process the table (see example below).
- it is also possible to designate several localised string tables. The string table can be controlled through compiler switches and conditional compilation.
- You can get by without recompilation if the strings are read from an external file. Windows programs do not only use this concept for string tables, but also for menus, dialog boxes and other elements.

## Example

```c
#include <stdio.h>

// string table
const char *message[] =
    {
    "Program will be terminated",
    "Enter a number between 0 and 5: ",
    "The input was not correct!",
    "Press F1 for Help",
    "Please wait...",
```

```
      "The program has unexpectedly quit.",
      };


int main()
  {
  int your_input;
  printf("Welcome to the string table test program\n\n");

  do
    {
    printf("%s\n\n",message[1]);
    scanf("%d",&your_input);
    fflush(stdin);

    if(your_input>=0 && your_input <=5)
      printf("Message: %s\n\n\n",message[your_input]);
    } while(your_input!=0);

  return 0;
  }
```

## Reference

See Reference section, category preprocessor, directives for conditional compilation.

# Local environment

## Application

When a program is executed, it runs within a local environment which determines how the program must behave with regard to certain language- and country-specific features. These local settings are, for example, the formatting of floating point numbers (with a comma or dot for separating decimals), the format of dates, the currency symbol used, and so on.

These settings are referred to as locale, and individual categories (date, currency system, character coding) within a locale are referred to as facets.

By default, a program runs under the default locale 'C', however, it can also use other locales, if the operating system or the compiler can provide them.

Furthermore, in C++, a program can define its own locales or replace parts of existing locales with its own settings (by creating a new locale as a copy of an existing locale and additionally passing the replacement for the relevant setting to the constructor).

## Implementation

In C the `setlocale()` function is used to switch facets. The selected locale influences the functionality of other C functions, for example `printf()`, `strftime()` or `tolower()`.

In C++, locales are created as objects of the `locale` class (in C++ it is also possible to have several `locale` objects in one program). These locales can be applied to streams with the `imbue()` method.

To work with existing locales, you must know their names.

The following locales are always available:

| | |
|---|---|
| "C" | A minimum environment for C compilers (initial locale for every program execution) |
| " " | The implementation-specific native environment of the platform |

Other available locales and the names assigned to them depend on your operating system and your compiler. Usual names are:

de_DE, De_DE, German, en_US, en_GB, and so on.

## Example

Using locales in C:

```
#include <stdio.h>
#include <locale.h>
#include <time.h>

int main()
{
  time_t ltime;
  struct tm *curtime;
  unsigned char str[100];

  setlocale(LC_ALL, "de_DE");
  time (&ltime);
  curtime = gmtime(&ltime);

  strftime((char *)str, 100, "%x", (const struct tm *)curtime);
  printf("Date specification for German locale: '%s'\n",str);

  setlocale(LC_ALL, "C");
  time (&ltime);
  curtime = gmtime(&ltime);
```

```
    strftime((char *)str, 100, "%x",(const struct tm *)curtime);
    printf("Date specification for C locale: '%s'\n",str);

    return 0;
}
```

Using locales in C++.

Establishing a locale with its own facet and applying the locale to the output stream.

```
#include <iostream>     // the locale settings may also be used
#include <locale>       // during overloading of the stream
                        // operators
#include <stdio.h>
using namespace std;

// user-defined facet which set a comma instead of a decimal point
class de_Num : public numpunct_byname<char> {
  public:
    de_Num(const char* name) : numpunct_byname<char>(name) {
      }
  protected:
    virtual char_type do_decimal_point() const {
      return ',';
      }
  };

int main(int argc, char **argv)
  {
  // user-defined locale with de_Num facet
  locale myloc(locale("C"), new de_Num(""));

  double value;
  cout << "Floating point number under C locale: \t" << 3.1415 << endl;

  // set locale for stream
  cout.imbue(myloc);
  cout << "Floating point number under new locale:\t" << 3.1415 << endl;

  return 0;
  }
```

Output:

```
Floating point number under C locale:     3.1415
Floating point number under new locale:   3,1415
```

## Tips

To be able to work with locales in C++ builder programs, you first need to activate the support for locales:

```
#define __USELOCALES__
```

In C, there is only one global locale, and in C++ locales are usually applied to individual streams with imbue(). However, you can also define one locale as the global C++ locale. For this, use the static method locale::global() (an alternative to setlocale()).

## References

See querying the settings of a locale.

See reference of the C runtime library, header file locale.h.

See reference of the C++ runtime library, classes for local settings.

# Querying the settings of a locale

## Application

You may not always want to change or adapt a locale immediately. Sometimes, you may wish to find out which settings are stored in a locale, to begin with.

## Implementation

In C, you copy the settings of the global locale into a lconv structure with the localeconv() function. Afterwards, you can read the individual settings from the structure.

In C++, the locales are represented by instances of the locale class. The individual settings are organised into categories (facets), for which there are separate classes. With the help of the global method has_facet() the facets of a locale can be returned and queried.

## Example

```
struct lconv ll;
struct lconv *conv = &ll;
conv = localeconv();
printf("Decimal point            : %s\n", conv->decimal_point);
printf("Thousands separator      : %s\n", conv->thousands_sep);
printf("Digit grouping           : %s\n", conv->grouping);
```

```
printf("Internat. currency symbol   : %s\n", conv->int_curr_symbol);
printf("Thousand sep. (currency)    : %s\n", conv->mon_thousands_sep);
printf("Grouping  (currency)        : %s\n", conv->mon_grouping);
printf("Plus sign  (currency)       : %s\n", conv->positive_sign);
printf("Minus sign  (currency)      : %s\n", conv->negative_sign);
printf("Fractions (ISO)             : %d\n", conv->int_frac_digits);
printf("Fractions    (currency)     : %d\n", conv->frac_digits);
printf("Currency symbol before/after pos. values
                            : %d\n", conv->p_cs_precedes);
printf("Space between. currency symbol and pos. values
                            : %d\n", conv->p_sep_by_space);
printf("Currency symbol before/after neg. values
                            : %d\n", conv->n_cs_precedes);
printf("Space between currency symbol and neg. values
                            : %d\n", conv->n_sep_by_space);
printf("Formatting of pos. curr. specs : %d\n", conv->p_sign_posn);
printf("Formatting of neg. curr. specs : %d\n", conv->n_sign_posn);
```

## Reference

See local environment.

# Category: miscellaneous

# Random numbers

rand()

## Application

A frequent and interesting problem encountered in programming is the creation of random numbers. Random numbers are not only required for the execution of numerous programming tasks, but are also frequently used for testing programs.

## Implementation

A random number is a sequence of digits which does not repeat itself even after thousands of digits and which does not show a pattern. Additional information on how such a sequence can be created can be found in any good book on algorithms. For practical purposes, it is usually sufficient to know that two powerful functions for creating random numbers are already defined in the C runtime library.

The rand() function generates an pseudo-random integer. The generated number lies in the range between 0 and the constant RAND_MAX. The function always produces the same sequence of random numbers, which is especially important for debugging programs. To generate a new number sequence at every program start-up, the random generator must be initialised with the srand() function, where srand() is passed a different number value at every program call (for example you can query and pass the current processor time which is coded in seconds; see time() function).

## Warning

Some compilers provide even more powerful random generators for professional applications (for example drand48() for the UNIX GNU compiler).

## Example

```
#include <stdlib.h>
#include <stdio.h>
#include <time.h>
#define MAX 100
// auxiliary function for comparison of two elements
int sortFunc(const void *a, const void *b)
  {
  int i = *((int *) a);
  int j = *((int *) b);
  if( i == j )
    return 0;
```

```
      else if (i < j )
        return -1;
        else
        return 1;
  }

int main(int argc, char** argv)
  {
  int i;
  time_t t;
  int values[MAX];
  int searchvalue;
  int* found;
  srand((unsigned) time(&t)); // srand(1) for debugging

  // generate random values between 0 und 99
  for(i=0; i<MAX; i++)
    {
    values[i] = rand() % 100;
    }

  // sort field
  qsort((void *)values, MAX, sizeof(int), sortFunc);

  scanf("%d",&searchvalue);
  fflush(stdin);

  // binary search in array
  found = (int *) bsearch (&searchvalue, values, MAX,
      sizeof(int), sortFunc);
  if(found)
    printf("The value %d is contained in the array\n",*gefunden);
    else
    printf("Value not found in the array\n");
  return 0;
  }
```

# Assembler

asm

## Application

The integration of assembler statements can be used by experienced programmers for runtime optimisation. Available assembler code modules can also be built into a program in this way.

## Implementation

With the help of the keyword asm assembler statements can be incorporated into the C/C++ source text. It can be used for inserting individual assembler statements

```
asm mov        dword ptr [ebp-4],12
asm mov        dword ptr [ebp-8],5
...
```

as well as for integrating assembler blocks

```
asm
  {
    mov        dword ptr [ebp-4],12
    mov        dword ptr [ebp-8],5
    ...
  }
```

## Warning

The precise syntax of the assembler statements may vary from one compiler to the next. Moreover, not all compilers support the ANSI keyword asm. The Microsoft Visual C++ compiler, for example, still uses the compiler-internal keyword asm in version 6.0.

Under DOS and Windows 3.x it was common amongst assembler programmers to use interrupts, either via direct calls or by implementing user-defined interrupt handlers. Under Windows 9x and NT, however, working with interrupts is restricted. The operating system controls the interrupt table and prevents the call of numerous interrupts. However, in return, it provides programmers with alternative concepts via new functions of the Windows API.

## Examples

```
#include <stdio.h>

int main()
{
  int var1, var2;
  int result;

  asm
  {
    mov        dword ptr [ebp-4],12
    mov        dword ptr [ebp-8],5
    mov        eax,dword ptr [ebp-4]
    imul       dword ptr [ebp-8]
    mov        dword ptr [ebp-12],eax
  }
```

```
    printf("Result = %d\n", result);
    return 0;
}
```

## Tips

The precise syntax of the assembler statements may depend on the integrated assembler which is used by your compiler. To familiarise yourself with the syntax, have your compiler create an asm file for your C++ source text.

- In case of the C++ builder, you only need to adopt asm statements into the source text. The compiler then automatically creates an asm file which you can load into the editor.

- In case of the Visual C++ compiler, you must switch to the page C/C++ in the dialog box of the project settings and select the Listing-Date category. Then you can, for example, select the Assembler with source text option in the Type of listing file field and specify in the field below the name of the asm file that is to be created. After rebuilding the program, you can load the asm file into the editor.

With the asm code you can also, for example, inform yourself about the addresses of local variables and parameters.

# Windows programming

## Application

When learning C/C++, you usually start with the creation of console programs (under Windows these are programs which run in the window of the MS-DOS prompt). One reason for this is that programming of console programs does not make high demands on the inexperienced programmer, so he can concentrate on learning C/C++.

However, more and more programs now run under graphic Windows interfaces. Many C++ programmers, therefore, dream of being able to program such window-oriented systems (for example Windows 95/NT or XWindows/OSF Motif under UNIX).

## Implementation

Whether you create console programs or graphic Windows applications, you are programming in the same language: C/C++. The reason that the creation of Windows programs is so difficult and requires a completely new set of programming skills for the beginner is that the Windows system makes high demands on the programs which are to run under it.

(The following remarks are based on Windows 95/NT, however, they also apply to X Windows and OSF Motif.)

- **Applications which run under a Windows system usually have a window,** known as the main window of the application.

- **Applications can create further windows.** Windows may also contain other windows. Thus, the well-known control elements (entry field, list fields and so on) are also windows whose functionality has already been implemented in the DLLs of the operating system.

- **Windows are the interfaces to the user.** Input and output occur through the windows. However, the functions and streams for input and output, which are defined in the runtime library, are unsuitable for Windows programs, as they cannot work with windows, but are dependent on a console.

- **Windows applications are event-oriented.** Mouse clicks and keyboard entries by the user are caught by the Windows system and are sent in a roundabout way through the application to the window to which the mouse click or keyboard entries refer. The window is responsible for receiving these event messages and, if necessary, responding accordingly.

- To allow the creation of applications which meet these requirements, Windows provides a collection of functions (including numerous macros and constants), known as **Windows API.**

- Apart from the central functions for the creation of windows and the processing of event messages, the API contains functions for every aspect of a Windows program (graphics, text processing, window management, access on the level of the operating system and so on).

- Unfortunately, the Windows PI is entirely written in C and, therefore, a beginner would see it as a confusing muddle of functions. Consequently, compilers such as the C++ Builder or Visual C++ provide their own class libraries, which encapsulate the most important functions of the Windows API and allow object-oriented Windows programming.

## Example

```
#include <windows.h>

// forward declaration
LRESULT CALLBACK WndProc(HWND, UINT, WPARAM, LPARAM);

// entry function, the arguments are passed
// to the function by Windows
```

```
int APIENTRY WinMain(  HINSTANCE hInstance, HINSTANCE hPrevInstance,
                       LPSTR     lpCmdLine, int       nCmdShow )
{
   HWND             hWindow;        // window handle
   MSG              Message;        // structure variable for messages
   WNDCLASS         WinClass;       // window class

   // first instance
   memset(&WinClass,0,sizeof(WNDCLASS));
   WinClass.style = CS_HREDRAW | CS_VREDRAW;
   WinClass.lpfnWndProc = WndProc;
   WinClass.hInstance = hInstance;
   WinClass.hbrBackground = (HBRUSH) (COLOR_WINDOW+1);
   WinClass.hCursor = LoadCursor(NULL, IDC_ARROW);
   WinClass.lpszClassName = "Windows-Programm";

   // register window class
   if(!RegisterClass(&WinClass))
      return(FALSE);

   // create main application window
   hWindow = CreateWindow("Windows Program",
                     "API Program",
                     WS_OVERLAPPEDWINDOW, 10, 10,
                     400,300,NULL,NULL,hInstance,NULL);
   ShowWindow(hWindow, nCmdShow);
   UpdateWindow(hWindow);

   // loop in which the event messages are intercepted
   while (GetMessage (&Message, NULL, 0, 0) )
      {
      TranslateMessage(&Message);
      DispatchMessage(&Message);
      }

   return (Message.wParam);
   }


// window function which handles the events of the window
LRESULT CALLBACK WndProc(HWND hWnd, UINT uiMessage,
                         WPARAM wParam, LPARAM lParam)
{
   char str[30] = "Mouse was clicked here";
   HDC dc;

   // answer messages with appropriate actions
   switch(uiMessage)
   {
      case WM_LBUTTONDOWN:
```

```
        // get device context for output in window
        dc = GetDC(hWnd);
        TextOut(dc, LOWORD (lParam), HIWORD (lParam) ,str,strlen(str));

        // release device context
        ReleaseDC(hWnd, dc);
        return 0;

  case WM_DESTROY:
        PostQuitMessage(0);         // destroy window
        return 0;
   default:
        return DefWindowProc(hWnd,uiMessage, wParam,lParam);
  }
}
}
```

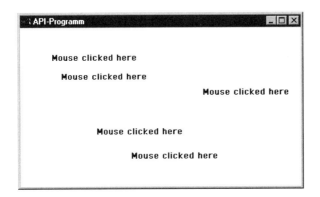

## Tips

The above example illustrates a typical frame of a Windows API program. However, beginners should not necessarily start programming in Windows through the API. More powerful compilers such as Visual C++ or Borland C++ permit an easier start with support through class libraries and wizards. RAD compilers such as C++ Builder take on windows programming without requiring intervention from the C/C++ programmer. They permit the composition of Windows interfaces and event handling by mouse click. This has the advantage that, after a short period of getting used to RAD programming, it is possible to create attractive Windows programs and to acquire knowledge of Windows API that is, required by all respectable Windows programmers, step by step.

# Database programming

## Application

Practically every application manipulates data, which may only be two `int` values which are multiplied. If the data quantities which are processed by a program increase above a certain amount, at a certain point you will need to know how best to manage the data.

## Implementation

In the simplest case, all data is kept in the working memory during the execution of the program. The data is stored and organised either:

- in individual variables,
- in arrays or dynamic fields, or
- in higher data structures (in the same way as they are implemented, for example, in STL containers).

If data is to be saved persistently between the program calls, data is usually saved in a file. This can be a simple binary file, in which data of the same type is stored in sequence without any gaps, or a text file, in which individual data is separated by special characters (for example, commas).

With the help of text files, it is also possible to create small databases by writing one data set into each line and separate the individual fields of a data set by commas (or other characters). Most professional database programs can read such files and convert them into their own format.

If larger data sets are to be managed, you start to save the data permanently in a database and only read the data which is currently needed, with the program.

If demands on the organisation of data in the database increase, it is recommended that a special database software for the management of the data in the database (such as Access or Oracle) is used, and that data is only queried with your own C/C++ program, if necessary, and new or modified data is written into the database.

For this, you require (apart from the database) a driver for the database as well as an API, a collection of functions with which the C/C++ program can control the database software and access the data in the database. More powerful compilers, such as Visual C++ or C++ Builder, provide special classes for the creation of a database connection and for database access.

# Example

Using an external file for saving data:

```cpp
#include <iostream>
#include <fstream>
#include <string>
#include <stdio.h>
using namespace std;

struct Demo {
  int value;
  char text[30];
  } structures[10];

int main()  {
  ifstream file_in;
  ofstream file_out;
  int element;
  struct Demo read_obj;

  // initialise array with structures
  int loop;
  for(loop=0; loop < 10; loop++)  {
    structures[loop].value = loop;
    sprintf(structures[loop].text,"%d. Structure Variable",loop);
    }

  // open output file
  file_out.open("Output.dat", ios_base::out);
  if (!file_out)  {
    cerr << "File could not be opened!\n";
    return 1;
    }

  // write array with structures to file
  file_out.write((char *)structures, sizeof(struct Demo)*10);
  file_out.close();

  // open input file
  file_in.open("Output.dat", ios_base::in);
  if (!file_in)  {
    cerr << "File could not be opened!\n";
    return 1;
    }

  // which structure shlould be read
  cout << "Which element should be read <0 - 9> : ";
  cin >> element;
```

```
// position file pointer
file_in.seekg(element*sizeof(struct Demo),ios_base::beg);

// read structure
file_in.read((char *) &read_obj,sizeof(struct Demo));

// display read structure on screen
cout << read_obj.text << endl;;
cout << read_obj.value << endl;

file_in.close();
return 0;
}
```

# Appendix

# Compatibility between C++ and C

In principle, the concept of C++ ensures that C code compiled with a C++ compiler behaves in exactly the same way when executed as if it had been compiled with a C compiler.

In some minor points, however, C++ deviates from the C semantics. The most important differences are:

- The data type of character literals is `int` in C and `char` in C++. This affects, for example, comparisons such as: `sizeof('c') == sizeof(int)`.

- The `main()` function cannot be called recursively.

- C++ carries out more rigorous type checks.

- In C++, a pointer to `void` can only be converted into a pointer to an object type by explicit type conversion.

- In C++, pointers to `const` objects cannot be converted into pointers to `void` without explicit type conversion.

- C++ does not support implicit function declarations with type specification.

- In C++, types cannot be defined in expressions (for example, in explicit type conversions).

- In C++, `switch` or `goto` statements cannot jump over a declaration containing an initialiser.

- In C++, a type alias defined with `typedef` and a class type out of a common scope cannot have the same name.

- In C++, `const` objects must be initialised.

- Automatic insertion of `int` in declarations without type specification does not exist in C++.

- In C++, variables of `enum` types can only be assigned values out of their `enum` type (the underlying `int` values cannot be assigned without explicit type conversion).

- In C++, a function declaration without a parameter list stands for a function that does not take over arguments (in C, this only means that the parameter list is not yet known).

- In C++, there is no Kernighan/Ritchie declaration of functions.

- In C++, an embedded class is local with respect to the surrounding class.

- The preprocessor switch `__STDC__` need not be defined for C++ compilers.

# ASCII table

| Dec | Hex | Char | Dec | Hex | Char | Dec | Hex | Char | Dec | Hex | Char |
|-----|-----|------|-----|-----|------|-----|-----|------|-----|-----|------|
| 0 | 00 | NUL | 32 | 20 | SP | 64 | 40 | @ | 96 | 60 | ' |
| 1 | 01 | SOH | 33 | 21 | ! | 65 | 41 | A | 97 | 61 | a |
| 2 | 02 | STX | 34 | 22 | " | 66 | 42 | B | 98 | 62 | b |
| 3 | 03 | ETX | 35 | 23 | # | 67 | 43 | C | 99 | 63 | c |
| 4 | 04 | EOT | 36 | 24 | $ | 68 | 44 | D | 100 | 64 | d |
| 5 | 05 | ENQ | 37 | 25 | % | 69 | 45 | E | 101 | 65 | e |
| 6 | 06 | ACK | 38 | 26 | & | 70 | 46 | F | 102 | 66 | f |
| 7 | 07 | BEL | 39 | 27 | ' | 71 | 47 | G | 103 | 67 | g |
| 8 | 08 | BS | 40 | 28 | ( | 72 | 48 | H | 104 | 68 | h |
| 9 | 09 | HT | 41 | 29 | ) | 73 | 49 | I | 105 | 69 | i |
| 10 | 0A | NL | 42 | 2A | * | 74 | 4A | J | 106 | 6A | j |
| 11 | 0B | VT | 43 | 2B | + | 75 | 4B | K | 107 | 6B | k |
| 12 | 0C | NP | 44 | 2C | , | 76 | 4C | L | 108 | 6C | l |
| 13 | 0D | CR | 45 | 2D | - | 77 | 4D | M | 109 | 6D | m |
| 14 | 0E | SO | 46 | 2E | . | 78 | 4E | N | 110 | 6E | n |
| 15 | 0F | SI | 47 | 2F | / | 79 | 4F | O | 111 | 6F | o |
| 16 | 10 | DLE | 48 | 30 | 0 | 80 | 50 | P | 112 | 70 | p |
| 17 | 11 | DC1 | 49 | 31 | 1 | 81 | 51 | Q | 113 | 71 | q |
| 18 | 12 | DC2 | 50 | 32 | 2 | 82 | 52 | R | 114 | 72 | r |
| 19 | 13 | DC3 | 51 | 33 | 3 | 83 | 53 | S | 115 | 73 | s |
| 20 | 14 | DC4 | 52 | 34 | 4 | 84 | 54 | T | 116 | 74 | t |
| 21 | 15 | NAK | 53 | 35 | 5 | 85 | 55 | U | 117 | 75 | u |
| 22 | 16 | SYN | 54 | 36 | 6 | 86 | 56 | V | 118 | 76 | v |
| 23 | 17 | ETB | 55 | 37 | 7 | 87 | 57 | W | 119 | 77 | w |
| 24 | 18 | CAN | 56 | 38 | 8 | 88 | 58 | X | 120 | 78 | x |
| 25 | 19 | EM | 57 | 39 | 9 | 89 | 59 | Y | 121 | 79 | y |
| 26 | 1A | SUB | 58 | 3A | : | 90 | 5A | Z | 122 | 7A | z |
| 27 | 1B | ESC | 59 | 3B | ; | 91 | 5B | [ | 123 | 7B | { |
| 28 | 1C | FS | 60 | 3C | < | 92 | 5C | \ | 124 | 7C | \| |
| 29 | 18 | CAN | 61 | 3D | = | 93 | 5D | ] | 125 | 7D | } |
| 30 | 19 | EM | 62 | 3E | > | 94 | 5E | ^ | 126 | 7E | ~ |
| 31 | 1A | SUB | 63 | 3F | ? | 95 | 5F | _ | 127 | 7F | DEL |

# ANSI table

For the characters from 32 to 127, the ANSI table is identical with the ASCII table. For the subsequent characters from 128 to 255. there are various code pages. Which code page is used depends on the configuration of the operating system and the current application. The following code table is typical for a German language installation.

| Dec | Hex | Char | Dec | Hex | Char | Dec | Hex | Char | Dec | Hex | Char |
|-----|-----|------|-----|-----|------|-----|-----|------|-----|-----|------|
| 128 | 80 | _ | 160 | A0 | | 192 | C0 | À | 224 | E0 | à |
| 129 | 81 | _ | 161 | A1 | ¡ | 193 | C1 | Á | 225 | E1 | á |
| 130 | 82 | , | 162 | A2 | ¢ | 194 | C2 | Â | 226 | E2 | â |
| 131 | 83 | ƒ | 163 | A3 | £ | 195 | C3 | Ã | 227 | E3 | ã |
| 132 | 84 | " | 164 | A4 | | 196 | C4 | Ä | 228 | E4 | ä |
| 133 | 85 | … | 165 | A5 | ¥ | 197 | C5 | Å | 229 | E5 | å |
| 134 | 86 | † | 166 | A6 | ≠ | 198 | C6 | Æ | 230 | E6 | æ |
| 135 | 87 | ‡ | 167 | A7 | § | 199 | C7 | Ç | 231 | E7 | ç |
| 136 | 88 | ^ | 168 | A8 | ¨ | 200 | C8 | È | 232 | E8 | è |
| 137 | 89 | ‰ | 169 | A9 | © | 201 | C9 | É | 233 | E9 | é |
| 138 | 8A | ≥ | 170 | AA | ª | 202 | CA | Ê | 234 | EA | ê |
| 139 | 8B | ‹ | 171 | AB | « | 203 | CB | Ë | 235 | EB | ë |
| 140 | 8C | Œ | 172 | AC | ¬ | 204 | CC | Ì | 236 | EC | ì |
| 141 | 8D | _ | 173 | AD | - | 205 | CD | Í | 237 | ED | í |
| 142 | 8E | _ | 174 | AE | ® | 206 | CE | Î | 238 | EE | î |
| 143 | 8F | _ | 175 | AF | ¯ | 207 | CF | Ï | 239 | EF | ï |
| 144 | 90 | _ | 176 | B0 | ° | 208 | D0 | √ | 240 | F0 | ≤ |
| 145 | 91 | ' | 177 | B1 | ± | 209 | D1 | Ñ | 241 | F1 | ñ |
| 146 | 92 | ' | 178 | B2 | Σ | 210 | D2 | Ò | 242 | F2 | ò |
| 147 | 93 | " | 179 | B3 | ∏ | 211 | D3 | Ó | 243 | F3 | ó |
| 148 | 94 | " | 180 | B4 | ' | 212 | D4 | Ô | 244 | F4 | ô |
| 149 | 95 | • | 181 | B5 | µ | 213 | D5 | Õ | 245 | F5 | õ |
| 150 | 96 | - | 182 | B6 | ¶ | 214 | D6 | Ö | 246 | F6 | ö |
| 151 | 97 | - | 183 | B7 | · | 215 | D7 | ∞ | 247 | F7 | ÷ |
| 152 | 98 | ~ | 184 | B8 | ‚ | 216 | D8 | Ø | 248 | F8 | ø |
| 153 | 99 | ™ | 185 | B9 | ∂ | 217 | D9 | Ù | 249 | F9 | ù |
| 154 | 9A | ● | 186 | BA | º | 218 | DA | Ú | 250 | FA | ú |

| Dec | Hex | Char | Dec | Hex | Char | Dec | Hex | Char | Dec | Hex | Char |
|-----|-----|------|-----|-----|------|-----|-----|------|-----|-----|------|
| 155 | 9B | › | 187 | BB | » | 219 | DB | Û | 251 | FB | û |
| 156 | 9C | œ | 188 | BC | π | 220 | DC | Ü | 252 | FC | ü |
| 157 | 9D | _ | 189 | BD | ∫ | 221 | DD | ≈ | 253 | FD | Δ |
| 158 | 9E | _ | 190 | BE | Ω | 222 | DE | ◊ | 254 | FE | |
| 159 | 9F | Ÿ | 191 | BF | ¿ | 223 | DF | ß | 255 | FF | ÿ |

# Glossary

**Abstract class:** an abstract class is a class that contains one or more purely virtual methods (methods without a definition part) and usually serves as an interface template for class hierarchies. No instances can be created from abstract classes.

**Buffer:** input and output operations via streams (for example, on stdin, cin or to and from files) are usually buffered by default to increase execution speed. When working with C++ stream classes, users can influence buffering themselves.

**Casting:** another term for explicit type conversion.

**Classes:** classes comprise and represent objects with common properties and behaviour.

**Class variable:** an element variable which is declared as static in a class and is jointly used by all instances of the class. (Class variables can be accessed directly via the class name.)

**Compilation unit:** all source text files translated by the compiler in one step into one object file are commonly called modules or compilation units. A compilation unit consists of an implementation file (with the file extension .c or .cpp) and all source text files whose contents are integrated directly or indirectly via #include statements.

**Constructor:** a special method called for the creation (instantiation) of objects of a class.

**Container:** a class that has been implemented to contain and manage data or objects of other classes. The different container classes of the C++ runtime library build on various higher data structures, such as arrays, lists or trees, which determine efficiency and the optimal application area of the containers.

**Copy constructor:** a constructor called with an argument of the type of its own class and used to create a new object on the basis of an existing object of its class.

**Declaration:** the introduction of a new identifier into a program source text.

**Default constructor:** a constructor that can be called without arguments.

**Definition:** the definition of an identifier (for a variable, function, type, etc.). Involves reservation of memory for variables and functions.

**Destructor:** a special method called for disintegration of the objects of a class.

**Encapsulation:** this means that real objects in their representation in the program are considered to consist of properties (data) and behaviour (methods). The properties and behaviour of an object are combined in the class that represents it. The concept of encapsulation entails the demand for abstraction and the design of sensible interfaces.

**Field:** a contiguous block of memory for objects of one data type; usually reserved in the form of an array or as a dynamic field via malloc() or new.

**Friends:** functions or methods which are assigned special access privileges by a class, so they can also access private and protected elements of that class.

**Header file:** source text file with the extension (.h, .hpp), which traditionally combined the declarations for the definitions of an implementation file (.c, .cpp).

**Information hiding:** the less programmers need to know about the call of a function, the more easily they can employ it. Many functions provided by C are employed without programmers knowing their source code. C++ applies this to the handling of classes. Classes provide programmers with methods allowing them to handle the objects of the class in the correct way. The class itself appears as a black box to the programmer.

**Inheritance:** classes can be combined into class hierarchies. Derived classes can assume (inherit) the properties of the higher-order class.

**Instance:** a variable of a class type.

**Instance variable:** an element variable which is declared in a class and of which each instance of the class receives a copy.

**Interface:** possibilities for information exchange between functions, classes, modules, etc. The interface of a function, for example, is given by its parameters, the return value or global variables. Classes, instead, provide public or protected methods or define friends. Interfaces should be as small as possible, but should not impair the sensible use of a class.

**Internationalisation:** the adaptation of a program for international use (taking into account country-specific features such as language, formatting time and date, etc.).

**Iterators:** pointer-like objects used in the C++ runtime library for accessing container elements.

**Locale:** a description of the local, country-specific environment in which a program is executed.

**Localisation:** the adaptation of a program to country-specific features, such as language, formatting time and date, etc.

**Methods:** methods are functions that belong to a class. They implement the behaviour shown by objects of the class (element functions).

**Module:** all source text files translated by the compiler in one step into one object file are commonly called a module or compilation unit. A compilation unit consists of an implementation file (with the file extension .c or .cpp) and all source text files whose contents are integrated directly or indirectly via #include statements.

**Multibyte character:** characters encoded with the aid of several bytes. The number of bytes may vary (usually used for storing multilingual texts, for example, English/ Chinese, in files).

**Null termination character:** a special character ('\0'), which indicates the end of a string in C/C++.

**Object orientation:** in object-oriented programming problems are solved by identifying objects, implementing them in the form of classes, and then proceeding to work with these classes. A large part of the programming effort goes into the implementation of an appropriate class for representing the objects. The remainder of the program is simplified because only methods of the classes are called. The methods themselves ensure that they are correctly executed. The advantage of this is the creation of better reusable code in the form of classes. Furthermore, the object-oriented perspective corresponds more to the human way of looking at things and classifying them than the handling of elementary data types.

**Objects:** objects denote real things that are models for a class. However, the term object is also used to denote a class instance.

**Overloading:** overloading is the assignment of several operations to one operator. At the same time, the term also denotes the declaration of several functions of the same name. In the case of operator overloading, the compiler can determine from the number and type of operands the operation to be executed. In the case of function overloading, the compiler resorts to the number and type of parameters to uniquely identify the function body to be called. Overloaded names must lie in a common validity range. The term is, however, sometimes also used in the context of class hierarchies and polymorphism, although the term overriding would be more precise in this context.

**Overriding:** overriding is the redefinition of an inherited function in a derived class. The aim is that the derived class reacts in a specific way to a corresponding function call. For a correct implementation it is required to declare functions that are to be overridden as `virtual`. Thus, overriding is the concept which makes polymorphism possible.

**Polymorphism:** this allows homonymous operations to be executed on different objects by overriding inherited methods. For example, you could derive two classes, circle and rectangle, from a common base class `GeomShape`. Both derived classes inherit the `draw()` method. Drawing a circle, however, requires completely different operations than drawing a rectangle. By overriding the inherited `draw()` method in the derived classes, it is possible to keep the name of the method and combine it with a class-specific implementation. Polymorphism of derived classes is a particularly interesting concept of object-oriented programming, which is best used in connection with virtual methods and base class pointers. In a wider sense, overloading of functions and operators can be also understood as a kind of polymorphism.

**Stream:** the flow of data between an input or output unit and the program.

**String:** a sequence of characters, terminated by a null termination character.

**STL:** part of the C++ runtime library. The core of the STL is constituted by containers, iterators and algorithms.

**Template:** a type-independent model for a function or a class out of which the compiler can, upon specification of the corresponding data types, create real functions or classes.

**White space:** characters that create spaces; such as space, tabs, new line break.

**Wide characters:** characters encoded using 16-bit or 32-bit values (as opposed to 8-bit ASCII or ANSI characters).

# Table Index

| Function / Command | Reference | Practice |
|---|---|---|
| ! | 94 | |
| − | 89 | |
| = | 91 | |
| -- | 89 | |
| != | 92 | |
| # | 208 | |
| ## | 209 | |
| #define | 83, 205 | |
| #elif | 207 | |
| #else | 207 | |
| #endif | 207 | |
| #error | 209 | |
| #if | 207 | |
| #ifdef | 208 | |
| #ifndef | 208 | |
| #include | 204 | |
| #line | 210 | |
| #pragma | 210 | |
| % | 88 | |
| & | 99 | |
| & (address) | 112 | |
| & (references) | 74 | |
| && | 93 | |
| ( ) (parameter list) | 137 | |
| () (type conversion) | 107 | |
| * | 89 | |
| * (pointer declaration) | 68 | |
| * (pointer dereferencing) | 68 | |
| + | 89 | |
| ++ | 89 | |
| , | 113 | |
| . | 96 | |
| .* | 97 | |
| ... | 143 | 527 |
| / | 88 | |
| : | 99 | |
| :: | 98 | |
| ::* (pointer to class elements) | 72 | |
| < | 92 | |
| << | 101 | |
| << (stream operator) | 102 | |

| Function / Command | Reference | Practice |
|---|---|---|
| <= | 92 | |
| <x>= | 90 | |
| = | 90 | |
| == | 92 | |
| -> | 97 | |
| > | 92 | |
| ->* | 95 | |
| >= | 92 | |
| >> | 102 | |
| >> (stream operator) | 101 | |
| ? | 112 | |
| [ ] (array declaration) | 53 | |
| [ ] (array indexing) | 53, 96 | |
| ^ | 100 | |
| { } | 10 | |
| \| | 100 | |
| \|\| | 93 | |
| ~ | 101 | |
| | | |
| abstract classes | 186 | |
| abstract methods | 186 | |
| access specifiers | | |
|   – in the class declaration | 162 | |
|   – in inheritance | 163 | |
| adapter for function objects | 454 | |
| advance() | 382 | |
| algorithms | 382 | 619 |
| allocator | 456 | |
| ANSI standard | 3 | |
| ANSI table | | 670 |
| arrays | 53 | 473 |
|   – access to elements | 54 | 473 |
|   – as function parameters | | 478 |
|   – compared to dynamic fields | | 473 |
|   – determine number of elements | | 479 |
|   – initialisation | 54 | |
|   – multidimensional arrays | 55 | |
|   – of base class pointers | | 556 |
|   – of class objects | 175 | 535 |
|   – of structures | | 481 |
|   – search | | 477 |

| Function / Command | Reference | Practice |
|---|---|---|
| – sort | | 475 |
| – strings | 58 | |
| – with elements of different data types | | 480 |
| ASCII table | | 669 |
| asm | | 657 |
| assembler | | 657 |
| assert() | 233 | |
| assignment operator | | 507, 541 |
| assignments | 90 | |
| associativity | 114 | |
| auto | 41 | |
| auto_ptr | 457 | 499 |
| | | |
| back_insert_iterator | 376 | |
| bad_alloc | 446 | 490, 492 |
| bad_cast | 446 | |
| bad_typeid | 446 | |
| base class objects | | |
| – assignment of derived objects | 91 | |
| – create | 180 | 535 |
| base class pointers | 72, 188 | 481, 556 |
| – and arrays | | 556 |
| – as parameters | | 558 |
| – conversion in pointers to derived objects | 107 | |
| base classes | 151 | |
| – access to hidden elements | 49 | |
| – direct | 182 | |
| – indirect | 182 | |
| – polymorph | 108 | |
| – virtual | 191 | |
| basic_filebuf | 406 | |
| basic_fstream | 410 | |
| basic_ifstream | 408 | |
| basic_ios | 395 | |
| basic_iostream | 402 | |
| basic_istream | 398 | |
| basic_istringstream | 404 | |
| basic_ofstream | 409 | |
| basic_ostream | 400 | |
| basic_ostringstream | 405 | |
| basic_streambuf | 396 | |

| Function / Command | Reference | Practice |
|---|---|---|
| basic_string | 411 | |
| basic_stringbuf | 402 | |
| basic_stringstream | 406 | |
| binary_function | 452 | |
| binary_negate | 453 | |
| binder for function objects | 451 | 628 |
| bit fields | | |
| – as bitset containers | 320, 350 | |
| – as structures | 63 | |
| bitset | 320, 350 | 614 |
| block scope | 44 | |
| bool | 36 | |
| break | 128 | |
| BubbleSort | | 475 |
| buffering | 230 | |
| | | |
| C/C++ | | |
| – alternative characters | 32 | |
| – ANSI standard | 3 | |
| – character set | 27 | |
| – compatibility between C++ and C | | 668 |
| – features | 3 | |
| – input and output | 18 | |
| – keywords | 30 | |
| – notation conventions | 5 | |
| – structure of programs | 5 | |
| – symbols | 30 | |
| – upper and lower case spelling | 5 | |
| call by reference | | 524 |
| cast operator | 79, 106 | |
| catch | 217 | 578 |
| cerr | 226 | |
| char | 36 | |
| char_traits | 411 | |
| character set | 27 | |
| character strings | 219 | |
| – access to individual characters | 59 | |
| – analyse | | 588 |
| – as arrays | 58 | |
| – as pointers to char | | 584 |
| – as string objects | | 586 |

| Function / Command | Reference | Practice |
|---|---|---|
|   – compare | 58 | 587 |
|   – copy | 59 | 585, 587 |
|   – initialise | 59 | |
|   – multibyte character | 222 | |
|   – string classes | 411 | |
|   – strtok() | | 588 |
|   – wide characters | 222 | 647 |
| cin | 226 | 594 |
| class (template parameter) | 195 | |
| class scope | 44 | |
| class templates | 195 | 565 |
|   – methods in class templates | 195 | |
| classes | 150 | 533 |
|   – abstract classes | 186 | |
|   – abstract methods | 186 | |
|   – access specifiers | 162 | 538 |
|   – access to base class elements | 166 | |
|   – access to elements | 163, 164 | 538 |
|   – arrays of objects | 173 | 536 |
|   – assignment operator | | 541 |
|   – base class pointers | 187 | 556 |
|   – closedness | 153 | |
|   – constant data elements | 155 | |
|   – const methods | 161 | |
|   – constant instances | 173 | |
|   – constructor list | 155 | |
|   – constructor | 168 | |
|   – conversion methods | | 546 |
|   – copy constructor | 170 | 541 |
|   – copy objects | | 541 |
|   – creation of embedded objects | | 536 |
|   – creation of inherited elements | 168, 182 | 536 |
|   – data elements | 156 | |
|   – default constructor | 168 | 535 |
|   – default methods | 172 | |
|   – destructor | 171 | |
|   – dynamic memory | | 495 |
|   – embedded objects | 158 | |
|   – encapsulation | 153 | |
|   – information hiding | 153 | |
|   – instance formation | 173 | |

| Function / Command | Reference | Practice |
|---|---|---|
| – methods | 158 | |
| – object-oriented programming | 152 | |
| – objects as data elements | 156 | |
| – of the C++ runtime library | 347 | |
| – overloading of operators | | 545 |
| – persistent classes | | 548 |
| – pointers as instance variables | | 543 |
| – prepare for containers and algorithms | | 623 |
| – recursive | | 484 |
| – static data elements | 154 | |
| – static methods | 160 | |
| – this pointer | 172 | |
| clog | 226 | |
| codecvt | 422 | |
| codecvt_base | 422 | |
| codecvt_byname | 423 | |
| collate | 424 | |
| collate_byname | 424 | |
| comma operator | 113 | |
| comments | 12 | |
| compare | | |
| – operators | 92 | |
| – strings | 58 | 583 |
| – structures | | 483 |
| compiler switches | | 572 |
| compiler | 21 | |
| – Borland C++ | 23 | |
| – C++ Builder | 24 | |
| – compiler switches | | 572 |
| – conditional compilation | 206 | 573 |
| – GNU compiler | 22 | |
| – standard conversions | 76 | |
| – Visual C++ | 25 | |
| complex | 435 | |
| conditional compilation | 206 | 573 |
| – compiler switches | | 572 |
| – debugging | | 573 |
| – portability | | 574 |
| conditional operator | 112 | |
| console programs | 7 | |
| const (data elements) | 154 | |

| Function / Command | Reference | Practice |
|---|---|---|
| const (methods) | 145, 161 | |
| const (parameters) | 80 | 524 |
| const (pointers) | 71 | |
| const (variables) | 41, 83 | |
| const_cast | 107 | |
| constants | 80 | |
| – #define | 82 | |
| – const variables | 83 | |
| – literals | 81 | |
| constructors | 168 | |
| – constructor list | 157, 182, 192 | |
| – conversion to class type | 170 | |
| – copy constructor | 170 | 541 |
| – default constructor | 168 | 535 |
| – explicit declaration | 169 | |
| – in inheritance | 180 | |
| – multiple inheritance | 182 | |
| containers | 347 | 614 |
| – associative containers | 348 | 616 |
| – bitset | 350 | 614 |
| – deque | 352 | 614 |
| – general characteristics | 347 | |
| – list | 355 | 614 |
| – map | 358 | 614 |
| – multimap | 358 | 614 |
| – multiset | 365 | 614 |
| – overview | | 614 |
| – priority_queue | 362 | 615 |
| – queue | 364 | 614 |
| – sequential containers | 348 | 615 |
| – set | 365 | 615 |
| – stack | 368 | 615 |
| – vector | 369 | 615 |
| continue | 28 | |
| conversion methods | | 546 |
| copy constructor | 170 | 541 |
| copy | | |
| – class instances | 170 | 541 |
| – strings | 58 | 584, 586 |
| cout | 226 | 594 |
| ctype | 420 | |

| Function / Command | Reference | Practice |
|---|---|---|
| ctype_base | 420 | |
| ctype_byname | 421 | |
| | | |
| data management | | 614, 663 |
| data types | 34 | |
| – arithmetic | 35 | |
| – arrays | 53 | 473 |
| – classes | 150 | |
| – coding | 35 | |
| – combined | 50 | |
| – conversion by compiler | 79 | |
| – elementary | 36 | |
| – enumeration types | 51 | 470 |
| – integer | 36 | |
| – literals | 80 | |
| – memory occupation | 37 | |
| – scalars | 35 | |
| – structures | 60 | 483 |
| – templates | 192 | |
| – unions | 64 | |
| – value range | 35 | |
| database programming | | 663 |
| debugging | | 573 |
| declaration | 32 | 634 |
| decrement | 88 | 508 |
| default | 122 | |
| defined | 208 | |
| definition | 32 | 634 |
| delete | 105 | 490 |
| – overloading | | 516 |
| deque | 352 | 614 |
| dereferencing | 68 | |
| destructor | 171 | |
| – in inheritance | 186 | |
| diagnostic messages | 209 | |
| difftime() | 247 | |
| distance() | 382 | |
| do | 127 | |
| double | 34 | |
| dynamic_cast | 107, 189 | 561 |

| Function / Command | Reference | Practice |
|---|---|---|
| elements, insert in programs | 32 | |
| else | 120 | |
| embedding | | |
| – creation of embedded objects | | 536 |
| – initialisation of embedded objects | 157 | |
| – versus friends | | 552 |
| – versus inheritance | 176 | 552 |
| encapsulation | 153 | |
| enum | 51 | 470 |
| enumeration types | 51 | 470 |
| – as sets | | 471 |
| – in switch branches | | 470 |
| – memory occupation | 52 | |
| equal_to | 453 | |
| errno | 234 | |
| escape sequences | 28 | |
| exception | 445 | |
| exceptions | 211 | 577 |
| – advantages and disadvantages | 211 | |
| – and dynamic memory | | 498 |
| – bad_alloc | | 492 |
| – catch | 216 | 578 |
| – define user-defined exception classes | 215 | 581 |
| – function declaration with throw | 215 | |
| – pass on | | 579 |
| – related functions | 218 | |
| – scheme of exception handling | 212 | |
| – specify handler scope | 217 | |
| – trigger | 214 | 579 |
| exit() | 128 | |
| extern | 41, 132, 145 | 634 |
| | | |
| FALSE | 36 | |
| fclose() | | 599 |
| features | 3 | |
| fgetc() | | 599 |
| fgets() | | 593 |
| fields, dynamic | | 473 |
| – access to elements | | 474 |
| – as function parameters | | 478 |
| – compared to arrays | | 473 |

| Function / Command | Reference | Practice |
|---|---|---|
| – search | | 477 |
| – sort | | 475 |
| – with elements of different data types | | 480 |
| file scope | 44 | |
| FILE | 225 | 599 |
| filebuf | | 610 |
| files | | 598 |
| – binary files in C | | 600 |
| – binary files in C++ | | 606 |
| – random access in C | | 602 |
| – random access in C++ | | 608 |
| – split file buffer (C++) | | 610 |
| – text files in C | | 598 |
| – text files in C++ | | 604 |
| flags | 62, 347 | |
| float | 36 | |
| floating point numbers | 38 | |
| fopen() | | 599 |
| for | 124 | 520 |
| fread() | | 602 |
| free() | | 488 |
| friends | 165 | 551 |
| – in templates | 195 | |
| front_insert_iterator | 377 | |
| fseek() | | 603 |
| fstream | | 604 |
| function adapters | 454 | 628 |
| function objects | 451 | 624 |
| function overhead | 142 | |
| function scope | 44 | |
| function templates | 194 | 565 |
| functions | 129 | 523 |
| – arrays as parameters | | 478 |
| – base class pointers as parameters | | 558 |
| – call by reference | 137 | 524 |
| – call by value | 136 | |
| – const parameters | | 524 |
| – default arguments | 139 | |
| – dynamic memory | | 495 |
| – function overhead | 142 | |
| – global variables | 135 | |

| Function / Command | Reference | Practice |
|---|---|---|
| – inline functions | 144 | |
| – main() | 133 | |
| – of the C standard library | 251 | |
| – overloading | 146 | 530 |
| – parameters | 134, 136 | |
| – pointers as parameters | | 524 |
| – recursive functions | | 527 |
| – reduce copying effort | | 524 |
| – references as parameters | | 502, 524 |
| – return value | 136 | |
| – specifiers | 145 | |
| – stack | 139 | |
| – 'static' variables | 135 | 526 |
| – trigger exceptions | 133, 214 | |
| – with any number of arguments | 143 | 528 |
| – without return value | 134 | |
| fwrite() | | 600 |
| glossary | | 672 |
| goto | 128 | |
| greater | 452 | |
| greater_equal | 452 | |
| gslice | 344 | |
| gslice_array | 344 | |
| header files | | |
| – avoid multiple calls | | 636 |
| – concepts | | 633 |
| – link | 18 | |
| – of the C standard library | 233 | |
| – of the C++ standard library | 317 | |
| heap | | 495 |
| hiding | 48 | |
| identifier | 5, 32 | |
| if | 119 | |
| ifstream | | 604 |
| increment | 88 | 510 |
| indirect_array | 443 | |
| information hiding | 153 | |
| inheritance | 174 | 551 |

| Function / Command | Reference | Practice |
|---|---|---|
| – access restrictions | 177 | |
| – access specifier | 177 | |
| – constructors | 180 | |
| – destructors | 186 | |
| – guidelines | | 555 |
| – loosen access rights | 179 | |
| – multiple inheritance | 182 | |
| – non-inheritable methods | 182 | |
| – overriding | 184 | |
| – polymorphism | 183 | 553 |
| – versus embedding | 176 | 552 |
| – versus friends | | 552 |
| inline functions | 144 | |
| input and output | 18, 223 | 591 |
| – buffering | 230 | |
| – cerr | 226 | |
| – cin | 226 | |
| – clog | 226 | |
| – cout | 226 | |
| – error handling in C++ | 229 | 596 |
| – files | | 598 |
| – formatted in C++ | 227 | 594 |
| – formatted in C | 225 | 592 |
| – formatting in C++ | 227 | |
| – functions in C | 226 | |
| – localise output | | 649 |
| – manipulators in C++ | 228 | 595 |
| – stderr | 225 | |
| – stdin | 225 | |
| – stdout | 225 | |
| – streams in C | 224 | |
| – streams in C++ | 226 | |
| – unformatted in C | 223 | |
| – unformatted in C++ | 223 | |
| insert_iterator | 377 | |
| instance formation | 173 | |
| int | 39 | |
| internationalisation | | 645 |
| – to localise output | | 649 |
| invalid_argument | 447 | |
| ios_base | 393 | |

| Function / Command | Reference | Practice |
|---|---|---|
| isprint() | 234 | |
| istream_iterator | 378 | |
| istreambuf_iterator | 379 | |
| iterator tags | 381 | |
| iterator_traits | 381 | |
| iterators | 372 | 617 |
|   – categories | 373 | |
|   – insert iterators | 376 | |
|   – return by container | | 618 |
|   – stream iterators | 378 | |
| | | |
| Kernighan, Brian | 2 | |
| keywords | 30 | |
| | | |
| length_error | 447 | |
| less | 452 | |
| less_equal | 452 | |
| libraries | | |
|   – create | | 643 |
|   – standard libraries | 16 | |
|   – use | | 642 |
| life span | 49 | |
| linker | 21 | |
| list | 355 | 614 |
| literals | 80 | |
| locale | 418 | 650 |
| localeconv() | 237 | 652 |
| localisation | | 645 |
|   – local environment | | 650 |
|   – localise output | | 649 |
|   – query locales | | 653 |
| log() | 238 | |
| log10() | 238 | |
| logic_error | 447 | |
| logical_and | 452 | |
| logical_not | 453 | |
| logical_or | 453 | |
| long | 37 | |
| longjmp() | 128 | |
| loops | 123 | |
|   – do-while | 127 | |

| Function / Command | Reference | Practice |
|---|---|---|
| – for | 124 | |
| – infinite loops | 125 | 520 |
| – termination statements | 128 | |
| – while | 126 | |
| | | |
| macros | | |
| – define | 204 | |
| – versus templates | 196 | |
| main() | 8, 133 | |
| – arguments | 133 | |
| malloc() | | 488 |
| manipulators | 228 | 595 |
| map | 358 | 614 |
| mask_array | 441 | |
| mem_fun() | 455 | |
| mem_fun_ref() | 455 | |
| mem_fun_ref_t | 455 | |
| mem_fun_t | 455 | |
| mem_fun1() | 456 | |
| mem_fun1_ref() | 455 | |
| mem_fun1_ref_t | 455 | |
| mem_fun1_t | 455 | |
| memory | | 495 |
| memory management | | 487 |
| – and exception handling | | 498 |
| – auto_ptr | | 499 |
| – in classes | | 497 |
| – in functions | | 495 |
| – pointers | 67 | |
| memory occupation | | |
| – enumeration types | 52 | |
| – floating point types | 38 | |
| – integer types | 37 | |
| memory | | |
| – release (delete) | | 490 |
| – release (free()) | | 488 |
| – reserve (malloc()) | | 488 |
| – reserve (new) | | 490 |
| menus | | 521 |
| messages | 425 | |
| messages_base | 425 | |

| Function / Command | Reference | Practice |
|---|---|---|
| messages_byname | 425 | |
| method adapter | | 628 |
| methods | 158 | |
|    – abstract methods | 186 | |
|    – constant | 161 | |
|    – in class templates | 196 | |
|    – non-inheritable methods | 182 | |
|    – overloading | 146 | |
|    – overriding | 184 | |
|    – static | 160 | |
|    – virtual methods | 184 | |
| minus | 453 | |
| modularisation | 13 | 632 |
| money_base | 427 | |
| money_get | 426 | |
| money_put | 427 | |
| moneypunct | 428 | |
| moneypunct_byname | 428 | |
| multibyte character | 2262 | |
| multi-file programs | 13 | 631 |
|    – cross-module use of elements | | 637 |
|    – header file and implementation file | | |
|    – hide elements in other files | | 638 |
| multimap | 358 | 614 |
| multiple inheritance | 190 | |
|    – circular references | 191 | |
|    – constructors | 180 | |
|    – name conflicts | 190 | |
|    – virtual base classes | 191 | |
| multiset | 365 | 614 |
| | | |
| namespaces | 45 | 464 |
|    – declare | 46 | 468 |
|    – extend | 46 | |
|    – insert into local validity ranges | | 468 |
|    – of the C++ runtime library | | 464 |
|    – std | | 464 |
|    – use elements from namespace | 46, 47 | 466 |
|    – use for larger projects | | 469 |
| negators for function objects | 453 | 628 |

| Function / Command | Reference | Practice |
|---|---|---|
| new | 103 | 490 |
|    – error handling | | 492 |
|    – overloading | | 516 |
|    – register handler function | | 493 |
| not_equal_to | 453 | |
| nothrow | | 490, 493 |
| num_get | 429 | |
| num_put | 430 | |
| numeric classes | 435 | |
| numeric_limits | 443 | 462 |
| numpunct | 431 | |
| numpunct_byname | 431 | |
| | | |
| ofstream | | 604 |
| operators, overloading | 115 | 509 |
| operators | 84 | 507 |
|    – address | 112 | |
|    – arithmetic | 87 | 511 |
|    – assignment operator | | 514, 545 |
|    – assignments | 90 | |
|    – associativity | 114 | |
|    – bit operators | 199 | |
|    – cast operator | 79, 106 | |
|    – comma operator | 113 | |
|    – comparison | 92 | |
|    – const_cast | 107 | |
|    – data access | 95 | |
|    – decrement | 88 | 508 |
|    – delete | 105 | 490 |
|    – dynamic_cast | 107 | |
|    – efficient use | | 508 |
|    – increment | 88 | 510 |
|    – logical | 92 | |
|    – new | 103 | 490 |
|    – overloading -- | | 510 |
|    – overloading () | | 513 |
|    – overloading ++ | | 510 |
|    – overloading << and >> | | 518 |
|    – overloading = | | 514 |
|    – overloading arithmetic operators | | 511 |
|    – overloading new and delete | | 516 |

| Function / Command | Reference | Practice |
|---|---|---|
|   – overloading | 115 | 509 |
|   – precedence | 114 | |
|   – references as return values | | 503 |
|   – reinterpret_cast | 109 | |
|   – signs | 87 | |
|   – sizeof | 111 | |
|   – static_cast | 108 | |
|   – stream operators | 102 | |
|   – synonyms | 114 | |
|   – typeid | 110 | |
| ostream_iterator | 379 | |
| ostreambuf_iterator | 380 | |
| out_of_range error | 447 | |
| overflow_error | 447 | |
| overloading | | |
|   – arithmetic operator | | 511 |
|   – assignment operator = | | 514 |
|   – decrement operator -- | | 510 |
|   – increment operator ++ | | 510 |
|   – new and delete | | 516 |
|   – of functions | 147 | 530 |
|   – of methods | 148 | |
|   – of operators | 115 | 509, 545 |
|   – operator () | | 513 |
|   – stream operators << >> | | 518 |
|   – versus templates | | 565 |
| overriding | 184 | |
| pair structure | 450 | |
| parameters | 136 | |
|   – copying address | 137 | 524 |
|   – copying value | 136 | |
|   – base class pointers as parameters | | 558 |
|   – const declaration | | 524 |
| persistence | | 548 |
| pointer_to_binary_function | 454 | |
| pointer_to_unary_function | 454 | |
| pointers | 66 | |
|   – application | 66 | |
|   – as function parameters | | 524 |
|   – as instance variables | | 543 |

| Function / Command | Reference | Practice |
|---|---|---|
| – as local variables | | 496 |
| – auto_ptr | | 499 |
| – base class pointers | 72, 187 | 555 |
| – constant pointers | 71 | |
| – dereferencing | 68 | |
| – initialisation | 68 | |
| – intelligent | | 500 |
| – ZERO pointer | 68 | |
| – pointer arithmetic | | 494 |
| – smart pointers | | 500 |
| – this | 72 | |
| – to character strings | 70 | |
| – to data elements | 71 | |
| – to functions | 70 | |
| – to methods | 71 | |
| – to static class elements | 72 | |
| – to void | 70 | |
| – versus references | | 501 |
| polymorphism | 183 | 553 |
| portability | | 574 |
| pow() | 239 | |
| pragma directives | 210 | |
| precedence | 114 | |
| precision of floating point numbers | | 463 |
| preprocessor | 202 | |
| – base symbol combination | 209 | |
| – conditional compilation | 206 | 573, 574 |
| – diagnostic messages | 209 | |
| – insert source code | 203 | |
| – macros | 204 | |
| – pragma directives | 210 | |
| – string formation | 208 | |
| – working principles | 202 | |
| printf() | | 592 |
| priority_queue | 362 | 615 |
| private | 162, 178 | 538 |
| program control | 118 | 519 |
| – branches | 118 | |
| – loops | 123 | |
| program creation | 21 | |
| program flow | 20 | |

| Function / Command | Reference | Practice |
|---|---|---|
| programs | | |
| – command line arguments | 133 | |
| – console programs | 7 | |
| – create | 21 | |
| – from several source files | 14 | 631 |
| – integrate assembler statements | | 657 |
| – modularise | 14 | |
| – structure | 5 | |
| – typical components | 8 | |
| – Windows programs | | 659 |
| protected | 162, 178 | 538 |
| ptr_fun() | 455 | |
| public | 162, 178 | 538 |
| putc() | | 592 |
| putchar() | 234 | 592 |
| puts() | | 592 |
| | | |
| qsort() | | 484 |
| queue | 364 | 614 |
| QuickSort | | 475 |
| | | |
| rand() | | 656 |
| RAND_MAX | | 656 |
| random numbers | | 656 |
| range_error | 447 | |
| recursion | | 527 |
| references | 73 | |
| – as function parameters | | 524 |
| – as parameters | | 502 |
| – as return values | | 503 |
| – const declaration | 75 | |
| – versus pointers | | 501 |
| register | 41 | |
| reinterpret_cast | 109 | |
| return value | 135 | |
| return | 126, 128, 135 | |
| return_temporary_buffer() | 457 | |
| reverse_iterator | 374 | |
| Ritchie, Dennis | 2 | |
| RTTI | 188 | |
| – with dynamic_cast | 189 | 561 |

| Function / Command | Reference | Practice |
|---|---|---|
| – with typeid | 189 | 563 |
| – with virtual methods | 188 | 559 |
| runtime_error | 446 | |
| scanf() | | 592 |
| search, in fields | | 477 |
| set | 365 | 615 |
| set_new_handler() | 447 | 493 |
| set_terminate() | 218, 448 | |
| set_unexpected() | 218, 448 | |
| setjmp() | 239 | |
| setlocale() | 237 | 651 |
| short | 37 | |
| sign | 88 | |
| signal() | 240 | |
| signed | 36, 39 | |
| sin() | 239 | |
| sizeof | 111 | 479 |
| slice | 436 | |
| slice_array | 436 | |
| smart pointers | | 499 |
| sort | | |
| – BubbleSort | | 475 |
| – errors | | 475 |
| – QuickSort | | 476 |
| – structures | | 483 |
| – specialisation, of templates | 200 | |
| sprintf() | | 612 |
| srand() | | 656 |
| sscanf() | 243 | 593, 612 |
| stack (for function calls) | 140 | |
| stack | 368 | 615 |
| standard constructor | 168 | 535 |
| standard conversions | 76 | |
| standard libraries | | |
| – algorithms | 382 | |
| – C functions | 251 | |
| – C header files | 233 | |
| – C | 233 | |
| – C++ header files | 318 | |
| – C++ | 317 | |

| Function / Command | Reference | Practice |
|---|---|---|
| – containers | 347 | |
| – diagnosis classes for exception handling | 445 | |
| – iterators | 372 | |
| – local classes | 417 | |
| – numeric classes | 435 | |
| – runtime type identification | 449 | |
| – stream classes | 391 | |
| – string classes | 411 | |
| – using elements | | 466 |
| – utilities | 450 | |
| – runtime type identification | 188 | |
| – with dynamic_cast | 189 | 561 |
| – with typeid | 189 | 563 |
| – with virtual methods | 188 | 559 |
| statements | 10 | |
| – if | 119 | |
| – if-else | 120 | |
| – menus | | 521 |
| – switch | 121 | |
| static (functions) | | 639 |
| static (global variables) | | 639 |
| static (local variables) | | 526 |
| static (methods) | 145, 159 | |
| static | 145 | |
| static_cast | 108 | |
| stderr | 225 | |
| stdin | 225 | |
| stdout | 225 | |
| STL | | 613 |
| stream classes | 390 | |
| streams | | |
| – buffering | 230 | |
| – error handling in C++ | 229 | 596 |
| – in C | 224 | |
| – in C++ | 226 | |
| – operators | 102 | |
| – share stream buffer (C++) | | 610 |
| – stream classes | 390 | |
| – string streams | | 612 |
| string classes | 410 | |
| string streams | | 612 |

| Function / Command | Reference | Practice |
|---|---|---|
| strings | 58, 221 | |
|   – access to individual characters | 59 | |
|   – analyse | | 588 |
|   – as arrays | 58 | |
|   – as string objects | | 586 |
|   – compare | 59 | 587 |
|   – copy | 59 | 585, 587 |
|   – initialise | 59 | |
|   – multibyte character | 222 | |
|   – pointer to char | | 584 |
|   – runtime type identification | 449 | |
|   – string classes | 411 | |
|   – strtok() | | 588 |
|   – wide characters | 222 | 647 |
| Stroustrup, Bjarne | 2 | |
| strtok() | | 588 |
| structure of programs | 5 | |
| structures | 60 | 483 |
|   – access to elements | 61 | |
|   – arrays of structures | | 483 |
|   – bit fields | 62 | |
|   – compare | | 483 |
|   – in C++ | 60 | |
|   – initialisation | 61 | |
|   – recursive | | 484 |
|   – sort | | 483 |
|   – with elements < 1 byte | 63 | |
| switch | 121 | 470, 521 |
| | | |
| templates | 192 | 565, 567 |
| templates | 192 | 565 |
|   – explicit instantiation | 199 | |
|   – explicit specialisation | 200 | |
|   – for classes | 195 | 567 |
|   – for functions | 194 | 565 |
|   – friend declarations | 195 | |
|   – implicit instantiation | 199 | |
|   – partial specialisation | 201 | |
|   – specialisation | 200 | |
|   – the STL containers | | 567 |
|   – versus macros | 193 | |

| Function / Command | Reference | Practice |
|---|---|---|
| – versus overloading | | 565 |
| terminate() | 218, 448 | |
| this pointer | 72, 172 | |
| this | 172 | |
| throw | 128,132 | 499, 579 |
| time() | 247 | |
| time_base | 432 | |
| time_get | 432 | |
| time_get_byname | 433 | |
| time_put | 434 | |
| time_put_byname | 434 | |
| time_t | 247 | |
| tolower() | 234 | |
| trigraph sequences | 29 | |
| TRUE | 36 | |
| try | 217 | 578 |
| type conversion | 78, 106 | |
| – cast operator | 106 | |
| – const_cast | 107 | |
| – dynamic_cast | 107 | |
| – reinterpret_cast | 109 | |
| – static_cast | 108 | |
| type definitions with typedef | 76 | |
| type identification | 106 | |
| – typeid | 110 | |
| type independence | 194 | |
| type_info | 449 | |
| typedef | 76 | |
| typeid | 189 | 562 |
| typename | 194 | |
| unary_function | 452 | |
| unary_negate | 453 | |
| uncaught_exception() | 445 | |
| underflow_error | 448 | |
| unexpected() | 218, 447 | |
| UNICODE | 222 | |
| uninitialized_copy() | 458 | |
| uninitialized_fill() | 458 | |
| uninitialized_fill_n() | 458 | |
| unions | 64 | |
| unsigned | | |

| Function / Command | Reference | Practice |
|---|---|---|
| using namespaces | 46 | 466 |
| utilities | 450 | |
| | | |
| va_macros | | 528 |
| valarray | 344 | |
| validity scopes | 44 | |
| value ranges | | |
|    – of floating point numbers | 37 | 463 |
|    – of integer data types | 37 | 460 |
| variables | 9, 34, 40 | |
|    – global | 49 | |
|    – hiding | 49 | |
|    – initialisation | 41 | |
|    – life span | 49 | |
|    – specifier | 41 | |
|    – visibility | 48 | |
| vector | 369 | 615 |
| virtual (base classes) | 175, 191 | |
| virtual (methods) | 145, 184 | 554, 559 |
| visibility | 48 | |
| void | 70, 132 | |
| volatile | 41, 146 | |
| | | |
| wchar_t | 37, 222 | 648 |
| wcout | | 648 |
| while | 126 | 520 |
| wide characters | 222 | 647 |
| Windows programs | | 659 |
| WinMain() | 6 | 661 |
| wprintf() | | 648 |
| wstring | | 648 |